THE ARTHUR OF MEDIEVAL LATIN LITERATURE

ARTHURIAN LITERATURE IN THE MIDDLE AGES

VI

THE ARTHUR OF MEDIEVAL LATIN LITERATURE

THE DEVELOPMENT AND DISSEMINATION OF THE ARTHURIAN LEGEND IN MEDIEVAL LATIN

edited by

Siân Echard

CARDIFF
UNIVERSITY OF WALES PRESS

Reprinted 2012 (twice)
Printed in paperback 2016

www.uwp.co.uk

British Library Cataloguing-in-Publication Data.
A catalogue record for this book is available from the British Library.

ISBN 978-1-78316-856-9
e-ISBN 978-1-78316-855-2

Typeset by Mark Heslington Ltd, Scarborough, North Yorkshire
Printed by CPI Antony Rowe, Chippenham, Wiltshire

PUBLISHED IN COOPERATION WITH

THE VINAVER TRUST

The Vinaver Trust was established by the British Branch of the International Arthurian Society to commemorate a greatly respected colleague and a distinguished scholar

Eugène Vinaver

the editor of Malory's Morte Darthur. *The Trust aims to advance study of Arthurian literature in all languages by planning and encouraging research projects in the field, and by aiding publication of the resultant studies.*

ARTHURIAN LITERATURE IN THE MIDDLE AGES

Series Editor

Ad Putter

I *The Arthur of the Welsh*, edited by Rachel Bromwich, A. O. H. Jarman and Brynley F. Roberts (Cardiff, 1991)

II *The Arthur of the English*, edited by W. R. J. Barron (Cardiff, 1999)

III *The Arthur of the Germans*, edited by W. H. Jackson and S. A. Ranawake (Cardiff, 2000)

IV *The Arthur of the French*, edited by Glyn S. Burgess and Karen Pratt (Cardiff, 2006)

V *The Arthur of the North*, edited by Marianne E. Kalinke (Cardiff, 2011)

VI *The Arthur of Medieval Latin Literature*, edited by Siân Echard (Cardiff, 2011)

VII *The Arthur of the Italians*, edited by Gloria Allaire and F. Regina Psaki (Cardiff, 2014)

VIII *The Arthur of the Iberians*, edited by David Hook (Cardiff, 2015)

CONTENTS

Preface ix
Ad Putter

Abbreviations xi

Introduction: The Arthur of Medieval Latin Literature 1
Siân Echard

Section One
The Seeds of History and Legend

1 The Chroniclers of Early Britain 9
Nick Higham

2 Arthur in Early Saints' Lives 26
Andrew Breeze

Section Two
Geoffrey of Monmouth

3 Geoffrey of Monmouth 45
Siân Echard

4 Geoffrey and the Prophetic Tradition 67
Julia Crick

Section Three
Chronicles and Romances

5 Latin Historiography after Geoffrey of Monmouth 85
Ad Putter

6 Glastonbury 109
Edward Donald Kennedy

7 Arthurian Latin Romance 132
Elizabeth Archibald

Section Four
After the Middle Ages

8 Arthur and the Antiquaries 149
James P. Carley

Bibliography 179

Index of Manuscripts 185
General Index 187

PREFACE

This book forms part of the ongoing series Arthurian Literature in the Middle Ages. The purpose of the series is to provide a comprehensive and reliable survey of Arthurian writings in all their cultural and generic variety. For some time, the single-volume *Arthurian Literature in the Middle Ages: A Collaborative History* (ed. R.S. Loomis, Oxford, 1959) served the needs of students and scholars of Arthurian literature admirably, but it has now been overtaken by advances in scholarship and by changes in critical perspectives and methodologies. The Vinaver Trust recognized the need for a fresh and up-to-date survey, and decided that several volumes were required to do justice to the distinctive contributions made to Arthurian literature by the various cultures of medieval Europe. *The Arthur of Medieval Latin Literature* is primarily devoted to medieval Arthurian texts composed in Latin, from all across Europe, but it also takes account of the interplay between Latin and vernacular traditions and of the influence of medieval Latin Arthurian writings on the literature of later periods, particularly that of the Early Modern period.

The series is mainly aimed at undergraduate and postgraduate students and at scholars working in the fields covered by each of the volumes. The series has, however, also been designed to be accessible to general readers and to students and scholars from different fields who want to learn what forms Arthurian narratives took in languages and literatures that they may not know, and how those narratives influenced the cultures that they do know. Within these parameters the editors have had control over the shape and content of their individual volumes.

Ad Putter, University of Bristol
(General Editor)

ABBREVIATIONS

AC	*Annales Cambrie*
ALMA	*Arthurian Literature in the Middle Ages*
DEB	*De excidio et conquestu Britannie*
ELH	*English Literary History*
EETS	Early English Text Society
FH	*Flores historiarum*
HB	*Historia Brittonum*
HE	*Historia ecclesiastica gentis anglorum*
HRB	*Historia regum Britannie*
ODNB	*Oxford Dictionary of National Biography*
RS	Rolls Series
VM	*Vita Merlini*

INTRODUCTION:
THE ARTHUR OF MEDIEVAL LATIN LITERATURE

Siân Echard

. . . codicem illum in Latinum sermonem transferre curaui[1]
[I have taken the trouble to translate the book into Latin]

In the preface to his *Historia regum Britannie* (*c.*1138), Geoffrey of Monmouth claims to be translating into Latin an ancient book in the British tongue, given to him by Walter, archdeacon of Oxford. The status of this book has been a subject of controversy ever since, and more than one of the essays in this collection will touch on Geoffrey's sources and possible motives. I open this introduction with the single line above, however, because it contains two crucial words – *codicem* and *Latinum*. Codex is an unequivocal word, an assertion of textual materiality, and Latin is the language of textuality in Geoffrey's day.[2] It is also the language of authority: Latin is, as Bakhtin puts it,'The word of the fathers'.[3] To be *litteratus* meant to be able to read and write Latin, and for much of the Middle Ages, such skills belonged largely to a clerical elite.[4] Even the rise of the vernaculars as vehicles for literary high art could not shake the status of Latin as the medium for certain kinds of knowledge, nor indeed the sense that codices are the proper repositories for that kind of knowledge. Latin, in short, was serious business. This is not to say Latin could not be satirical, irreverent, subversive, funny – it could be all of these things.[5] There was also a great deal of bad Latin in the Middle Ages, pedestrian, overreaching, or just plain wrong. But for the educated *litterati*, Latin came as part of a package with a certain kind of education, one that included self-conscious awareness of matters of style at the level of word, argument and form.[6]

Geoffrey asserts that he has accepted Walter's commission with humility: 'I have not collected flowery words from foreign gardens, but have instead been content with my own rustic style and my own reed pipe.'[7] His readers are expected to recognize the modesty topos and its classical antecedents, and they are expected as well to see the degree to which his preface invokes what we might think of as the community standards for medieval Latin histories. Geoffrey names his source, compliments his patron, and asserts straightforward practice while also displaying technical skill.[8] Similarly when Geoffrey closes his history by warning other historians 'to keep silent about the kings of the Britons, because they do not have the book in the British language which Walter, archdeacon of Oxford, brought from Wales',[9] he is targeting very precisely the habits of mind of his contemporaries by asserting that he possesses a written source which they do not. They may suspect that he is lying – indeed some of them charged that he was – but part of the overwhelming success of Geoffrey's *Historia* can be attributed to his historiographical skill, even if in the service of what William of Newburgh (1135/6–*c*.1198) would call *ridicula figmenta*.[10] Geoffrey would not be the only Latin historian to fabricate a useful documentary source, nor is he the only Latin historian to embellish 'fact', embracing the latitude granted by history's acknowledged place as one of the rhetorical arts.[11] Geoffrey's opening and closing remarks amount to a greeting to his peers: if they are also an implicit challenge, or the sly acknowledgement of a long joke at their expense, it is important to recognize that the terms are the shared inheritance of Latinity.

This volume, then, is rather different from those that have preceded it. While other Arthurian traditions can be treated through a lens that to some extent at least aligns language with ethnic or geographical identities, the Latin tradition is the product of a shared language and a particular kind of culture, but the language is not a birth tongue. Instead, like the attendant culture, it was acquired through education. There is no one geographical place to which this tradition can be assigned. There is perhaps a sense that Arthur appropriately belongs to the British – when a transplanted Italian, Polydore Vergil (*c*.1470–1555), raised questions about two foundational British heroes (Brutus and Arthur), the response from English historians suggested nationalistic pride and a touch of xenophobic hostility.[12] But British is a vexed term – many of the works to be dealt with in these pages were produced at the time of the Angevin kings, for example, a period in which a Latinate courtier-cleric might find himself in the service of an empire that included parts of what we now call England and France. Geoffrey opens his *Historia* with the account of the founding of Britain by the Trojan refugee Brutus, but Geoffrey's own sympathies and ethnicity – was he Norman? Breton? Welsh? – have long been a matter of debate. There is pre-Galfridian material in this collection as well, some of it with clear indebtedness to the Welsh tradition, and some of it hostile to the Britons even as it originates from them (I am thinking here of a figure such as Gildas). What Bede (673/4–735) had to say about the linguistic situation of Britain in his day remains more or less true for much of the period with which this book deals: '[Britain] . . . has five languages, just as the divine law is written in five books. These are the English, Welsh, Irish, Pictish, and Latin languages.' Bede goes on to note that 'Latin, by means of the study of scriptures, has become common to all,'[13] and this is the significant point. While many of the most influential texts dealt with in the pages to follow can be designated Anglo-Latin, the status of Latin as the intellectual lingua franca allowed Latin Arthurian material to spread widely during the Middle Ages, beyond the already multilingual and multi-ethnic confines of Geoffrey's world. Godfrey of Viterbo (*c*.1125–96) drew on Geoffrey's *Historia* for *Pantheon*, his universal chronicle. Johannes de Hauvilla (fl. *c*.1184), a master at the cathedral school at Rouen, introduces Gawain as a character in his verse-satire the *Architrenius*. Caesarius of Heisterbach (*c*.1180–*c*.1240) made use of Geoffrey's Merlinian prophecies. And these are only a few examples of the reach of Latin Arthurian material. A. G. Rigg has argued that 'the Latin writers of England and Wales [in the twelfth and thirteenth centuries] . . . achieved a reputation across Europe that their vernacular counterparts never rivalled, before or since.'[14] Arthur was not their only export, but he was certainly one of the most popular.

In stressing, as I have done thus far, the shared Latinate ethos of the schoolmen, I do not wish to imply that this background produced uniformity in their written work. Geoffrey announces that he is writing a *historia*,[15] and many of the writers to be dealt with in this collection also produced what we classify as histories and chronicles. But there are other genres here, and many forms and styles, and it is one of the goals of this collection to give our readers some sense of this variety. While Geoffrey's *Historia* is well known to modern students of the vernacular Arthurian traditions, the classicizing versification of his work by William of Rennes (*c.*1236) is not. The 'ridiculous figments' William of Newburgh derides in Geoffrey's *Historia* can also be found in such Latin romances as the *Historia Meriadoci*, or in the *mirabilia* section of the *Historia Brittonum*. The pages to follow will introduce readers to saints, monsters, knights, werewolves, and to many Arthurs. We begin with Nick Higham's survey of the chroniclers of early Britain, an essay whose subjects include polemic, annals and chronicles. Andrew Breeze traces the outlines of both the British Latin saints' lives and the scholarly reception of those lives and their rather unexpected Arthurs. Geoffrey of Monmouth receives his due in two essays, one my own overview of what it might mean to Geoffrey to write (Arthurian) history, and the other, Julia Crick's investigation of the reach and influence of his Merlinian prophecies. Ad Putter takes on Arthurian historiography after Geoffrey, showing the range of responses the *Historia regum Britannie* provoked, from stern disapproval (William of Newburgh) to opportunistic deployment (Gerald of Wales) to exuberant expansion (the *Vera historia de morte Arthuri*). Edward Donald Kennedy explores how the traditions linking Arthur to Glastonbury developed, and how the Latin Glastonbury texts existed in a kind of mutual feedback loop with the growing vernacular literature relating to Arthur and the grail. Elizabeth Archibald's texts include Latin romances about Gawain and Meriadoc, and one about Arthur's encounter with a king turned werewolf. In this last text, *Arthur and Gorlagon*, Arthur is looking for an answer to the question posed in vernacular loathly lady stories: what do women most desire? The answer is no easier to find in Latin than it is in Middle English. Finally, James Carley takes us out of the Middle Ages to delineate Arthur's afterlife in the early modern world. Latin is still the common language of the antiquaries with whom Carley deals, even as Arthur is written into English nationalist scripts. Here too there is variety, as Tudor readers of the Arthurian past disagreed both about the king's existence and what, if he did exist, that might mean. But Carley shows that the Latin Arthurian tradition remained influential, and engrossing, centuries after its origins in the early texts with which we began. Like his vernacular counterparts, the Latin Arthur is a versatile and charismatic figure, offering both those who write about him, and those who read about him, an entry into many possible worlds.

Notes

[1] Geoffrey of Monmouth, *The History of the Kings of Britain: An Edition and Translation of De gestis Britonum*, ed. Michael D. Reeve (Woodbridge, 2007), ch. 1 (hereafter *HRB*). Translations are my own.

[2] For example, Gabrielle Spiegel, writing about the rise of vernacular history in the thirteenth century, has written that Latin was 'a "high," learned, written, and fully textualized language, the vernacular a "low," basically oral language'; *Romancing the Past: The Rise of Vernacular Prose Historiography in Thirteenth-Century France* (Berkeley, 1993), p. 66. I discuss the significance of Geoffrey's use of Latin in '"Hic est Artur": reading Latin and reading Arthur', in Alan Lupack (ed.), *New Directions in Arthurian Studies* (Cambridge, 2002), pp. 49–67.

[3] M. M. Bakhtin, *The Dialogic Imagination*, ed. Michael Holquist, trans. Caryl Emerson and Michael Holquist (Austin, 1981), p. 342.

[4] See, for example, M. T. Clanchy, *From Memory to Written Record: England 1066–1307*, 2nd edn (Oxford, 1993), p. 186.

[5] As amply demonstrated by Martha Bayless, *Parody in the Middle Ages: The Latin Tradition* (Ann Arbor, 1996).

[6] Michael Clanchy points out that 'the basic training of the schools was in the use of language' (p. 215), and goes on to argue that it is not therefore surprising that it should be the Latinate schoolmen who experimented with developing literary forms for the vernacular; in other words, they were uniquely suited by their education to be aware of the possibilities and limitations of language and form.

[7] *HRB*, ch. 2: 'infra alienos ortulos falerata uerba non collegerim, agresti tamen stilo propriisque calamis contentus.'

[8] Antonia Gransden details these *topoi* in 'Prologues in the historiography of twelfth-century England', in Daniel Williams (ed.), *England in the Twelfth Century* (Woodbridge, 1990), pp. 55–81.

[9] *HRB*, ch. 208: 'quos de regibus Britonum tacere iubeo, cum non habeant librum illum Britannici sermonis quem Walterus Oxenefordensis archidiaconus ex Britannia aduexit.'

[10] William of Newburgh, *The History of English Affairs*, Bk I, ed. and trans. P. G. Walsh and M. J. Kennedy (Warminster, 1988), *Prooemium*, p. 28. For more on the response of other historians to Geoffrey's work, see the contributions by Julia Crick and Ad Putter to this volume.

[11] On forgeries see, for example, Alfred Hiatt, *The Making of Medieval Forgeries: False Documents in Fifteenth-Century England* (London, 2004). There are many discussions of the rhetorical nature of medieval history (for a selection, see the notes to my essay in this volume). Nancy F. Partner, describing classical history, provides a succinct summary when she notes that 'History absorbed some of [rhetoric's] dominant concerns, especially persuasiveness, *gravitas*, order, and a special kind of verisimilitude with a flexible link to verifiable accuracy'; 'The new Cornificius: medieval history and the artifice of words', in Ernst Breisach (ed.), *Classical Rhetoric and Medieval Historiography* (Kalamazoo, 1985), p. 11.

[12] See James Carley's contribution to this volume.

[13] Bede, *Bede's Ecclesiastical History of the English People*, ed. Bertram Colgrave and R. A. B. Mynors (Oxford, 1969), I.1: 'Haec in praesenti iuxta numerum librorum quibus lex diuina scripta est, quinque gentium linguis unam eandemque summae ueritatis et uerae sublimitatis scientiam scrutatur et confitetur, Anglorum uidelicet Brettonum Scottorum Pictorum et Latinorum, quae meditatione scripturarum ceteris omnibus est facta communis.' The translation is my own.

[14] A. G. Rigg, *A History of Anglo-Latin Literature, 1066–1422* (Cambridge, 1992), p. 2.

[15] In his new edition of the *HRB*, Michael D. Reeve calls Geoffrey's work *De gestis Britonum*, pointing out that a small but significant group of manuscripts uses that title, and that Geoffrey uses it

himself at the end of his *Vita Merlini*. Reeve urges that no arguments should be founded on the more familiar form of the title (Reeve, *The History of the Kings of Britain*, p. lix). Geoffrey does however open by announcing that he has been searching for a *historia* of British kings, and he closes as well by saying that he has been writing about their *historia*. I retain the term, then, not simply for its familiarity, but also because later assumptions about 'history' and 'fiction' have long governed how readers have reacted to the Latin Arthurian tradition, something I discuss in 'Latin Arthurian literature', in Norris J. Lacy (ed.), *A History of Arthurian Scholarship* (Cambridge, 2006), pp. 62–76.

Section One

The Seeds of History and Legend

> [Arthur] was enflamed with excessive passion for the girl and filled with evil thoughts . . . but [his companions], to prevent him, said, 'You should not commit such an outrage, for it is our custom to help the weak and the troubled.'[1]

In this excerpt from the Welsh-Latin *Vita Cadoci*, King Arthur, seated on a hill and playing dice with Cei and Bedwyr, reacts to a drama taking place below him. Gwynllyw, ruler of Gwynlliog, is fleeing Brychan, king of Brecon. Gwynllyw had wished to marry Brychan's daughter Gwladus, and when Brychan refused, Gwynllyw kidnapped her. Brychan's army is about to overtake the pair when they pass in front of Arthur. Arthur's first emotion on spying Gwladus is lust (*libidine*), and his first impulse is wickedness (*scelus*). He asks his companions to seize Gwladus for him, and is only reluctantly dissuaded from what was in essence a planned rape. He eventually aids Gwynllyw instead, and the union of Gwynllyw with Gwladus results in the birth of Cadog, the saint whose life this is.

This incident might surprise readers familiar with Arthur as the great and heroic king of the Britons. But in the British Latin saints' lives, as Andrew Breeze's essay in chapter 2 outlines, Arthur is often portrayed as a 'Celtic chieftain of uncertain temper and dubious morals'. Here we might note the general tone of Gildas's *De excidio et conquestu Britannie*, the sixth-century polemic discussed by Nick Higham in the first chapter in this section. Gildas wrote with passionate disgust about the degeneracy of (his own) British people and their rulers, declaring, 'For it was always the custom of our people, just as it now is, to be weak when it comes to turning back enemies, and to be strong in raising civil war . . . to be powerless, as I say, in pursuing the standard of peace and truth, and strong when it comes to wickedness and lies.'[2] For Gildas, the arrival of the Saxons was a just punishment from God, and while he mentions what will come to be known as Arthur's greatest victory, at Mount Badon, he never names the figure who for a time stems the Saxon tide. Two later texts that deal with the same period, the *Historia Brittonum* and *Annales Cambrie*, do name Arthur, but Higham argues that these works have their own (non-Arthurian) imperatives. These, he writes, are 'Arthurs developed retrospectively for specific and very immediate purposes, with no universal claim on reality centuries earlier'. Like the Arthurs of the saints' lives, these versions of the king are subordinated to the larger ideological schemes of the texts in question. Breeze similarly outlines the contemporary politics in Wales which might lie behind both the Latin texts and some of the vernacular Welsh material with which they must be compared. None of the texts in this section is focused exclusively, or even significantly, on Arthur. Instead, Higham's essay on pre-Galfridian Arthurian material, and Breeze's survey of the Latin saints' lives, demonstrate the range of uses to which Arthur could be put at the birth of the Latin Arthurian tradition.

SE

Notes

[1] *Vita Sancti Cadoci*, in *Vitae sanctorum Britanniae et genealogiae*, ed. A. W. Wade-Evans (Cardiff, 1944), p. 26: 'libidine in amorem adolescentule nimium succensus, ac iniqua cogitatione plenus . . . At illi prohibentes eum dixerunt, 'Absit a te tantum scelus patrari, nos enim soliti sumus inopes anxiosque iuuare.' My translation.

[2] Gildas, *The Ruin of Britain and Other Works*, ed. Michael Winterbottom (London, 1978), ch. 21: 'Moris namque continui erat genti, sicut et nunc est, ut infirma esset ad retundenda hostium tela et fortis esset ad civilia bella . . . infirma, inquam, ad exequenda pacis ac veritatis insignia et fortis ad scelera et mendacia.' My translation.

1

THE CHRONICLERS OF EARLY BRITAIN

Nick Higham

As a figure of Latin literature, Arthur derives from the central Middle Ages and most particularly the fertile mind of the British cleric responsible for the *Historia Brittonum* (*HB*). This work was arguably written in 829–30 in Gwynedd and under the patronage of King Merfyn, who was then in his fourth regnal year.[1] *HB* appears, however, to have been composed by an author with greater personal experience of the southern March and south-east Wales than of north-west Wales.[2] This is particularly clear as regards his collection of marvels (chs 67–75): several comparatively detailed narratives relate to the south east (chs 67–74), including instances which betray a personal presence in these vicinities, and these contrast with the very brief listing of four marvels relating to Anglesey, offered in as many sentences, which along with two somewhat fuller Irish stories seem to have been appended to the author's initial foray into this particular genre.

The *HB* is far from being an attempt at what we might consider history, but was presented as a kind of sermon,[3] carrying a nationalist, dynastic and ideological agenda and – like other early medieval narratives – seeking to manipulate the past to serve present needs.[4] The popularity of *HB* during the Middle Ages led to numerous recensions, which have in turn made establishment of the primary text and its authorship problematic. The following will focus specifically on the Harleian text, on the assumption that it is the earliest and closest to the original.[5]

First, we should place this work in its immediate political and cultural context. In the early ninth century, British kingship was limited to the extreme west, specifically to Strathclyde, Wales and Cornwall, and contemporary historical perspectives were necessarily conditioned very largely by the creation of Anglo-Saxon England across what had formerly been the economic and demographic heartland of the Roman diocese. This author clearly has very little accurate knowledge of the Roman/medieval interface but displays familiarity with a 'Loss of Britain' story which stemmed ultimately from Gildas's *De excidio et conquestu Britannie* (*DEB*: *Concerning the Loss and Lament/Complaint of Britain*).[6] Gildas, writing at an ill-defined point in the very late fifth or early sixth century, portrayed the Britons as if latter-day Israelites,[7] so God's chosen people, but interpreted Roman-period and sub-Roman history, and particularly the arrival of the Saxons in Britain, as indicative of recurring episodes of cowardliness and sinfulness, via which they had brought down divine punishment upon themselves. In his opening remarks he compared their present and recent history to that which Jeremiah had lamented concerning the fall of Jerusalem to

Nebuchadnezzar,[8] and offered a blueprint for the recovery of divine protection via moral reform and a return to obedience to God, which had not, however, been achieved by the close of the work.

While Gildas's vision retained the expectation of future redemption, Bede's influential *Historia ecclesiastica gentis anglorum* (*HE*), completed in 731 and based as regards the fifth century very largely on his reading of Gildas, further developed this negative portrayal by reference to British unwillingness to convert the Anglo-Saxons, rejection of Rome's authority, and refusal to accept Catholic practices (as regards the dating of Easter and the tonsure).[9] Bede, therefore, portrayed the Britons in the present (i.e. the early eighth century) as a community stubbornly unresponsive to righteous Catholic attempts at inclusion and in a sense outside the Christian fold, 'opposed by the power of God and man alike', with their place as the Lord's elect within Britain having been taken by the English whom he foreknew.[10]

Such views on the comparative value of English and Britons were unlikely to be welcomed by the audience of *HB*. Merfyn seems to have come from the Isle of Man to seize power in Gwynedd *c.*825/6,[11] just as Mercian efforts to conquer Wales collapsed: the death of King Coenwulf in 821, the deprivation of his brother and successor, Ceolwulf I, in 823, and then Beornwulf's defeat and death in East Anglia in 825 left the most powerful Anglo-Saxon kingdom of the previous century in crisis and Egberht of the West Saxons as the most powerful figure in southern England, and capable of extending his protection to Welsh rulers. Mercia's failure following a generation characterized by military intervention in Wales provided the space for a new nationalist rhetoric in Gwynedd. The author of the *HB* was thereby encouraged to contradict Bede, highlighting Britons as having in the past been militarily successful,[12] as effective missionaries to both the Irish and the Northumbrians,[13] and as characteristically beloved of the Lord.[14] In contrast, he presented the English as of dubious morality, recently pagan and lacking in courage,[15] and, implicitly at least, looked forward to ultimate British victory against the invader. We have, therefore, *inter alia* the prophetic story of the struggle between the red dragon of the Britons and the white one of the English, which posits three heroic but unsuccessful attempts to throw the Saxons back and then a final triumph which has the red dragon pursuing the defeated enemy overseas.[16] Via the campaigns of Vortimer, Arthur and Urien, the author implied that the first three attempts had already occurred,[17] so only the final, successful war of expulsion remained to be achieved. Merfyn was, therefore, being established rhetorically as a potential pan-British war leader, whose destiny was to expel the English from Britain. Several references to the Isle of Man, from which he arguably derived, seem to have been included for their topical relevance, and Cunedda,[18] who had much earlier supposedly come from the north to eject invaders from Wales, the red dragon itself, Vortimer, Arthur and Urien should all, perhaps, be read as metaphors for the present king, whose infamous freckles (he was known as Merfyn Frich) may well imply that he had reddish hair.[19]

An essential precondition of the success of this narrative was effective moral positioning of the Britons as a people, and there is a reaction herein against both Gildas and Bede. The putative sins of the Britons were re-focused in the *HB* on the single figure of Vortigern,[20] whom Bede had named as responsible for the initial invitation to the Saxons.[21] Vortigern was depicted, therefore, as thoroughly evil – as incestuous, lecherous, cowardly, criminal and heathen, and having suffered the consequences in the manner of his death. To balance his moral impact, a series of virtuous individuals were introduced through whom divine approval of the Britons could be illustrated and carried forward. The prophetic boy-child Emrys arguably derives from a foundation story attached to the hillfort of Dinas Emrys,[22] which has been conflated with the figure of Ambrosius Aurelianus whom both Gildas and Bede had named, to produce a Christ-figure (as the child with no father) and Moses-figure, in the context of his contest with the magicians of Pharaoh.[23] Vortipor, Vortigern's putative son, seems to have been developed as the obverse of his father, so as a brave, far-sighted and successful warrior, combating his father's Saxon allies.[24] His presentation has debts to Gildas and Bede and his short battle-list is arguably apocryphal, given the presence of English place-names, so there is no reason to think him historical. St Germanus is herein a conflation of the historical bishop of Auxerre who visited Britain in 429, as Bede reported,[25] and St Garman, whose cult developed primarily in eastern Wales and to whose *Life* the author referred,[26] but developed for rhetorical effect again as a Moses- and Christ-figure to confront the Satanic Vortigern. St Patrick, the British missionary bishop to the Irish, was then presented as if an antidote to Vortigern, his triumphs for the Lord coming immediately after the latter's death. The author relied here on comparatively late hagiographical material from Ireland and set out quite explicitly to portray Patrick as a British type of Moses.[27] Each of these figures was developed to rhetorical effect for a particular purpose, therefore, primarily via biblical imagery. Particularly for an audience versed in the Testaments, these somewhat stereotypical characterizations served to rebut the assertion that the Britons were either by their nature cowardly or had in the era of Vortigern and as a consequence of his actions for ever lost divine favour. Although some obviously originated as historical figures, it was not their historicity that was central to their depiction here but their adaptability to the author's rhetorical purposes.[28]

Arthur *miles* is the last of this cast of characters developed so as to present the Britons as both courageous and beloved of the Lord, and his story closes this section of the *HB*, comprising chapter 56. This chapter heralds the shift to the final 'historical' section (chs 57–65) which was constructed around a group of Anglian genealogies, annotated so as to provide details of 'British' interest, again primarily in praise of the types of achievement already noted. So, here the successes of Cædwallon, Cunedda and Urien all feature as illustrations of British military prowess,[29] Outigern provides an exemplar of British courage,[30] and Rhun is credited with converting Edwin of Northumbria to Christianity.[31] In contrast, the English are termed *ambrones* (best translated here as 'savages'),[32] their earliest bishop was said to be the very late figure of Egbert (bishop, then archbishop of York, 732–66),[33] which were it true would imply a real tardiness in accepting conversion, and the narrative closes with Penda's victories over his neighbours achieved as a non-believer through Satanic powers.[34]

Let us focus, therefore, on chapter 56. The first two sentences signal the growing menace posed by the number of Saxons in Britain and how authority passed from Hengist on his death to his son:

> At that time the English increased their numbers and grew in Britain. On Hengest's death, his son Octha came down from the north of Britain to the kingdom of the Kentishmen, and from him are sprung the kings of the Kentishmen.[35]

Arthur does not occur here or in the last two sentences, which revert to the same theme and the arrival with reinforcements of barbarian kings from Germany. The 'Arthurian' passage is strictly, therefore, just 186 words long, and embedded within a chapter which acts as a bridge between the preceding section, based on British and Irish material, and that which follows, which was structured around English material. It is inserted between two somewhat derivative sets of remarks about the Saxons, which apparently were drawn largely from Bede, whose various references to Hengist, Octa, Oeric, Ida and the influx of immigrants from Germany they loosely paraphrase.[36]

The 'Arthurian' filling of this Saxon sandwich seems entirely original to the text, and the construction should arguably be read as this author's, and not a result of his copying some pre-existing source. There is a clear logic to the ordering of these three blocks. The first 'Saxon' section establishes the threat. The 'Arthurian' text then proclaims British successes against the invader under God's protection, which spells out very clearly just where this episode and the participants within it belong in providential history. Then the second 'Saxon' passage describes the response of the defeated English, who brought in overwhelming forces from Germany along with their kings. In very general terms, therefore, it was the Britons who won the victories named, who fought heroically, and who enjoyed the support of both Christ and the Virgin Mary on the battle field. That they finally lost is acknowledged only by default and is to be understood against the moral juxtapositioning of the two sides. Like Bede writing of Rædwald (in *HE* II.12), for example, this author felt that it was acceptable to acknowledge the victory of the 'baddies' provided they had overwhelming numerical superiority. Therefore mass migration by the English was an essential part of this explanation of the loss of Britain.

The 'Arthurian' passage in chapter 56 consists of a single, introductory sentence which contextualizes Arthur and positions him within the author's vision of contemporary 'British society', followed by a group of eight interconnected sentences detailing eleven of his glorious victories. There is a brief concluding sentence, which credits Arthur with fantastic achievements at the twelfth battle, of Badon, then provides a separate and concluding phrase of just six words which sums up and emphasizes his achievements. That he was in this conclusion 'victorious in all his campaigns',[37] connects neatly with the introductory sentence, in which 'Arthur fought against them [the Saxons] in those days, together with the kings of the British'; but he was their 'leader in battle'.[38]

There are several features which spring immediately to our attention. One is a sense of *déjà vu*: there are significant parallels between this passage and that describing the campaigns of Vortimer in chapters 43 and 44, even down to use of some of the same language and similar structures – most noticeably their respective battle-lists, both of which were biblically numbered.[39] A second is the sense in which, excluding chapter 73 (see below), Arthur is entirely contained within this specific context, and has no part to play in this text other than as an iconic, Christian, British war-leader against the Saxons in this rhetorical interlude inserted between two references to Saxon immigration and the growth of Anglo-Saxon power inside Britain. His exploits are used here to break up the otherwise depressing story of Saxon occupation, for powerful ideological and rhetorical purposes. Arthur provides a very necessary 'feel-good' factor at this point in the tale. A third is Arthur's status as *miles* and *dux*, by which he is exclusively being celebrated in this chapter as a warrior and leader in battle. The annotated contents list which precedes the main text of the *Historia* in Morris's edition refers to Arthur as *rex belligerus* ('warlike king') but this introductory apparatus is absent from the Harleian and Chartres texts, which are the earliest available, so are arguably a late addition: it is important to note that there is no hint of royal status in chapter 56.[40] A fourth is the looseness of Arthur's chronological positioning. That might not be a matter of much concern in some other early medieval texts, but this author was as interested in the passage of time as was Bede and was careful to make sure he located such figures as Vortigern with some precision (if not necessarily accurately). Arthur is, by contrast, located only by the phrase *In illo tempore* ('At that time') with which the author began his initial remarks about the Saxons, then the *Tunc* ('then') with which he began the Arthurian passage proper. Thereafter, Ida and other unnamed Anglo-Saxon kings were introduced as a consequence of an appeal to Germany '*dum* they were defeated in all their battles'.[41] There is no attempt even to denote the number of years across which Arthur purportedly won his great battles, and so his years of service, to compare with the regnal years which occur in the following sections.

Finally, this passage is infused with biblical number. This is only to be expected, perhaps, since so too are the previous sections dealing with Germanus and Patrick, but the fact does little to inspire confidence in the detail. So, for example, Arthur's name occurs three times and he fought twelve battles. This emphasizes the rhetorical construction of the text. If we look in a little more detail at the points in this story at which his name actually appears, the first reference introduces Arthur as the overall military leader, leading the warriors of the British kings; the second stresses his achieving victory while bearing the emblems of the Virgin and slaughtering the *pagani* under the protection of both Mary and Christ, and the third positions him as the superhuman hero who killed 960 men in a single charge at Badon. The twelve battles necessarily equate Arthur with the Saviour, so confirming and reinforcing the connections made in the second reference to 'Our Lord Jesus Christ'.

We have, therefore, an Arthur portrayed as the paramount military leader of the Britons, an invariably successful Christian soldier and a great warrior who personally achieved heroic deeds under divine protection. He is constructed against the numerous but pagan Saxons, whose death and destruction God encompassed via the heroic Arthur as an agent of divine will. Arthur is, therefore, a saviour figure and a warrior type of the messiah for his people.

Gildas had referred to the council advising the *superbus tyrannus* (whom Bede later called Vortigern) to call in the Saxons as 'the silly princes of Zoan', as has been said, 'giving foolish advice to Pharaoh'.[42] However, he thereafter abandoned this analogy with the history of the Israelites in Egypt and turned to the deeds of the Assyrians,[43] and then the sack of Jerusalem by the Babylonians as parallels appropriate to the present,[44] as the principal biblical metaphors by which to inject meaning into his account of the Saxon revolt, the killing or enslavement of his people, the destruction of Britain's towns and the parlous condition of the Britons in the present. In contrast, the author of the *HB* seems to have been particularly attracted by this comparison between Vortigern and Pharaoh, and developed the analogy much further. His St Patrick was, therefore, explicitly paralleled with Moses, and constructed as a prophet-figure for the Britons whose role it was to lead them from a metaphorical Egypt – ruled by the inimical Vortigern – to the Promised Land. Patrick begins as a captive among the Irish in the time of Vortigern, much as the Israelites were captives in Pharaoh's Egypt. Thereafter (ch. 54), he preached the Gospel for forty years, achieved many miracles and

> fasted for forty days and forty nights on the summit of Eile hill; and on that hill that reached to the skies, he gently asked three petitions for those of the Irish who had received the faith . . . On that hill he blessed the peoples of Ireland, and he climbed it in order to pray for them and to see the fruits of his labour.[45]

The positioning of Patrick as a Moses figure is to this point implicit, although far from difficult to decipher. Thereafter, in chapter 55, the connection is made explicit, for

> In four ways Patrick is like Moses: in talking with an angel in the burning bush; secondly he fasted on a mountain for 40 days and 40 nights; thirdly, both alike were 120 years old; fourthly no man knows his tomb . . . The matter demands that more should be said of St. Patrick, but nevertheless I must be brief, to shorten my sermon.[46]

Our author based this on Irish hagiographical texts, primarily Tirechan's *Memorandum*, but he was biblically literate and presumably knew that the later passages derive verbatim from the last chapter of the Book of Deuteronomy. In verse 9 thereof, reference is made to Joshua, whose Book follows. Joshua is presented in the Bible as the universally victorious martial leader of his people, under God's guidance, who led the Israelites across the Jordan, picking up twelve stones (to represent the twelve tribes into which he divided his people) from the river bed as they crossed. During the first twelve chapters of this book, he won battle after battle against the Canaanites under divine guidance and took control of the land. Just as the great prophet Moses was succeeded by the war-leader Joshua, therefore, so too was the British Moses-figure, St Patrick, followed in this text by the British Joshua-figure of Arthur. The twelve tribes of Israel, the twelve stones and the twelve chapters of the Book of Joshua which detail his victories are paralleled by Arthur's twelve victories over the Saxons.[47] This parallel is entirely implicit, but the author made it relatively simple to unravel for those of his audience who knew the Bible. At the start of Judges, the book which follows Joshua, we find: 'After the death of Joshua the children of Israel consulted the LORD, saying, who shall go up before us against the Canaanites, to be the leader in battle?' The phrase used of Joshua's role is *dux bellum*, a somewhat tautological phrase meaning 'war-leader of war', or 'general in war'. The author of the *HB* used almost the same phrase of Arthur, who *ipse dux erat bellorum.* Since there immediately follows the list of twelve battles, the author perhaps substituted the plural in recognition of these numerous individual engagements. This is the only occurrence of these two words in combination in the Bible, and it seems very likely that our author derived it from this passage.

Arthur was, therefore, being constructed here as a Joshua figure, to sustain the metaphorical vision of the Britons as the latter-day Israelites of Exodus. This construct should be put alongside that already established of Arthur as a type of the warrior-Christ to provide a package of biblical influences on the ways in which he was developed in this text. Joshua and Jesus were, of course, identical names in Hebrew, and the connection between the two seems to have been widely recognized in the early Middle Ages. It seems very likely that it was both the Book of Joshua and the numbering of the apostles which encouraged the author to provide Arthur with twelve battles, particularly seeing that he struggled to reach this total. He seems to have appropriated battles from all sorts of existing narratives, none of which necessarily had anything previously to do with an Arthur-figure, Badon included, and even placed four (numbers two to five) on a single river (the *Dubglas*), which suggests that his imagination may have been unequal to the task of assembling twelve individual candidates.

The Arthur of the *HB* was, therefore, developed in defence of the positioning of the Britons within the history of salvation, and to contest divine approval of Anglo-Saxon domination of Britain in the present, which, the author was here implying, resulted from overwhelming military superiority rather than its accordance with God's plan for Britain. His connections with both Joshua and Christ were apparently intended to parallel the positioning of Patrick as a type of British Moses, making a complimentary doublet of God-beloved British characters, so implying that even after the *adventus Saxonum* during the reign of Vortigern the Britons remained a chosen people of the

Lord. By contrast, in chapter 56 the Saxons were represented explicitly as unwarlike pagans and implicitly as Canaanites, whom God did not favour and whose land would ultimately be reconquered by the latter-day Israelites; that is, the Britons.

The Arthur that we have articulated here is, therefore, very largely a product of biblical metaphor, but it is important to explore the author's sources. Many of the materials used in this work seem only to date to the late eighth or early ninth century, so to the generation of its author or perhaps of his parents.[48] Take, for example, the list of *civitates*, which it is usually assumed was original to the *Historia* and written by the same author, although it follows the *Annales* and genealogies in the Harleian text. While the total of twenty-eight towns arguably derives from Gildas,[49] he named far fewer and the actual sites chosen are not consistent with a date much earlier than 800, even if some of the unidentified names have not been made up by the author.[50] The English genealogical material includes Offa's son Ecgfrith, so is unlikely to predate the sole year in which he actually reigned (796). This English-derived material was therefore not quite up to date when incorporated in the *Historia* c.829/30, but it was only one generation adrift. Nor was the 'British' or 'Irish' material much nearer contemporary with the events it purported to describe. While Patrick is generally thought of as a fifth century figure, the author of the *HB* seems not to have had access to his surviving works but depended on later hagiographical material written in support of Armagh's claims on his cult, around the third quarter of the seventh century. Germanus of Auxerre is closely dated to the mid-fifth century but the author of the *HB* does not seem to have had access to the *Life* written by Constantius, but depended rather on a *Life* of the Powysian St Garman which seems to have conflated these two figures and is unlikely to have been particularly ancient *c*.829.[51] The *HB* is, therefore, highly retrospective as regards its earlier figures and cannot be relied upon without independent verification as evidence for the sub-Roman epoch. If we focus specifically on chapter 56, it has been suggested that a vernacular battle-poem of the kind known to have celebrated the careers of particular Welsh warrior kings underlies the Arthurian list of battles,[52] but there is little substance to the proposal. Although all the battles are named in the vernacular, so too were other battles in this text, so there is no particular reason to identify a single vernacular source. This view has latterly relied far too heavily on the ingenious assumption that a mistranslation resulting from confusion between Old Welsh *iscuit* (shield) and *iscuid* (shoulder) has resulted in the depiction of an Arthur carrying 'the image of St Mary the perpetual virgin on his arms', when it should have read '. . . on his shield',[53] but given the biblical imagery this might perhaps be read symbolically rather than literally, as a depiction of Arthur carrying a picture of Mary as if in a religious procession, in which case no mistranslation occurred. In practice, the battles selected seem previously to have belonged to a variety of other contexts, Badon to the wars of Gildas's Ambrosius, for example, and *urbs legionis* to the Northumbrian victory over Powys highlighted by Bede,[54] and to have derived from pre-existing texts, both Latin and Old Welsh, and very different dates. As Kenneth Hurlstone Jackson opined long since, it seems safest to view this list as historically spurious.[55]

Arthur's battle-list looks as contrived as that provided for Vortimer, therefore, and it would be perilous to argue that this passage of the *HB* can offer insights into the actual achievements of a historical figure via its repetition of significantly earlier source materials that are no longer extant. The author's most obvious sources here should be viewed as Gildas, who initially described warfare between Britons and Saxons leading up to *mons Badonicus*, and Bede, who paraphrased that same account and added further, perhaps apocryphal detail. This was combined with several references to the Bible and a variety of local folktales and campaigns previously associated with heroic figures of Welsh tradition or the British North.

That a warrior Arthur was already a hero of Welsh folklore by this date is illustrated in this same text, in the list of *mirabilia* ('marvels'),[56] two of which feature a figure of this name:

> There is another wonder in the region which is called Builth. There is a pile of stones there and one stone positioned on top of the heap has the footprint of a dog on it. When he hunted the boar *Troynt*, *Cabal*, who was the hound of Arthur the warrior, made an imprint on the stone, and Arthur afterwards collected up the heap of stones under the stone in which was the footprint, and it is called *Carn Gabal*. And men come and carry the stone in their hands for the space of a day and a night, and on the next day it has returned to the top of the pile.[57]

The site is identified as Carn Gafallt, in the upper valley of the Wye, and this story alludes to the boar hunt which also features in the story of *Culhwch and Olwen*, the earliest surviving text of which dates to around 1000.[58] The coincidence of the name of Arthur's dog, *Cabal* (meaning 'horse': modern Welsh *ceffyl*) and this hill name was perhaps the catalyst for the development of an etymological story centred on Arthur which this author borrowed from the locale. To this the author added:

> There is another miracle in the region of Ergyng [Archenfield]. There is there a grave next to a spring, which is called *Llygad Amr*, and the name of the man who is buried in the tumulus is *Amr*; he was the son of the warrior Arthur, and he himself killed him in that very place and buried him. And men come to measure the grave, which is sometimes six feet long, sometimes nine, sometimes twelve, sometimes fifteen. Whatever length you measure on one occasion, you do not repeat that measure, and I have tried myself.[59]

Again, this is a wonder-tale derived from etymological roots, since *Amr* is the stem of the river-name Gamber. Arthur's introduction here perhaps derives from the superficial similarity of the two names – recall after all the connection made earlier in the *HB* between the eponymous Trojan, Brutus, and Britain. The story of a legendary warrior killing his own son finds parallels in Irish legend with the story of *Aided Óenfir Aífe*.[60]

Both stories demonstrate the pre-existence of Arthurian folktales in the early ninth century and our author's interest in them, and it seems quite possible that he historicized Arthur for his own rhetorical purposes from this source.[61] Clearly, none of his hero-figures herein should be counted historical on his evidence alone. The survival of Patrick's own works and Vortigern's early naming, perhaps by Gildas, certainly by Bede, provides independent verification of their historicity. But in this incarnation, at least, Germanus is arguably more fiction than fact, and Vortimer may even have been this author's invention. Given the virtual absence of earlier references, therefore, the non-contemporaneity and rhetorical style of the *HB* must count against it as evidence by which to establish Arthur's historicity in a recognizable form, let alone distinguish his role and/or his dates.

The *Annales Cambriae* ('Welsh Annals': hereinafter *AC*) have often been interpreted as providing the necessary second strand of evidence capable of confirming the figure of Arthur presented by the *HB* as a bona fide historical figure but that is perhaps a little naïve. Before turning in detail to the Arthurian entries, however, we should establish the overall context of this brief chronicle. The *AC* close with an entry for the year 954 detailing the death of Rhodri, one of the sons of Hywel Dda (whose death in 950 was also included), and it was most probably written within a year or so of the final entry. It was arguably composed at St David's in the heart of Hywel's erstwhile primary kingdom of Dyfed, then under the rule of his son Owain. Hywel, herein uniquely termed 'king of the Britons', had ruled all of Deheubarth (Dyfed and Ceredigion), Powys and Gwynedd in the last eight years of his long reign (904–50), but dynastic rivals had re-secured Gwynedd on his death and had waged a successful war against his sons, who were defeated at the battle of Carno in 951 and whose very survival probably seemed in doubt in 954. In 955, three Welsh kings, namely Iago of Gwynedd and Powys, Morgan of Morgannwg, and Owain, Hywel's son, were witnesses to King Eadred's grant of Alwalton to one Ælfsige Hunlafing,[62] which implies that they had congregated at the English court, presumably under English pressure to signal an end to their conflicts, in the months before Eadred's death in November of the same year.

The *AC* were probably written, therefore, at a time of political crisis in south-west Wales, under a king who had suffered defeat at the hands of dynastic rivals across the previous few years, and whose best hope of survival lay in attracting English support against his own near relatives. It is noticeable that the nationalistic rhetoric that we find in the *HB* is distinctly lacking in the *AC*, perhaps due to King Owain's reliance at this point on the hope of English protection from his Welsh enemies.

The underlying structure of this set of annals was established by Kathleen Hughes in 1973:[63] the earliest material is based on an Irish original now lost but closely related to the Chronicle of Clonmacnoise,[64] to which had been added northern British and English material covering the early seventh to late eighth centuries and a set of annals composed locally detailing the mid-790s onwards, in the aftermath of Welsh acquiescence in the Catholic dating of Easter in 768 and a period of intense Mercian pressure on Wales generally. The two Arthurian entries derive from the earliest section, so it is this on which we will focus here.

The *AC* are particularly sparse across the first century, conventionally dated from 444,[65] and most of this material is of Irish provenance, reflecting the author's reliance on an Irish chronicle source. If we exclude the death of Gildas, which he arguably took from his Irish annals, there are only seven distinctly 'British' entries between the years 444 and 612, as follows:

> [516]: The battle of Badon, in which Arthur carried the cross of our Lord Jesus Christ for three days and three nights on his shoulders and the Britons were victors.
> [537]: The battle of Camlann, in which Arthur and Medraut fell, and there was a great mortality [i.e. plague] in Britain and in Ireland.
> [547]: The great mortality [i.e. plague] in which died Maelgwyn, king of Gwynedd.
> [573]: The battle of Armterid.
> [580]: Gwrgi and Peredur died.
> [584] Battle against the Isle of Man [from Irish annals] and burial of Daniel of the Bangors.
> [595]: King Dunawd died.[66]

After the mid-century, the British material arguably relates predominantly to northern Britain and derives from northern sources.[67] The burial of Daniel is the only 'Welsh' addition to these 'northern' entries, which the author perhaps derived from a *Life* now lost but associated with the principal cult site of Bangor in Gwynedd. However, such hagiographical works are so rarely provided with dates – let alone accurate dates – that there seems no good reason without further evidence to assume that Daniel's inclusion in these annals was based on anything more sophisticated than guesswork. Similarly, there seems little reason to suppose that the author had good information regarding the obit of King Maelgwyn. There is no evidence within this text that he was personally familiar with Gildas, whose work clearly implies the king to have been his own adult contemporary,[68] making it improbable that Gildas should have died, as the *AC* records, in 570, but Maelgwyn in 547.[69]

There seems little contextual reason, therefore, to accept the two Arthurian entries as chronologically accurate and this impression is compounded by an exploration of the author's sources. It has often been argued that this section of the *AC* was based on related but not identical material to that used by the author of *HB*, but such are the similarities of language used that it seems very likely indeed that the principal source for the Arthurian entries in the *AC* was the *HB* itself: of the thirty-one words in the Latin original in the two entries for 516 and 537, taken together, nineteen occur in *HB* chapter 56, and a further seven occur in *HB* chapters 57 and 63, including, in the latter, the phrase 'for three days and three nights'. While the annalist clearly did not copy out entire sentences, he does seem to have based his entries very firmly on the construction of Arthur in the earlier work, which is not, of course, effectively dated.

The very different political circumstances of authorship seem to have required a fundamentally different type of Arthur here than in the *HB*. There is no mention of Arthur's enemies at all, let alone pejorative language attached to them. Instead, the image of an Arthur carrying the image of St Mary, which we find in *HB* chapter 56 in the context of his eighth battle, becomes an Arthur bearing Christ's cross for three days and three nights, implying connections with Simon the Cyrenian carrying the cross for Jesus,[70] via whom we are offered an Arthur who is less the martial type of Christ or Joshua of the *HB* and more a symbolic Christ-helper. This new image of Arthur has no retrospective validity, however, reflecting as it arguably does the author's impulse to avoid entries which might be prejudicial to his patron's claims on the good services of the English court of the day in reconciling him with his enemies.[71]

Of the five words not clearly sourced, one is a personal name, Medraut, and another a place- or battle-name, Camlann. There is no good reason to suppose that Medraut should be considered Arthur's enemy here, although that was how he was developed subsequently, particularly by Geoffrey of Monmouth. The battle name is not otherwise known from early sources, and given the locality of authorship there is a possibility that both names should be sought primarily in south-west Wales.[72] The author of the *AC* was presumably familiar with the genealogy of the native kings of Dyfed, in which the name Arthur appears thirteen generations before Owain,[73] so the Arthur of the *HB* was perhaps here being re-imagined as a hero of Dyfed and forebear of the present king, and included in a new set of annals as a means of introducing a figure capable of carrying current dynastic meanings into early sections of a chronicle which were otherwise virtually without local material.

Given the chronological imprecision of the *HB* regarding Arthur, as already noted, it may be profitable to explore the precise dates chosen for his appearances in the *AC*. These entries were introduced to that part of the *Annales* which derives primarily from an early tenth-century Irish chronicle, so should probably be viewed as original to the author of the mid-tenth-century *AC*. Given their heavy reliance on the text of the *HB*, they cannot have been written before the early ninth century at earliest. We can be confident, therefore, that these entries can have no claim to contemporaneity with the events they claim to describe.[74] Given that Patrick's activities immediately precede Arthur's in the *HB*, the author of *AC* may well have felt encouraged to define the period appropriate to Arthur by reference to the death of Patrick, which his Irish source placed in 457. The gap between 457 and 516 looks somewhat substantial, however, for this logic to have been overly persuasive. An alternative is to argue that the author knew Bede's *Chronica majora* of 725, which locates the battle of Badon in the period 474–91, then added the forty-four years which are associated with that battle by both Gildas and Bede, giving a time-frame of 518–35.[75] Given the underlying imprecision of dating across this text, the inclusion of Arthurian entries in 517 and 537 seems to fit this explanation quite effectively, but this does require our author to have dispensed with Ambrosius' responsibility for this battle, as was acknowledged in Bede's *Chronica*. It additionally requires the author to have had access to this text, which is possible but far from certain, particularly given the numerous attacks which St David's had suffered at the hands of the Vikings over the previous century.

Alternatively, one might argue that successive references to plague years *c*.546 and 550 in the Irish annals enabled the author to fix the death of King Maelgwyn, who *HB* implied was an approximate contemporary of Ida of Northumbria, whose reign Bede had fixed at 547–59, at or approximate to the earlier of these two dates. Such required Arthur's death to precede 547 but the eleven battles listed before Badon may have been read to imply that Arthur should be located in the latter part of this time period. His positioning in 516 and 537 in *AC* may, therefore, have been comparatively arbitrary, with sources available to the author doing little more than suggest that his activities be located in the latter part of a time period stretching from 457 to 547.

The Arthurian entries in *AC* are not, therefore, obviously based on early and reliable source material. Rather they betray a heavy reliance on the *HB* itself, which was not written until 829–30. Differences between these texts arguably derive from the different contexts in which their authors were working, rather than their access to different pre-existing materials for comment on Arthur. While the *HB* was a narrative designed to extol British moral and military virtues and claim past victories over the Sassenachs, written in the early years of Merfyn's reign in Gwynedd, in the particular context of the collapse of Mercian power, *AC* was written over a century later in the shadow of a Welsh court where fear of Gwynedd was the dominant domestic agenda and an effort was arguably being made to cultivate the English court to obtain protection from inter-dynastic conflict. These texts pursue very different and in some senses diametrically opposing political agendas, but both authors centred their works in the same Welsh cultural milieu, and it is arguably that shared cultural identity which led each author to write his own version of Arthur into his text. Neither should be read as if a narrative likely to have been primarily reflective of historical fact concerning the distant past, or outside the immediate context in which each was framed. Rather, theirs were Arthurs developed retrospectively for specific and very immediate purposes, with no universal claim on reality centuries earlier. That need not mean that Arthur was entirely fictional but it does mean that these versions do not of themselves, singly or in combination, provide a secure foundation on which to build a historical figure. That *HB* and *AC* have since so often been read as if providing evidence capable of both locating and outlining the reign of a historical King Arthur is due to a deep misunderstanding of the texts themselves and the mutability of the stories each offers in the face of the immediate political and dynastic contexts within which each was written.

Notes

1 The *Historia Brittonum* offers a variety of dating strategies among which, in ch. 16, 'From the year when the Saxons first came to Britain to the fourth year of king Merfyn, 429 years are reckoned' (A primo anno, quo Saxones venerunt in Brittanniam, usque ad annum quartum Mermini Regis, supputantur anni CCCCXXVIIII) seems to imply that it was written in Merfyn's fourth regnal year. See n. 5 below for bibliographical references.

[2] David N. Dumville, 'The historical value of the *Historia Brittonum*', *Arthurian Literature*, 6 (1986), 6; the author's name is given as Nennius in Corpus Christi College, Cambridge, MS 139, and a small number of MSS derivative therefrom, but this may well be a late addition to the work: see the various arguments against this ascription offered by David Dumville, 'Some aspects of the chronology of the *Historia Brittonum*', *Bulletin of the Board of Celtic Studies*, 25 (1974), 439–45, and for by P. J. C. Field, 'Nennius and his history', *Studia Celtica*, 30 (1996), 159–65.

[3] The author referred to it as a *sermo* in ch. 55, although this text was not one which would have lent itself to recitation as a whole.

[4] For discussion of the historicity and purposes of *HB*, see particularly Dumville, 'The historical value'; Thomas Charles-Edwards, 'The Arthur of history', in Rachel Bromwich, A. O. H. Jarman and Brynley F. Roberts (eds), *The Arthur of the Welsh* (Cardiff, 1991), pp. 15–32; Nicholas J. Higham, *King Arthur: Myth-Making and History* (London, 2002), pp. 119–65.

[5] David Dumville has begun to provide scholarly editions of the several recensions but to date only one has been published: *Historia Brittonum*, III: *The 'Vatican' Recension,* ed. David N. Dumville (Cambridge, 1985). The earliest surviving recension is that contained in Harleian MS 3859, which has been edited by Theodor Mommsen in his *Chronica Minora Saec. IV, V, VI, VII*, iii, *Monumenta Germaniae Historica*, AA xiii (Berlin, 1898), pp. 147–222, then Edmund Faral, *La Légende arthurienne. Études et documents, les plus anciens textes*, III (Paris, 1929), pp. 5–62. The most accessible text today is that provided by John Morris in his *Nennius: British History and the Welsh Annals* (London, 1980), pp. 50–84, with an English translation on pp. 9–43, but this posthumously published text has additions from later sources which are not always easy to distinguish and the introduction was little more than a series of notes before the author's untimely death, which offer a highly improbable view of the contemporaneity and historicity of the author's sources.

[6] The most accessible text is in *The Ruin of Britain and Other Documents*, ed. Michael Winterbottom (London, 1978), pp. 87–142, with a translation on pp. 13–79, which is based on the text as established by Mommsen, *Chronica Minora,* III, pp. 25–88.

[7] *DEB* I.13.

[8] *DEB* I.5, at the close of two chapters which collectively stress the awfulness of God's wrath concerning comparatively minor misdemeanours committed by his people.

[9] *Bede's Ecclesiastical History of the English Church and People*, ed. Bertram Colgrave and R. A. B. Mynors (Oxford, 1969), I.22, II.2; V.23.

[10] *HE*, V.23: 'et diuina sibi humana prorsus resistente'; I.22: 'Sed non tamen diuina pietas plebem suam, quam praesciuit, deseruit; quin multo digniores genti memoratae praecones ueritatis, per quos crederet, destinauit.'

[11] David P. Kirby, 'British dynastic history in the pre-Viking period', *Bulletin of the Board for Celtic Studies*, 27 (1976), 97–8: Merfyn held power for an unusual period, until 844.

[12] See, for example, *HB*, 27–30.

[13] See, for example, *HB*, 50–5, 63.

[14] See, for example, *HB*, 47, for St Germanus as if an Old Testament prophet, and *HB*, chs 50–5 for St Patrick.

[15] See, for example, *HB*, ch. 44: 'They fled to their keels and were drowned as they clambered aboard them like women' (et ipsi in fugam versi usque ad ciulas suas mersi sunt in eas muliebriter intrantes), in which the author was perhaps deliberately contesting Gildas's use of *muliebriter* ('like women') of the Britons (*DEB* VI.2) by transferring it to their opponents, while adopting his same, Old English, term for ships: *ciulas*.

[16] *HB*, ch. 42.

[17] *HB,* chs 43–4, 56, 63.

[18] *HB*. chs 14, 62.

[19] Higham, *King Arthur*, p. 160.

[20] *HB*, chs. 37–42, 45–7.

[21] *HE*, I.15.

[22] Dumville, 'Historical value', 9–11.

[23] Higham, *King Arthur*, p. 136.

[24] *HB*, chs 43–4.

[25] *HE*, I.17–21, based on the late fifth-century *Vita Germani* by Constantius: Bruno Krusch and Wilhelm Levison (eds), *Passiones vitaeque sanctorum aevi Merovingici cum supplemento et appendice*, Scriptores rerum Merovingicarum (Hanover, 1920), VII, pp. 225–83.

[26] *HB*, ch. 47: 'This is the end of Vortigern, as I found it in the *Liber beati Germani*' (Hic est finis Guorthigirni, ut in Libro beati Germani repperi). Dumville suggests, in 'Historical value', that this life is likely to have been written in the years around 800.

[27] *HB*, chs 50–5, based largely on Tirechan's *Memorandum*, in *The Patrician Texts in the Book of Armagh,* ed. Ludwig Bieler (Dublin, 1979), pp. 122–79.

[28] As Patrick Sims-Williams rightly remarks, there is no clear division in terms of types of knowledge at this date between history and myth: 'The emergence of Old Welsh, Cornish and Breton orthography: 600–800: the evidence of Archaic Old Welsh', *Bulletin of the Board of Celtic Studies*, 38 (1991), 35.

[29] *HB*, chs 61, 62, 63.

[30] *HB*, ch. 62.

[31] *HB*, ch. 63: once again the forty days here implies parallels with both Moses and Christ, while at the same time besting the 'thirty-six days' with which Bede credited Paulinus' missionary effort at Yeavering; *HE* II.14.

[32] *HB*, chs 57, 63. Gildas used *ambrones* in a similar way, terming the raiding, pagan Irish and Picts *ambrones lupi*, which Winterbottom translates as 'greedy wolves': *DEB* XVI. This use of the term may have encouraged our author to deploy it for the Saxons.

[33] *HB*, ch. 61.

[34] *HB*, ch. 65.

[35] *HB*, ch. 56: 'In illo tempore Saxones invalescebant in multitudine et crescebant in Brittannia. Mortuo autem Hengisto, Ochta, filius ejus, transivit de sinistrali parte Brittanniae ad regnum Cantorum, et de ipso orti sunt reges Cantorum.'

[36] See *HE*, I.15; II.5; V.24; and I.15, respectively, but with additional, but probably imaginative, details added.

[37] *HB*, ch. 56: 'in omnibus bellis victor extitit.'

[38] *HB*, ch. 56: 'Tunc Arthur pugnabat contra illos in illis diebus cum regibus Brittonum, sed ipse dux erat bellorum.'

[39] In *HB*, ch. 43, Vortimer is credited with having besieged the Saxons three times on Thanet, then, in ch. 44, although four battles are intimated, only three are named.

[40] See Morris, *Nennius*, pp. 50–8. Compare the opening of the text in Faral, *Légende Arthurienne*, III.4–5, which provides both Harleian MS 3859 and Chartres MS 98 in parallel. Arthur's royal status in the annotated contents bears close parallels with the treatment of Urien in ch. 63, who similarly was depicted as a warrior king leading a confederacy of other kings.

[41] *HB*, ch. 56: 'Et ipsi, dum in omnibus bellis prosternebantur.'

[42] *DEB* XXIII.2: 'ut ita dicam, sub unius tecti culmine invitabant: "stulti principes," ut dictum est, "Taneos dantes Pharaoni consilium insipiens".' Vortigern was named, however, in the late twelfth-century Avranches MS of *DEB*, written at Mont Saint Michel, which was in this respect apparently similar to that which Bede used: Avranches Bibliothèque Municipale Codex no. 162.

[43] *DEB* XXIV.2.

[44] *DEB* I.4–5.

[45] *HB*, ch. 54: 'Quadraginta diebus et quadraginta noctibus in cacumine collis Eile jejunavit . . .; in quo colle in aere imminente tres petitiones pro his qui fidem ex Hibernensibus receperunt elementer postulavi . . . In illo autem tumulo benedixit populis Hiberniae, et ideo ascendit, ut oraret pro eis et videret fructum laboris sui.'

[46] *HB*, ch. 55: 'Quattuor modis aequantur Moyses et Patricius: id est angelo colloquente in rubo igneo; secundo modo, in monte quadraginta diebus et quadraginta noctibus jejunavit; tertio modo, similes fuerunt aetate CXX annis; quarto modo sepulchrum illius nemo scit, sed in occulto humatus est, nemine scient . . . Res autem exigebat amplius loqui de sancto Patricio, sed tamen pro compendio sermonis volui breviare.'

[47] Higham, *King Arthur*, pp. 141–4.

[48] Dumville, 'Historical value', p. 8–11.

[49] *DEB* III.2.

[50] A possibility mooted by K. H. Jackson, 'Nennius and the twenty-eight cities of Britain', *Antiquity,* 12 (1938), 44–55.

[51] See Molly Miller, *The Saints of Gwynedd* (Woodbridge, 1979), p. 98. The literary model of a saint triumphing over a wicked king is a commonplace of British hagiography in the tenth and eleventh centuries, and the treatment of Germanus and Vortigern in *HB* implies access to an early version of a hagiography of this type. For further discussion of the appearance of Arthur and related figures in Welsh Latin hagiography, see the essay by Andrew Breeze in this volume.

[52] Initially by H. M. Chadwick and N. K. Chadwick, *The Growth of Literature,* I (Cambridge, 1932), pp. 154–5.

[53] This suggestion was already in circulation in the mid-nineteenth century: Thomas Jones, 'The early evolution of the legend of Arthur', *Nottingham Medieval Studies*, 8 (1964), 5; see also Rachel Bromwich, 'Concepts of Arthur', *Studia Celtica*, 10–11 (1975–6), 163–81. The passage is *HB,* ch. 56: 'imaginem sanctae Mariae perpetuae virginis super humeros suos'.

[54] *HE* II.2.

[55] K. H. Jackson, 'Once again Arthur's battles', *Modern Philology*, 43 (1945), 44–57.

[56] *HB*, chs 67–75, with the Arthurian examples at 73.

[57] *HB,* ch. 73: 'Est aliud mirabile in regione quae dicitur Buelt. Est ibi cumulus lapidum et unus lapis superpositus super congestum cum vestigio canis in eo. Quando venatus est porcum Troynt, impressit Cabal, qui erat canis Arthuri militis, vestigium in lapide, et Arthur postea congregavit congestum lapidum sub lapide, in quo erat vestigium canis sui, et vocatur Carn Cabal. Et veniunt homines, et tollunt lapidem in manibus suis per spatium diei et noctis, et in crastino die invenitur super congestum suum.'

[58] *Culhwch and Olwen: An Edition and Study of the Oldest Arthurian Text*, ed. Rachel Bromwich and D. Simon Evans (Cardiff, 1992).

[59] *HB*, ch. 73: 'Est aliud mirabile in regione quae vocatur Ercing. Habetur sepulcrum juxta fontem, qui cognominatur Licat Amr, et viri nomen: qui sepultus est in tumulo, sic vocabatur Amr; filius Arthuri militis erat, et ipse occidit eum ibidem et sepelivit. Et veniunt homines ad mensurandum tumulum in longitudine aliquando sex pedes, aliquando novem, aliquando duodecim, aliquando quindecim. In qua mensura metieris eum in ista vice, iterum non invenies eum in una mensura, et ego solus probavi.'

[60] Charles-Edwards, 'The Arthur of history', p. 16.

[61] As argued convincingly by Oliver Padel, 'The nature of Arthur', *Cambrian Medieval Celtic Studies*, 27 (1994), 1–31, although the name Arthur does seem to derive from the Latin Artorius, rather than an Old Welsh form, as one might expect of a folkloric figure. This conundrum is perhaps best resolved on the assumption that Arthur originates from the legendization of a pre-existing figure, such as Artorius Castus: see K. Malone, 'Artorius', *Modern Philology*, 22 (1925), 367–74. Most recently, see Thomas Green, *Conceptions of Arthur* (Stroud, 2007), pp. 177–201.

[62] *Anglo-Saxon Charters*, ed. A. J. Robertson (Cambridge, 1939), no. 30.

[63] Kathleen Hughes, 'The Welsh Latin chronicles, *Annales Cambriae* and related texts', *Proceedings of the British Academy*, 59 (1973), 233–58.

[64] See K. Grabowski and David Dumville, *Chronicles and Annals of Medieval Ireland, and Wales: The Clonmacnoise-Group* (Woodbridge, 1984), for discussion.

[65] As Edmond Faral, *La Légende arthurienne*, II.44, although later scholars have generally preferred a start date of 445 or 447. For wider discussion of the Arthurian entries in context, see Higham, *King Arthur,* pp. 193–217.

[66] *AC* 516: 'Bellum Badonis, in quo Arthur portavit crucem Domini nostri Jhesu Christi tribus diebus et tribus noctibus in humeros suos et Brittones victores fuerunt.'

AC 537: 'Gueith Camlann in qua Arthur et Medraut corruerunt, et mortalitas in Brittannia et in Hibernia fuit.'

AC 547: 'Mortalitas magna in qua pausat Mailcun rex Genedotae.'

AC 573: 'Bellum Armterid.'

AC 580: 'Guurci et Peretur . . . moritur.'

AC 584: 'Bellum contra Euboniam et depositio Danielis Bancorum.'

AC 595: 'Dunaut . . . rex moritur.'

[67] See Molly Miller, 'Historicity and the pedigree of the North Countrymen', *Bulletin of the Board of Celtic Studies*, 26 (1975), 255–80, and 'The commanders at Arthuret', *Transactions of the Cumberland and Westmorland Antiquarian and Archaeological Society*, ns 75 (1975), 96–118. This material represents what David Dumville has described as the historical horizon of native British record, although that need not imply that it was a particularly accurate record: Dumville, 'Historical value', p. 9.

[68] *DEB* XXXIII–XXXVI. Maelgwyn was here Latinized as Maglocunus and termed *insularis draco* ('dragon of the island').

[69] See David N. Dumville, 'Gildas and Maelgwyn: problems of dating', in Michael Lapidge and David N. Dumville, eds, *Gildas: New Approaches* (Woodbridge, 1984), pp. 51–9.

[70] Luke 23:26.

[71] Higham, *King Arthur*, p. 207.

[72] Early attempts to associate Camlann with the Cornish river Camel were set aside by Jackson, 'Arthur's battles'.

[73] Faral, *La Légende arthurienne*, II.51. These Harleian genealogies derive from Owain's reign and from his kingdom, so the author of the *AC* had good reason to be familiar with any legends concerning this Arthur.

[74] *Contra* the claims for contemporaneity made, for example, by Leslie Alcock, *Arthur's Britain* (Harmondsworth, 1971), p. 40.

[75] H. Wiseman 'The derivation of the date of the Badon entry in the *Annales Cambriae* from Bede and Gildas', *Parergon*, ns 17, 2 (2000), 1–10.

2

ARTHUR IN EARLY SAINTS' LIVES

Andrew Breeze

Unexpected evidence for Arthurian tradition occurs in early hagiography. Here nine texts are relevant, all in Latin. Two deal with the Breton saints Efflam and Goeznovius, and six with the Welsh saints Cadog (who has two *Lives*, one by Lifris and another by Caradog of Llancarfan), Carannog, Gildas (another *Life* by Caradog of Llancarfan), Illtud and Padarn. Separate from these is *De miraculis S. Mariae Laudunensis* by Herman of Tournai, sometimes called Herman of Laon, who described a journey by canons of Laon from Exeter to Bodmin in 1113 and the evidence for Arthur they saw on the way, including his chair and oven. Although these various Celtic saints lived in the fifth and sixth centuries, their lives date from the eleventh and twelfth, and are often little more than folklore. Hence the general appearance of Arthur in them as a Celtic chieftain of uncertain temper and dubious morals. Yet the representation of Arthur in the texts is more varied than one might think, so that commentators reach differing conclusions on their implications for his legend.

Study of the documents effectively began in Victorian Wales. *Lives* of Cadog, Carannog, Illtud and Padarn became available in 1853 in an edition by the Revd William Jenkin Rees (1772–1855), based on the work of his nephew, the Revd Rice Rees (1804–39) of St David's College, Lampeter.[1] The elder Rees edited these and *Lives* of other Celtic saints from London, British Library, MS Cotton Vespasian A. xiv, a volume written about 1200 at Monmouth. Unfortunately his edition reproduces the errors of the manuscripts and adds hundreds of its own, so that since its publication even mild-mannered scholars have abused it as 'execrable'. Nevertheless, it advanced knowledge of Arthurian legend by putting into print many early texts, which on the whole show the king in an unflattering light. To the *Lives* edited by Rees may be added the 'second' *Life* of Gildas, by Caradog of Llancarfan (active in the 1130s), which is perhaps most accessible in the edition by Hugh Williams of Bala.[2]

The work of Rees and Williams allowed a basis for comments on Arthur by Baring-Gould and Fisher in their compendium of Celtic hagiography. They referred to 'altercations' between Cadog and Arthur, after the saint for seven years gave sanctuary to a warrior called Llyngesog Lawhir ('long-hand'), who had killed three of Arthur's men. Cadog had to give Arthur cattle in compensation, but lost nothing thereby (as we see below). Baring-Gould and Fisher also mentioned Carannog's altar, appropriated by Arthur, who was ruling in Somerset, but recovered by the saint after he rid the area of a dangerous dragon. Arthur's dealings with Gildas were more robust. This saint had a troublesome brother called Huail, and Arthur had him killed, according to a late tradition at Ruthin in north Wales, where a stone in St Peter's Square marks the spot. On this Baring-Gould and Fisher remarked crisply that Huail 'was a vulgar marauder, who richly deserved his fate. Arthur was perfectly justified in executing him for his depredations.' They also alluded to Illtud, who left home and visited the court of his cousin Arthur, called 'a great conqueror', though the story rather strangely says nothing of his extraordinary achievements.[3]

These samples from Baring-Gould and Fisher show the mixed press that Arthur received from medieval hagiographers. Hence the puzzled comment of Hugh Williams, after discussion of the tyrant Maelgwn Gwynedd (d. 547) denounced by Gildas: 'Arthur, on the other hand, was seemingly a prince whose heart was given to the Church and the saints, though with strange shortcomings, if we have regard to some of the *Vitae*.'[4] Those 'strange shortcomings' were looked at in professional detail by Sir Edmund Chambers. Besides drawing attention to Breton-Latin material, he distinguished between the negative picture given by most hagiographers and that of Caradog of Llancarfan in his *Life* of Gildas, who followed what Chambers saw as a popular view of Arthur as a hero-king.[5] Implicit within that comment is a distinction between a 'lay' view of Arthur, seen as a glorious victor, and an 'ecclesiastical' one, where he is little more than an upper-class troublemaker.

Extracts from the *Lives* of Cadog, Padarn and Carannog were also published by Faral (who referred as well to the testimony of the Laon canons).[6] The four main passages may be summarized as follows.

The first of these is the prologue to the life of Cadog, which tells how Gwynllyw, king of Glywysing (between the rivers Tawe and Usk of South Wales), wished to marry Gwladus, daughter of Brychan, ruler of the area round Brecon. But Brychan refused. The princess being beautiful, Gwynllyw advanced on Brychan's domains with three hundred troops. They found her at Talgarth (not far from Brecon), chatting to her sisters outside her room, and took her by force. Brychan, in his distress, mustered an army. Although he attacked Gwynllyw and his men at Boch Rhiw Carn (unlocated, but somewhere in south-east Wales) and killed two hundred of them, Gwynllyw escaped with the princess. On his retreat he met Arthur, Cai and Bedwyr playing dice on top of a nearby hill. Arthur desired to possess the maiden, Cai and Bedwyr dissuaded him; when Gwynllyw maintained that the territory there was his, Arthur vanquished Brychan, and Gwynllyw returned with Gwladus to his home on the hill, ever since called 'Gwynllyw's Hill'.

A second extract deals with Cadog himself. For seven years he concealed a chief called Llyngesog, who had killed three of Arthur's warriors. Arthur heard where he was, came with troops to the river Usk, and agreed to accept cattle as compensation. Although he stipulated that they should be red in front and white behind, the saint was able to produce them. But when he led them across the river Usk (at a point near Tredunnock, upstream from Caerleon) and Cai and Bedwyr hurried forward to seize them, they at once turned into bundles of fern. They were later found safe in their owner's field. Impressed at Cadog's powers, Arthur begged his forgiveness and granted his sanctuary the privilege of asylum.

Faral noted an analogue to the above in the life of Padarn. The saint, resting after a journey to Jerusalem and back, was approached by 'a certain tyrant', Arthur, who (to Padarn's indignation) tried to take by violence the tunic he was wearing. At Padarn's wish the earth swallowed Arthur up to the chin. Arthur begged forgiveness, the earth delivered him up, and he was Padarn's continual patron ever after.

The last extract is from the *Life* of Carannog. He was travelling from his native region of Ceredigion to the river Severn, where his portable altar floated away before him. He travelled onwards and met the local rulers Cadwy and Arthur, who lived at Dindraithou (by Dunster, Somerset). Arthur was hunting a monster snake, which had devastated the land of Carrum (Carhampton, near Dunster). At Arthur's request Carannog summoned the snake with his prayers, it came 'with a great noise like a calf running to its mother, and it bent its head before the servant of God like a slave obeying his lord with humble heart'. Carannog led it like a lamb, would not let it be killed, let it go (its taming being an instance of God's power), and it troubled no one ever after. He also recovered his altar, which Arthur had tried to use as a table, but which flung into the distance anything placed upon it.

Faral commented perceptively on the personality changes of Arthur in these four texts, as follows. He recognized that in all of them Arthur is a ruler of power and authority. There was good reason for this. By showing how their saint got the better of Arthur, the monks both glorified their patron and defended their interests. They knew Arthur would (up to a point) be respected by the secular rulers of their day. So these tales helped to safeguard possessions in Glamorgan, Ceredigion, Somerset, and even Cornwall (at Crantock, near Newquay). At the same time the monks had little love for Arthur. His government tended to be unjust and cruel, and always depended on force. Even if the expression *tyrannus* that they use for him did not have its modern sense, they had no admiration for him. Arthur is not the prodigious champion of *Historia Brittonum*, who accomplishes wonderful feats, nor does he have the magnanimity shown in later romance. He is dominated by lust, greed and rage, which are instincts of an animal, and like an animal he is rebuffed by God's servants. Faral noted further that this is hardly due to any trace of paganism. He thought it had more to do with the sordid realities of secular power in medieval Wales, as monks and others would know from weary experience. If they had been presented with a picture of Arthur as the hero beyond reproach and mirror of perfection, they would have laughed in one's face. Nevertheless, the tales of Arthur in saints' *Lives* must have helped his legend (as well as those of Cai and Bedwyr) to grow, with unforeseen consequences.

In the same year that Faral published his study, the Canadian-Irish historian James Kenney published a useful guide to some of the *Lives*. He noted how Caradog's life of Gildas exalts Arthurian links with Glastonbury, and also referred to editorial work on Cadog, Carannog and Padarn.[7] In a brief account of the subject the Chadwicks summarized the tale of Arthur, Cadog and the cattle that turn into ferns, and pointed out that the tale is there to 'explain' both a place-name and a privilege. They also noted that Cadog, active about the year 450, could not have known Arthur, active some fifty years later. Elsewhere they remarked that Arthur, with Cai and Bedwyr, is often linked with saints' lives from south-east Wales, where his conduct is 'not always much to his credit', as in the prologue to the life of Cadog, where he wishes to waylay what they call 'a fugitive and his wife' (= Gwynllyw and the abducted princess).[8]

In the 1930s significant contributions were made by scholars in the USA. J. S. P. Tatlock came to grips with Herman's account of the Laon canons in Cornwall, vindicating its authenticity against the doubts of Faral.[9] Grant Loomis collected and translated the passages from the saints' lives, and was corrected by Margaret Schlauch on one *Life* with no relevance here.[10] Tatlock later dealt with problems of dating the lives, though few will now accept all his conclusions on their postdating Geoffrey of Monmouth's writings of the late 1130s.[11] Research on the subject gained a better footing in 1944 with Wade-Evans's edition of texts in London, British Library, MSS Cotton Vespasian A. xiv and Titus D. xxii.[12] It also benefited from the publication of Tatlock's posthumous study of Geoffrey of Monmouth and his predecessors, reproducing some material published in *Speculum*.[13] Researchers could thus work with increased confidence.

Amongst writers of the 1950s are Rachel Bromwich, who refers to dispersed allusions to Arthur in early Welsh poems, triads and saints' lives as evidence that he really existed as a British leader in the anarchy of post-Roman Britain, after which he became an 'increasingly prominent figure in native saga, drawing into his orbit' many characters from originally quite separate stories.[14] (One may say that few scholars now accept such material as in any way historical evidence for Arthur.) Canon Elliott-Binns of Truro reported on the canons of Laon (whose cathedral had burnt down in 1112) in Cornwall. He noted how the relics of Our Lady of Laon cured a girl of blindness in Bodmin, but, when a quarrel broke out with the Cornishmen on whether Arthur was still alive, the miracles stopped. He further quoted the Cornish historian Charles Henderson for identification of Arthur's chair and oven as Crockern Tor and the King's Oven on Dartmoor, in Devon.[15] Kenneth Jackson, although he always looked with a cold eye on theories of Arthur as a North British ruler, cited the legend in Caradog's life of Gildas of a vendetta between Arthur and the chieftain Huail, Gildas's brother. Their father was Caw of Pictland, a robber giant living north of Bannog, the massif of the Campsie Fells (where Bannockburn rises) between Glasgow and the Upper Forth. The tale hints at other legends of Strathclyde otherwise lost.[16]

R. S. Loomis provided a contentious survey of the Arthurian legend before 1139, where he discussed the Laon canons in Cornwall, and the *Life* of Gildas by Caradog of Llancarfan. He followed Tatlock in seeing Herman as incorporating, after over thirty years, two reports of 1113 made by the canons on a fund-raising tour of England. It shows that the Cornish regarded Arthur as a Cornishman and a ruler of Cornwall long before Geoffrey of Monmouth's fantasies of his court at Tintagel and final battle of Camlan at nearby Camelford. Herman's materials show Arthur was likewise a hero amongst the Bretons. Arthur again appears as hero in Caradog's *Life* of Gildas. This tells of a feud between Arthur and Huail, Gildas's brother (who figures as well in the eleventh-century *Mabinogion* tale of *Culhwch and Olwen*). It recounts further the abduction of Guinevere in a version resembling that later told by Chrétien de Troyes, with Caradog's Melwas (king of Glastonbury and its environs) corresponding to Chrétien's Meleagant. Loomis accepted Tatlock's arguments that *Vitae Gildae* predated the work of Geoffrey, and was perhaps written in the early 1130s. But he took issue with Tatlock's views on Arthur and hagiography, allegedly showing him as a 'lewd, blustering, somewhat ridiculous *tyrannus*' and implying he was 'an obscure and absurd figure among the Welsh' until Geoffrey of Monmouth transformed him. Loomis disagreed. He thought the *Lives* were poor evidence for Arthurian tradition, since 'monkish' prejudice would always try to run down Arthur's greatness.[17] On that point one may say two things. The tale of Culhwch and Olwen is surely by a clerical author, showing how Welsh monks enjoyed a good story about Arthur; but the *Lives* of the saints are a different kind of narrative. They are not primarily about entertainment, but about land rights and legal immunities—hence their negative picture of secular rulers. The framers of the US Declaration of Independence, who believed that kings tended to be a troublesome lot, would here have seen eye to eye with the monks, unlike Professor Loomis of New York City.

Kathleen Hughes placed *Lives* of Cadog and other saints within the context of monasticism in Norman Wales, regarding them as an attempt to assimilate Celtic saints to a new political order. Her concern was less with the text of the *Lives* than with their compiler at (as is now agreed) Monmouth, who brought together material of diverse origins to exalt these saints. This is why she said nothing on their allusions to Arthur.[18] From a different point of view, Proinsias Mac Cana mentioned a strange tale of Cadog told by Lifris, of how his monks mutilate the horses of a local robber-chief by cutting their lips and ears off as their owner slept. As Mac Cana dated the work of Lifris to about 1090, the tale could be a source for a similar outrage on horses in the *Four Branches of the Mabinogi*, written in the late 1120s or so.[19] A summary account of writings in the 1130s by Caradog of Llancarfan was made by Sir John Lloyd in the Welsh equivalent of the *Dictionary of National Biography*.[20] The 1950s ended with R. S. Loomis's encyclopaedia of 1959, still fundamental for research. Loomis made some important comments on our material. He cited the *Life* of Gildas by Caradog as evidence for Arthurian tradition in the south-west, since Arthur musters troops in Devon and Cornwall to rescue Guinevere from Melwas's stronghold at Glastonbury; while the adventures in Cornwall of the nine canons of Laon, and how one of their servants quarrelled with a Cornishman who insisted that Arthur was still alive, indicate the strength there of Arthurian tradition before Geoffrey of Monmouth. Loomis followed Faral and Tatlock in seeing the Breton-Latin account of Goeznovius, which mentions Arthur's victories, as postdating Geoffrey, despite the date 1019 of its introduction. He considered the *Life* of St Efflam perhaps as old as the twelfth century, but surely independent of Geoffrey. Its chief interest is in showing how Arthur, for all his prowess as a warrior, nevertheless yielded to a saint who performed miracles. Loomis consistently argued that these texts by clerical authors hardly proved Arthur was no hero for the laity, especially in Brittany, where the Bretons were amongst his most active propagandists.[21]

In the 1960s the work of Lifris was briefly discussed by Kenneth Jackson, who described the tale of the cows that turn into bundles of fern as a standard international folktale, 'being used and modified by a monkish compiler of a saint's life, as so often happened in medieval hagiography'.[22] Christopher Brooke has his own view of the figure of Arthur as described by Lifris. In both stories told of him Arthur is described as a hero, 'yet portrayed as a tricky, savage, frivolous man'. He thinks this was hardly invented by Lifris, even if he was the first to add Arthur to the story of St Cadog. Arthur appears before Cadog's birth, in the tale of his parents' marriage, and then in a group of stories about sanctuary, where Arthur confirms the saint's rights, as do other potentates, including Maelgwn Gwynedd himself from north-west Wales. Brooke thinks the story of the abduction of Brychan's daughter by Gwynllyw is due to Lifris and not an old motif at all. [23] A sober and valuable paper by Thomas Jones of Aberystwyth on the Arthurian legend before Geoffrey of Monmouth has had less attention than it deserves, because its first appearance was in Welsh, and its second in the journal of a provincial university. It makes the useful point that Herman's account of the canons provides the first evidence for the myth of Arthur's return, believed in by Welsh, Cornish, and Bretons.[24]

In an unconventional book on religion and the Celts, the Welsh bard and minister Pennar Davies made an original comment. He observed that, although Welsh saints are usually made out to be of royal ancestry, descending from Macsen, Cunedda, Brychan or the like, their communities are continually at odds with secular authority. Davies had an explanation for this phenomenon. He thought the monastic order would, sooner or later, inevitably be opposed to political order, and that enmity would arise between 'prince and abbot'. Hence, he argued, the unsympathetic picture of Arthur in monastic texts. Even if disputes between Arthur and Cadog or Arthur and Carannog are resolved amicably, there is a bitter struggle between Arthur and Padarn. Davies referred back on this to the opposition in the lives of Brynach, Cybi, Padarn and Tydecho to Maelgwn Gwynedd, to say nothing of the diatribes of Gildas against the rulers of his day. He saw there a struggle of Church and State, sometimes between a king and a saint who were brothers.[25] His thoughts are stimulating. Davies (1911–96), head of a Nonconformist college in Swansea, in 1979 illegally entered and switched off a television transmitter station in west Wales. For this he was fined; his son was sent to prison. Life imitated art: it seems clear that Davies saw Celtic saints as Welsh Nonconformists, who were bound in conscience to deny to Caesar what was not Caesar's, and to the BBC what was not the BBC's. His remarks are thus amongst the more novel interpretations of Arthur and the saints, where the king had a role which is today occupied by the British establishment, Whitehall, the media and so on. Even if one sees over-literalism in Davies's reading of texts (perhaps characteristic of an evangelical inheritance), it does not lack point.

Thomas Jones discussed references to Arthur and Gildas's brother Huail, whose tale was relocated from Scotland to north Wales, at Ruthin, where a stone in front of Barclay's bank records that Arthur struck off Huail's head there. Jones noted how in the version of the tale recorded by Elis Gruffydd (d. 1552), the 'soldier of Calais' (who attended the Field of the Cloth of Gold in 1521), Arthur is unheroic, so that Huail is able to injure his knee and mock him when he hobbles. Jones saw the analogies for this picture of Arthur as in the *vitae*, and not in the histories or romances. He also cited a University of Wales MA thesis of on Arthur and the saints, though this has unfortunately not been noticed much.[26] R. M. Wilson of Sheffield thereafter cited the work of Lifris and Caradog of Llancarfan on Arthur, as well as Herman of Laon's account (in volume 106 of Migne's *Patrologia Latina*) of Arthur's seat and oven somewhere between Exeter and Bodmin, and how there was nearly bloodshed at Bodmin when a servant of the Laon canons had a quarrel with a cripple who said Arthur was still alive.[27]

The archaeologist Leslie Alcock used accounts of Cadog and Padarn as a comment on Arthur in *Annales Cambriae*, which were put together as we now have them in the earlier tenth century. The annal for 518 represents Arthur as a Christian hero, who 'carried the cross of Our Lord Jesus Christ on his shoulders for three days and three nights and the Britons were victors'. Here many have taken 'shoulders' as a mistranslation of the Welsh for 'shield' and the whole clause on Arthur as an interpolation.[28] But Alcock disagreed. He thought Arthur was not regarded as a Christian hero until Geoffrey of Monmouth transformed him in the 1130s, and that the British Church was openly hostile to him. The *Life* of Cadog, written about 1090, portrays him as 'lustful and perverse'; the *Life* of Padarn, of about 1120, shows him as an 'avaricious tyrant'. He concluded that 'no scribe brought up in that tradition would interpolate a reference to Arthur as a Christian hero.' He hence regarded the annal as authentic and early.[29] Yet no historian or philologist has taken Alcock's view seriously. Many will feel that early Welsh clerics were as varied as the rest of us, with many of them enjoying tales of their favourite hero, so that they might make him out as a better Christian than their sources implied.

A different image of Arthur appears in essays of Canon Doble, the Cornish hagiographer. His editor noted how allusions to Arthur in the *Lives* of Cadog, Carannog, Padarn, Illtud and Gildas are 'not very respectful', which he saw as continuing the conflict of Church and State embodied by Gildas and Maelgwn Gwynedd in the sixth century. Doble himself told how Illtud, once his education was over, left his native Brittany for Arthur's court in Wales, where he 'was honourably received and munificently entertained', but which he left for the court of the king of Glamorgan, who made him commander of his forces on account of 'his most subtle eloquence and incomparable intellect'. Doble rejected Tatlock's view that the writer took his description of Arthur's court in south-east Wales from Geoffrey. It must be earlier and independent, and in any case the writer made little of it.[30] But it is of interest in pointing to Arthurian glamour before Geoffrey. In a convenient overview of early Glamorgan literature, C. W. Lewis summarizes discussion of MS Cotton Vespasian A. xiv and mentions the 'many stories circulating in south-east Wales and the border' as shown by the *Vitae*. His references are useful in showing that

Arthur is called both 'bravest of heroes' and treaty-maker in the work of Lifris.[31] He thinks this enhanced Arthur's dignity.

John Morris gave much attention to Celtic hagiography. Though a professional historian at London University, Morris sometimes wrote of Arthur in the language of a revivalist preacher. He contrasted the Arthur of the eleventh-century *Culhwch and Olwen*, who rules a court attended by heroes, with the 'more rugged attitude' of the saints' *Lives*. In them Arthur is 'plebeian and nationalist', a 'foreign lowland enemy, cruel, lascivious and fearful'. At Llanbadarn Fawr in Ceredigion this ruler demands Padarn's fine tunic; in south-east Wales, he burns with lust for a princess abducted by Gwynllyw, and has to be restrained by Cai and Bedwyr, who remind him he should be helping 'the needy and distressed'. Morris suggested that Cai and Bedwyr are evidence for the New Arthur (chivalrous and respectful to women) that was edging out the Old Arthur (who was not). If the prologue to the *Life* of Cadog dated from the 1090s, like the life, it would predate Geoffrey's work by some forty years. But it is the Old Arthur who appears in the life itself, energetically pursuing Llyngesog, general of the British, and demanding a hundred cows as compensation for his offence. We find the same Arthur in Somerset, using an altar as a table, and in North Britain, in the tale of Huail from the life of Gildas, where he seeks out and puts to death this young warrior and then goes home 'pleased to have killed his strongest enemy'. As for Illtud's visit to Arthur, he is there shown as a 'remote suzerain' whose court abounds in soldiers, and who gives the saint 'honours' and 'high favour'. Morris thought all these accounts reflected the Arthur of popular traditions preserved by the monks. The humble people of Wales had come to see Arthur as an alien and hostile overlord.[32] Morris thus presented an interpretation of Arthur strikingly different from those of R. S. Loomis or Leslie Alcock. Loomis distinguished a lay and 'popular' Arthur, who was every inch a hero, from the rather unsuccessful Arthur of monkish detractors. Morris, in contrast, saw no distinction between lay and monastic tradition. He believed that popular tradition was actually preserved by the monks, and it treated Arthur in what we would now call post-colonial terms, as a foreign tyrant.

Yet another point of view is presented by Siân Victory. She observes that Lifris is a far less sober hagiographer than his contemporary Rhygyfarch, who wrote of St David. Lifris delights in exuberant native folklore: revenge for him is 'swift and merciless', and miracles 'often bizarre'. She finds the same colour and savagery in the *Mabinogion* and Irish sagas. A murdered man rises from the grave, 'wet and bloody, of maimed and horrid aspect'; horses have their lips and ears sliced off; Arthur's cattle-tribute turns into worthless bundles of fern. This she calls 'entertainment' rather than didacticism (others, more gravely, have seen it as the fantasies of a sadist), although she is careful to state how the information set out by the text and its interpolations on Llancarfan's estates safeguarded its rights when the Normans handed it over to St Peter's Abbey, Gloucester.[33]

Rachel Bromwich in her edition of the Triads observes how the saints' lives show relocation of Arthurian themes in Wales, even though she thinks his original associations were with North Britain. As for his depiction as a tyrant king who provides a 'foil to holy men' in different parts of Wales, she considers this indicates the way that late clerical writers borrowed from secular tradition, as they did with Maelgwn of Gwynedd.[34]

In a serious and unromantic study of monastic property, Wendy Davies nevertheless underlines the Celtic aspect of Welsh saints' lives, where their allusions to Arthur and other heroes of vernacular tradition resemble those of Irish and Breton hagiography, but contast with English and other continental *vitae*. She makes the further point that Arthur's granting of rights of sanctuary to Cadog goes beyond its normal associations. The right is, rather, one of *nawdd*, a principle of Welsh law by which individuals were immune from distraint.[35] In her history of Wales she (like a good historian) does not mention Arthur, yet she provides updated information on the writings of Lifris. She thinks he wrote his life of Cadog probably in the 1070s or 1080s, but that it was afterwards interpolated from the later life of Cadog by Caradog. The tale of Arthur's cattle-tribute would be due to Lifris. She follows Wade-Evans for the dates of other *Lives*: those of Carannog from the early twelfth century, and written at Llangrannog on the Ceredigion coast; that of Illtud from about 1140, perhaps at Llantwit Major in Glamorgan; and that of Padarn from about 1120 at Llanbadarn Fawr.[36] A bibliography of all the lives discussed here, excepting that by Herman of Tournai (who was not a Celt, and who wrote on the miracles of a saint rather than the life), is given by Lapidge and Sharpe, who date the Breton-Latin *vita* of Euflamus or Efflam to the later twelfth century.[37]

Accounts of Gildas are usefully collected and examined by Elissa Henken.[38] She is followed by James Carley, who sets out traditions of Arthur's execution of Huail, and his rescue of Guenevere from Glastonbury.[39] The figure of Arthur in the *Vitae* was analysed by Jeff Rider, who stresses that the material forms 'the most extensive surviving body of Arthurian texts' written before Geoffrey of Monmouth arrived on the scene in the late 1130s. He plays down the notion that Arthur's role is merely conventional. He argues that in only two of these texts is Arthur a tyrant riding for a fall at saintly hands, and thereafter (duly abashed) granting lands or privileges or both. Elsewhere Arthur 'plays a role more heroic than royal, grants nothing, acts in concert with the saint, or is simply thrown in for "historical" relief. The figure of Arthur in these lives is, in fact, more remarkable for its diversity than for its unanimity.'[40] Even if it is unclear what a 'unanimous figure' is, this emphasis on Arthur's diverse aspects is a reasonable one.

Brynley Roberts stands back from the material to make the point that the Welsh hagiographers followed well-known conventions. They wrote to glorify the saint as local hero, founder of a Church and defender of its privileges in both life and death. The *vitae* are 'ecclesiastical hero-tales' with a strong local interest, where the saint will come into conflict with secular magnates (like Arthur), but invariably best them by force or miracles or both. The king has to grovel to the hero-saint, who retires with rights, privileges and prestige intact or enhanced. Roberts feels that, although all the lives present Arthur negatively, some are more negative than others. The life of Illtud describes a visit to Arthur's magnificent court, where he is 'dazzled by the generosity and splendour of all he sees'. Even though nothing more is said of Arthur, the incident shows that such visits were part of the storytelling of the day, as in *Culhwch and Olwen*.[41]

The careful edition by Rachel Bromwich and Simon Evans of that very text stresses its author's clerical learning. This inevitably blurs the line made between 'ecclesiastical' and 'lay' by some critics, especially those unfamiliar with vernacular Welsh writing. Bromwich and Evans here note the unique status of the life of Cadog by Lifris of Llancarfan. They describe it as the one saint's *Life* by a Welshman that mentions Arthur and certainly predates Geoffrey of Monmouth's *Historia regum Britannie* of 1138. Only in this life are Cai and Bedwyr named, and its explanations of *Boch Rhiw Carn*, and of *Rhyd Gwrthebau* (on the Usk near Tredunnock), are typical of Celtic place-name lore. They hence usefully emphasize the Celtic aspects of Arthur in the work of Lifris, which they think were known directly to *Culhwch and Olwen*'s author.[42]

A paper of 1994 by Oliver Padel makes a substantial and original contribution to the subject. His guiding and persuasive principle is that Arthur never existed, and that it is therefore foolish to relate his appearance in later narratives to any historical figure. Such texts are mere legends. Arthur's acts and deeds in *vitae* thus find their parallels in stories of Fionn mac Cumhaill, the traditional hero of popular tales in Ireland and Gaelic Scotland (a point made by the Dutch scholar A. G. van Hamel in a British Academy lecture of 1934). Nobody thinks Fionn existed. To treat Arthur as a historical character, even though he so much resembles Fionn, is hence to chase a will-o'-the-wisp.[43]

Although Ceri Davies of Swansea mentions the 'wonders and miraculous deeds' set out by Lifris, and his desire to assert the rights of Llancarfan against Norman claims, his real interest is classical learning, where Cadog's desire to study Priscian, Donatus and the seven liberal arts tells us more about Lifris than about Cadog.[44] John Koch provides a useful survey of approaches to the *Lives*, especially those of Cadog by Lifris and of Gildas by Caradog, as well as the Breton-Latin *Life* of Goeznovius, where the date of 1019 in its introduction, with its famous summary of the legendary history of Britain (including Arthur's victories against the Saxons and on the Continent), still has defenders, especially in Brittany, despite a curious similarity there to the fictions of Geoffrey of Monmouth.[45]

Although it has passed unnoticed in the English-speaking world, what is easily the most extensive study of the present subject was completed in 1997 by Dr Torres Ascensio, of the department of Latin at Barcelona University.[46] This truly massive dissertation has separate chapters on the *vitae* of Cadog, Carannog, Padarn, Gildas, Efflam, Illtud and Goëznou. It also discusses the *vitae* of Cenydd and Dyfrig, clearly influenced by Geoffrey of Monmouth. Her thesis, excluding bibliography and index, has 1,050 pages, and was reproduced on microfiche in 1999 (the present writer has a copy). It is most unfortunate that her book based on the thesis (mentioned below) curtails its contents and leaves out most of its bibliographical references, since it is they, rather than any conclusions that Dr Torres comes to, which are perhaps its most valuable part.

In contrast to the above are comments on the *vitae* by the editor of this volume.[47] They are brief: but their implications are of the first importance, her approach here being stimulating and original. She sees the six Welsh-Latin lives as all concerned with the education of a ruler. She notes that Arthur's episodic appearance in these narratives and his routine discomfiting have been linked to the stock hagiographical figure of the Recalcitrant King. Yet against that she says Arthur is not always the saint's adversary. When Carannog reaches the lands of Arthur, he obtains information on the whereabouts of his lost altar in return for taming a blatant beast. For Illtud, Arthur merely provides the stage-setting for a conventional renunciation of military glory; after a brief visit to Arthur's court, Illtud goes on to Glamorgan to be converted by Cadog. Perhaps that is why the account of court life is so perfunctory. In the life of Padarn, Arthur is the stereotypical tyrant whom the saint must subdue. In all these narratives Arthur has little more than a walk-on part to make a point. But in the life of Cadog he has more individuality. We meet him on a hillside, dicing with Cai and Bedwyr; he is inflamed with lust for Gwladus, abducted by Gwynllyw; his companions restrain him; he thus instead aids Gwynllyw, the consequence being the birth of Cadog, the child of Gwynllyw and Gwladus. Siân Echard here compares Arthur with Pwyll of Dyfed in the *Four Branches of the Mabinogi*, who she thinks is often persuaded against first impulses by his advisers. (This is not quite correct. The main person who does that is Rhiannon, for a reason implied by note 58.) Echard concludes that the representation of Arthur, who encounters an adventure while sitting on a hill, here retains characteristics of Welsh vernacular secular narrative, as with Pwyll's encounters at the mound of Arberth. This 'process of narrative appropriation or interpenetration' she sees as still clearer in the episode of Llyngesog and the transformed cattle. She points out how Arthur refuses the cows allocated as his compensation by a council of nobles, and insists on red-and-white ones. Arthur thus subverts a tribunal's decision. Cadog takes that in his stride, and Arthur acknowledges defeat and vanishes from the narrative, where he has not even secondary interest, but mere 'name recognition', in the language of modern advertising. Siân Echard's approach is, in short, a most illuminating one, which provides a series of fresh insights into early Welsh narrative as a whole.

In a summary of the Celtic background to Arthur, Ceridwen Lloyd-Morgan refers to the life of Gildas by Caradog of Llancarfan, writing for the monks of Glastonbury in the 1120s or 1130s, and telling of the abduction of Guinevere by Melwas, who both figure as well in an early Welsh dialogue poem of the queen and the knight.[48] Though it does not mention saints' lives, an ingenious paper by Ken Dark should be mentioned as arguing for a historical Arthur, in part from the sudden appearance of this rare name in early Christian Britain and Ireland.[49]

In a volume of the Writers of Wales series Oliver Padel makes various points in discussion of the *vitae*. These lives are late. Their authors had few data at hand. Arthur appears in the texts, all predating Geoffrey of Monmouth, as a means of glorifying the saint and his monastery. Hence his role as an antagonist vanquished by the saint. But he is not entirely blackened. In the tale of Cadog and the cattle Arthur is styled *rex*, apparently the first known instance of this. He may be capricious, but is not shown as pagan or anti-Christian, so that in the first life of Carannog discussed here Arthur 'joyfully received a blessing' from the saint on his arrival in Somerset. In general, Padel see the Arthur of these Latin texts and the Welsh vernacular ones as similar: a leader of men, living in a fairy-tale world of dragons and transforming cattle, spoiled but well-meaning, and not malevolent or ill-disposed to Christianity or the saints, unlike the Maelgwn Gwynedd of legend. A further point has implications unsuspected by Dr Padel. In a parenthesis on Arthur's attempts to seize Gwladus from Gwynllyw he comments that the lady's opinion 'is not considered'.[50] In a male-authored text, no surprise. It contrasts with the *Four Branches of the Mabinogi*, which say much on the feelings of women: a wife's grief on losing a foster-child; Blodeuedd's falling in love with a man not her husband; Goewin's account of being raped, where she speaks with dignity, but is careful to state that 'everyone in the court knew about it.' This concern for and interest in the feelings of women would be curious if those tales were, as some assert, the work of a man.

David Dumville, in the course of general comments on hagiography and the Age of the Saints in Celtic Christianity, ascribes the writing of London, British Library, MS Cotton Vespasian A. xiv to Monmouth, and not Brecon, as earlier writers suggested.[51] Comments on some of our texts appear in Nick Higham's survey of the Arthurian legend. Arthur's 'oven' seen by the Laon canons may be an old furnace on east Dartmoor (at British National Grid Reference SX 674812); the 'seat' seems unknown, unless it was at Warbstow, between Launceston and Tintagel. The image of Arthur as ruler and hero of the Cornish people (now twice conquered and dispossessed) in Herman's account contrasts with that in Caradog's *Life* of Cadog, where Arthur rules all Britain. Both versions therefore have their own political slant.[52] K. M. Wickham-Crowley puts the lives into a Glamorgan group (the work of Lifris, Caradog and their school) and a Ceredigion one (for Carannog and Padarn), and thinks the Protean aspects of Arthur in the *Lives* (king, would-be rapist, hero, bandit, Christian, thief) made him a useful subject for Lawman.[53]

The *vitae* and the Laon canons figure in the book of Dr Torres Ascensio's thesis, though it is not one from which English-speaking scholars are likely to learn anything new, unlike the thesis itself.[54] Ceridwen Lloyd-Morgan's volume on the Celtic Arthur, though saying nothing on the *vitae*, reminds us of the legacy of Loomis's bogus analogies and dud etymologies, long rejected by professional Celticists, but unfortunately still taken seriously by others.[55]

In an encyclopaedia of Arthuriana, Alan Lupack describes the Breton-Latin legend of St Goeznovius as perhaps the earliest of the *Lives* to mention Arthur, though the date 1019 of its preface is often disputed. Its account is of interest in referring to Vortigern's invitation of the Saxons to Britain and to Arthur's victories in Britain and Gaul, as well as to an ambiguous hint that Arthur did not die but was merely 'called from human activity' at the end of his life. Of Illtud he notes that the saint is Arthur's cousin and desires to 'visit the court of a great conqueror'. Lupack contrasts these positive images of Arthur with the unconventional ones elsewhere, where he sees Arthur as a mere foil to a particular saint or to God himself. In the *Life* of Carannog, Arthur is on a dragon-hunt when he meets the protagonist; much the same happens in the Breton-Latin *Life* of Efflam, where Arthur also pursues a dangerous dragon. When Arthur meets Padarn, he is 'pierced with the sin of avarice' and demands with menaces the saint's tunic. In the life of Cadog by Lifris, Arthur's supposed duty to 'help the needy and distressed', so that he should rescue Princess Gwladus and not rape her (his original intention), is described as his 'traditional role'. So Lupack views Arthur as a long-standing Christian hero, unlike commentators cited above. As for the account of Gildas written about 1130 by Caradog of Llancarfan, Lupack emphasizes Arthur's killing of Huail, the way Gildas forgives him, his doing of penance, and the mediation of Gildas in restoring Guinevere to him after Melwas had kidnapped her and hidden her away in his castle at Glastonbury, after which Arthur and Melwas in gratitude give lands in Somerset to the Glastonbury monks.[56] The Laon canons figure briefly in a recent paper by Oliver Padel.[57] The tales of the *Mabinogion*, which cannot be divorced from those of our saints, now appear in a new translation, which sums up research of the last two decades or so, and thereby opens wide the door to future investigators.[58]

It will be seen that passages on Arthur and the saints have generated more discussion than one might have thought. Three aspects of them may be stressed in conclusion. First, although there are disagreements on how Arthur is shown in them, recent writers tend to see Arthur as represented more positively than was previously thought. Second is the question of popular tradition. There is no consensus on whether the lives represent a clerical 'deviant reading' of Arthurian lore, as Loomis maintained, or whether they preserve popular legends intact, as John Morris argued. This brings us to our third point. If we are fully to understand these passages and the traditions behind them, we must look more closely at vernacular texts. Naturally, this demands a certain effort for medievalists, few of whom are at home in the Welsh language. But it has to be done.

It is on this last point that the concise but pregnant comments of Siân Echard on the *Mabinogion* show the way ahead. Her relating of the saints' *Lives* to the *Four Branches of the Mabinogi* has a dual significance. The very fact that the *Four Branches*, written before the publication of Geoffrey of Monmouth's *Historia*, never mention Arthur or his heroes (though they mention much else) requires explanation. Either the author had good reason to ignore him, or else Arthur was not a predominant figure in Welsh narrative before Geoffrey of Monmouth. Of these two possibilities the first seems the likelier. The four tales consistently exalt the political status and dynasties of Gwynedd and Dyfed (and in the fourth branch treat, with remarkable delicacy, a war between the two). As Arthur had no original part in the traditions of Gwynedd or Dyfed, the author of the tales had no special reason to refer to him. Also deserving consideration is what the *Four Branches* and the *vitae* say about government and kingship, including political education and decision-making. There is a task here for researchers. Their analyses will here surely cast a flood of light on Wales in the decades about 1100, when Lifris and Caradog wrote down their views of politics and society, shortly before the author of the *Four Branches* gave her views of the same, when she composed these tales in the late 1120s or thereabouts.[59]

All the above was written in 2007. When the present volume was ready for printing in early 2009, the editor asked the writer to add to it, as follows. Here we may cite the new Academy of Wales encyclopaedia, with five relevant articles: on Arthur, Cadog, Caradog of Llancarfan, Illtud and Padarn. Although they are by anonymous contributors and lack bibliographical data, which is a disadvantage, they still sum up current thinking in the University of Wales on Arthur and his legend. They make these points. The article on Arthur mentions him in early *Lives* of saints and other sources as a 'leader of a band of wondrous warriors who free the land of dragons, giants, and oppressors'. (It makes no reference to Arthur as himself being an oppressor.) Yet it mentions another strand in his tradition, persisting strongly in Cornwall and Brittany as well as in Wales: the 'messianic belief that Arthur had not died and would one day return to restore his nation's freedom'. This we know of thanks to Herman of Tournai (= Herman of Laon) and the adventures that the Laon canons had in Devon and Cornwall. On Cadog, we hear that he founded a monastic school at Llancarfan (in Glamorgan) and that the twelfth-century *Life* of him by Lifris of Llancarfan is 'of questionable historical value'. Caradog of Llancarfan, active in about 1135, appears as the author of *Lives* of Cadog, Gildas, and perhaps of Illtud. But the entry on Illtud in contradiction attributes the Latin *Life* of him to a twelfth-century Norman cleric. It denies that the life has any historical basis, claiming that Illtud's cruel rejection in it of his wife reflects a Norman campaign against Welsh married priests and hereditary ecclesiastical offices. (Naturally, if Illtud's life is the work of a Norman, it casts new light on its representation of Arthur.) As for Padarn, the brief account of him states that his Latin life was written at Llanbadarn in about 1120, and is 'not dependable historically'.[60]

In summing up the above, we may both look back and look forwards. On the first we may feel that a compilation of opinion on these Latin texts indicates diversity rather than consensus. This may have value in distinguishing between beholders and what is beheld. On the second, it is clear that we are still far from a thorough and complete understanding of the material. This brings us back to its relation to vernacular narrative in this period, and particularly the *Four Branches of the Mabinogi*.[61] Although often ignored or rejected without discussion (the reaction known to scientists as the 'Semmelweiss Reflex'), there is evidence to date the last to the 1120s or early 1130s, and to regard them as the work of an author of high rank, who was familiar with the traditions of Gwynedd and Dyfed alike, and was ardent for the political advancement of each. If these dates and this provenance can be accepted, they offer a template against which the Arthurian passages in Latin hagiography can be gauged. With the *Four Branches* as a measure of comparison, it will become easier to discuss the dating, popular or semi-learned origins, audience, and ideological component of Arthur in Latin documents of the eleventh and twelfth centuries, including the Latin *Lives* of Efflam and Goeznovius in Brittany, and those of Cadog, Carannog, Gildas, Illtud and Padarn in Wales.

Notes

[1] W. J. Rees (ed.), *Lives of the Cambro-British Saints* (Llandovery, 1853).

[2] Hugh Williams (ed.), *Gildae De excidio Britanniae* (London, 1899), pp. 390–413.

[3] Sabine Baring-Gould and John Fisher (eds), *Lives of the British Saints* (London, 1907–13), II, pp. 29, 81; III, pp. 106, 285, 304, 305.

[4] Hugh Williams, *Christianity in Early Britain* (Oxford, 1912), p. 349.

[5] E. K. Chambers, *Arthur of Britain* (London, 1927), pp. 242, 262–4.

[6] Edmond Faral, *La Légende arthurienne: Les plus anciens textes des origines à Geoffroy de Monmouth* (Paris, 1929), pp. 228–33, 236–44.

[7] J. F. Kenney, *The Sources for the Early History of Ireland: Ecclesiastical* (New York, 1929), pp. 176–8, 179–80.

[8] H. M. and N. K. Chadwick, *The Growth of Literature: The Ancient Literatures of Europe* (Cambridge, 1932), pp. 102, 146.

[9] J. S. P. Tatlock, 'The English journey of the Laon canons', *Speculum*, 8 (1933), 454–65.

[10] C. Grant Loomis, 'King Arthur and the saints', *Speculum*, 8 (1933), 478–82; Margaret Schlauch, 'Saints Tryphina and Hirlanda', *Speculum*, 10 (1935), 161–2.

[11] J. S. P. Tatlock, 'The dates of the Arthurian saints' legends', *Speculum*, 14 (1939), 345–65.

[12] A. W. Wade-Evans (ed.), *Vitae sanctorum Britanniae et genealogiae* (Cardiff, 1944).

[13] J. S. P. Tatlock, *The Legendary History of Britain* (Berkeley, 1950).

[14] Rachel Bromwich, 'The character of the early Welsh tradition', in Nora Chadwick (ed.), *Studies in Early British History* (Cambridge, 1954), pp. 83–136.

[15] L. E. Elliott-Binns, *Medieval Cornwall* (London, 1955), pp. 261–2, 412–13.

[16] K. H. Jackson, 'The Britons in southern Scotland', *Antiquity*, 29 (1955), 77–88.

[17] Roger Sherman Loomis, *Wales and the Arthurian Legend* (Cardiff, 1956), pp. 180–3, 214–15.

[18] Kathleen Hughes, 'British Museum MS Cotton Vespasian A. xiv ("Vitae Sanctorum Wallensium"): its purpose and provenance', in Nora Chadwick (ed.), *Studies in the Early British Church* (Cambridge, 1958), pp. 183–200.

[19] Proinsias Mac Cana, *Branwen, Daughter of Llŷr* (Cardiff, 1958), pp. 158–9.

[20] J. E. Lloyd, 'Caradog of Llancarfan', in *The Dictionary of Welsh Biography* (London, 1959), p. 67.

[21] R. S. Loomis, 'The oral diffusion of the Arthurian legend', in R. S. Loomis (ed.), *Arthurian Literature in the Middle Ages* (Oxford, 1959), pp. 52–63.

[22] K. H. Jackson, *The International Popular Tale and Early Welsh Tradition* (Cardiff, 1961), pp. 105–6.

[23] C. N. L. Brooke, 'St Peter of Gloucester and St Cadoc of Llancarfan', in Nora Chadwick (ed.), *Celt and Saxon* (Cambridge, 1963), pp. 258–322.

[24] Thomas Jones, 'The early evolution of the legend of Arthur', *Nottingham Medieval Studies*, 8 (1964), 3–21.

[25] Pennar Davies, *Rhwng Chwedl a Chredo* (Caerdydd, 1966), pp. 60–1.

[26] Janem Mary Williams, 'Y darlun o Arthur ym mucheddau'r saint ac yn englynion *Ymddiddan Arthur a'r Eryr*' (MA thesis, University of Wales, 1966); Thomas Jones, 'Chwedl Huail', in Thomas Jones (ed.), *Astudiaethau Amrywiol* (Caerdydd, 1968), pp. 48–66.

[27] R. M. Wilson, *The Lost Literature of Medieval England*, 2nd edn (London, 1970), pp. 104–5.

[28] For further discussion of this reference, see the essay by Nicholas Higham in this volume.

[29] Leslie Alcock, *Arthur's Britain* (Harmondsworth, 1971), p. 53.

[30] G. H. Doble, in D. Simon Evans (ed.), *Lives of the Welsh Saints* (Cardiff, 1971), pp. 47, 105, 125–6.

[31] Ceri Lewis, 'The literary tradition of Morgannwg', in T. B. Pugh (ed.), *Glamorgan County History: The Middle Ages* (Cardiff, 1971), pp. 449–554.

[32] John Morris, *The Age of Arthur* (London, 1973), pp. 120–3.

[33] Siân Victory, *The Celtic Church in Wales* (London, 1977), pp. 116–17.

[34] Rachel Bromwich (ed.), *Trioedd Ynys Prydain*, 2nd edn (Caerdydd, 1978), pp. 275, 438.

[35] Wendy Davies, 'Property rights and property claims in Welsh *vitae* of the eleventh century', in *Hagiographie, cultures, et sociétés IVe–XIIe siècles* (Paris, 1981), pp. 515–33.

[36] Wendy Davies, *Wales in the Early Middle Ages* (Leicester, 1982), p. 208.

[37] Michael Lapidge and Richard Sharpe, *A Bibliography of Celtic-Latin Literature* (Dublin, 1985), pp. 15–17, 36–7, 264.

[38] Elissa Henken, *Traditions of the Welsh Saints* (Woodbridge, 1987), pp. 135–40.

[39] J. P. Carley, *Glastonbury Abbey* (Cambridge, 1988), pp. 95–6.

[40] Jeff Rider, 'Arthur and the saints', in Valerie Lagorio and Mildred Leake Day (eds), *King Arthur through the Ages* (New York, 1990), I.3–21.

[41] Brynley F. Roberts, '*Culhwch ac Olwen*, the triads, saints' lives', in Rachel Bromwich, A. O. H. Jarman and Brynley F. Roberts (eds), *The Arthur of the Welsh* (Cardiff, 1991), pp. 73–95.

[42] Rachel Bromwich and D. Simon Evans (eds), *Culhwch and Olwen: An Edition and Study of the Oldest Arthurian Text* (Cardiff, 1992), pp. lxxix–lxxx.

[43] Oliver J. Padel, 'The nature of Arthur', *Cambrian Medieval Celtic Studies*, 27 (1994), 1–31.

[44] Ceri Davies, *Welsh Literature and the Classical Tradition* (Cardiff, 1995), pp. 13–16.

[45] J. T. Koch, 'The Celtic lands', in N. J. Lacy (ed.), *Medieval Arthurian Literature: A Guide to Recent Research* (New York, 1996), pp. 239–322.

[46] Gloria Torres Ascensio, 'La "Materia de Bretaña" en la literatura latina medieval. La leyenda artúrica en la hagiografía celtolatina medieval' (PhD thesis, University of Barcelona, 1999).

[47] Siân Echard, *Arthurian Narrative in the Latin Tradition* (Cambridge, 1998), pp. 198–200.

[48] Ceridwen Lloyd-Morgan, 'The Celtic background', in W. R. J. Barron (ed.), *The Arthur of the English* (Cardiff, 1999), pp. 1–9.

[49] Ken Dark, 'A famous Arthur in the sixth century?' *Reading Medieval Studies*, 26 (2000), 77–95.

[50] Oliver J. Padel, *Arthur in Medieval Welsh Literature* (Cardiff, 2000), pp. 37–47.

[51] David N. Dumville, *Saint David of Wales* (Cambridge, 2001), p. 4.

[52] Nicholas J. Higham, *King Arthur: Myth-Making and History* (London, 2002), pp. 59, 90, 219, 220, 230.

[53] Kelley Wickham-Crowley, *Writing the Future: La3amon's Prophetic History* (Cardiff, 2002), pp. 103–4.

[54] Gloria Torres Ascensio, *Los orígenes de la literatura artúrica* (Barcelona, 2003), pp. 113–64.

[55] Ceridwen Lloyd-Morgan, 'Introduction', in Ceridwen Lloyd-Morgan (ed.), *Celtic Arthurian Material* (Cambridge, 2004), pp. 1–8.

[56] Alan Lupack, *The Oxford Guide to Arthurian Literature and Legend* (Oxford, 2005), pp. 22–4.

[57] Oliver J. Padel, 'Evidence for oral tales in medieval Cornwall', *Studia Celtica*, 40 (2006), 127–53.

[58] Sioned Davies (tr.), *The Mabinogion* (Oxford, 2007), p. 239.

[59] Cf. Andrew Breeze, 'Did a woman write the *Four Branches of the Mabinogi*?' *Studi Medievali*, 38 (1997), 679–705.

[60] Anon., 'Arthur', 'Cadog', 'Caradog of Llancarfan', 'Illtud', and 'Padarn', in John Davies, Nigel Jenkins, Menna Baines, and Peredur I. Lynch (eds), *The Welsh Academy Encyclopedia of Wales* (Cardiff, 2008), pp. 37–8, 102, 114, 390, 643–64.

[61] Bernhard Maier and Stefan Zimmer (eds), *150 Jahre 'Mabinogion'. Deutsch-Walisische Kulturbeziehungen* (Tübingen, 2001); Andrew Breeze, *The Origins of the 'Four Branches of the Mabinogi'* (Leominster, 2009).

Section Two
Geoffrey of Monmouth

> He was a lover of peace, for he gave law to a savage people in such a way that no one was harmed by anyone else. He treated the holy cleric with just control, and allowed both the powerful and the humble to be ruled by justice. He was generous and gave much away, and kept very little. He was all things to all men, doing whatever was fitting, the flower of knights, the glory of kings and the pillar of the kingdom.[1]

In the Latin Arthurian texts discussed in Section One, King Arthur was a sometimes peripheral, even ignoble figure. While those texts, and the early vernacular traditions to which they doubtless bore some relationship, demonstrate the existence of a pre-Galfridian body of Arthurian material, it was Geoffrey of Monmouth, and more particularly his *Historia regum Britannie*, that gave rise to the great Arthurian traditions in both Latin and the vernacular. The significance of Geoffrey's *Historia*, and of Arthur in that *Historia*, cannot be overstated. At the same time, as the essays in this section will show, neither Arthur nor the *Historia* were Geoffrey's only preoccupations. The lines quoted above describe, not King Arthur, but King Rodarch. They are uttered as a lament after Rodarch's death by his wife Ganieda, sister to Merlin, and the text in which this description of an ideal king is found, is Geoffrey's *Vita Merlini*. Arthur himself is not important in the *Vita Merlini*, but that work, like the *Historia regum Britannie*, shows Geoffrey's persistent interest in both human rulers and the larger forces which shape and perhaps circumscribe their rule. Geoffrey's Arthur takes up the lion's share of the *Historia regum Britannie*, but he is nevertheless one king among many, carefully placed by Geoffrey in a sweep of history which rolls inexorably onwards. Ganieda's lament underlines a grim reality: the end of that sweep, no matter how excellent the king, is always death.

While the *Vita* seems to have circulated scarcely at all, Geoffrey's Merlin, thanks largely to the *Prophetie Merlini* section of the *Historia regum Britannie*, is a figure of equal or perhaps even greater importance to Arthur, at least in the learned Latin tradition. As Julia Crick argues in her essay in this section, learned readers, conversant with prophetic traditions more generally, felt 'intellectual sympathy' with Geoffrey's presentation of prophecy, even as they might also deploy these prophecies to their own political ends. Merlin was for them, Crick writes, 'a figure of enigma and of revelation', one who continued to be of interest for centuries after Geoffrey presented him to the Latin-speaking world. At the end of the *Vita Merlini*, Merlin gives up his prophetic gift and turns to prayer, but Crick shows just how many readers were more than willing to perpetuate Merlin's voice across time.

SE

Notes

[1] Geoffrey of Monmouth, *Life of Merlin, Vita Merlini*, ed. and trans. Basil Clarke (Cardiff, 1973), line 696–702:

> Pacis amator erat, populo nam jura feroci
> sic dabat ut nulli vis inferretur ab ullo.
> Tractabat sanctum justo moderamine clerum,
> jure regi populos summos humilesque sinebat.
> Largus erat nam multa dabat, vix quid retinebat.
> Omnibus omnis erat faciens quodcumque decebat,
> flos equitum regumque decor regnique columpna. (My translation)

3

GEOFFREY OF MONMOUTH

Siân Echard

> I had found nothing about the kings who lived here before the Incarnation of Christ, nor indeed anything about Arthur and all the many others who succeeded after the Incarnation . . . Walter, archdeacon of Oxford . . . [gave me] a certain very ancient book in the British language, which continually and in order, in most beautiful language, displays the deeds of all these men, from Brutus, the first king of the Britons, up to Cadwallader, the son of Cadwallo. Thus at Walter's request, I have taken the trouble to translate the book into Latin.[1]

In the Dedication to his *Historia regum Britannie* (*HRB*), Geoffrey of Monmouth famously asserts that his work is a translation of an ancient British book which preserves the whole sequence of Britain's history, from the time of its founding to the reign of the last British (as opposed to Saxon) king.[2] Geoffrey's claim, and the work it introduced, attracted immediate attention, both positive and negative. Other contemporary historians had been engaged in the writing of Britain's early history and were thus familiar with the available sources.[3] They knew that there were enormous holes in the written record for early British history. The rapid absorption of Geoffrey's British history into the British chronicle tradition suggests the eagerness with which Geoffrey's *Historia* was welcomed as a solution for those *lacunae*, but there were also expressions of overt scepticism.[4] Today, Geoffrey's contribution to the Arthurian tradition is usually measured in terms of his presence at the beginning of a coherent literary tradition; along with Chrétien de Troyes in the vernacular realm, he is credited as a founder of the enduring Arthurian story. It is Geoffrey who tells us of Arthur's conception; Geoffrey who connects Merlin to that story; Geoffrey who takes Arthur to war with Rome, in the company of knights such as Gawain, Kay and Bedevere; and Geoffrey who tells us of Arthur's death in his final battle with Mordred. Many details familiar to us from the later vernacular tradition are absent from Geoffrey's *Historia* – Guinevere is Arthur's wife, but there is no Lancelot; Mordred is Arthur's nephew and enemy but not his bastard son; Arthur and his knights never seek the Grail; and so on. But it is Geoffrey who provides the first consecutive Arthurian narrative, and I will discuss this narrative in due course. I have chosen to open this overview with Geoffrey's dedication, however, because it underlines that Geoffrey is *not* writing just about Arthur, but also about the kings who came both before and after the Incarnation. Arthur is by this preface placed firmly in a line that extends from Brutus, the Trojan refugee guided to the island by the goddess Diana, to Cadwallader, the last British king to rule before the final Saxon conquest. The Brutus foundation story looms almost as large in Geoffrey's afterlife as does the Arthuriad, and even at the beginning of the eighteenth century, Geoffrey's first English translator devotes considerable attention to defending both the British book and the foundation story.[5] While the Arthuriad occupies about a third of the *Historia*, it is best understood, then, in relation to the rest of the work. Arthur may be Britain's greatest king, but for Geoffrey at least, his achievements were inevitably framed by the triumphs and disasters of his predecessors and successors. The evocation of this larger picture in Middle English Arthurian narratives, most famously captured as the *Gawain*-poet's description of a history of 'blysse and blunder', suggests that at least some of Geoffrey's medieval inheritors similarly saw Arthur as one of many.[6]

A backward journey through the few known facts of Geoffrey of Monmouth's life allow us to trace a general outline of his background and milieu. In 1151, he was appointed bishop of St Asaph in Wales, but the ongoing turmoil in the region may have prevented him taking up his seat before his death, in 1154 or 1155. He was, then, a cleric – although his ordination predated his election to the bishopric by only a week, he was a scholar and thus would have been in orders of some sort most of his life. The fact that he attained a bishopric also suggests that he was in favour with the powerful men of his day, since such positions were often rewards for service. He dedicates the *Historia* to Robert of Gloucester, who from 1139 led his half-sister Matilda's armies in her fight against their cousin Stephen of Blois for the throne of England (though Julia Crick suggests that the dedication probably predates Robert's break with Stephen).[7] Geoffrey's signature appears on a number of documents from Oxford between the years 1129 and 1151, sometimes with the designation 'magister', and from this sparse documentary record we can deduce that he was well educated and probably based in that city, though perhaps educated in France. The epithet Monemutensis, meaning from Monmouth, in south Wales, was once taken as evidence that he was Welsh, though it is more common today to suggest he was of Breton extraction.[8]

The argument over Geoffrey's origins matters in part because it may speak to his mobilization of British source materials, as well as to his probable attitude towards those materials.[9] While there may not have been a 'British book', there most certainly was a tradition of Welsh Arthurian poetry and of Welsh nationalist prophecy, and Geoffrey's work, particularly his treatment of Merlin, clearly echoes some of this material. Some critics have wondered if Geoffrey's 'book' is not in fact a place-holder for his access to oral traditions richer in his own time than their scattered survivals today suggest. In the Dedication to the *HRB* he refers positively to the oral traditions concerning the kings of the Britons: 'their deeds are worthy of eternal praise, and they were joyfully and by memory preached by many people, as if they had been written down.'[10] As I have argued elsewhere, this overt recourse (or claim of recourse) to oral tradition is a stunning move from a writer of Latin history.[11] Medieval historians did not share our understanding of 'fact' and 'fiction': as a branch of rhetoric, history was properly embellished in ways we might regard as essentially literary.[12] History was a didactic and revelatory mode, and its 'truth' was not always understood to reside in such things as accuracy of numbers or dates.[13] Geoffrey's contemporary John of Salisbury, for example, prefaced his *Policraticus*, a work rooted in the political and court culture of his day, with these words: 'I do not promise that all the things which are written here are true, but, whether they be true or false, they will be of use to the reader.'[14] In the famous biblical maxim, all that is written, is for our doctrine – but there were proprieties to be observed, particularly in the scholarly milieu in which Geoffrey moved. William of Newburgh's well-known attack on the veracity of Geoffrey's *Historia* registers a precise degree of shock when he notes that Geoffrey clothed his 'fables . . . with the honourable name of history by presenting them with the ornaments of the Latin tongue'.[15] For William, Geoffrey's use of Latin is tantamount to a claim to utility – to doctrine – applied to (vernacular oral) fables. Whether Geoffrey actually could have accessed Welsh tradition in its original language remains a point of some debate,[16] but the more interesting matter here is his bold claim to find the matter of history in a people's memory and oral tradition.

That historical memory is, for Geoffrey, also written across the landscape, retrievable through its linguistic traces. The *HRB* is full of anecdotes about how geographical features, cities and regions got their names. Geoffrey is of course often inventing these stories, but the important point is his desire to root his history in the physical, often using the linguistic to do so.[17] Britain is named for Brutus, and its three main divisions for his sons:

> Brutus then slept with his wife Innogin and by her he had three famous sons, whose names were Locrinus, Albanactus, and Kamber. These three, when twenty-four years after his arrival their father left this world, buried him within the city that he had founded, and divided the kingdom of Britain amongst themselves, each succeeding [his father] in his own particular region. Locrinus, who was the first-born, took the middle part of the island, which afterwards was called Loegria, according to his name. Kamber took that area which is across the Severn River. It is called Wales now, but for a long time it was called Kambria, after his name, for which reason the people of this country call themselves Kambri in the British tongue. Albanactus, the youngest, took the region which is called Scotland in our language today, and he gave it the name Albany, from his own name.[18]

These names combine the plausible and the fanciful in a way most characteristic of Geoffrey. On other occasions, the invention is more obvious and even outrageous, at least to later centuries of readers. Consider, for example, the story of Corineus, Brutus' right-hand man. Brutus names his newly found land for himself, and then distributes land to his followers, one of whom is Corineus, who had taken a major role in the Trojan victory at Tours, prior to the landfall in Britain. Then, Geoffrey tells us,

> Corineus, following the example of his leader, called the portion of the kingdom which had fallen to his choice Corineia, from his own name, and he also called his people Corineians. He could have had the first choice of provinces, before all the others who came there, but he preferred that region which is now called Cornubia, either from the horn of Britain, or through a corruption of the aforementioned name.[19]

There is an appearance of scholarly objectivity here, as Geoffrey allows for two possible explanations for the name, and even introduces the idea of corruption over time. But do those possibilities have equal status? For the first, 'Cornwall' might indeed derive from the Celtic word for horn and the Saxon word used for (Celtic) foreigners; so, Cornwall is the horn of the Celts. But Corineus himself is another matter. Geoffrey probably adopted the name from the *Aeneid*, where one Corynaeus fights with Aeneas against Turnus.[20] Although in the few lines in which he appears Corynaeus is a formidable warrior – he sets a foe's beard ablaze and then wrestles him to the ground – he otherwise bears no relation to the character in *HRB*, and J. S. P. Tatlock suggests Geoffrey found the name appealing simply because it could be used to provide an etymology for Cornubia, Cornwall.[21]

Geoffrey follows this bit of etymological invention by attaching narrative to naming in his account of Corineus' battle with the Cornish giant Gogmagog. Corineus, we are told, 'delighted in fighting with giants',[22] and this giant makes for a particularly exciting encounter:

> Then the battle began – Corineus advanced, and the giant advanced, each trapping the other in the shackles made by their arms. They vexed the air with their laboured breath. Without delay, Gogmagog crushed Corineus with all his strength, breaking three of his ribs, two on the right side, and one on the left. Corineus was furious and called on all his strength and hoisted Gogmagog onto his shoulders, and he raced, with all the speed he could muster under that weight, to the nearby seashore. Then, having come upon a very high cliff, he gleefully shook off that monster, which he was carrying on his shoulders, and hurled him into the sea. The giant, falling onto the jagged rocks, was torn into a thousand pieces, and stained the water with his blood. And that place, having taken its name from the giant's fall, is called Gogmagog's Leap to this day.[23]

The fight began in the port where Brutus had landed; that is, at Totnes. The city is on an estuary, and Corineus would therefore have had to run some six to nine miles to reach the coast (and as Tatlock points out, he would not have found a steep cliff when he got there).[24] The point here is not so much the flawed geography or the fantastical quality of the story, however, but rather, that there is a story at all. This place-name is apparently unattested anywhere except in *HRB* (unlike, say, Britain or Albany), and while it may well be true, as Tatlock suggests, that Geoffrey is here embellishing a local, Celtic tradition,[25] his choice to recount this episode in the first place says much about his methods. The giant is twelve feet tall; the fight is lively, engaging; the Latin prose is balanced and carefully constructed; and the encounter prefigures Arthur's own, even more elaborate, giant-fight, with the giant of Mont Saint Michel. The episode is, in short, part of the literary fabric of the *HRB* – a fabric that makes modern readers in particular uncomfortable in the face of something claiming to be 'history'. Surely Geoffrey is writing imaginative fiction, clothed (as William of Newburgh has it) in both the language and, although here more fitfully, the accoutrements of history (linguistics, onomastics, toponymics, translation . . .). And yet before we leave the realm of giants to consider Arthur himself, a note of caution needs to be sounded. Geoffrey's giants are not merely entertaining and outlandish, and it would be misleading to see them simply as proof of the gleeful literary game which many commentators (myself included) have seen in Geoffrey's work.[26] A curious footnote in the transmission of the *HRB* illustrates the degree to which even the most apparently fantastical elements of Geoffrey's narrative worked their way into the British historical imagination.

De origine gigantum (or *De gigantibus*) is a Latin prose translation of a thirteenth- or early fourteenth-century Anglo-Norman poem called *Des grantz geanz*. In their edition of the Latin work, James Carley and Julia Crick argue it was produced at Glastonbury, some time in the 1330s.[27] The narrative recounts how the island of Albion was discovered by Albina and her twenty-nine sisters, Greek princesses who had been set adrift for plotting to murder their husbands. They land on the island which the eldest, Albina, calls Albion; they then consort with incubi and thus become the mothers of the giants who rule the island until Brutus arrives. This brief summary makes clear why the piece might be treated, as indeed it was, as a preface to several manuscript copies of *HRB*.[28] Like the story of Brutus, it is a myth of origin, linking name and narrative; like Geoffrey's own procedure, it fills in a *lacuna* in attested history, in this case a hole Geoffrey left himself, by neglecting to tell his audience where giants such as Gogmagog came from. Geoffrey's later audience participates in the synthetic activity of history-making, then, by adding this layer to his origin myth. In a similar move, some later readers would add the Latin *Vera historia de morte Arthuri*, a Celtically-inflected account of Arthur's death, to the bald ending provided by Geoffrey.[29] And the additional details are not simply narrative housekeeping. For early modern readers, for example, both the Albina and the Brutus stories played a part in the often competing discourses of nationalism, so that it was important to flesh out Geoffrey's account.[30] Geoffrey's *Historia* might be read for its narrative appeal, for its ideological utility, or for some combination of these impulses; and important as Arthur is, he is not the only contributor to the text's enduring allure.

Thus far, I have made some suggestions about how to understand the first part of Geoffrey's title – what the term *historia* might mean to medieval producers and readers in general, as well as in Geoffrey's rather more idiosyncratic approach.[31] Arthur's historicity in particular has been a source of constant interest to many readers, perhaps especially so for the scholarly medieval and early modern readers/writers discussed in the contributions to this volume. For Geoffrey, however, I would argue that we need to put as much emphasis on the second word of the title – on Arthur as a *rex* among *reges*, as one of the many kings, to return to the words of Geoffrey's preface, who ruled in Britain both before and after the Incarnation of Christ. Here again, the opening of the *HRB* offers us a way to understand that emphasis. The first king we spend any significant time with is Brutus himself, and his path to rule is a violent one. Brutus is said to be 'overflowing with joy'[32] after his troops' grisly destruction of the Greek camp, for example, and as I have argued elsewhere, this initial violent slaughter is shown by Geoffrey to be the necessary first event on the path to Brutus' eventual kingship of Britain.[33] Belinus and Brennius conquer Rome with similar violent gusto, slaughtering thousands and even hanging noble Roman hostages outside the city gates to compel its surrender (chapter 43). Violence is not necessarily always negatively portrayed here, but the early chapters of *HRB* show a preoccupation with power and those who exercise it.

This exercise of power can be benevolent. Good kings often follow their violence with peace-making activities. They may build roads, like Belinus (chapter 39), or establish laws, like Dunvallo Molmutius (chapter 34); they often build or repair cities that then, in Geoffrey's persistent linkage of place with person, bear their names – London for Lud (chapters 22 and 53), Leicester for Leir (chapter 31), and so on. And once Geoffrey reaches the Christian era, his good kings often distinguish themselves by fighting non-Christians and then by rebuilding churches and caring for the victims of war. A notable example of this kind of king can be found in the run-up to the Arthuriad, in the person of Aurelius, the rightful ruler who reclaims the throne from the treacherous Vortigern. He is a great warrior – 'strong on foot and stronger on horseback' – but once he wins his victories, 'His whole attention was turned to the restoration of the realm, the rebuilding of the churches, the renovation of peace and laws, and the ordering of justice.'[34] It is worth noting the figures of repetition (polyptoton in the first quotation) and parallelism (the tricolon in the second) Geoffrey deploys here in his descriptions – it is as if the strength and excellence of Aurelius are further underlined by the polishing of Geoffrey's prose.

And yet Aurelius does not govern long. He falls victim to poisoning, thus exemplifying a common pattern throughout the *HRB*, wherein even the best of kings die, often as a result of treachery. Geoffrey's history is one of kings in the plural – an account of power struggles, triumphs and defeats, and, inevitably, of death and succession. Because the Arthuriad occupies so much of the *HRB*, and because readers interested in Arthur often abstract this section from the whole of Geoffrey's history, it is easy to forget this frame and its implications. But two aspects of Geoffrey's treatment of Arthur serve to connect him to the larger frame. One is Arthur's death, which in Geoffrey's handling is bald and completely lacking in the mystery later attached to it. I will return to that death at the end of this essay. The other is the prophet Merlin, and it is to this enigmatic figure that I now turn.

It is helpful to pause for a brief plot summary of the events leading up to Arthur's reign in the *HRB*. As discussed above, Geoffrey's history opens with the flight of Trojan refugees, led by Brutus, and traces their arrival in Britain and how their descendants divide and govern the island. The first widely documented historical events with which Geoffrey has to deal are Julius Caesar's invasion, and the later, successful Roman invasion and settlement. Geoffrey treats the Romans in his characteristic fashion, interweaving familiar events with unfamiliar ones and unlikely interpretations (for example, he credits the baths at Kaerbadum/Bath to the British king Bladud (chapter 30) and not to the Romans).[35] When the Romans eventually leave Britain, the Britons fall prey to the invading Saxons, and Geoffrey's narrative now picks up the story of the struggles between Britons and Saxons as also recorded in Gildas and Bede. It is against the backdrop of this conflict that Geoffrey introduces the descendants of Constantinus, the brothers Constans, Aurelius Ambrosius and Uther Pendragon. After Constantinus is murdered by a Pict, the treacherous Vortigern seizes the opportunity presented by internecine strife over which of the brothers is to succeed to the throne, and manoeuvres Constans, hitherto a monk, from the cloister to a kingdom. Soon enough Vortigern arranges for Constans' death and seizes the throne for himself, and shortly thereafter enters into an alliance with the Saxons Hengist and Horsa. The relationship is a troubled one, and eventually Vortigern finds himself on the run from his erstwhile allies. Seeking to build an impenetrable fortress tower, he is stymied by the tower's repeated collapse. His magicians tell him that the mortar must be sealed with the blood of a fatherless boy, and his soldiers scour the countryside and bring Merlin to him.

I have noted that it is common for modern readers to treat the Arthuriad as separable from the rest of the *Historia*; this is in fact a habit among some medieval readers as well. William of Rennes, for example, pauses in his thirteenth-century metrical Latin adaptation of *HRB* when he reaches the point of bringing Arthur to the throne, and inserts a new invocation, appealing to the muses to aid him in the praise of one who outstrips the heroes of the classical past:

> Bright Caliope, come from Helicon, with the band of your sisters with you, and moisten my hollow, thirsty breast with your sacred spring; for I do not presume to describe the deeds of Arthur in verse without you, lest I should seem to demean them. Homer could not succeed without your willing it, nor Ovid, nor Virgil, nor Tullius himself, since Arthur surpasses Achilles in praise by as much as Achilles surpasses Thersites. The author of the *Aeneid* would have preferred the praises of Arthur to the story of old Anchises, [for those praises] are worthy of the Maeonian bard; grave Lucan would have fallen silent about the deeds of Caesar, and old Thebes would have lacked its eternal fame, had the deeds of Arthur preceded these poets. But lest so great a hero should perish without praise, I will try to lift up the praise of this invincible prince.[36]

Geoffrey had also paused his account, but not, tellingly, at precisely the same place. Instead, it is at the moment in *HRB* when the soldiers bring Merlin to Vortigern that Geoffrey suddenly suspends the narrative and inserts a second preface. Merlin tells Vortigern that the tower is resting on a pool, which conceals two dragons, one red and one white. When the lake is drained and the dragons begin to fight, Merlin breaks forth into prophetic speech, but not before Geoffrey once again claims, as he did at the beginning of *HRB*, to be a mere translator:

> Love of your nobility, Alexander, bishop of Lincoln, compelled me to translate from British into Latin the prophecies of Merlin, before I had finished the history of the deeds of the British kings which I had begun. I had intended first to complete that work, and then to write this one, lest while the labour of both pressed upon me, my sense might prove too weak for either.[37]

There are obvious similarities to the opening of *HRB*. Geoffrey figures himself as a humble translator, not an innovator. His role is that of mediator between British tradition and Latin readers, here in the person of Alexander, bishop of Lincoln. Both the history Geoffrey has hitherto been writing, and prophecies of all sorts with their attendant commentary traditions, are precisely the sort of reading material favoured by educated courtier-clerics.[38] Geoffrey's own interest in this tradition is suggested, not merely by the Merlin section of the *Historia*, but also by the fact that he apparently returned to Merlin for his last work, the *Vita Merlini*.

In his *Vita Merlini*, a poem surviving in only one manuscript and of considerably later date than the *HRB*,[39] Geoffrey displays wide knowledge of the Welsh poems that deal with Merlin and his prophecies,[40] but this Merlin is not a member of Arthur's court. He is (as in the Welsh poetic tradition) a king of the south Welsh, driven mad after a battle. The crazed prophet takes refuge in the woods, but is brought thence by his sister Ganieda to the court of her husband King Rodarch, where he displays his prophetic knowledge before escaping again to the forest. The plot of the poem involves several such captures and escapes, interspersed with both ecstatic prophecy and, later, learned discussion about such geographic features as islands, springs and lakes, the latter between Merlin and the fictional Welsh bard Taliesin. The poem ends with Merlin and Taliesin's resolution to live in the forest in the service of God. Merlin gives up his prophetic voice, which is taken up by his sister Ganieda, who also joins him in the forest.

The poem, as even this brief sketch surely indicates, is a strange creation, not at all like the coherent, highly accessible *HRB*, though it shares some of its interests (I am thinking here of the geographic discussions as well as Merlin's prophecies). The poem may be a cerebral game for its creator or a few insiders – the opening lines announce, 'I prepare myself to sing the madness of Merlin, the prophetic bard, and the jocose muse.'[41] The *musa jocosa* may suggest a playful stance, though it is clear from the occasionally grotesque moments in the plot – as when Merlin kills his former wife's new husband with a set of stag's antlers – that playfulness is not the same as lightness. The prophecies are often connected with Merlin's laughter, but Merlin is laughing at such things as Ganieda's infidelity to her husband, and the imminent death of a young man who is buying patches for his new shoes, ignorant of the fact that he is about to drown on the way home. Many of the longer prophetic passages recall Welsh nationalist prophecy, and dwell on the fate of the Britons and the coming of the Saxons. Merlin speaks here against the 'madness of the Britons',[42] a tendency towards internecine strife even at moments of crisis that Geoffrey also deplores in the *HRB*. Even more, the prophetic passages imagine a world in which all positive human structures disappear:

> Then peace and faith and virtue will all depart, and there will be civil war throughout the lands, and man will betray his fellow, and no friend will be found. The husband, despising his wife, will mate with whores, and the wife will join with whomever she desires, despising her husband. Honour for the churches will not remain, and the order will perish. Then bishops will bear arms, then they will follow the camps, they will place towers and walls on sacred ground and give to soldiers what they ought to give to the poor.[43]

In the *HRB*, Geoffrey's good kings (Arthur among them, as we will see), often reveal themselves by caring for families and the poor, establishing peace, and restoring and fostering law and religion. Here in the *Vita*, Merlin predicts a future in which none of these efforts will have lasting purchase. A few lines after this particular passage, Merlin remarks that he has already predicted this future to Vortigern (lines 681–3), thus connecting the *Vita Merlini* to the *HRB*. Later, another prophetic section includes a sort of précis of the *Historia*.

The connections made here between the enigmatic, mad prophet of the *Vita* and the fatherless boy prophesying before Vortigern are important to the overall tone of the *HRB*. The *Vita* ends with an explicit turn to Christ, thus perhaps offering a counter to the grim future imagined in passages like the ones quoted above. The analogous passages in the *HRB* have no similar resolution. Merlin's prophecies in the *HRB* pass through cryptic references to recognizable historical events both before and after the prophet's time, to increasingly dense predictions of unspecified internal warfare and strife with a growing reliance on animal imagery, to, finally, an apocalyptic imagination of the heavens going to war with mankind:

> The splendour of the sun will languish in the amber of Mercury, and there will be horror among those who see this. Mercury of Arcady will change its shield, and the Helmet of Mars will call to Venus. The helmet of Mars will cast a shadow, and the rage of Mercury will cross over its orbit. Iron Orion will bare its sword, and watery Phoebus will torment the clouds. Jupiter will leave its ordained paths and Venus will desert its appointed lines. The anger of the star Saturn will fall and kill mortals with a curved sickle . . . The oceans shall surge up and the dust of the ancients shall be made new in a stroke of light. The winds will do battle with a dire blast, and they shall make noise among the stars.[44]

For Robert Hanning, this is a vision of history '[dissolving] into nothingness'.[45] In the *Vita*, a similarly bleak prophetic imagination – displaying what Jan Ziolkowski has called 'a hopelessness that any divine order governs events in the human world'[46] – is perhaps offset by Ganieda's final call: 'Christ, bring aid to your people, quiet the lions, and, having brought an end to war, given peaceful quiet to the kingdom.'[47] It is also true that while both Merlin and Ganieda have recourse to animal and celestial imagery in the *Vita*, they are for the most part predicting the Saxon and Norman oppressions of the Britons. The prophetic Merlin of *HRB*, on the other hand, moves from that recognizable world of Welsh nationalist prophecy towards this more terrifyingly general and apocalyptic future, after which he simply stops, and the narrative picks up again as if nothing had happened, after Vortigern and his men pronounce their amazement at what they have heard.

Merlin's prophecies interrupt the flow of *HRB*, as Geoffrey's second preface acknowledges. There is no obvious plot impact as a result of Merlin's prophesying (except of course that Vortigern abandons the plan to use Merlin's blood as mortar for the tower). Furthermore, Merlin's character shifts once Geoffrey settles into the account of Arthur's reign. After his prophetic outburst, Merlin is treated in the narrative as a wise man and adviser, and there seems to be a deliberate avoidance of anything particularly mystical in the depiction. Merlin supervises the transportation of the Giant's

Ring (Stonehenge) from Ireland and its erection on Salisbury Plain, but it is his 'machines' and his genius that get the credit.[48] Here he is working for Aurelius, who wishes to set up a memorial to the Britons killed by Saxon treachery at Mount Ambrius. Later, Merlin works for Uther and alters Uther's appearance so that he can sleep with Ygerna, but he does so with 'drugs', not with magic.[49] Merlin disappears from the narrative after this point, having nothing in fact to do with Arthur beyond having predicted his birth to Uther in response to a comet that appears at Aurelius' death (chapter 133), but the enigmatic, gnomic prophecies preceded by the second preface, by virtue of their positioning in the *HRB*, remain in the mind to colour Arthur's reign.

The *Prophetie Merlini* precede the defeat of Vortigern and Hengist by the admirable Aurelius, and while the deaths of both Aurelius and Uther by poison are in keeping with the dark tone of many of the prophecies, we soon find ourselves in the Arthuriad proper, in which everything, it seems, conspires to urge us to forget the various framings of Arthur's story. Arthur is, we should remember, a king who like the rest of the kings in the *HRB* is part of history – and while history *may* be divinely ordered, it may also be tending, as Merlin's prophecies seem to suggest, towards meaningless chaos.[50] But the things we are told about Geoffrey's Arthur, and the way he is presented to us, seem designed to emphasize the singularity of this greatest of kings. As the sometimes breathless pace of the *Historia* slows to linger over Arthur's reign, the audience runs the risk of losing sight of the larger forces of history, in the contemplation of the individual's role.

And what an individual Arthur is. We have met impressive kings before, but Arthur seems precociously perfect (and, as the following quotation suggests, pragmatic to boot):

> Now Arthur was a youth of fifteen years, of outstanding virtue and generosity. His innate goodness gave him such great grace that he was loved by almost all the people. Having been initiated into the kingship, he displayed his customary generosity. Such a great multitude of soldiers flocked to him that he began to run out of gifts to distribute. But one who combines generosity with righteousness, even if he is temporarily without money, will not be harmed by perpetual poverty. Arthur, because his strength was linked with generosity, decided to harass the Saxons so that he could enrich the household which served him with their wealth. Righteousness also moved him, for he ought by hereditary right to have the rule of the whole kingdom.[51]

Other kings have been great (and brutal) warriors, but Arthur is marked out by formal attention to his arming, including the naming of his weapons, and when he enters the fray, his deeds are prodigious:

> Arthur himself was clothed in a breastplate worthy of so great a king, and he placed on his head a golden helmet, sculpted in the likeness of a dragon. On his shoulders was his shield, called Pridwen, on which the image of the blessed Mary, mother of God, was depicted, so that she was continually called to his memory. He was girded with his sword Caliburn, the best of swords, made in the island of Avalon, and a spear called Ron adorned his right hand; this spear was long and broad, well-suited for battle . . . Taking out his sword Caliburn, he called out the name of holy Mary and rushed into the dense ranks of the enemy. Whomsoever he touched, he killed with a single blow, calling upon God. Nor did he cease his attack until with Caliburn alone he had killed four hundred and seventy men.[52]

This passage also makes clear Arthur's explicitly Christian identification. While other kings in the Christian era, as I have noted, perform such pious deeds as rebuilding churches, Arthur is the first to be figured as an anti-pagan crusader.[53] In the passage above he calls on Mary and on God. Similarly, in the speech to his troops before this battle begins, he speaks as a warrior for the faith, and his urgings are echoed by Bishop Dubricius, who explicitly links Britain to Christianity:

> Men marked with the Christian faith, remember the love of your homeland and your fellow citizens, and let their death by the perfidy of the pagans be an eternal reproach to you, unless you stir yourselves to defend them. Fight for your country, and if death should come, suffer it for that country. For this is a victory and a cure for your souls. For indeed, whosoever offers his life for his brothers, shows himself as a living sacrifice to God and cannot be doubted to follow Christ, who deigned to offer his life for his brothers.[54]

The potent combination of Arthur's personal gifts and weapons with the divine sanction implied by Dubricius and seemingly confirmed by Arthur's victories, encourages us to see Arthur as special or unique, and Geoffrey continues in this vein for some time. Arthur's defeat of the Saxons is followed by his subduing of the Scots, the Picts and the Irish and his installation of the British princes Loth, Urien and Auguselus in the territories they had lost at the advent of the Saxons. This imperial activity is presented positively, as '[returning] the whole country to the dignity of its original (*pristinam*) state'.[55] The word *pristina* is a powerful one, connoting a sense of ultimate origins – Arthur returns the island of Britain to what should be its ideal state, to the condition of wholeness which Brutus first imposed upon it. If we should happen to remember, with concern, that this pristine state was immediately followed by the carving out of separate territories by Brutus' descendants, we are perhaps at this point distracted by the spectacle of Arthur's apparently inevitable rise.

Internal conquest is followed by external campaigns, as Arthur learns that the kings of foreign lands are fortifying against him: 'And when Arthur was told about this, exalting himself since he was feared by so many, he decided to conquer all Europe.'[56] Translators often translate *extollens* as 'exulted', a good rendering of Arthur's bloodthirsty delight, but the more literal 'exalted himself' is apt as well – both senses create a thread that links Arthur to all those other conquering kings we have temporarily put to the side. We have seen Brutus overflowing with joy at the carnage on the battlefield. Dunvallo the lawmaker 'overthrew cities and towns' and 'subjugated the whole land' on his way to the throne.[57] Geoffrey's Leir laments his changed circumstances specifically in terms of his martial past, remembering 'that time when, with so many hundreds of thousands of men I used to batter down the walls of cities and lay waste the provinces of my enemies'.[58] I do not wish to suggest that there is any moralizing or condemnation attached to Arthur's European activities (though certainly later adaptors sometimes try to locate a moment when Arthur goes too far). What I am tracing here is a tension between Arthur's super-excellence, and an all but submerged sense that he is nevertheless a king among kings, following, and subject to, patterns we have seen before.

Arthur's campaigns in Norway and Gaul are triumphs, and after their successful conclusion, the narrative momentum of the *HRB* seems to pause again, in this case for the set-piece of Arthur's plenary court. Geoffrey provides a detailed (and apparently largely accurate) description of the city of Caerleon on Usk, where Arthur holds this gathering.[59] This description is followed by a long list of the dignitaries attending the court, a list punctuated only by *occupationes* in which Geoffrey tells us he has neither the time nor the space to describe all the marvels of the occasion. Religious ceremonies are followed by feasting, and feasting by jousts, and here Geoffrey sounds the notes of proto-romance:

> Britain at that time had arrived at such a state of dignity that it excelled all other realms in the abundance of its riches, the luxury of its ornaments, and the courtliness of its inhabitants. Whatever knight of that country was famous for prowess wore clothing and arms of one colour. The women, too, fashionably attired in the same colours, would have nothing of the love of any man, unless he had been proven three times in battle. The women, then, were made chaste and more virtuous, and the soldiers more brave for the love of them. When they had been refreshed by the feasting, they went outside the city to take part in various sports. Then the knights took part in equestrian competition, feigning battle. The ladies, watching from the tops of the walls, playfully incited love's furious flames.[60]

The emphasis on the role of women in inciting knightly behaviour foreshadows the preoccupations of the vernacular romances which were to develop after Geoffrey. *Facetia*, a word that occurs twice in this passage, describes a courtliness which has hitherto not been a particular focus in the *HRB*; if Arthur has in one sense returned Britain to its pristine state, he has also elevated it to a new level, a position above all other realms in the known world. The word's meaning is difficult to represent with a single, English equivalent. It is one of a cluster of courtly terms – others include *urbanitas*, *decorum*, *jocus* (this latter also in the above passage) – that epitomize a kind of civilized behaviour valued in the courtly culture of the high Middle Ages, perhaps particularly as it relates to the educated courtier-clerics who doubtless formed part of Geoffrey's readership.[61] The plenary court, then, seems to be introducing a new moment, a further evolution, in British history; and yet it is at this precise moment that the harbingers of a return to war arrive. Into this scene of peacetime excellence, twelve Roman ambassadors intrude to demand that Arthur render tribute to Rome, as had his ancestors before him. The request is of course rejected, Arthur pointing out that he has as much claim to tribute from the Romans, and then Arthur and his army set off for France. The encounter with the Romans is, however, postponed by Arthur's combat against the giant of Mont Saint Michel, and here again Geoffrey seems to be delaying the march of Arthur's history towards its final end. Instead we pause for the account of the abduction and death of Helena, duke Hoel's niece; a conversation between Bedevere and the girl's nurse, who recounts her own rape at the giant's hands, and then Arthur's determination to meet the giant in single combat.

I suggested above that Corineus' encounter with Gogmagog is later echoed in Arthur's encounter with the giant of Mont Saint Michel. In both cases, the hero meets the giant in single combat, the giant attempts to crush the hero, and the hero wins – but the important point of resemblance lies not in the details of the fight (which otherwise differ), but rather in the *type* of incident it represents. The encounter between Corineus and Gogmagog is exciting and described with some literary verve; as with all else concerning Arthur, Geoffrey lavishes even more narrative space and artistry on the fight with the giant of Mont Saint Michel. Here is the climax of the struggle:

> He had already seized [his club], and struck the king's raised shield with such force that the sound of the blow filled all the shore and utterly deafened his ears. Arthur, burning with bitter rage, struck him a blow on the forehead with his raised sword, and while it was not mortal, it caused blood to stream over his face and into his eyes, blinding him. The giant defended his forehead from a lethal wound with his club, but blinded by the flowing blood, he surged forward even more fiercely, and like a boar rushing on a hunter along his spear, he rushed at the king along the other's sword, and seizing him around the waist, he began to force him to his knees on the ground. And then Arthur, recovering his strength, quickly escaped and swiftly advanced, striking now here, now there with his sword, never resting until with a fatal stroke he had penetrated that part of the giant's head which protected his brain. The hateful creature cried out and, like an oak tree uprooted by powerful winds, fell with a loud crash. The king immediately laughed.[62]

As in the encounter between Corineus and Gogmagog, the passage is marked by careful attention to the creation of excitement, the mimicry of action in the prose (*nunc hinc nunc illato*), and the evocation of sight and sound. Arthur's burning rage and vocal delight are the larger-than-life attributes of the epic hero. One might suspect Geoffrey of approaching parody when Arthur immediately compares this fight to another combat he has apparently had with yet another giant, but there is no doubt that the run-up to the final movement of the Arthuriad continues to mark Arthur out as uniquely gifted, even as the parallels to strong figures of the past should perhaps give rise to some anxiety. Geoffrey has shown us many times that history may pause briefly – for an impressive martial feat, a display of regal power, a period of the peaceful quiet for which Ganieda calls at the end of the *Vita Merlini* – but it always moves forward, and one king is inevitably followed by another. We should not be surprised that this is true of Arthur as well, but Geoffrey's structure trips us up, making the shock of Arthur's death all the greater.

After the interlude at Mont Saint Michel, Arthur moves on to encounter Lucius and his armies. Arthur ends his military career as he began it, linking victory to the potential spoils as he promises his troops, 'we will seize [Rome], and take possession of it, and thus you will have gold, silver, palaces, towers, castles, cities, and all the other spoils of victory.'[63] The battle which follows is carefully described, with much attention paid to tactics. It occurs in several waves, the first of which brings about the death of Bedevere and the mortal wounding of Kay. Gawain fights Lucius in single combat, and Arthur draws Caliburn, rallies his men, and attacks with the fury that carried him to victory at Mount Badon. The first sign that things are about to change, however, comes with the conclusion of the battle. Despite Gawain's heroics, and Arthur's savage ferocity, Lucius' death is oddly flat: 'Then Lucius the emperor, in the middle of the crowd, died on someone's lance.[64] The emperor does not perish at the hands of Arthur or of one of his named heroes; he simply falls in battle, with thousands of others. The narrative briefly refocuses on the exploits of individual men when it tells of the burial of Bedevere and Kay, but almost immediately, as Arthur prepares to march on Rome, the news reaches him that, back in Britain, his nephew Mordred has usurped both throne and queen.

At this point Geoffrey again pauses his narrative, as he did before Merlin's prophecies. Here, as in the opening of the *HRB*, he turns to the figure of the British book: 'Nor will Geoffrey of Monmouth, most noble consul, be silent about this. Instead he will, with his lowly pen and briefly, set forth the battles which that famous king fought with his nephew upon his return to Britain after his famous victory, as he found them in the aforementioned British book, and has also heard them from Walter of Oxford, a man most learned in many histories.[65] The appeal to the 'lowly pen' is a familiar modesty topos – in the similar passages at the opening of the *HRB* and before the *Prophetie* there are similar apologies – but here the topos also signals a genuine shift in style, as Geoffrey returns to the swift, matter-of-fact narrative of events that forms the basic ground and canvas of the *HRB*. There are no set speeches, no single combats, and most striking, there is no death-scene for Arthur. Instead we read simply, 'But that most famous king Arthur was mortally wounded. He was taken thence to the island of Avalon, for the healing of his wounds. He passed the crown of Britain to his cousin Constantine, son of Cador duke of Cornwall, in the year of our Lord 542.'[66]

Arthur is not *said* to be dead here, and the reference to Avalon could be taken to suggest the Breton hope, the idea that Arthur would one day return to his people.[67] As I have noted above, the anonymous *Vera historia de morte Arthuri*, which provides far more detail in an appropriately mystical atmosphere, is appended to Geoffrey's brief description in some manuscripts, suggesting perhaps the dissatisfaction of some readers with Geoffrey's summary dismissal of Arthur. But whatever some readers might think of it, Geoffrey's plan is quite clear. Immediately after the crown passes to Constantine, he returns us to the relentless cycle of strife that has characterized most of British history: 'And after he had been crowned, the Saxons and the two sons of Mordred rebelled against him, but they were unable to prevail against him, and instead, after many battles, one fled to London, and the other to Winchester, attempting to capture these cities.'[68] Several kings follow in rapid succession, each accorded a bald paragraph noting succession, reign and death. The overall impression is of a firm return to history, to business as usual after the temporary holiday represented by the Arthuriad. The contrast is not complete, as there are still narrative interludes on the way to the final Saxon domination, but there is nothing as sustained as Arthur's reign, and the end comes fairly quickly. Cadwallader, the last British king, finally gives up his attempt to reclaim the island from the Saxons when an angelic voice instructs him that 'God did not wish the Britons to rule any longer over the island of Britain, until that time should come which Merlin had prophesied to Arthur'.[69]

Merlin of course never prophesied to Arthur in Geoffrey's *HRB* – the *Prophetie Merlini* are made in the presence of Vortigern, while the explication of the comet foretelling Arthur's birth is offered to Uther. In the *Vita Merlini*, Merlin speaks in the forest, at Rodarch's court, and to Taliesin, but never to Arthur. And the prophecies of both Merlins, as I have noted above, are dark and even apocalyptic; in other words, there is little comfort in the words of the angelic voice. History stands framed in prophecy – the *HRB* begins with Diana and ends with the Angel, while the Arthuriad begins with Merlin, before returning us again to history. This structure suggests that there is something beyond or behind the human scale of history, but it does little to make that something clear or comforting. History is also, in Geoffrey's hands, dressed in 'ornate words',[70] the literary language and rhetorical effects the equally rhetorical modesty topoi repeatedly deny – here the 'something' beyond and behind history is the process of telling it, of human craft and art. Geoffrey is, in the end, rather like Merlin. He can see what is going to happen; he can, for a time, make history stand still – but he too is, finally, a spectator, one who can show, but not change, what he knows. The ancient British book, then, is not merely a stand-in for Geoffrey's access to Welsh tradition, or a cover for his own imagination. It also serves to materialize a paradox in the writing of history. All that is written, is for our doctrine – but the lesson seems often to be about our powerlessness in the face of history, and herein lies the grimmest interpretation of Arthur's death. At the end of the *Vita Merlini*, Ganieda counsels a turn to Christ, and in the *HRB*, many kings, once we reach the Christian era, make a Christian end. Arthur does not. In the ambiguous retreat to Avalon, he is simply gone, with no death-scene and no tomb. Geoffrey's book was to carry Arthur to centuries of fame. Geoffrey did not coin the phrase 'the once and future king', but he may fairly be said to have made the epithet possible. Yet as I hope to have shown, for Geoffrey Arthur remains one of the *reges Britannie*, the men who both stride across the landscape of British history, and are ultimately consumed by it.

Notes

[1] Geoffrey of Monmouth, *The History of the Kings of Britain: An Edition and Translation of De gestis Britonum*, ed. Michael D. Reeve (Woodbridge, 2007), ch. 1: 'nichil de regibus qui ante incarnationem Christi inhabitauerant, nichil etiam de Arturo cetersique compluribus qui post incarnationem successerunt repperissem . . . Walterus Oxenefordensis archidiaconus . . . quendam Britannici sermonis librum uetustissimum qui a Bruto primo rege Britonum usque ad Cadualadrum filium Caduallonis actus omnium continue et ex ordine perpulcris orationibus proponebat. Rogatu itaque illius ductus . . . codicem illum in Latinum sermonem transferre curaui.' Translations are my own, not out of any disrespect for the excellent work of Neil Wright as a translator of the cited edition, but rather out of old habit, and to underline the occasional interpretive point.

[2] Geoffrey repeats the claim at the end of the *Historia*, ordering other historians to keep silent about the kings of the Britons, 'because they do not have the book in the British language which Walter, Archdeacon of Oxford, brought from Wales, which I have made the effort to translate into Latin' (cum non habeant librum illum Britannici sermonis quem Walterus Oxenefordensis archidiaconus ex Britannia aduexit, quem . . . hoc modo in Latinum sermonem tranferre curaui; ch. 208).

[3] For a discussion of the available sources for early British history, see the contributions by Nick Higham and Andrew Breeze in this volume. While most critics believe Geoffrey is fabricating the book, Geoffrey Ashe has considered the possibility of a written source; see '"A certain very ancient book": traces of an Arthurian source in Geoffrey of Monmouth's *History*', *Speculum*, 56 (1981), 301–23.

[4] For a discussion of the early reaction of contemporary historians to Geoffrey's work, see Ad Putter's contribution to this collection.

[5] See Aaron Thompson, *The British History, Translated into English from the Latin of Jeffrey of Monmouth. With a large Preface concerning the Authority of the History* (London, 1718). James Carley's contribution to this collection documents the attitudes of early modern antiquarians to both Brutus and Arthur, and traces some of the nationalist currents that were at play in the famous 'battle of the books'; see also Jennifer Summit, *Memory's Library: Medieval Books in Early Modern England* (Chicago, 2008), p. 119. A recent discussion of Geoffrey's treatment of the Troy story is Francis Ingledew, 'The Book of Troy and the genealogical construction of history: the case of Geoffrey of Monmouth's *Historia regum Britanniae*', *Speculum*, 69 (1994), 665–704.

[6] *Sir Gawain and the Green Knight*, ed. J. R. R. Tolkien and E. V. Gordon (Oxford, 1930, 1963), line 18.

[7] Julia C. Crick, 'Monmouth, Geoffrey of (*d.* 1154/5)', in *Oxford Dictionary of National Biography*, Oxford University Press, 2004 (*http://www.oxforddnb.com/view/article/10530*, accessed 15 July 2009).

[8] For a full discussion of Geoffrey's biography, see Michael J. Curley, *Geoffrey of Monmouth* (New York, 1994), the article by Crick cited in n. 7, and the introduction to Reeve's edition.

[9] See n. 16 below for the main lines of argument as to Geoffrey's ethnic origins and linguistic abilities.

[10] *HRB*, ch. 1: 'gesta eorum digna aeternitate laudis constarent et a multis populis quasi inscripta iocunde et memoriter praedicentur.'

[11] See Siân Echard, '"Hic est Artur": reading Latin and reading Arthur', in Alan Lupack (ed.), *New Directions in Arthurian Studies* (Cambridge, 2002), pp. 49–67.

[12] Christopher Brooke, for example, sees Geoffrey's primary motive as 'the desire to display the literary gifts of a historian'; C. N. L. Brooke, 'Geoffrey of Monmouth as a historian', in C. N. L. Brooke *et al.* (eds), *Church and Government in the Middle Ages: Essays Presented to C. R. Cheney on his 70th Birthday* (Cambridge, 1976), p. 90. Many studies of medieval history writing include specific discussion of the truth/fiction distinction. See Suzanne Fleischman, 'On the representation of history and fiction in the Middle Ages', *History and Theory*, 22 (1983), 278–310; Nancy Partner, '"The new Cornificius": medieval history and the artifice of words', in Ernst Breisach (ed.), *Classical Rhetoric and Medieval Historiography* (Kalamazoo, 1985), pp. 5–59; Ruth Morse, *Truth and Convention in the Middle Ages: Rhetoric, Representation, and Reality* (Cambridge, 1991); the introduction to Gabrielle M. Spiegel, *Romancing the Past: The Rise of Vernacular Prose Historiography in Thirteenth-Century France* (Berkeley, 1993); Barbara Sargent-Baur, 'Veraces historiae aut fallaces fabulae?' in Norris J. Lacy (ed.), *Text and Intertext in Medieval Arthurian Literature* (New York, 1996), pp. 25–39; Monika Otter, *Inventiones: Fiction and Referentiality in Twelfth-Century English Historical Writing* (Chapel Hill, 1996); and Jon Whitman, 'Alternative scriptures: story, history, and the canons of romance', *New Medieval Literatures*, 8 (2006), 1–44.

[13] There are many general scholarly discussions of medieval attitudes towards the writing of history. In addition to the studies listed in n. 12 above, see, for example, William M. Brandt, *The Shape of Medieval History* (New Haven, 1966); R. W. Southern, 'Aspects of the European tradition of historical writing, 1: The classical tradition from Einhard to Geoffrey of Monmouth', *Transactions of the Royal Historical Society,* 20 (1970), 173–96 and 'Aspects of the European tradition of historical writing, 3: History as prophecy', *Transactions of the Royal Historical Society*, 22 (1972), 159–80; Antonia Gransden, *Historical Writing in England c.550 to c.1307* (London, 1974); Nancy Partner, *Serious Entertainments: The Writing of History in Twelfth-Century England* (Chicago, 1977); Janet Coleman, *Ancient and Medieval Memories: Studies in the Reconstruction of the Past* (Cambridge, 1992); and, for Arthurian history in particular, Laurie A. Finke and Martin B. Shichtman, *King Arthur and the Myth of*

History (Gainesville, 2004), and Robert M. Stein, *Reality Fictions: Romance, History, and Governmental Authority, 1025–1180* (Notre Dame, 2006).

[14] John of Salisbury, *Policraticus*, in J.-P. Migne (ed.), *Joannis Saresberiensis Opera Omnia*, Patrologia Latina, 199 (1855), Prol.: 'qui non omnia, quae hic scribuntur, vera esse promitto; sed sive vera, seu falsa sunt, legentium usibus inservire.'

[15] William of Newburgh, *The History of English Affairs, Book I*, ed. and trans. P. G. Walsh and M. J. Kennedy (Warminster, 1988), *Prooemium*, p. 28: 'fabulas . . . Latini sermonis colorem honesto historiae nomine palliavit.' I discuss William's response to Geoffrey's *Historia* on p. 52 of '"Hic est Artur"'.

[16] J. S. P. Tatlock writes 'there is proof that [Geoffrey] knew at least some Welsh', though he argues that the evidence shows Geoffrey to have been of Breton origin; *The Legendary History of Britain* (Berkeley, 1950), pp. 445, 443. T. D. Crawford, 'On the linguistic competence of Geoffrey of Monmouth', *Medium Aevum*, 51 (1982), 152–62, suggests a Norman-French origin, but argues as well that the text of the *HRB* makes clear a 'certain competence in Welsh', pp. 153, 154. Brynley Roberts agrees that Geoffrey, who he thinks is probably of Breton origin, made use of oral material and knew traditional Welsh material and story, but he appears less convinced than either Tatlock or Crawford as to the depth of Geoffrey's knowledge of Welsh; see 'Geoffrey of Monmouth, *Historia regum Britanniae*, and *Brut y Brenhinedd*', in Rachel Bromwich, A. O. H. Jarman, Brynley F. Roberts and Daniel Huws (eds), *The Arthur of the Welsh: The Arthurian Legend in Medieval Welsh Literature* (Cardiff, 1991), pp. 97–116. In the same volume, however, J. E. Caerwyn Williams notes that there are indications the Welsh and Bretons could understand each other in the Middle Ages: 'Brittany and the Arthurian legend', pp. 253–4. For a recent argument as to Geoffrey's sympathies, see Michael Faletra, 'Narrating the matter of Britain: Geoffrey of Monmouth and the Norman colonization of Wales', *Chaucer Review*, 35 (2000), 60–85.

[17] Andrew Breeze comments in this volume on a similar approach in the Welsh-Latin life of St Cadog, wherein we learn, among other things, how Gwynllyw's Hill got its name.

[18] *HRB*, ch. 23: 'Cognouerat autem Brutus Innogin uxorem suam et ex ea genuit tres inclitos filios, quibus erant nomina Locrinus, Albanactus, Kamber. Hii, postquam pater in .xx.iiii anno aduentus sui ab hoc saeculo migrauit, sepelierunt eum infra urbem quam condiderat et diuiserunt regnum Britanniae inter se et secesserunt unusquisque in loco suo. Locrinus, qui primogenitus fuerat, possedit mediam partem insulae, quae postea de nomine suo appellata est Loegria; Kamber autem partem illam quae est ultra Sabrinum flumen, quae nunc Gualia uocatur, quae de nomine ipsius postmodum Kambria multo tempore dicta fuit, unde adhuc gens patriae lingua Britannica sese Kambro appellat; at Albanactus iunior possedit patriam quae lingua nostra his temporibus appellatur Scotia et nomen ei ex nomine suo Albania dedit.'

Tatlock devotes a considerable portion of his *Legendary History* to the dissection of Geoffrey's place-names. Of the main divisions, he argues that 'Albania' is a deliberate archaism on Geoffrey's part, since the contemporary usage was 'Scotia' (p. 8); of Loegria, he remarks that Geoffrey never uses 'Anglia', but always the Welsh-derived Loegria (p. 19); and that Geoffrey uses both Latin forms for Wales – Kambria and Guallia (p. 62) Welsh forms included Cymru and, for the whole island, ynys Prydain.

[19] *HRB*, ch. 21: 'At Corineus portionem regni quae sorti suae cesserat ab appellatione etiam sui nominis Corineiam uocat, populum quoque suum Corineiensem, exemplum ducis insecutus. Qui cum prae omnibus qui aduenerant electionem prouinciarum posset habere, maluit regionem illam quae nunc uel a cornu Britanniae uel per corruptionem praedicti nominis Cornubia appellatur.'

[20] See Tatlock, *Legendary History*, p. 116; Corynaeus appears in *Aeneid* VI.228, IX.571, and XII.298.

[21] Tatlock, *Legendary History*, p. 116. Similarly there is a 'Turonus' or Turnus in *HRB*, offered as the reason for the naming of the city of Tours, but this is not the Turnus of the *Aeneid*, although it seems likely Geoffrey picked the name out of the *Historia Brittonum*, which recounts that Brutus was exiled because of the death of Turnus at Aeneas' hand, and that he founded a city in Gaul called Turnis (ch. 10).

[22] *HRB*, ch. 21: 'delectabat enim eum contra gigantes dimicare.'

[23] *HRB*, ch. 21: 'Inito deinde certamine, instat Corineus, instat gigas, et alter alterum uinculis brachiorum adnectens crebris afflatibus aera uexant. Nec mora, Goegmagog, Corineum maximis uiribus astringens, fregit ei tres costas, duas in dextro latere, unam uero in sinistro. Vnde Corineus compulsus

in iram reuocauit uires suas et imposuit illum humeris suis et quantum uelocitas pro pondere sinebat ad proxima littora cucurrit. Deinde, summitatem excelsae rupis nactus, excussit se et praedictum letabile monstrum, quod super humeros suos ferebat, infra mare proiecit. At ille, per abrupta saxorum cadens, in mille frustra dilaceratus est et fluctus sanguine maculauit. Locus autem ille, nomen ex praeciptatione gigantis adeptus, Saltus Goegmagog usque in praesentem diem uocatur.'

[24] See Tatlock, *Legendary History*, p. 56. He points out that it was this latter problem, rather than the distance from Totnes to the sea, that led later commentators to suggest locations such as Dover Cliff or Plymouth Hoe.

[25] Tatlock, *Legendary History*, pp. 53–6 discusses in detail all possible explanations for this particular place-name.

[26] Geoffrey's intentions as a historian have long been a matter of discussion. Many readers have found evidence of satire, playfulness or parody in *HRB*. See, for example, R. W. Hanning, *The Vision of History in Early Britain: From Gildas to Geoffrey of Monmouth* (New York, 1966); C. N. L. Brooke, 'Geoffrey of Monmouth as a historian', pp. 77–91; Valerie I. J. Flint, 'The *Historia regum Britanniae* of Geoffrey of Monmouth: parody and its purpose: a suggestion', *Speculum*, 54 (1979), 447–68; John Gillingham, 'The context and purposes of Geoffrey of Monmouth's *History of the Kings of Britain*', *Anglo-Norman Studies*, 13 (1991), 99–118, and my *Arthurian Narrative in the Latin Tradition* (Cambridge, 1998). Many of the general studies of medieval historiography cited above also deal with Geoffrey's work.

[27] James P. Carley and Julia Crick, 'Constructing Albion's past: an annotated edition of *De origine gigantum*', in James P. Carley (ed.), *Glastonbury Abbey and the Arthurian Tradition* (Cambridge, 2001), p. 347. The essay appeared first in *Arthurian Literature*, 13 (1995), 41–114. For a translation of the Latin text, see Ruth Evans, 'Update. Gigantic origins: an annotated translation of *De origine gigantum*', *Arthurian Literature*, 16 (1998), 197–211.

[28] See Carley (ed.), *Glastonbury Abbey*, pp. 7–8, and James P. Carley, 'A Glastonbury translator at work: *Quedam narracio de nobili rege Arthuro* and *De origine gigantum* in their earliest manuscript contexts', *Nottingham French Studies*, 30 (1991), 5–12. For a discussion of the text's appearance as a prologue to *HRB*, see Julia Crick, *The Historia regum Britannie of Geoffrey of Monmouth, 4: Dissemination and Reception in the Later Middle Ages* (Woodbridge, 1991), p. 30. Crick notes that the text appears prefacing the *HRB* in two manuscripts, and appears with it, though separated by other works, in two others, and was added to two further copies in later hands, and Carley, 'A Glastonbury translator', cites its appearance in several other historical collections, p. 11, n. 25. The Anglo-Norman version appears as a preface to the *Brut* chronicle in some MSS; see Carley and Crick, 'Constructing Albion's past', pp. 352–3.

[29] See Ad Putter's contribution to this volume.

[30] See James P. Carley's contribution to this volume, as well as May McKisack, *Medieval History in the Tudor Age* (Oxford, 1971); Patricia Ingham, *Sovereign Fantasies: Arthurian Romance and the Making of Britain* (Philadelphia, 2001); Alan MacColl, 'The construction of England as a Protestant "British" nation in the sixteenth century', *Renaissance Studies*, 18 (2004), 582–608; Helen Cooper, *The English Romance in Time: Transforming Motifs from Geoffrey of Monmouth to the Death of Shakespeare* (Oxford, 2004), p. 24; Christopher Baswell, 'Troy, Arthur, and the languages of "Brutis Albyoun"', in Robert M. Stein (ed.), *Reading Medieval Culture* (Notre Dame, 2005), pp. 170–97; and Anke Bernau, 'Myths of origin and the struggle over nationhood in medieval and early modern England', in Gordon McMullan and David Matthews (eds), *Reading the Medieval in Early Modern England* (Cambridge, 2007), pp. 106–18; and 'Beginning with Albina: remembering the nation', *Exemplaria*, 21 (2009), 247–73.

[31] I am parsing the long-popular version of the title, *Historia regum Britannie*, here in order to make a point about Geoffrey as a history-writer, but I should note the views of Geoffrey's most recent editor, Michael D. Reeve. Reeve prefers to call Geoffrey's work *De gestis Britonum*, a title found in a small but significant group of early manuscripts, and used by Geoffrey himself in his *Vita Merlini* (Reeve, *The History of the Kings of Britain*, p. lix). I think we may still, however, consider what it means to Geoffrey to write history, given his frequent use of the term and his obvious awareness of the conventions of medieval historiography.

[32] *HRB*, ch. 14: 'maximo gaudio fluctuans'.

[33] See '"But here Geoffrey falls silent": death, Arthur, and the *Historia regum Britannie*', in Karen Cherewatuk and Kevin Whetter (eds), *The Arthurian Way of Death: The English Tradition* (Cambridge, 2009), pp. 17–32.

[34] *HRB*, chs 120, 127: 'fortis pede, fortior equo'; 'Tota intentio ipsius uersabatur circa regni restitutionem, ecclesiarum reformationem, pacis ac legis renouationem, iusticiae compositionem.'

[35] See my '"Whyche thyng semeth not to agree with other histories . . .": Rome in Geoffrey of Monmouth and his early modern readers', *Arthurian Literature*, 26 (2009), 109–29, for a discussion of Geoffrey's persistent reorientation of Romano-British history in favour of the Britons.

[36] William of Rennes, *Gesta regum Britannie*, in Neil Wright (ed.), *The Historia regum Britannie of Geoffrey of Monmouth V: Gesta regum Britannie* (Woodbridge, 1991), VII.11–26:

> Candida Caliope, cetu comitante sororum
> Ex Elicone ueni pectusque arentis inane
> Sacro fonte riga; neque enim describere gesta
> Arturi metrice ne detractare uiderer
> Presumo sine te. Nil hic prodessest Homerus,
> Nil Naso, nil Uirgilius, nil Tullius ipse
> Absque tuo nutu, quia quantis fortis Achilles
> Tersitem excedit, tantis prefertur Achilli
> Laudibus Arturus. Cuius preconia uatis
> Meonii condigna modis Eneidos auctor
> Hystorie ueteris Anchise preposuisset,
> Lucanusque grauis tacuisset Cesaris actus,
> Et ueteres Thebe caruissent perpete fama,
> Si precessissent Arturi gesta poetas.
> Sed ne depereat tantus sine laudibus heros
> Principis inuicti laudes extollere conor. (my translation)

This new invocation is found at the beginning of Book VII, while the stories of Constans and Vortigern occupied Books V and VI; Merlin's prophecies appear in a sharply truncated form in Book VI. For a study of William's work, see Rosemary Morris, 'The *Gesta regum Britanniae* of William of Rennes: an Arthurian epic?' *Arthurian Literature*, 6 (1986), 60–123.

[37] *HRB*, ch. 110: 'Coegit me, Alexander Lincolniensis praesul, nobilitatis tuae dilectio prophetias Merlini de Britannico in Latinum transferre antequam historiam perarassem quam de gestis regum Britannorum inceperam. Proposueram enim illam prius perficere istudque opus subsequenter explicare, ne dum uterque labor incumberet sensus meus ad singula minor fieret.'

[38] For a discussion of the role of prophecy in the academic traditions and tastes of the period, see Southern, 'Aspects of the European tradition of historical writing, 3: History as prophecy' (1972); Marjorie Reeves, 'History and prophecy in medieval thought', *Medievalia et Humanistica*, 5 (1974), 51–75; and *The Prophetic Sense of History in Medieval and Renaissance Europe* (Brookfield, VT, 1999); and Richard Trachsler, Julien Abed and David Expert (eds), *Moult obscures paroles: étude sur la prophétie médiévale* (Paris, 2007). For Geoffrey's particular deployment of the prophetic tradition, see Jan Ziolkowski, 'The nature of prophecy in Geoffrey of Monmouth's *Vita Merlini*,' in James L. Kugel (ed.), *Poetry and Prophecy: The Beginnings of a Literary Tradition* (Ithaca, 1990), pp. 151–62; and Julia Crick, 'Geoffrey of Monmouth, prophecy, and history', *Journal of Medieval History*, 18 (1992), 357–71, as well as her contribution to this collection. The particular contemporary importance of Merlin's prophecies is discussed by Jean Blacker, 'Where Wace feared to tread: Latin commentaries on Merlin's *Prophecies* in the reign of Henry II', *Arthuriana*, 6 (1996), 36–52; and Karen R. Moranski, 'The *Prophetie Merlini*, animal symbolism, and the development of political prophecy in late medieval England and Scotland', *Arthuriana*, 8 (1998), 58–68.

[39] It may be dated some time between 1148 and 1151; for a review of attempts to fix a more precise date, see Curley, *Geoffrey of Monmouth*, pp. 110–11.

[40] Basil Clarke notes particularly the Myrddin story as it appears in the Welsh poem 'Afallennau'; this is the oldest Myrddin material in Welsh, to be dated to anywhere between 850 and 1050; *Life of Merlin: Vita Merlini* (Cardiff, 1973), p. 1 (hereafter *VM*). For a complete list of possible Welsh source material, see Curley, *Geoffrey of Monmouth*, pp. 115–18. For recent assessments of the relationship between Geoffrey of Monmouth, Welsh prophecy, and the Merlin story, see A. O. H. Jarman, 'The Merlin legend and the Welsh tradition of prophecy', in Bromwich *et al.* (eds), *The Arthur of the Welsh*, pp. 117–45; O. J. Padel, 'Geoffrey of Monmouth and the development of the Merlin legend', *Cambrian Medieval Celtic Studies*, 51 (2006), 37–65; and Nikolai Tolstoy, 'Geoffrey of Monmouth and the Merlin legend', *Arthurian Literature*, 25 (2008), 1–42.

[41] *VM*, lines 1–2: 'Fatidici vatis rabiem musamque jocosam / Merlini cantare paro.'.I discuss the *Vita*'s invocation of the jocose muse in *Arthurian Narrative in the Latin Tradition*, pp. 217–19.

[42] *VM*, line 580: 'rabiem Britonum'.

[43] *VM*, lines 661–9:

> Tum pax atque fides et virtus omnis abibit,
> undique per patrias committent prelia cives
> virque virum prodet, non invenietur amicus.
> Conjuge despecta meretrices sponsus adibit
> sponsaque cui cupiet despecto conjuge nubet.
> Non honor ecclesiis servabitur, ordo peribit.
> Pontifices tunc arma ferent, tunc castra sequentur,
> in tellure sacra turres et menia ponent
> militibusque dabunt quod deberetur egenis.

[44] *HRB*, ch. 117: 'Splendor solis electro Mercurii languebit, et erit horror inspicientibus. Mutabit clipeum Stilbon Archadiae, uocabit Venerem galea Martis. Galea Martis umbram conficiet, transibit terminos furor Mercurii. Nudabit ensem Orion ferreus, uexabit nubes Phoebus aequoreus. Exibit Iupiter licitas semitas, et Venus deseret statutas lineas. Saturni sideris liuido corruet et falce recurua mortales perimet . . . In ictu radii exurgent aequora, et puluis ueterum renouabitur. Confligent uenti diro sufflamine et sonitum inter sidera conficient.'

[45] Hanning, *The Vision of History*, p. 172.

[46] Ziolkowski, 'The nature of prophecy', p. 160.

[47] *VM*, lines 1516–.17: 'Christe, tuo populo fer opem, compesce leones, / da regno placidam bello cessante quietem!'

[48] *HRB*, ch. 130: 'machinationes', 'ingenium'.

[49] *HRB*, ch. 137: 'medicaminibus'.

[50] I discuss Geoffrey's treatment of the forces controlling history in *Arthurian Narrative* and, more recently, in '"For Mortals are Moved by these Conditions": fate, fortune and providence in Geoffrey of Monmouth', in Norris J. Lacy (ed.), *The Fortunes of King Arthur* (Cambridge, 2005), pp. 13–28.

[51] *HRB*, ch. 143: 'Erat autem Arturus quindecim annorum iuuenis inauditae uirtutis atque largitatis, in quo tantam gratiam innata bonitas praestiterat ut a cunctis fere populis amaretur. Insignibus itaque regiis iniciatus, solitum morem seruans largitati indulsit. Confluebat ad eum tanta multitudo militum ut ei quod dispensaret deficeret. Sed cui naturalis inest largitio cum probitate, licet ad tempus indigeat, nullatenus tamen continua paupertas ei nocebit. Arturus ergo, quia in illo probitas largitionem comitabatur, statuit Saxones inquietare, ut eorum opibus quae ei famulabatur ditaret familiam. Commonebat etiam id rectitudo, cum tocius insulae monarchiam debuerat hereditario iure obtinere.'

[52] *HRB*, ch. 147: 'Ipse uero Arturus, lorica tanto rege digna indutus, auream galeam simulacro draconis insculptam capiti adaptat, humeris quoque suis clipeum uocabulo Pridwen, in quo imago sanctae Mariae Dei genitricis inpicta ipsum in memoriam ipsius saepissime reuocabat. Accinctus ergo Caliburno

gladio optimo et in insula Auallonis fabricato, lancea dextram suam decorat, quae nomine Ron uocabatur. Haec erat ardua lataque lancea, cladibus apta . . . Abstracto ergo Caliburno gladio, nomen sanctae Mariae proclamat et sese cito impetu infra densas hostium acies immisit. Quemcumque attingebat Deum inuocando solo ictu perimebat, nec requieuit impetum suum facere donec quadringentos septuaginta uiros solo Caliburno gladio peremit.'

53 Several scholars have noted similarities between the anti-Saxon rhetoric of *HRB* and the preaching of the Crusades. See, for example, Geraldine Heng, *Empire of Magic: Medieval Romance and the Politics of Cultural Literacy* (New York, 2003); Lawrence Warner, 'Geoffrey of Monmouth and the de-Judaized Crusade', *Parergon*, 21 (2004), 19–37; and Stein, *Reality Fictions*.

54 *HRB*, ch. 147: 'Viri Christiana professione insigniti, maneat in uobis conciuium uestrorum pietas et patriae, qui proditione paganorum exterminati uobis sempiternum erunt opprobrium nisi ipsos defendere institeritis. Pugnate pro patria uestra et mortem si superuenerit ulto pro eadem patimini. Ipsa enim uictoria est et animae remedium. Quicumque etenim pro confratribus suis mortem inierit uiuam hostiam se praestet Deo Christumque insequi non ambigitur qui pro fratribus suis animam suam dignatus est ponere.'

55 *HRB*, ch. 152: 'tocius patriae statum in pristinam dignitatem reduxisset'.

56 *HRB*, ch. 154: 'Cumque id Arturo notificatum esset, extollens se quia cunctis timori erat, totam Europam sibi subdere affectat.'

57 *HRB*, ch. 34: 'Denique per patrias supradictorum interemptorum uagando subuertit urbes et oppida populumque potestati suae summittit; et cum totam insulam omnino subiugasset, fecit sibi diadema ex auro insulamque in pristinum statum reduxit.'

58 *HRB*, ch. 31: 'illius temporis memoria quo tot centenis millibus militum stipatus et moenia urbium diruere et prouincias hostium uastare solebam.'

59 Tatlock, *Legendary History*, notes that most of the description seems to reflect real knowledge of the place; p. 70. The prominence of Caerleon as an ecclesiastical centre, however, seems largely to be Geoffrey's invention, and Tatlock suggests he may have been motivated by contemporary conflict between St David's and Llandaff; p. 71. Both Christopher Brooke ('Geoffrey of Monmouth as an historian') and Valerie Flint ('Parody and its purpose') also entertain the possibility that part of Geoffrey's purpose or interest is to intervene in, or to satirize, contemporary ecclesiastical squabbles.

60 *HRB*, ch. 157: 'Ad tantum etenim statum dignitatis Britannia tunc reducta erat quod copia diuitiarum, luxu ornamentorum, facetia incolarum cetera regna excellebat. Quicumque uero famosus probitate miles in eadem erat unius coloris uestibus atque armis utebatur. Facetae etiam mulieres, consimilia indumenta habentes, nullius amorem habere dignabantur nisi tercio in milicia probatus esset. Efficiebantur ergo castae et meliores et milites pro amore illarum probiores. Refecti tandem epulis, diuersi diuersos ludos compositiuri campos extra ciuitatem adeunt. Mox milites, simulacrum proelii ciendo, equestrem ludum componunt. Mulieres in edito murorum aspicientes in furiales amores flammas more ioci irritant.'

61 The terms are traced in C. Stephen Jaeger, *The Origins of Courtliness: Civilizing Trends and the Formation of Courtly Ideals 939–1210* (Philadelphia, 1985). I draw extensively on Jaeger's discussion in the 'Introduction' to *Arthurian Narrative in the Latin Tradition*.

62 *HRB*, ch. 165: 'ille . . . iam ceperat eam regemque in interpositum clipeum tanto conamine percussit quo sonitu ictus et tota littora repleuit et aures eiusdem ultra modum hebetauit. Arturus uero, acri ignescens ira, erecto in frontem ipsius ense uulnus intulit, tametsi non mortale, unde tamen sanguis in faciem et oculos eius profluens eorundem excaecauit aciem; interposuerat namque clauam ictui et frontem suama letai uulnere muniuerat. Excaecatus autem profluente sanguine acrior insurgit et uelut aper per uenabulum in uenatorem ita irruit per gladium in regem et complectendo eum per medium coegit illum genua humi flectere. Arturus itaque, reuocata uirtute, ocius elabitur et celeriter nunc hinc nunc illinc nefandum gladio diuerberabat, nec requieuit donec letali uulnere illato totum mucronem capiti impressit qua cerebrum testa protegebatur. Exclamauit uero inuisus ille et uelut quercus uentorum uiribus eradicata cum maximo sonitu corruit. Rex ilico in risum solutus.'

63 *HRB*, ch. 169: 'petitam capiemus, captam autem possidebimus, et sic aurum, argentum, palatia, turres, oppida, ciuitates, et ceteras uictorum diuicias habebitis.'

[64] *HRB*, ch. 175: 'Tunc tandem Lucius imperator, infra turmas occupatus, cuiusdam lancea confossus interiit.'

[65] *HRB*, ch. 177: 'Ne hoc quidem, consul auguste, Galfridus Monemutensis tacebit, sed ut in praefato Britannico sermone inuenit et a Waltero Oxenefordensi, in multis historiis peritissimo uiro, audiuit, uili licet stilo, breuiter tamen propalabit, quae proelia inclitus ille rex post uictoriam istam in Britanniam reuersus cum nepote suo commiserit.'

[66] *HRB*, ch. 178: 'Sed et inclitus ille rex Arturus letaliter uulneratus est; qui illinc ad sananda uulnera sua in insulam Auallonis euectus Constantino cognato suo et filio Cadoris ducis Cornubiae diadema Britanniae concessit anno ab incarnatione Domini .dlxii.'

[67] At least one manuscript adds the phrase 'may his soul rest in peace' (Anima eius in pace quiescat) after the reference to Arthur's death, and Michael Faletra notes the insertion as part of his own argument that Geoffrey for one did not mean to develop the Breton hope; see Michael A. Faletra, trans., *The History of the Kings of Britain* (Peterborough, 2008), p. 200, n. 1. Contemporary Latin satire of the idea can be found in Étienne de Rouen's *Draco Normannicus* of 1167/9, which includes an exchange of letters between Henry II and a bombastic Arthur, who now lives in the Antipodes. For a discussion, see Mildred Leake Day, 'The letter from King Arthur to Henry II: political use of the Arthurian legend in *Draco Normannicus*', in Glyn S. Burgess and Robert A. Taylor (eds), *The Spirit of the Court* (Woodbridge, 1985), pp. 153–7, as well as the introductory material in her edition and translation, *Latin Arthurian Literature* (Cambridge, 2005), pp. 47–54; I discuss the text in my *Arthurian Narrative in the Latin Tradition*, pp. 85–93.

[68] *HRB*, ch. 179: 'Illo igitur insignito, insurrexerunt Saxones et duo filii Modredi nec in eum praeualere quiuerunt, sed post plurima proelia diffugiendo unus Lundonias, alter uero Guintoniam ingressus eas optinere coeperunt.'

[69] *HRB*, ch. 205: 'Nolebat enim Deus Britones in insulam Britanniae diutius regnare antequam tempus illud uenisset quod Merlinus Arturo prophetauerat.'

[70] *HRB*, ch. 2: 'falerata uerba'.

4

GEOFFREY AND THE PROPHETIC TRADITION

Julia Crick

At the close of his *Historia regum Britannie* Geoffrey of Monmouth dropped into the narrative an apparently simple story whose meanings continued to unfold long after his death. Cadwallader, the exiled king of Britain, contemplating defeat, had consulted Alan, king of Brittany: should he abandon his kingdom to the Saxons, as an angelic voice had advised him, or could contrary advice be found in written revelation? Alan decided the issue. Consulting and scrutinizing various prophetic books his research produced nothing to contradict the angelic message; Cadwallader consequently renounced his throne, travelling to Rome to die in 689.[1] This story served an obvious narrative purpose, marking the expiry of the prophetic mandate which had sustained the Britons in power since the time of Brutus. Simultaneously, it functioned as aetiology: it explained why the Welsh no longer ruled Britain. At the same time, however, Geoffrey performed a piece of literary sophistry, because the political meaning of the passage was undercut by an earlier section in the *Historia*, in which Merlin had foretold Cadwallader's return.[2] Geoffrey also used the episode to confront his readers. Alan's inspiration came from three named sources, he reports: the prophecies of the Sibyl, the Prophecy of the Eagle, and the Prophecies of Merlinus Ambrosius. As it happens only the first of these was indeed available in the seventh century when Alan is meant to have read them; the second, the Prophecy of the Eagle, attributed to Merlinus Sylvester, is here attested for the first time, and the last, the *Prophetia Merlini*, the core of Geoffrey's own *Historia*, was arguably Geoffrey's own creation.[3] In the story, then, Geoffrey, ostensibly depicting a reader in ancient times, modelled how future readers might use his own text.[4]

The passage and its complexities illustrate Geoffrey's artifice.[5] He initiated an interplay between prophecy and history which readers continued in the centuries in which his work circulated as fact. Medieval readers studied the prophecies of Merlin much as Alan was said to have done, alongside other prophecy, and sought in them understanding of present and future as well as past. Scribes copied them into prophetic collections; readers found in them reference not just to English history to the time of Henry I, but to events in their own present or recent past: the loss of the Norman dominions of the English Crown in 1204, the accession of Edward II in 1307, the Black Death of 1347, the fifteenth-century present.[6] But for those who examined the past, no less than those who looked to the future, the prophecies issued difficult challenges. Was Merlin pagan or Christian? By what authority did he prophesy? If, as Geoffrey said, he was fathered by an incubus, then was his birth demonic? These were potent questions for readers throughout the Middle Ages but especially at the point at which Merlin made his entry into Latin literature, in the middle years of the twelfth century, at the intersection of monastic and scholastic culture, where patristic and scriptural authority collided with that of the pagan classics. One user of the prophecies, stung by criticism from a high-placed colleague, pleaded 'Read and understand the scriptures, I beg: for not everything is found in Cato'.[7] Most readers would have understood the situation in reverse. Merlin spoke to new learning, as a rule, to schoolsmen equipped to question the nature of God's hand in human affairs.[8]

Without doubt the figure of Merlin challenged and continues to challenge readers, evoking contradictory and sometimes inconsistent responses. Orderic Vitalis, first known reader of Geoffrey's Merlinian prophecies, understood their function immediately.

> Men well read in histories can easily apply his predictions, if they know the lives of Hengist and Katigern, Pascent and Arthur, Æthelberht and Edwin, Oswald and Oswy, Cædwalla and Alfred, and other rulers of the Angles and Britons up to the times of Henry I and Gruffudd, who still, uncertain of their lot, await the future events that are ordained for them.[9]

He recognized them as both spent prophecy – as a cipher for Insular history from remote antiquity to the present – and as live prediction, as a potential resource for men in power; to those living in daily jeopardy, whether political or personal, or carrying immense responsibilities and taking decisions without the comfort of hindsight, the prophecies could promise enlightenment. Some writers responded less sympathetically, omitting the prophecies and passing over them in silence. Henry of Huntingdon failed to report the prophecies at all in the letter which he wrote to the Breton Warin after his encounter with Geoffrey's History at the Norman monastery of Bec in 1139.[10] Wace and Gaimar likewise omitted the prophecies. One sixteenth-century reader resorted to violence, excising from his copy of Geoffrey's *Historia* the folios containing the prophecies, and noting in the margin: 'here are excised the obscene predictions of Merlin, now condemned at last by the Council of Trent'.[11]

Henry of Huntingdon's silence has been interpreted as incredulity – a tiny number of twelfth-century readers, all with serious reason to distrust the message of the prophecies, did respond thus, but it is important to suspend disbelief.[12] As the excision of the prophecies demonstrates, omission did not necessarily betoken indifference: the prophecies could be construed as a threat to the moral or political order.[13] Nevertheless, it will be argued here that however incendiary their potential, in the hands of a significant number of readers the prophecies provoked the kind of intellectual and political responses logged by Orderic; they offered reassurance, solace, historical exegesis, intellectual stimulus, on the one hand, and political direction on the other.[14] Such conclusions are provisional, of course: response to the prophecies can only be gauged by examining reader reaction and manuscript transmission, two bodies of evidence not yet systematically explored.[15] Nevertheless plenty of evidence warrants the conclusion that the prophecies gained a significant purchase on the attention of readers, a grip which extended beyond political partisanship to intellectual sympathy.

First it is important to clarify terms. Geoffrey was not the only source of Merlinian tradition or native British prophecy in the twelfth century: Welsh and Latin texts circulated and were cited in Britain and abroad.[16] Geoffrey himself recognized the existence of two prophets called Merlin: Merlinus Ambrosius of the *Historia regum Britannie* and Merlin Caledonius, or *Silvestris*, the wild man whose life Geoffrey is supposed to have written in Latin verse at the end of his career.[17] Despite the popularity of his *Prophetia Merlini Ambrosii*, the Life of the Merlin *Silvestris* hardly circulated, and the vaticinations of that Merlin, later known as the Prophecy of the Eagle, were not collected in Geoffrey's lifetime, and for this reason will receive only passing mention here. Merlinus Silvestris is important nevertheless as a counterfoil to the Merlin of Geoffrey's history, as a source of political anxiety, perhaps, and certainly as a potential source of confusion. This was the Merlin recognized and generally respected by Gerald of Wales, who claimed to have discovered and collected his prophecies in Welsh, but who forbore to comment on them.[18] This was also the Merlin whom Higden compared, apparently favourably, with the other Merlin, the son of an incubus, whom he judged to have prophesied less lucidly.[19] Often, however, annotators failed to discriminate between the two Merlins and Merlinian prophecy circulated without precise attribution, a conflation which did not necessarily damage the credibility of either figure.[20]

Merlin Ambrosius rapidly became entrenched in Anglo-Norman culture. As Paul Zumthor showed in his doctoral study of Merlin published in 1943, the story of Merlin closely echoed that of the biblical prophet, Daniel, and his utterances belonged to a recognizable genre: other non-biblical prophets, like pseudo-Methodius or the Tiburtine Sibyl, spoke prophecies of a recognizably biblical sort.[21] This may explain why, as Southern noted in a classic article, prophecy constituted 'matter of grave intellectual concern to serious and practical men'.[22] Indeed bishops feature prominently among Merlin's earliest known students: Alexander, bishop of Lincoln (1123–48), dedicatee of the *Prophetia Merlini*; his successor, Robert de Chesney (1148–66), to whom Geoffrey's *Vita Merlini* was dedicated; Robert I or II of Exeter (1138–55, 1155–60), dedicatee of the first commentary on the *Prophetia Merlini*, by John of Cornwall; and three others who cited the prophecies before 1170: Arnulf, bishop of Lisieux (1141–81), Thomas Becket, archbishop of Canterbury (1162–70) and Gilbert Foliot, bishop of London (1163–87), nephew of Robert Chesney, the first dedicatee.[23]

One important aspect of the impact of the *Prophetia Merlini* was their appeal beyond the immediate political constituency to which they spoke. As with the *Historia* in which they were imbedded, they immediately reached the Continent and provoked comment. Within Geoffrey's lifetime two continental writers had mined them for information about their own times, one, Orderic Vitalis, in the Anglo-Norman realm, the same political sphere as Geoffrey; the other, Suger, abbot of Saint-Denis, writing from enemy territory.[24] These are the earliest attested readers. Within a generation, by *c*.1170, two further continental writers had written full-length works inspired by or dependent on the prophecies. Alanus, a member of a religious order who had spent his childhood in Lille, completed a seven-book commentary, the *explanatio*, in effect a full-length history of early medieval Britain, nearly 300 pages in the printed edition;[25] Stephen of Rouen's *Draco Normannicus*, not only alluded to the dragons of Merlin's prophecy but quoted individual prophecies in connection with events in his own day including the death of King Stephen (1154).[26] Within fifty years Geoffrey's text had reached Italy, where it was quoted by Joachim of Fiore in his *Vita sancti Benedicti*, *c*.1186/7.[27] At the time of the loss of the continental dependencies of the English Crown, in the opening years of the thirteenth century, the text was again circulating at the French court, being cited by Guillaume le Breton, and in Germany where Frederick Barbarossa commissioned a French translation.[28] The work was used by Godfrey of Viterbo at the end of the twelfth century and Caesarius of Heisterbach in the first quarter of the thirteenth.[29] Within Britain the text received early attention, being known in Becket's circle, championed allegedly by Henry II and certainly known to his poets, and provoking Gerald of Wales to frame his account of Henry's invasion of Ireland as a prophetic history, a *historia vaticinalis*.[30] The Galfridian narrative of early British history, to which Merlin belonged as a royal counsellor, advising and assisting various kings, albeit with the benefit of supernatural gifts, found a place in tens of histories of England in the high and later Middle Ages.[31] Merlin's predictive power was recognized as active beyond these shores as well and his prophecies were interpreted for continental audiences in the light of their own national histories.[32]

There is every indication that Merlinian prophecy was treated as authoritative, even with a reverence almost accorded to scripture.[33] As Matthias Kaup has noted, the *Prophetia* was the first non-biblical prophetic text to sustain an exegetical tradition.[34] Copies of the *Prophetia* were intensively glossed, both interlineally and marginally, and some were formally laid out as lemmata to take an interlinear and marginal gloss, in the manner of a glossed Bible or other authoritative text worthy of exegesis.[35] This exegetical tradition reached its fullest form in Alan's commentary, the *Explanatio in prophetiam Merlini Ambrosii*, in which a sequence of passages from the *Prophetia* was dissected in each of seven books, Books I–III dealing with historical time but books IV–VII ranging into apocalyptic and eschatological speculation.[36] Almost contemporary with this, but very different in character, John of Cornwall's early versification of the *Prophetia*, with extensive marginal gloss, represents a different kind of response, a display of eloquence and erudition befitting a schoolsman, bearing thick glosses, as were many copies of the Prophecies themselves, attesting the engagement of readers with this challenging text.[37] This vigorous exegetical tradition remains only partly explored: the six continuous commentaries published by Jacob Hammer before his death in the 1950s need to be set aside the much larger body of unpublished glossed texts, fifteen or more.[38]

The extent of the commentary tradition, much of still it unexplored, indicates something of Merlin's purchase on the attention of medieval readers. His utterances (*dicta*) indeed carried special authority both within Geoffrey's history and outside it. Rubrics directed the attention of readers to this portion of the *Historia*.[39] The *Prophetia* remained the only part of the vulgate text of Geoffrey's *Historia* to enter the First Variant version unrevised.[40] Outside the *Historia*, the prophecies circulated as an independent text or were intruded into other texts. They were rendered into Latin verse, and into Anglo-Norman, French, English and Icelandic prose, but there is some evidence that the language of the original was accorded particular respect. The text remained in Latin when inserted into French narratives, like Langtoft's Chronicle, while Matthew Paris and Peter Langtoft incorporated the Latin text verbatim and entire into portions of narrative which otherwise constituted extensive reworkings of Galfridian material, as did the anonymous authors of the *Flores* and *Eulogium historiarum*.[41] It is striking that vernacular versions circulated apparently less freely than the Latin text: the various French translations enjoyed very limited dissemination and no complete English translation survives from the Middle Ages.[42]

The special authority of the *Prophetia Merlini* is further suggested by their treatment within historical writing of other kinds. Texts of the prophecies intruded into larger-scale histories attracted glosses which were recognized as commentaries in their own right.[43] The text of the *Prophetia* interpolated into Matthew Paris's *Historia anglicana*, for example, received heavy interlinear and marginal glossing in more than one hand, some annotators cross-referencing passages in the accompanying history in which individual prophecies were revealed.[44] A note added at the foot of the folio records that the prophecy 'Venedotia will run red with a mother's blood' [*HRB*, ch. 113.85] was fulfilled in north Wales in 1138.[45] The same active relationship between the *Prophetia Merlini* and historical writing is attested half a century earlier in Roger of Howden's *Historia*, where an annotator, possibly Howden himself, recorded in the margin four passages from the *Prophetia* at critical points in the narrative: the arrival of the Normans, the accession of Henry I, his death, and the accession of Stephen.[46] The *Prophetia* could thus be said to have occupied a place in the consciousness of individuals writing, annotating, and copying historical texts in the high Middle Ages, at least in England.

That is not to say that the prophecies remained on the page. There is ample evidence that they were talked about, that they became the stuff of rumour and the subject of invective; there is even a suggestion that they became self-fulfilling, in that they were reported to have guided action. The prophecies first can be seen coming to life amid the troubled politics of Henry II's reign. In the space of a decade, first the ecclesiastical and then the secular hierarchies of the Anglo-Norman realm were rent by crises of authority: the exile of Becket after his refusal to submit to royal justice in 1164, his attempt to excommunicate bishops who colluded with the king, the shock of his murder in 1170, and the war of 1173–4 when Henry II's enemies abroad and at home joined forces to install on the throne his son, the young Henry. It is clear that in the febrile atmosphere of royal and episcopal courts, in England but probably also abroad, the prophecies were known and deployed. Ralph of Diceto, Henry's courtier, states emphatically that at a truly auspicious moment for Henry II and his cause, the capture of the king of Scots, William IV, which ended the revolt of the young Henry in 1174, the actions of the captors were influenced by Merlinian prophecy. They imprisoned William in the castle of Alan of Brittany at Richmond, 'so that the prophecy should be fulfilled: Upon its [Scotland's] jaws will be placed a bridle, made in the bay of Brittany' [*HRB,* ch. 114].[47]

Merlinian prophecy was talked about in these years, or so contemporaries repeatedly reported. John of Salisbury, writing in 1166, relayed to Thomas Becket news of the military advances of Henry II, in these terms:

> It is said that the time is at hand when the eagle of the broken covenant, according to Merlin's prophecy, shall gild the bridle, which is being given to his boar or being forged now in the Breton peninsula [HRB, ch. 114]. I have had certain news since I wrote my last letter that he has suffered heavy loss at the assault of Fougères: those among us who are for the French still grieve for it.[48]

Two years before, the wrath of Henry, their political master, had sent John and Becket into exile when Becket refused to submit to secular jurisdiction. The gulf which opened up lasted more than six years and ended only after Becket's murder in 1170. Becket and his followers, able and ambitious men, were reduced to penury and disgrace on a point of principle, and brought down their followers and their families with them; Henry, threatened with interdict and diplomatic ostracism, guarded his position as *rex Dei gratia*; the clergy left to uphold the dignity of the English Church in the absence of the metropolitan, threatened with excommunication by their archbishop and charged with shameful collusion.[49] The direness and dislocation of the politics of these years were not only evident with the hindsight which Becket's biographers commanded. Protagonists writing in the 1160s did so in fear, anticipating interception, and expressed themselves obliquely, avoiding direct reference to the king, requesting anonymity for themselves.[50] One such was Arnulf, bishop of Lisieux, who maintained neutrality in the dispute but who, in a long and secret letter of advice to Becket in 1165, again connected Henry's campaigns with Merlinian prophecy.

> He [Henry] was even disposed, so they say, to act more mildly in many ways, so that . . . he can quickly return to put down the audacity of the Welsh before the Scots and the Bretons make an alliance with them and Albion, as prophesied, begins to be shamed [HRB, ch. 114]. He is coming therefore to obey orders . . . judging it better for the moment to surrender something of the haughtiness of his former pride than to wait until all or most of what has been predicted comes to pass to his destruction. Farewell.[51]

In the following year, another of Becket's intimates, Herbert of Bosham, exhorted Pope Alexander III to act in support of the exiles, again alluding to Henry's interest in Merlin. Merlin was Henry's prophet (*suus propheta*) and Herbert, in a series of veiled biblical allusions, conjured images of apocalyptic foreboding, reminding the pope of the example of Belshazzar who ignored the prophet Daniel, and lost his kingdom, Ezekiel who foretold the destruction of the earth, if God willed it, before finally quoting the *Prophetia Merlini*:

> he who boasts that we will offer our backs and cut out the tongues of bulls just as his prophet, Merlin, prophesied among other things long before about him, just as he boasts: 'and the tongues of bulls shall be cut off'. [HRB, ch. 116][52]

What exactly Merlin meant to the scholars of the 1160s and 1170s is a matter of doubt: responses to the prophecies were rarely consistent and were often ironic or ambivalent. They indicate that Merlin was a matter for bishops and popes; that talk about Merlinian prophecies permeated widely as rumour;[53] even that Merlinian prophecy offered a form of running reference to royal action, permitting oblique commentary on political events. Unmistakably, Henry II paid close attention to the prophecies and this had potential consequences for his followers. Wace pre-empted reprisal, so Jean Blacker has argued, by omitting the prophecies from his history strategically, in order to escape their interpretation; Gerald of Wales professed himself unable to meet Henry II's request for a commentary on the prophecies of Merlinus Sylvestris lest the truth proved unpalatable to the great.[54] The courtier Peter of Blois cited the *Prophetia* in a work addressed to the king and so later incurred charges of sycophancy.[55] Certainly, there was enough here to raise the hackles of the Becket party. John of Salisbury, in particular, in a letter to the community of Canterbury, treated the prophecies with icy disdain. He warned them of a scheme hatched by the bishop of London, Gilbert Foliot, to appropriate metropolitan authority, 'underpinned by a prophecy of Merlin *nescio quo repletus spiritu*'.[56] John's intention was polemical – Foliot constituted Becket's rival and bitterest clerical enemy whom Becket had excommunicated and so started a war of invective – but his aim was sure.

By what spirit was Merlin inspired? Peter of Blois had exposed himself to criticism on the same issue, and he responded by accusing his attacker of following pagan Gods: 'Surely I never proposed that Merlin be placed in the catalogue of holy prophets who are from this world, but I put you among the prophets of Baal, I count you among the forty prophets of Achab, who prophesied to him falsely.' His accuser was evidently a bishop versed in classical texts as he continues

> Or, because you have taken upon yourself in the destiny of a prelate, I deem you colleague to the supreme high priest Caiaphas, who in that cruel court, in which the innocent Christ was condemned to death 'since he was high priest for that year, he prophesied' [John XI.51]. Read and understand the scriptures, I beg: for not everything is found in Cato.[57]

One wonders whether his anonymous enemy could have been John of Salisbury himself, elevated to the bishopric of Chartres (1176–80) where Peter held a canonry at the same time.[58] Whatever the case, the intellectual difficulties with Merlin remained unresolved. Perhaps a century after John, the author of the *Flores historiarum* voiced continuing doubts about the nature of Merlin's prophetic inspiration: 'some people used to say that he [Merlin] had exhausted the prophetic spirit and, in the obfuscating manner of demons, had spoken in riddles with double meaning [following] the example of Balaam; but other people say otherwise'.[59]

Although Merlin drew opprobrium from the political opponents of factions who championed him, not all opposition to him can be explained away as political partisanship. Unease was inspired in some by the figure of Merlin himself. Prophets existed, but Merlin was neither Christian nor human and some readers struggled with the story of the magical conception of Merlinus Ambrosius, who Geoffrey had claimed was the son of an incubus. Alanus, author of the full-length commentary written 1167–74, sought to rationalize this: Merlin, he wrote, was the son of a high-born mother.[60] John Bale later explained Merlin's conception as the product of an illicit union between a Roman consul and a vestal virgin, an explanation accepted by the seventeenth-century annotator of Cambridge, University Library, MS Peterborough E.648, who reproduced the information.[61] William of Newburgh, anticipating Merlin's later critics, derided the story about the incubus and condemned the prophecies as false, although he did accept that they had a basis in Welsh tradition (Geoffrey translating and editing them) and he conceded that incubi were attested in sacred writings.[62] Others who used the prophecies, such as Gervase of Tilbury, simply reported that Merlin's paternity was unknown.[63] More commonly, however, readers adhered to Geoffrey's incubus story and attempted to deal with the consequences. Jerome, Isidore and Servius before them had noted the existence of incubi; Augustine in *De civitate Dei* had discussed reports of the corporality of spirits, notably stories that demons, some called incubi, could take on human form and mate with women. He suspended judgement on the veracity of these stories, but did note that tales of miscegenation were supported by biblical authority.[64] Patristic guidance on this difficult matter did not pass unquestioned in the twelfth century, however, in scholastic circles at least, and scholars sought to understand how demons could create life, or to find a rational explanation for the phenomena reported.[65]

Readers' anxieties about Merlin's birth are apparent in the transmission of Geoffrey's history, both in the accretion of annotations and in rewriting of the text. A fourteenth-century annotator of the manuscript of Geoffrey's *Historia*, now Exeter Cathedral Library, MS 3514, reinforced the Galfridian story of Merlin's birth by copying into the margin Augustine's statement on incubi and thus lending patristic authority to the statement in the text.[66] One twelfth-century continental reader adopted an agnostic position, that Merlin's paternity was unknown, reporting the incubus story as hearsay, and again seeking the origin for his prophetic spirit, appealing to scripture for examples of bad people able to predict the future: Caiaphas the high priest and the prophet Balaam.[67] Other readers rewrote the text to incorporate statements of doubt. One passage, about Merlin's birth, beginning 'Merlinus iste' found in a dozen manuscripts dating from the twelfth century onwards, also reports Merlin's paternity as unknown, attributing the incubus story to Merlin's mother.[68]

If the problem of Merlin's paternity became problematic as scholars in the twelfth century worried over the practicalities and limitations of demonic intervention in human affairs, acceptance of other elements of Merlin's message also challenged orthodox belief. The astrological element of the prophecies, which overwhelms the text in the closing section, was a case in point.[69] Geoffrey chose to depict Merlin Caledonius as a star-gazing sage, deriving knowledge of the future by observing of the night sky from his mansion of seventy windows.[70] Southern connected astrology very closely with prophecy and he and others have noted how it functioned as a branch of scientific learning under the patronage of the English prelacy, a group particularly touched by Merlinian prophecy as we have seen.[71] With its roots in pagan learning, its association with divination and the occult, and its powerful appeal to the political, astrology had many features in common with Merlinian prophecy, not least its heterodox associations: by whose inspiration was it rendered valid? Like secular prophecy judicial astrology, prediction according to the stars, attracted criticism. Finally, in the 1270s, it was condemned outright, although this did not impede the use of astrology in courts in the later Middle Ages.[72]

Commentators tended to focus on the earlier, more historically intelligible part of the prophecies, but the astrological content of the prophecies will also have influenced their reception.[73] Henry II, whose engagement with the *Prophetia Merlini* is strongly attested, has been identified as an early student of astrology; Adelard of Bath dedicated his treatise on the astrolabe to one Henry, usually interpreted as the future Henry II, and noted the importance of such knowledge for those in public affairs.[74] Becket, a former friend of the king, was also drawn to astrology, although his friend, John of Salisbury, famously condemned astrological practices.[75] These sympathies mirror quite closely attitudes to the prophecies of Merlin: Becket, like Henry, seems to have been drawn to them while John retained a firmly sceptical stance, citing the *Prophetia Merlini* as hearsay when he was not actively hostile. Astrological works commonly circulated with prophetic texts, and manuscripts of the prophecies were no exception.[76] Library lists make reference to the presence of Merlinian prophecies within a computus manuscript written by John de Bruges, *c.*1240, from Coventry, or a volume of scholarly texts, including a lapidary, inventoried in the library of Dover Priory in 1389.[77]

The reception of the prophecies, both within Geoffrey of Monmouth's history and outside it, demonstrates the potency of prophecy and its ambivalence to medieval readers, within the Anglo-Norman realm and beyond: while still live, a source of arcane and illicit knowledge, morally and politically dangerous, attractive to the powerful, lapped up by the prelacy; once spent, widely accepted as a form of historical revelation, although matter inappropriate for casual rewriting or easy interpretation. Much more needs to be said. The manuscript-tradition preserves evidence of reader reaction not only in articulated form, as glossing, but as a host of textual juxtapositions which suggest something of reception.[78] Merlinian prophecies occur in association with texts on rebellion, with astrology, with law and statutes or other constitutional documents.[79] Readers and owners included not simply men who lived in the world

– secular men, *curiales*, prelates, intellectuals – but those living more structured lives in the cloister.

The indications are that by the later Middle Ages the figure of Merlin had become utterly familiar, a prophetic voice whose validity was confirmed by the course of recent history. An annotator working *c.*1400 copied into a handsome volume from St Albans a double acrostic which encrypted the name of the white monk Roger Horte and the date of his death (1370) in doggerel purporting to be prophecy of Merlin Ambrosius.[80] Whether, as the annotator claimed, the poem formed an epitaph inscribed on a marble tomb, or whether it was a learned game or even a parody, such monastic experimentation with Merlinian prophecy and with Latin verse demonstrates how readers embraced Merlin as a figure of enigma and of revelation.[81]

Notes

[1] *Geoffrey of Monmouth: The History of the Kings of Britain. An Edition and Translation of the De gestis Britonum (Historia Regum Britanniae)*, ed. and trans. Michael J. Reeve and Neil Wright (Woodbridge, 2007) (*HRB*), ch. 206. On the conflation of Cadwaladr with Ceadwalla, king of Wessex, see D. N. Dumville, 'Brittany and "Armes Prydein Fawr"', *Études celtiques*, 20 (1983), 143–59, at p. 153. Parts of this paper were presented in preliminary form at the symposium on Medieval Prophecy, at Swansea University, 23 May 2008. I owe thanks to the organizers for this opportunity and to the participants, especially to Lesley Coote and Anke Holdenried, for profitable discussion. I am grateful to Catherine Rider and Jane Whittle for bibliographical leads and to Sjoerd Levelt for reading and commenting on a draft.

[2] *HRB*, ch. 115.110. In the later Middle Ages the Welsh were charged with investing hope in Merlinian prophecy: Julia Marvin, 'Arthur authorized: the prophecies of the Prose *Brut* Chronicle', *Arthurian Literature*, 22 (2005), 84–99, at 94–5.

[3] For the Sibyl see *Sibyllinische Texte und Forschungen. Pseudomethodius, Adso und die Tiburtinische Sibylle*, ed. Ernst Sackur (Halle, 1898), pp. 177–87; for the Prophecy of the Eagle see *Gottfried's von Monmouth, Historia regum Britanniae, mit literar-historischer Einleitung und ausführlichen Anmerkung, und Brut Tysilio, altwälsche Chronik in deutsche Uebersetzung*, ed. A. Schulz (Halle, 1854), pp. 463–5; H. L. D. Ward, *Catalogue of Romances in the Department of Manuscripts in the British Museum*, 3 vols (London 1883–1910), I.292–8; see also below, n. 21; for the Galfridian prophecies *HRB*, chs 112–18. On the reception of these texts see Lesley A. Coote, *Prophecy and Public Affairs in Later Medieval England* (Woodbridge, 2000), pp. 44–71.

[4] On the passage see Paul Zumthor, *Merlin le prophète. Un thème de la littérature polémique de l'historiographie et des romans* (Lausanne, 1943), pp. 35–6.

[5] This passage may have resonated with readers in other ways as well. Readers familiar with models of pagan kingship derived from classical fiction will have recognized the image of the literate monarch, seeking knowledge and enlightenment in books on matters of practical politics: Hilary M. Carey, *Courting Disaster: Astrology at the English Court and University in the Later Middle Ages* (Basingstoke, 1992), pp. 25–6, 28–9. Those at the French court may have felt reassurance that the prophecy which sustained their own ruling dynasty had been renewed only recently: see Gabrielle Spiegel, 'The *Reditus regni ad stirpem Karoli magni*: a new look', *French Historical Studies*, 7 (1971), 145–74, esp. pp. 146–50; John W. Baldwin, *The Government of Philip Augustus: Foundations of French Royal Power in the Middle Ages* (Berkeley, 1986), pp. 367–71.

[6] On reaction see Caroline D. Eckhardt, *The* Prophetia Merlini *of Geoffrey of Monmouth: A*

Fifteenth-Century English Commentary (Cambridge, MA, 1982) and the useful hand-list of English prophecy manuscripts in Coote, *Prophecy*, pp. 239–80. Also Jean Blacker, 'Anglo-Norman verse prophecies of Merlin', *Arthuriana*, 15 (2005), 1–125, at p. 12; Julia Crick, 'Geoffrey of Monmouth, prophecy and history', *Journal of Medieval History*, 18 (1992), 357–71, at 367–8; Helen Fulton, 'Prophecy and the deposition of Richard II', *Arthurian Literature*, 22 (2005), 64–83, esp. 73–80. Also Marvin, 'Arthur'. On 1204 see *Radulphi de Coggeshall Chronicon Anglicanum*, ed. Joseph Stevenson, RS 66 (London, 1875), p. 146. The connection with the Black Death was made by an annotator in New York, Columbia University, MS Plimpton 266 (*olim* Phillips 26052), fol. 29r: 'Anno sequente cepit maxima mortalitas hominum in Anglia qualis non fuerant sextentis annis elapsis sicut ex dictis Merlini prophetie et ex gestis Anglorum qui Britonibus successerunt satis constabat' (compare *HRB*, ch. 112.3). See also below, n. 32.

[7] Peter of Blois, *De inuectiua*, *Patrologia Latina*, ed. Jacques-Paul Migne, 221 vols (Paris, 1844–65), 207, cols. 1113–26, col. 1124. See below, n. 57.

[8] Compare the comments of Carey, *Courting Disaster*, pp. 14, 24, 27–8.

[9] *The Ecclesiastical History of Orderic Vitalis*, ed. and trans. Marjorie Chibnall, 6 vols (Oxford, 1969–80), VI.386–8 (*Historia ecclesiastica,* XII.47): 'Historiarum gnari eius dicta facile poterunt intelligere, qui nouerint ea quae contigerunt Hengist et Catigirno, Pascent et Arturo. Aedelberto ac Edwino, Osualdo et Osuio, Cedwal et Elfredo, aliisque principibus Anglorum et Britonum usque ad tempora Henrici et Gritfridi, qui dubia sub sorte adhuc imminentia prestolantur, quae sibi diuinitus ineffabili dispositione ordinatur.' Orderic perhaps encountered the *Prophetia* as a separate text circulating outside the context of the *Historia*, as discussed by C. D. Eckhardt, 'The *Prophetia Merlini* of Geoffrey of Monmouth: Latin manuscript copies', *Manuscripta*, 26 (1982), 167–76, at 169–72.

[10] Neil Wright, 'The place of Henry of Huntingdon's *Epistola ad Warinum* in the text-history of Geoffrey of Monmouth's *Historia regum Britanniae*: a preliminary investigation', in Gillian Jondorf and D. N. Dumville (eds), *France and the British Isles in the Middle Ages and Renaissance: Essays by Members of Girton College, Cambridge, in Memory of Ruth Morgan* (Woodbridge, 1991), pp. 71–113, esp. p. 77.

[11] Edinburgh, National Library of Scotland, MS Adv. 18.4.5, 67v: *The Historia Regum Britannie of Geoffrey of Monmouth, II: The First Variant Version: A Critical Edition*, ed. Neil Wright (Cambridge, 1988), p. xci: 'hic absciduntur obscene predictiones Merlini. Utpote per concilium Tridentum ultimum condemnate.' On the condemnation see Zumthor, 'Merlin', pp. 113–14.

[12] Wright noted that Henry avoided reference to supernatural stories: 'The place', p. 77.

[13] In 1307, the year of Edward I's death, an English official was warned of anticipated Scottish resurgence following the reported discovery of prophecies of Merlin: M. O. Anderson, 'The Scottish materials in the Paris manuscript, Bib. Nat. latin 4126', *Scottish Historical Review*, 28 (1949), 31–42 at p. 34.

[14] See below, n. 41. For discussion of the reception and function of prophecy in later medieval England see Lesley Coote, 'A language of power: prophecy and public affairs in later medieval England', in Bertrand Taithe and Tim Thornton (eds), *Prophecy: The Power of Inspired Language in History 1300–2000* (Stroud, 1997), pp. 17–30. See also R. R. Davies, *Conquest, Coexistence and Change: Wales 1063–1415* (Oxford, 1987), pp. 435–7.

[15] The possibilities of each method are suggested in Zumthor, *Merlin*, and Eckhardt, *The Prophetia Merlini*. Coote's study, a powerful exposition of the potential of manuscript evidence, ranges far beyond Galfridian prophecy, but is confined to reception in England: *Prophecy*, esp. pp. 1–11. The reception of Merlinian prophecy in France, Italy and Spain is treated in the various contributions to Richard Trachsler et al. (eds), *Moult obscures paroles. Études sur la prophétie médiévale* (Paris, 2007).

[16] *Expugnatio hibernica: The Conquest of Ireland by Giraldus Cambrensis*, ed. and trans. A. B. Scott and F. X. Martin (Dublin, 1978), pp. 293, n. 29; 313, nn. 161–2; Michael T. Curley, 'A new edition of John of Cornwall's *Prophetia Merlini*', *Speculum*, 57 (1982), 217–49, at 224–31; M. E. Haycock, 'Merlin (*supp. fl.* 6th cent.)', *Oxford Dictionary of National Biography* (Oxford, 2004) (*http://0-www.oxforddnb.com.lib.ex.ac.uk/view/article/19711*, accessed 22 September 2008); O. J. Padel, 'Geoffrey of Monmouth and the development of the Merlin legend', *Cambrian Medieval Celtic Studies*, 51 (2006),

37–65; Nikolai Tolstoy, 'Geoffrey of Monmouth and the Merlin legend', *Arthurian Literature*, 25 (2008), 1–42, at 6–11, 20–34. Padel posits a greater degree of Galfridian influence in Welsh tradition than does Tolstoy.

[17] *Life of Merlin: Geoffrey of Monmouth, Vita Merlini*, ed. and trans. Basil Clarke (Cardiff, 1973). On the authorship see Julia C. Crick, 'Monmouth, Geoffrey of (*d.* 1154/5)', *Oxford Dictionary of National Biography*, Oxford University Press, 2004 (*http://0www.oxforddnb.com.lib.exeter.ac.uk/view/article/10530*, accessed 13 March 2009).

[18] Above, n. 16.

[19] *Polychronicon Ranulphi Higden monachi Cestrensis* . . ., ed. Churchill Babington and Joseph Rawson Lumby, 9 vols (London, 1865–86), I.418, line 222.

[20] See further below, n. 48.

[21] Zumthor, *Merlin*, pp. 26–30. See also Michael J. Curley, 'Animal symbolism in the Prophecies of Merlin', in Willene B. Clark and Meradith T. McMunn (eds), *Beasts and Birds of the Middle Ages* (Philadelphia, 1989), pp. 151–63, esp. 152–4, 156–8. On the Sibyl see Anke Holdenried, 'The Bedan recension of the *Sibylla Tiburtina*: new manuscript evidence and its implications', in Michael W. Herren, C. J. McDonough and Ross G. Arthur (eds), *Latin Culture in the Eleventh Century: Proceedings of the Third International Conference on Medieval Latin Studies, Cambridge, September 9–12 1998*, 2 vols (Turnhout, 2002), I.410–43. See also Marvin, 'Arthur', pp. 85–6 and n. 6.

[22] R. W. Southern, 'Aspects of the European tradition of historical writing, 3: History as prophecy', *Transactions of the Royal Historical Society*, 22 (1972), 159–80 (168).

[23] On the appeal to bishops see further Tolstoy, 'Geoffrey', pp. 6–7, 39–42.

[24] *Vie de Louis VI le Gros*, ed. and trans. Henri Waquet, 2nd edn (Paris, 1964), pp. 98–105.

[25] *De prophetia ignota: Eine frühe Schrift Joachims von Fiore*, ed. Matthias Kaup, Monumenta Germaniae Historica Studien und Texte, 19 (Hanover, 1998), pp. 128–9. On authorship see Crick, 'Geoffrey', p. 370.

[26] *Chronicles of the Reigns of Stephen, Henry II and Richard I*, ed. Richard Howlett, RS 82, 4 vols (London, 1884–9), II.589–781 at 654–5, 663. *Prophetia anglicana, Merlini Ambrosii Britanni . . . una cum septem libris explanationum in eandem prophetiam . . . Alani de Insulis* (Frankfurt, 1603).

[27] *De prophetia ignota*, ed. Kaup, pp. 87–9; 141, n. 266.

[28] Eckhardt, *The Prophetia Merlini*, pp. 27; 85, n. 61; Franz Kampers, *Kaiserprophetieen und Kaisersagen im Mittelalter. Ein Beitrag zur Geschichte der deutschen Kaiseridee* (Munich, 1895), p. 112.

[29] *Patrologia Latina*, ed. Migne, 198, cols 1001B–1003C; *The Dialogue on Miracles: Caesarius of Heisterbach (1220–1235)*, trans. H. von E. Scott and C. C. Swinton Bland, 2 vols (London, 1929), I.139 (Bk I, ch. 12).

[30] For an overview see Curley, 'A new edition', pp. 219–22. Above, n. 16, and below, n. 54.

[31] The Rolls Series volumes include more than thirty such works; for commentary see Robert Huntington Fletcher, *The Arthurian Material in the Chronicles, especially those of Great Britain and France* (Boston, 1906). See nn. 26, 41, 44, 46–7, 52, 59

[32] Julien Abed, 'La traduction française de la *Prophetia Merlini* dans le Didot-Perceval (Paris BnF, nouv. acq. fr. 4166)', in Trachsler et al. (eds), *Moult obscures paroles*, pp. 81–105, at 92–4; Géraldine Veysseyre, '"Metre en roman" les prophéties de Merlin: voie et détours de l'interprétation dans trois traductions de l'*Historia regum Britannie*', ibid., pp. 107–66, at 149–50, 155–9.

[33] They are sometimes called *scriptura*: *Annals of Burton*, s.a. 1259 'ut scriptura Merlini Silvestris impleretur': *Annales Monastici*, Henry Richards Luard (ed.), RS 36, 4 vols and index (London, 1864–9), I.487.

[34] *De prophetia ignota*, ed. Kaup, p. 124.

[35] On the implications see Malcolm B. Parkes, 'The influence of the concepts of *ordinatio* and *compilatio* on the development of the book', in *Scripts, Scripts and Readers: Studies in the Communication, Presentation and Dissemination of Medieval Texts* (London, 1991), pp. 35–69, at 36–7. In London, BL Cotton Claudius B. vii, fols 224r–230v, a mid-thirteenth-century product of the St Albans–Westminster

school, to judge from the line drawings, the *Prophetia* text was treated quite differently from others in the volume. The interlinear and marginal glosses were written in the script of the rest of the volume while the prophecies were copied in formal bookhand (semi-quadrata), nearly twice the size of the standard script of the volume, and ruled at twice the distance. The interlinear and marginal glosses were printed by Jacob Hammer, 'A commentary on the *Prophetia Merlini* (Geoffrey of Monmouth's *Historia regum Britanniae*, Book VII)', *Speculum*, 15 (1940), 409–31.

[36] *De prophetia ignota*, ed. Kaup, pp. 128–9, 132–40, 142–4; Crick, 'Geoffrey', pp. 368–70.

[37] Biblioteca apostolica Vaticana, MS Ottoboni lat. 1474 s. xiii$^{in.}$, illustrated by Curley, 'John of Cornwall', p. 230; for a comparably densely glossed Galfridian manuscript see BnF lat. 6232, below, n. 67. For analysis of the treatment of two lemmata at the hands of various glossators see Claire Wille, 'Le dossier des commentaires latins des *Prophetie Merlini*', in Trachsler et al. (eds), *Moult obscures paroles*, pp. 167–84.

[38] Eckhardt, *The* Prophetia Merlini, pp. 10–15. Additional commentaries in Galfridian manuscripts are found in Julia C. Crick, *The Historia Regum Britannie of Geoffrey of Monmouth, III: A Summary Catalogue of the Manuscripts* (Cambridge, 1989), nos. 16, 28, 37, 65, 66, 70, 80, 90, 112, 121, 125, 137, 149, 154, 164, 177, 178, 186. Wille estimates 'une vingtaine' and identifies an additional glossed manuscript of the *Prophetia Merlini* (BnF lat. 14465): 'Le dossier' p. 168 and n. 4. See also Crick, 'Geoffrey' and below, n. 41.

[39] Julia C. Crick, *The Historia Regum Britannie of Geoffrey of Monmouth, IV: Dissemination and Reception in the Later Middle Ages* (Cambridge, 1991), pp. 123–43.

[40] *The Historia*, ed. Wright, pp. xvii–xx.

[41] On Anglo-Norman, Blacker, 'Anglo-Norman verse prophecies'; on Gunnlaugr Leifsson's Icelandic translation, Karl G. Johansson, 'Översättning och originalspråkstext i handskriftstradereringens våld – Merlínusspá och Voluspá i Hauksbók'', in Susanne Kramarz-Bein (ed.), *Neue Ansätze in der Mittelalterphilologie/Nye veier i middelalderfilologien. Akten der skandinavistischen Arbeitstagung in Münster vom 24. bis 26. Oktober 2002,* Texte und Untersuchungen zur Germanistik und Skandinavistik, 55 (Frankfurt am Main, 2005), pp. 97–113 (I have not been able to consult this item); on Langtoft, *The Chronicle of Pierre de Langtoft*, ed. Thomas Wright, RS 47, 2 vols (London, 1866–8), I.114; *Eulogium (historiarum siue temporis): Chronicon ab orbe condito usque ad annum domini M.ccc.lxvi a monacho quodam Malmesburiensi exaratum*, ed. Frank Scott Haydon, RS 9, 3 vols (London, 1858–63), II.284–301; *Flores historiarum*, ed. Henry Richards Luard, RS 95, 3 vols (London, 1890), I.27–36. The interpolation of a French translation of the *Prophetia Merlini* into a French text, Robert de Boron's *Merlin*, is discussed by Abed, 'La traduction'.

[42] On the circulation of the French translations, see Veysseyre, '"Metre en roman"', p. 109; on English see Eckhardt, *The Prophetia Merlini*, pp. 17–19.

[43] Eckhardt cites two examples, in Matthew Paris's *Chronica maiora* and Waurin's Chronicle: *The Prophetia Merlini*, pp. 12–13 (below, n. 44). The texts of prophecies copied into the *Eulogium* and the *Flores* were also lightly glossed: above, n. 41; *Eulogium*, ed. Haydon, II.287, n. 3.

[44] 'Hoc impletum anno domini MLXXXIX, scilicet secundo folio secundi libri': *Matthaei Parisiensis monachi Sancti Albani Chronica majora*, ed. Henry Richards Luard, RS 57, 6 vols and index (London, 1872–83), I.198–215, at 206, no. 62. The glosses are clearly heterogeneous in origin (Cambridge, Corpus Christi College, MS. 26, fols 33va–35rb): see below, n. 73.

[45] Matthew's account of the wreck of the White Ship, anticipated in *HRB*, ch. 113.84, contains the marginal note 'hos appellau*it* Merlin*us* calamist*ra*tos id est effeminatos'; *HRB*, ch. 113.81: Cambridge, Corpus Christi, MS 26, 111va.

[46] *Chronica Magistri Rogeri de Houedene*, ed. William Stubbs, RS 51, 4 vols (London, 1868–71), I.lxxv; 113, n. 2,; 157, n. 1; 187, n. 5; 190, n. 9. London, British Library, MS Royal 14.C. ii, fols 51r, 73r, 86r, 87r.

[47] 'ut adimpleretur illud propheticum': *Radulfi de Diceto decani Lundoniensis opera historica: The Historical Works of Master Ralph de Diceto, Dean of London*, ed. William Stubbs, RS 68, 2 vols (London,

1875), I.384. The prophecies of Merlin Sylvester were similarly invoked: the *Annals of Worcester* records King John's burial in the cathedral church between St Oswald and Wulfstan 'ut uerificetur illud quod dictum est in Merlino: Et inter sanctos collocabitur': *Annales Monastici*, ed. Luard, IV.407. See also above, n. 33.

[48] John of Salisbury to Becket, letter 99: 'Instat enim tempus, ut aiunt, quo Aquila rupti federis, iuxta Merlini uaticinium, frenum deauratura est, quod apro eius datur, aut modo fabricatur in sinu Armorico. Nam, sicut accepi pro certo, postquam priores litteras exaraueram, in accessu Filgeriarum graue dampnum perpessus est, quod adhuc deplorant apud nos amici Francorum.' *The Correspondence of Thomas Becket, Archbishop of Canterbury 1162–1170*, ed. and trans. Anne Duggan, 2 vols (Oxford, 2000), I.453–55. On the campaign, which ended in the deposition of the Duke of Brittany, Conan II, see J. A. Everard, *Brittany and the Angevins: Province and Empire 1158–203* (Cambridge, 2000), pp. 40–2, 55.

[49] The story is told by Adrian Morey and C. N. L. Brooke, *Gilbert Foliot and his Letters* (Cambridge, 1965), pp. 147–87. On Becket and his followers see Frank Barlow, *Thomas Becket* (London, 1986), esp. pp. 126–35.

[50] Arnulf of Lisieux to Becket, letter 45: *The Correspondence*, ed. Duggan, I.183–201 at 200–1.

[51] Ibid.: 'Disposuit etiam, sicut aiunt, in plerisque mitius agere, ut . . . ipse celeri reditu ad reprimendam Gualensium reuertatur audaciam, priusquam cum eis Scotti Britonesque conueniant, et Albania, sicut prophetatum est, incipiat indignari. Venit igitur imperata facturus . . . utilius estimans aliquid ad tempus de fastu ueteris supercilii sequestrare, quam expectare ut in perniciem eius que predicta sunt omnia uel pleraque concurrant. Valete.'

[52] *Epistola* 156: 'qui eo quod ex adverso non ascenderimus gloriatur nos terga praebuisse et linguas taurorum abscidisse; sicut propheta suus Merlinus inter caetera istud longe ante de eo (sicut gloriatur) vaticinatus est: "Et linguas," inquit, "taurorum abscidet".' *Materials for the History of Thomas Becket*, ed. James Craigie Robertson, 7 vols (London, 1875–85), V.285–94, at 291–2 (my translation). Gerald reported that the same prophecy was fulfilled at the Council of Clarendon, when Becket broke with the king: *Expugnatio*, ed. Scott and Martin, pp. 218–19, lines 33–6.

[53] As Gerald suggested: *Expugnatio*, ed. Scott and Martin, pp. 106–7 lines 24–7.

[54] Jean Blacker, '"Ne vuil sun livre translater": Wace's omission of Merlin's prophecies from the *Roman de Brut*', in Ian Short (ed.), *Anglo-Norman Anniversary Essays* (London, 1993), pp. 49–59; *Expugnatio*, ed. Scott and Martin, pp. 254–7.

[55] Below, n. 57.

[56] 'Fretus est oraculo Merlini qui, nescio quo repletus spiritu, perhibetur ante aduentum beati Augustini, Anglorum apostolo, uaticinatus esse . . .': *Epistola* 292: *The Letters of John of Salisbury*, ed. and trans. W. J. Millor and H. E. Butler, rev. Christopher N. L. Brooke, 2 vols (Oxford, 1955–79), II.666–9. On the circumstances see Morey and Brooke, *Gilbert Foliot*, pp. 149–62; also Christopher N. L. Brooke, *The Church and the Welsh Border in the Central Middle Ages* (Woodbridge, 1986), pp. 24–6. Compare this letter, composed in 1169, with that addressed to Becket three years earlier (above, n. 48).

[57] *De inuectiua, Patrologia Latina*, ed. Migne, 207, cols. 1113–26, at col. 1124 (my translation): 'Non solum Merlinum, sed et te prophetam voco; nam propheta es Antichristi: jam enim per te operatur mysterium iniquitatis. Sane nunquam Merlinum ponendum decrevi in catalogo sanctorum, qui a saeculo sunt, prophetarum, sed te et ipsum constituo inter prophetas Baal, annumero inter quadringentos prophetas Achab, qui ei in mendacio divinabant: vel, quia in sortem sacerdotii es assumptus, collegam summo sacerdoti Caiphae te adjungo, qui in eo crudeli consistorio, in quo Christus innocens condemnabatur ad mortem, cum esset anni illius pontifex, prophetavit. Scripturas, quaeso, lege et intellige: non enim omnia inveniuntur in Catone.' On the text and its author see John D. Cotts, 'Peter of Blois and the problem of the court in the late twelfth century', *Anglo-Norman Studies*, 27 (2004), 68–84.

[58] On John's career see David Luscombe, 'Salisbury, John of (late 1110s–1180)', *Oxford Dictionary of National Biography*, Oxford University Press, September 2004; online edn, May 2006 (*http://0www.oxforddnb.com.lib.exeter.ac.uk/view/article/14849*, accessed 18 September 2008); on Peter's, *John le Neve, Fasti ecclesiae Anglicanae 1066–1300, VIII: Bath and Wells*, ed. D. E. Greenway (London, 2001), pp. 28–9.

[59] 'Dicebant namque nonnulli illum Phitonicum spiritum exhausisse et more demonum obscure et amphibologice enigmatizasse exemplo Balan, aliis aliter affirmantibus': *Flores historiarum*, ed. Luard, I.234.

[60] *Prophetia anglicana*, p. 6.

[61] [John Bale,] *Scriptorum illustrium maioris Brytannie quam nunc Angliam et Scotiam uocant Catalogus* . . . (Basel, [1557–9]), p. 48.

[62] *Chronicles*, ed. Howlett, I.1–408, II.409–500 at p. 12.

[63] *Gervase of Tilbury, Otia imperialia: Recreation for an Emperor,* ed. and trans. S. E. Banks and J. W. Binns (Oxford, 2002), I.17, pp. 96–7.

[64] '*unde,* et *Incubi* dicuntur ab *incumbendo,* hoc est, *stuprando*': Isidore, *Etymologiae*, 8.11.103; *De civitate Dei*, XXV.23. Maaike van der Lugt, 'The *Incubus* in scholastic debate: medicine, theology and popular belief', in Peter Biller and Joseph Ziegler (eds), *Religion and Medicine in the Middle Ages* (York, 2001), pp. 175–200, at 178–80.

[65] Maaike van der Lugt, 'La personne manquée: démons, cadavers et opera vitae du début du xiie siècle à Saint Thomas', *Micrologus*, 7 (1999), 205–21, esp. 212–15; also Lugt, 'The *Incubus*'; Alison M. Peden, 'Macrobius and medieval dream literature', *Medium Aevum*, 54.1 (1985), 59–73, at p. 64.

[66] *De civitate Dei*, XV.22 (quoted in Exeter, Cathedral Library, MS 3514, p. 158). Noted by Hammer, 'Bref commentaire', p. 112, and *The Historia*, ed. Wright, pp. lxxxii–lxxxvi. The manuscript contains material of Welsh and Cistercian origin and is provenanced to Whitland.

[67] Paris, BnF lat. 6232: Crick, *The Historia . . . IV*, p. 91. The script indicates that the manuscript was copied on the Continent (?France).

[68] Crick, *The Historia . . . IV*, pp. 90–1.

[69] This element is discussed sympathetically and its structure analysed by Blacker, 'Anglo-Norman verse prophecies', pp. 11–17, see also pp. 116–19.

[70] *Life of Merlin*, ed. and trans. Clarke. This passage was discussed by Nathalie Koble, 'Un univers romanesque en expansion. Les *prophécies de Merlin* en prose du pseudo-Richard d'Irlande', in Drachsler et al. (eds), *Moult obscures paroles*, pp. 185–217, at 185–6.

[71] Southern, 'Aspects', pp. 170–3; R. W. Southern, *Robert Grosseteste: The Growth of an English Mind in Medieval Europe*, 2nd edn (Oxford, 1992), pp. 101–7; Roger French, 'Foretelling the future: Arabic astrology and English medicine in the late twelfth century', *Isis*, 87 (1996), 453–80, esp. 462–3. On reception by prelates see Jean Patrice Boudet, *Entre science et nigromance. Astrologie, divination et magie dans l'Occident médiéval (xiie–xve siècle)* (Paris, 2006), pp. 158, n. 1; 159; 163–8. I thank Dr Catherine Rider for bringing this volume to my attention.

[72] For full discussion of the acceptance and rejection of astrology in the twelfth and thirteenth centuries see Boudet, *Entre science et nigromance*, pp. 35–278, and on condemnation see ibid., pp. 239–58.

[73] One text of the prophecies annotated throughout was interpolated into the *Chronica maiora*, ed. Luard (above, nn. 44–5). The annotations cluster in the early sections, which caused Eckhardt to date the commentary to the twelfth century, but examination of the manuscript suggests that what Luard printed as a single work was a collection of disparate glosses added in more than one hand. On the distribution of glosses in the final part of the *Prophetia* see Wille, 'Le dossier', pp. 171, 182.

[74] Charles Homer Haskins, *Studies in the History of Mediaeval Science* (Cambridge, MA, 1924), pp. 28–9; he dates the text 1142x1146. Boudet, *Entre science et nigromance*, p. 168.

[75] Boudet, *Entre science et nigromance*, pp. 89–07; *Ioannis Saresberiensis* Policraticus *I–IV*, ed. K. S. B. Keats-Rohan (Turnhout, 1993), pp. 57–117 (*Policraticus*, I.11–13, II.15–19); *Frivolities of Courtiers and Footprints of Philosophers, being the First, Second, and Third Books and Selections from the Seventh, and Eighth Books of the* Policraticus *of John of Salisbury* , trans. Joseph B. Pike (New York. 1972), pp. 40–99. On John see Carey, *Courting Disaster*, pp. 29–30.

[76] The connection is quite clear from manuscripts listed in Coote's hand-list: *Prophecy*, pp. 239–80; on the Merlinian manuscripts see pp. 241, 243, 246, 254–5, 274.

[77] *English Benedictine Libraries: The Shorter Catalogues*, ed. Richard Sharpe et al., Corpus of British Medieval Library Catalogues, 4 (London, 1996), p. 111 (no. 14); *Dover Priory*, ed. William P. Stoneman, Corpus of British Medieval Library Catalogues, 5 (London, 1999), p. 163 (no. 413).

[78] Anke Holdenried has championed this type of evidence in examining reception of the Sibylline prophecies: 'Aspects of the English reception of the *Sibylla Tiburtina*: prophecy and devotion', in Nigel Morgan (ed.), *Prophecy, Apocalypse and the Day of Doom: Proceedings of the 2000 Harlaxton Symposium* (Donington, 2004), pp. 118–38.

[79] London, British Library, Royal 8 D. iii, from Ramsey, in association with letters about the Barons' War of 1264: J. P. Gilson, 'The parliament of 1264', *English Historical Review*, 16, 63 (1901), 499–501; *The Libraries of King Henry VIII*, ed. James P. Carley, Corpus of British Medieval Library Catalogues, 7 (London, 2001), p. 122 (no. 626). Merlinian prophecy was found with Magna Carta in a volume from the Premonstratensian abbey of Titchfield, Hants, whose remnant is now shelved as Oxford, Bodleian Library, MS Digby 154: *The Libraries of the Cistercians, Gilbertines and Premonstratensians*, ed. David N. Bell, Corpus of British Medieval Library Catalogues, 3 (London, 1992), pp. 228–9 (no. 162).

[80] London, British Library, MS Royal 4 D. viii, fol. 1r. Printed by David Casley, *A Catalogue of the Manuscripts of the King's Library: An Appendix to the Catalogue of the Cottonian Library* (London, 1734), pp. 55–6.

[81] The importance of 'systematic rationalization' and learned intervention in the dissemination of prophetic ideas in the later Middle Ages has been discussed by Steven Justice, 'Prophecy and the explanation of social disorder', in *Prophecy*, ed. Morgan, pp. 139–59.

Section Three

Chronicles and Romances

> In the meantime, while the bishops are celebrating the final rites, the air thunders, the earth shakes, tempests pour down from the heavens, lightning flashes, and the various winds blow from their various quarters. Then, after the shortest time, a mist followed which, absorbing the brightness of the lightning, wrapped the guards of the king's body in such blindness that they saw nothing, although their eyes were open. This mist persists from terce to nones; the air never grows quiet from the crashing thunder as the time goes by. And finally, when the mist is gone and calm restored, they find no part of the royal body.[1]

As noted in the essays in the last section, Geoffrey of Monmouth tells us much about Arthur's life, but shockingly little about his death. The Breton hope – the notion that Arthur was not dead, but would one day return to aid his people – finds little traction in Geoffrey's *Historia*. Geoffrey's Arthur goes to Avalon, but it is never suggested that he might come back, and Geoffrey simply moves on to the exploits of other British rulers. The lines quoted as the epigraph to this section might speak to readerly dissatisfaction with Geoffrey's summary dismissal of his most arresting king. They are drawn from the *Vera historia de morte Arturi*, an elaborate account of Arthur's death that provides all the fireworks Geoffrey eschewed. This account is found attached to Geoffrey's *Historia* in some manuscripts. As Ad Putter notes in his essay in the following section, it may have arisen in part out of jurisdictional disputes (he argues that the story is intended to show Arthur wishes to be buried at Aberconwy Abbey and not at Glastonbury), but I cite it here because it shows as well the extent to which chronicle and romance can be intertwined. The story, as Putter illustrates, has a decidedly Celtic flavour. Elizabeth Archibald suggests, in her contribution to this collection, that it may be intended to evoke the Resurrection; certainly there is an important mystical quality added to Arthur's death that was absent in Geoffrey. The full-blown Latin romances dealt with by Archibald show that the Latin Arthurian tradition could move from the world of chronicle into what we might think of as straightforward fiction, but the chronicle traditions traced here by both Putter and Edward Donald Kennedy make clear the extent to which our categories of 'fact' and 'fiction' fail us in the face of many Latin Arthurian texts. As Putter puts it, 'By medieval standards, the Latin chroniclers . . . wrote history as it should be written' – and history could include the mysterious storm of the *Vera historia*, or the Glastonbury traditions which developed in conversation with vernacular romances, as well as what we may have been conditioned to think of as 'proper' history. The romances dealt with by Archibald, for their part, share some of the concerns of the chronicles (and one even calls itself a *historia*), and again display the exchange between Latin and vernacular traditions. Kennedy rightly points to a growing divide between scholarly and popular attitudes towards Arthurian tradition, but the long list of Latin Arthurian texts dealt with in this section nevertheless underlines the hold that Arthur had on even the Latinate imagination.

SE

Notes

[1] *Vera historia de morte Arthuri*, in Michael Lapidge, 'An edition of *De vera historia de morte Arthuri*', *Arthurian Literature*, 1 (1981), 90: 'Interim, episcopis exequias celebrantibus, aer tonat, terra nutat, desuper crebro irruunt tempestates, fulgura choruscant, aureque diuerse uariis se alternant uicibus. Demum, interposita breuissimi temporis morula, aeris subsecuta est caligo que fulgurum absorta est claritatem et tanta cecitate regii corporis obuoluit custodes, ut apertis oculis nihil uiderent. Hec ab hora tertia usque ad nonam perdurat assidue; aer nullo tempore celebris horarum uicibus a tonitrui quiescit tumultu. At deinde, cum caligo subducitur et serenitas restituitur, corporis regii nullas repperunt reliquias.' My translation.

5

LATIN HISTORIOGRAPHY AFTER GEOFFREY OF MONMOUTH

Ad Putter

The vigorous tradition of Arthurian historiography in Latin following Geoffrey's *Historia regum Britannie* (*HRB*) is one of the most neglected areas of modern scholarship. Robert Huntington Fletcher's *The Arthurian Material in the Chronicles* (Boston, 1906) and Laura Keeler's *Geoffrey of Monmouth and the Late Latin Chronicles: 1300–1500* (Berkeley, 1946) offer indispensable overviews of the vast amount of extant material, but their surveys also reveal how deplorably inaccessible much of the relevant material was (and still is): some of the most interesting Arthurian chronicles can only be read in manuscripts or early printed editions.

It is impossible to cover the available material in a single chapter, so by way of introducing some of the landmarks of the chronicle tradition, I propose to address some larger questions that go the heart of the tradition as a whole. What is it about Geoffrey's *HRB* that excited or troubled later medieval chroniclers? And what is it that prompted them to rewrite Galfridian history and to combine it with other sources?

I: Geoffrey's Earliest Readers: 1136–1220

To answer these questions, we need to begin by appreciating that medieval readers generally regarded Geoffrey's *Historia* as genuine national history. William of Newburgh, Geoffrey of Monmouth's most incisive critic, is a rare exception in this regard. William's *Historia rerum Anglicarum* is a history of England from the Norman Conquest until the reign of Richard the Lionheart.[1] It breaks off suddenly (presumably because William died) with an account of a mysterious shower of rain mixed with blood that allegedly took place in Andelys in 1198. Since William did not concern himself with Dark Age Britain, he did not have to engage with Geoffrey on the same historical ground; but that did not stop him from taking a good swipe at Geoffrey in the Preface. Here he writes that the great authority for English history is Bede; for the history of the Britons, the most reliable source is Gildas. Since Gildas denounces his own race, he must be impartial; and so the Welsh really must be an inferior race, for there can be no suspicion that the truth is disguised when a Briton, speaking of Britons, says they were cowardly and faithless. Recently, however, a mendacious writer called Geoffrey 'Arthur' (a nickname given to him because he has provided in Latin a history of King Arthur) has seen fit to pervert the Latin language, the language of truth,[2] in order to exalt the Britons above all other races, even the English. However, since the latter conquered the Welsh, the English were actually their masters, and Geoffrey has it the wrong way around when he depicts Arthur and his successors lording it over the English. Geoffrey of Monmouth was thus dismissed by William of Newburgh as a preposterous liar who reinvented history to flatter the Welsh.

Although William's animosity against *HRB* is patently fanned by his pro-English and anti-Welsh sentiments, he provides genuine insight into Geoffrey's creative design. He is insightful, for example, about Geoffrey's ingenious handling of Merlin's prophecies. Many of these, William says, are *not* Merlin's – he evidently thought some were – but spurious additions due to Geoffrey's own invention (*ex proprio figmento*).[3] Because these additions tally with events that are narrated later on in the *HRB* or have taken place since, they trick the reader into believing that all of Merlin's prophecies are true: 'Moreover, as would have been easy for him to do, he attuned his inventions to events that had occurred before or during his time, in such a way that they could bear a concordant interpretation.'[4] Finally, William puts his finger on the competitive spirit that led Geoffrey to imagine Arthur as emulating the feats of other legendary conquerors. For example, Geoffrey has Arthur conquer all Northern lands up to and including Thule (Iceland), 'so that the flattering words addressed to the Roman Augustus – "The distant Thule shall confess thy sway" [Virgil, *Georgics* 1.30] – might apply to that Briton'.[5] Arthur's later triumphs against the Romans and their exotic allies (Phrygians, Parthians, Egyptians, etc.) are designed to conjure up the image of Alexander, whose achievements Arthur surpasses as if his little finger were broader than Alexander's back. As a key to Geoffrey's biography of Arthur, William's notion of mimetic rivalry is genuinely useful, since Arthur really does take after Alexander in *HRB*.[6] Of all of Geoffrey's critics, William of Newburgh seems to come closest to getting the point of *HRB*.

The two other early chroniclers who comment on Geoffrey's *HRB*, Henry of Huntingdon and Gerald of Wales, are often regarded as enlightened sceptics, but their engagement with *HRB* shows, if anything, how deeply they were taken in by it. By the time Geoffrey's *HRB* was written, *c.*1136, Henry of Huntingdon had already published his first edition of the *Historia Anglorum*.[7] This included a skeletal account of Arthur and his twelve battles (based on 'Nennius'), sandwiched between the years 527 and 530, years which are fleshed out with more reliable information taken from the *Anglo-Saxon Chronicle*. In 1139, Henry wrote a letter to his friend Warinus Brito (Warin the Briton). While Henry had been visiting the monastery of Bec, the librarian, Robert of Torigny, had shown him a copy of Geoffrey's *HRB*. Henry says that the discovery of this history stupefied him because his own researches for the *Historia Anglorum* had yielded very little or nothing that could form the basis of a history of the Dark Ages, so that he had not been able to say much about that period. His expression of amazement at seeing *HRB* could be taken as evidence of Henry's unusual 'exercise of critical judgement',[8] but this would be rather misleading. What amazed Henry is that the gap in the historical record has been filled, and it is precisely to make good his own omission in the *Historia Anglorum* that he immediately sent Warinus a synopsis of *HRB*. As Neil Wright has shown,[9] to avoid any conflicts with other historical authorities (especially Bede, 'Nennius' and Henry's own history), Henry omitted or silently emended a few details in *HRB*. All this suggests that he regarded it as providing a body of evidence that needed to be reconciled with the evidence of others. His approach, then, is not precociously modern but typical of medieval writers. As C. S. Lewis put it:

> They are bookish. They are indeed very credulous of books. They find it hard to believe that anything an old *auctour* has said is simply untrue . . . Obviously their *auctours* will contradict one another . . . If, under these conditions, one also has a great reluctance flatly to disbelieve anything in a book, then there is obviously both an urgent need and a glorious opportunity for sorting out and tidying up. All the apparent contradictions must be harmonised. A Model must be built which will get everything in without a clash; and it can do this only by becoming intricate, by mediating its unity through a great, and finely ordered, multiplicity.[10]

Henry's letter to Warinus provides the missing piece in his own historical model, and we shall get more out of Henry's letter (and other Latin Arthurian chronicles) if, instead of expecting 'exercise of critical judgement', we cultivate a taste for 'finely ordered multiplicity'.

To this end, it is worth noting that bookish respect for authority paradoxically spawns its own kind of inventiveness, particularly when there are gaps in the *auctour*'s account. The most significant gaps in *HRB* are in its threadbare account of Arthur's death at the end of a much longer list of casualties: 'The illustrious king Arthur too was mortally wounded; he was taken away to the island of Avallon to have his wounds tended, and, in the year of Our Lord 542, handed over Britain's crown to his relative Constantinus, son of Cador duke of Cornwall.'[11] There are many unanswered questions here, which excited later imaginations. Does Arthur make a 'good end' in the religious sense? Who killed Arthur, who Mordred, and how did Arthur die? Indeed, did he actually die? Merlin's earlier prophecy to Vortigern that the end of the Boar 'shall be unknown'[12] has prepared us for open-endedness, and the possibility that Arthur has not died is again suggested by the 'Angelic voice' which at the close of *HRB* announces to Cadwallader that the Britons will not regain their freedom 'until the time came which Merlin had foretold to Arthur'.[13] This announcement raises a further question, for not only does it provide hope that Arthur may one day return to free the Britons, but tantalizingly it informs us that *Merlin* prophesied that moment to Arthur. How can this be when Merlin's last recorded act in *HRB* is to preside over Arthur's conception?

The reason for dwelling on these enigmas in *HRB* is that they tickled the imaginations of later historians, including Henry of Huntingdon. Having supplied a summary of *HRB* for his friend Warinus, Henry becomes suddenly expansive when he reaches Arthur's death and can take inspiration from all that Geoffrey does *not* say:

> With a few men he pursued him [i.e. Mordred] as far as Cornwall, and came upon him and his many followers. When he realized that he was unable to retreat, he said: 'Companions, let us put

> a high price on our deaths. I will now cut off the head of my nephew and betrayer with my sword. After that, death will be sweet'. Thus he spoke, and using his sword to make a way through the enemy line, he took hold of Mordred's helmet, in the midst of his men, and severed the armoured neck with one stroke of his sword, as if it were a head of corn. But he received so many wounds in doing so that he also fell. But the Bretons, your ancestors, refuse to believe that he died. And they traditionally await his return.[14]

This dramatic showdown between Arthur and Mordred has no warrant in *HRB* but shows a writer firmly in the grip of Geoffrey's fantasy, filling one of the lacunae in Geoffrey's account in the same way that Geoffrey had filled the gaping hole in early British history. Together, Geoffrey and Henry are 'builders of a great model' of British history, and their later scribes completed the collaboration. In some of the manuscripts of *HRB*, Henry's amplified ending is substituted for Geoffrey's, and vice versa the summary of Geoffrey in Henry's letter to Warinus was added (probably on Henry's own initiative) to later editions of the *Historia Anglorum*.[15]

Gerald of Wales's relationship to Geoffrey of Monmouth was also much more involved than scholars used to think.[16] The older view that he was contemptuous of Geoffrey's history is based on a passage in the second redaction (*c*.1197) of the *Itinerarium Cambriae*,[17] which tells the story of Meilyr, the soothsayer of Caerleon-on-Usk who was plagued by demons:

> When he was harassed beyond endurance by these unclean spirits, Saint John's Gospel was placed on his lap, and then they vanished immediately, flying away like so many birds. If the Gospel were afterwards removed and the *History of the Kings of Britain* by Geoffrey of Monmouth put there in its place, just to see what would happen, the demons would alight all over his body, and on the book, too, staying there longer than usual and being even more demanding.[18]

Demons cannot abide St John's Gospel[19] but love Geoffrey of Monmouth. Whether this is a dig at Geoffrey's historical fraudulence is not entirely clear, however: Gerald's target may well have been the secularism of Geoffrey's entertainment. In any event, it is important to note that his critique takes the form of a story that is itself as fantastical as anything in *HRB*. It might thus occur to readers of Gerald (as doubtless it had to Gerald himself) that the demons would have loved his work too.

Moreover, Gerald made avid use of Geoffrey's history. In *The Conquest of Ireland*, first issued (*c*.1189) by Gerald under the title *Vaticinalis Historia* (*The Prophetic History*),[20] Merlin's prophecies are cited at every turning-point in the history in order to persuade us that the colonization of the Irish was destined to happen. At the end of the history, Gerald promises a continuation, which was to consist of an authoritative Latin translation of Merlin's authentic prophecies, excluding those that Gerald and a team of Welsh linguists had shown to be spurious interpolations by later writers. Unfortunately, Gerald's intentions were overtaken by grave events. Gerald's original patron, King Henry II, died in 1189, and Gerald seems to have decided that, in the resulting climate of insecurity, it would be dangerous to meddle any further with political prophecy.[21]

The problem of chronology posed by Geoffrey's treatment of Merlin also exercised Gerald. To recapitulate, in *HRB* one 'Merlin Ambrosius' utters prophecies to Vortigern, who rules after the arrival of the Saxons, i.e., *c*.450 AD; but at the very end of the *Historia*, the Angelic Voice mentions Merlin as having prophesied the future to Arthur (*c*.540). Can Merlin really have lived that long? Gerald provides a neat solution:

> There were two Merlins. The one called Ambrosius, who thus had two names, prophesied when Vortigern was King. He was the son of an incubus and he was discovered in Carmarthen, which means Merlin's town, for it takes its name from the fact that he was found there. The second Merlin came from Scotland. He is called Celidonius because he prophesied in the Calidonian Forest. He is also called Silvester, because once when he was fighting he looked up into the air and saw a terrible monster. He went mad as a result and fled to the forest where he passed the remainder of his life as a wild man of the woods. This second Merlin lived in the time of Arthur. He is said to have made more prophecies than his namesake.[22]

The chronological difficulties in Geoffrey of Monmouth's story thus failed to dislodge Gerald's belief that Merlin was real; Gerald simply absorbed the problem by making his model more intricate: there were two Merlins, not one – hence the apparent contradictions in the modern record.

Another good example of this process of recuperative revision is the theory, canvassed by Gerald in *Descriptio Cambriae*, that Gildas had a brother, a Scottish chieftain, whom Arthur killed. When Gildas discovered this, 'he threw into the sea a number of outstanding books which he had written in . . . praise [of the Britons] and about Arthur's achievements'.[23] Lewis Thorpe noted sceptically that 'Apart from the fact that Gildas was born on the south bank of the Clyde there is no evidence to support any of this.' But Gerald did possess evidence of sorts. *The Life of Gildas* (*c*.1140) by Caradoc of Llancarfan, 'confirms' that Gildas had a brother whom Arthur killed, thus causing great hostility between the two. There is also the fact that Gildas does not mention Arthur in his *De excidio Britannie*. To modern sceptics, this omission might seem to militate against the historicity of Arthur, but to Arthurian believers like Gerald the omission suggested, on the contrary, that Gildas must have had a reason for overlooking Arthur. It was thus plausible for Gerald to suggest that Gildas hated Arthur, and that, in Gerald's words, 'as a result, you will find no book which gives an authentic account of that great prince'.[24] Once again the historical model is adjusted to harmonize the contradictions, so that the very thing that tells against King Arthur's existence – Gildas's silence about him – now speaks in its favour.

The crowning achievement of Gerald's collusion with Geoffrey of Monmouth is the foundation myth of St David's, which, as Gerald argued, had once been the seat of an archbishopric. Such a claim was bound to be contentious. Since the time of Henry I, the Welsh Church had been subject to the English. England had two archbishoprics (York and Canterbury), Wales had none, and the bishoprics it did have (St David's, Bangor, Llandaff and St Asaph's) came under the jurisdiction of Canterbury. Around the same the time as Geoffrey of Monmouth was writing *HRB*, both the bishops of Llandaff and St David's were advancing claims that 'by ancient tradition' their sees had been, and should again be, archbishoprics.[25] The case made by St David's went even further: its archbishop had supposedly once been the primate of an independent Church in Wales, accountable not to Canterbury but directly to Rome.

Since the hierarchical organization of the Church into archbishoprics and bishoprics was actually a comparatively recent development, the problem faced by anyone claiming ancient metropolitan status was that historical proof was necessarily lacking. However, where evidence did not exist, it could be fabricated, and *HRB* proved useful for this purpose, because on at least a couple of occasions Geoffrey projected back onto the past the present hierarchical structure of primates and metropolitans. One such occasion is Merlin's obscure prophecy to King Vortigern:

> Religion will be destroyed again and archbishoprics will be displaced. London's honour will adorn Canterbury, and the seventh pastor of York [= Samson?; cf. *HRB*, paras. 130, 151] will dwell in the kingdom of Armorica [= Brittany]. St David's will wear the pallium of Caerleon . . .[26]

The last item of this prophecy has a bearing on one of the most memorable scenes in the Arthurian section of Geoffrey's *HRB*, the occasion of Arthur's coronation:

> Now that the feast of Whitsun was imminent, Arthur, delighted at his great triumph, decided to hold court immediately, wearing the royal crown upon his head . . . Among those attending were . . . the three archbishops of the metropolitan sees: London, York, and Caerleon. Archbishop Dubricius of Caerleon [was] primate of Britain and papal legate . . . The saintly Dubricius relinquished his position as archbishop, being eager to live as a hermit. His place was taken by the king's uncle David . . . Archbishop Samson of Dol was replaced by Teliaus, a distinguished priest of Llandaff.[27]

The most intriguing suggestion here is that Wales could indeed boast a metropolitan see, though Geoffrey mischievously places it, not in Llandaff or St David's, where the Welsh wanted it most, but in Caerleon – a place that had nothing going for it except for some Roman ruins that hinted at former glory.[28]

Gerald, whose great ambition in life was to become not just the bishop of St David's but its archbishop, realized that Geoffrey's sidelights on ecclesiastical history gave him plenty of ammunition. In 1199 he travelled to Rome to present his case for the 'ancient dignity' of St David's to Pope Innocent III.[29] The argument he put forward there is wonderfully surreal. Gerald asked Pope Innocent to think back to the time when Britain became Christian, when two holy men, Faganus and Duvianus, converted King Lucius to Christianity:

> So Britain was organized by these holy men in such a way that in the western part of this island – now called 'Wales' (an adulterated word) but more properly Kambria, named after Kamber, Brutus' son – the city of Legions was the metropolis, with twelve suffragan bishops . . . Dubricius, archbishop of Caerleon, ceded the honour to David, who transferred the Metropolitan Sea to St David's [Menevia], as was foretold by our prophet Merlin long before in the following manner: 'St David's will wear the pallium of Caerleon.' Now, we had at St David's twenty-five archbishops in succession, of whom the first was St David and the last St Samson, who sailed to Brittany, taking the pallium with him.[30]

In this madness readers will immediately recognize Gerald's debt to Geoffrey of Monmouth. According to Geoffrey, Brutus, founder of Britain, had given Wales to his son Kamber; it was thenceforth called *Kambria*. Gerald's claim that St David's was once a metropolitan church is supported with reference to the primacy of Dubricius and his successor St David, who transferred the pallium (the vestment worn by the pope and archbishops) to St David's, so fulfilling Merlin's prophecy: 'St David's will wear the pallium of Caerleon.' To explain how St David's subsequently lost that pallium, Gerald needs Samson, who is named as the Archbishop of Dol in *HRB*, but who (according to Celtic tradition) had been born in Wales.

Gerald's opponents, the agents of the archbishop of Canterbury, dismissed this history of St David's as an outrageous fiction, a 'fable of Arthur'.[31] Gerald's reliance on *HRB* and Merlin must have left him vulnerable to the charge that he was a *fabulator* rather than a historian. The pope's response to Gerald's myth was more encouraging. According to Gerald, the single issue he raised was how St Samson could have been the last bishop of St David's when it was common knowledge that he had been archbishop of York:

> Giraldus expounded to him how St David's metropolitan rank had disappeared when Samson, the last Archbishop of St David's, fled overseas to Brittany to escape the yellow plague . . . But when he heard this, the pope replied: 'Surely this Samson of Dol had been archbishop of York.' But to this Giraldus replied, 'No, with respect, father, the chronicles of Dol also confirm that this Samson was ours and not from somewhere else . . . The people of York have been misled by the identical name; for they also once had an archbishop called Samson'.[32]

If the pope's response is genuine, he, too, may have been reading Geoffrey of Monmouth, for (as far as I am aware) Samson's flight from York and his subsequent reappearance as archbishop of Dol are 'facts' that have no independent existence outside *HRB*. And again Gerald deals with the pope's objection by multiplying personalities. Just as there were two Merlins, so there were two Samsons, one archbishop of York, the other of St David's; and it is the latter, not the former, who transferred the pallium to Dol.

Gerald's use of *HRB* shows that he largely believed it or found it expedient to do so. His response to any contradictions between *HRB* and other authorities was not to jettison Geoffrey's history but to complicate it in such a way that the contradictions could be understood as the products of historical complexity.

II: Geoffrey of Monmouth in the Age of the Universal Chronicle: 1220–1350

Gerald and Henry of Huntingdon stand at the beginning of a long history of creative responses to Geoffrey. As we move later into the thirteenth century, Geoffrey's influence on Latin historiographers becomes more far-reaching but also more complicated, since he now influenced medieval poets and chroniclers not only directly but also indirectly. Poets working in French or English often knew Galfridian 'history' from vernacular translations such as Wace's *Brut* and the Prose *Brut*. And while many chroniclers in the Latin tradition still went directly to Geoffrey, they could also access HRB indirectly in various 'universal' histories (histories of the world from Creation up to the present) which offered sober summaries of Arthur's reign. These universal histories played a crucial role in mediating Geoffrey's narrative and in establishing it as official history.

On the Continent, perhaps the most influential universal history was Vincent of Beauvais's *Speculum historiale* (*c.*1255). The textual history of the Arthurian section in Vincent's *Speculum historiale* (book 20, chapter 59 in the printed edition[33]) is itself an instructive example of King Arthur's gradual infiltration into the domain of 'fact'. Vincent's main source was not Geoffrey of Monmouth himself but Sigebert of Gembloux, who in the early twelfth century produced a universal history up to the year 1111. Later in the twelfth century, an anonymous continuator, a Cistercian monk at Ourcamp, enlarged Sigebert's *Chronographia* by interpolating extracts from Geoffrey's *HRB*.[34] The extracts are hedged about with expressions both of doubt and of scholarly enthusiasm. Arthur's coronation is entered under the year 470, with the following note:

> Now, if we put our faith in the account of this history, then the deeds of that famous king Arthur (who reigned over Britain after his father Utherpendragon) should be inserted at this particular point in time. But because we do not find any mention of him in other histories, and because the aforementioned *History of the Britons* [i.e. *HRB*] is neither entirely explicit nor entirely silent about the chronological dating of the years in which Arthur and many other reigned, we do not affirm these doubtful matters to be true, nor, however, do we withhold from the reader this historical account, which was recently translated from Welsh into Latin.[35]

Geoffrey's dubious claim to have translated his history from Welsh was evidently accepted by the interpolator, but he did not overlook the dearth of corroborating evidence. The lack of any clear dates in Geoffrey's Arthurian section (the date of Arthur's vanishing, AD 542, being the only exception) was another problem, and one that naturally weighed heavily with this and other monastic readers who had been brought up in the annalistic tradition of historiography. However, since Geoffrey's dates were vague, there was also nothing to prevent the Ourcamp interpolator from placing the reign of Arthur earlier in time (in the late fifth century). Indeed, this dating was in one respect superior to Geoffrey's, since it avoided the chronological error that Geoffrey committed when situating Arthur's Roman War in the time of the Emperor Leo. As the interpolator knew,[36] Leo died in 473, so that, *if* Arthur indeed fought against the forces of Emperor Leo, it could not have happened when Geoffrey claims it did. The Ourcamp interpolator therefore protests when he mentions, in his entry for the year 542, that *HRB* assigns to this year Arthur's foreign conquests *sub Leone imperatore*: 'Therefore all these aforementioned things seem to have no credible authority if we compare them with other histories.'[37]

The interpolator's revised dating of Arthur's deeds to the years of the Emperor Leo (*c*.470) was silently accepted by Vincent of Beauvais in his *Speculum historiale*. Recounting the interpolated Arthurian section in Sigebert's *Chronographia*, Vincent was aware that Arthur's deeds were the subject of popular stories, not perhaps all credible (*licet plura esse fabulosa videantur*). However, he raises no other questions about Arthur's historicity. Significantly, he deletes the Ourcamp interpolator's above-cited protestation and proceeds simply to summarize Arthur's glorious reign. Although the more colourful elements of Geoffrey's story (e.g. Merlin's magic) are missing, Arthur still features as a superhuman hero. As in Geoffrey, he single-handedly kills 470 Saxons with his sword Excalibur. With Vincent of Beauvais's imprimatur, the story of Arthur passed readily into later chronicles, Latin and vernacular.[38] Arthur's future on the Continent was made.

In England, the universal chronicle also offered Geoffrey of Monmouth safe passage through to later medieval historians. Two of the most important conduits are the various versions of the *Flores historiarum* (*FH*) and Ranulph Hidgen's *Polychronicon* (*c*.1350). *FH* exists in various versions. The earliest was compiled at St Alban's (*c*.1200), another influential version is Matthew Paris's *Cronica majora* (*c*.1253), a third and later version, much indebted to Matthew Paris but with some independent elaborations, is attributed – spuriously, it is now believed – to Matthew of Westminster (*c*.1326),[39] who will be the focus of my discussion.

All *FH* versions represent attempts to reconcile Geoffrey with other historical authorities and to anchor Arthurian events more securely to known dates and events by supplying the *supputatio annorum* ('computation of years') that readers like the Ourcamp interpolator expected to find in proper history. The highlights of Arthur's career are accordingly keyed to specific years and other events of historical note. The results are very funny (no doubt unintentionally so). Here are some entries in Matthew of Westminster's *FH*:

> AD 521. Boethius, having been long an exile, was put to death by Theoderic, king of the Goths. The same year, news was brought to Arthur that the Scots and Picts had besieged king Hoel . . . [40]
>
> AD 536. Saint Benedict, according to some accounts, departed to Christ. Likewise king Arthur, desiring to reduce the countries of Gaul under his power, having prepared a fleet, committed the protection of the whole of Britain and his wife to Mordred, his nephew.[41]

It will be observed that, unlike the continuator of Sigebert's *Chronographia*, *FH* accepts Geoffrey of Monmouth's periodization (Arthur dies AD 542); but it does not follow *HRB* blindly. For instance, *FH* silently removes all mention of a Roman emperor named Leo, calling the emperor Justinian instead. It also emends the name of the pope: 'There was also at that time Walwan, the son of the before-mentioned Lother, a youth of twelve years of age, who had been entrusted to pope Vigilius to bring up, and who received from him also the belt of military service.'[42]The passage has been lifted verbatim from *HRB*, except that the pope's name has been changed from Sulpicius to Vigilius (recorded as pope during this period in Martin of Troppau's influential *Chronicle of the Popes* (see n. 38)). The emendations neatly remove any impediments to Geoffrey's periodization.

With the same adroitness, *FH* rearranges Geoffrey's narrative into an annalistic chronicle, extracting from *HRB* the key events of Arthur's illustrious reign and rearranging them, interspersed with other historical milestones, across a precise temporal range, from AD 516 (Arthur's succession to the throne) to 542. A comparison between *HRB* and *FH* is instructive. *HRB* tells us that Arthur, having slaughtered many Saxons, allowed the remaining ones to leave Britain on condition that they would not return. As the Saxons sail away, they immediately regret this arrangement and head back to Britain. *FH* does some intelligent cutting and pasting. Arthur's decision to grant the Saxons a safe retreat is the final entry for the year 518. In 519, Justus becomes emperor of the Romans for eight years, and Boethius writes *The Consolation of Philosophy*. In 520, the Saxons renege on their promise and return to Britain. The two years' lapse between the Saxons' departure and return makes their change of heart comprehensible and helps to spread the historical matter evenly across the temporal canvas.

The circumstances surrounding Arthur's death are also rationalized in *FH*. Because Arthur's bones had been 'discovered' at Glastonbury (*c.*1191), Geoffrey's statement that his body was carried off to Avalon to be healed now needed qualification: Avalon, *FH* explains, is the historic name of a place now called Glastonbury. If, in spite of Arthur's bones, the Britons believe that Arthur will one day return, that is because the early histories make no mention of either his death or his burial place. 'Matthew of Westminster' inherited this argument from his main source (Matthew Paris) but was not content to leave the matter there. The historians' silence about Arthur's death seemed to him to need explanation, so he supplied one based on a psychological reconstruction of Arthur's intentions:

> The dying king kept himself from sight, so that his enemies might not insult his misfortunes, nor his friends be grieved. On which account, as the histories say nothing of the death of Arthur or of his burial, the nation of the Britons, out of the greatness of their affection for him, contend that he is still alive.[43]

In other words, the reason why no historian reports Arthur's death is that no one was present to witness it when it happened. The ambiguity surrounding his death is thus a historical accident.

A second influential and widely disseminated later chronicle to transmit *HRB* is Ranulph Higden's *Polychronicon*, translated into English by John Trevisa in 1387.[44] Higden (d.1364) was a Benedictine monk at St Werburgh's abbey in Chester. His history starts with Creation and ends with Higden's present. For the period of Arthur's rule, his main authorities were Geoffrey of Monmouth, Henry of Huntingdon, William of Malmesbury and Martin of Troppau's *Chronicle of the Popes*. From these, Ranulph, too, gathered that Geoffrey got the pope's name wrong. As he points out, the correct name is Justinian, the fifth pope after Leo. He also points out that, given the pre-eminence attributed to Arthur by Geoffrey, it is suspicious that no other historians praise Arthur. Trevisa, Ranulph's translator, has no time for such quibbles. It is true, he concedes, that some of Geoffrey's names are unexpected, but rulers do and did have multiple names and these often vary from place to place: 'ofte an officer, kyng, oþer emperour haþ many dyuers names, and is diverselyche i-nempned in many dyvers londes'.[45] Nor should we expect exact agreement between different authorities when even the Gospel lives of Jesus differ amongst each other.

Trevisa's defensiveness might give the misleading impression that Hidgen was attacking *HRB*, but in actual fact Trevisa's arguments owe something to Hidgen's own defensive manoeuvring. Admittedly, Higden points out that chroniclers from other nations do not mention any Arthur, despite his many foreign conquests, but for this oddity he himself offers a possible explanation:

> But perhaps it is the habit of any nation to extol one of their own with excessive praises. This often happens, as Josephus says, because of the beauty of the history, or for the sake of the readers' pleasure, or to exalt one's own bloodline.[46]

From this perspective, the British partiality for Arthur is quite natural.

Higden's most original contribution to Arthurian historiography is further testimony to his belief in Arthur's historicity. From his reading of Henry of Huntingdon, Ranulph gathered that the king of Wessex in the early sixth century was Cerdic: '*Henry, book II* . . . This year the kingdom of the West Saxons was begun under Cerdic and Kynric.'[47] The apparent contradiction between Henry of Huntingdon and Geoffrey of Monmouth (who has Arthur as sole sovereign) inspires an inventive compromise. After years of making a nuisance of himself, Cerdic (a Saxon enemy in *HRB*) is offered a peace deal by Arthur:

> In some chronicles[48] it is reported that Cerdic frequently fought with Arthur and, although Cerdic was repeatedly overcome, he rose up to fight even more eagerly on another occasion. Finally Arthur, worn out by fighting, after twenty-six years, and having received pledges from Cerdic, gave him Hampshire and Somerset, which part he called Wessex.[49]

By this arrangement, King Arthur and King Cerdic can coexist in harmony, and Hidgen's sources can both be right. Geoffrey of Monmouth and Henry of Huntingdon have been reconciled.

As *FH* and Higden's *Polychronicon* suggest, the development of Galfridian history in later chronicles is towards a more restrained and rationalized narrative, in which form *HRB* was transmitted to many later readers and writers. However, this section would not be complete without a mention of two eccentric productions from the period: *Gesta regum Britannie* and *De vera historia de morte Arthuri*.

Gesta regum Britannie, from the first half of the thirteenth century, is a vast Latin versification of *HRB* in an ornate classicizing style.[50] One of the manuscripts attributes the poem to William of Rennes, who may, however, have been the scribe rather than the poet. Book VII, the first of three devoted to King Arthur, begins with an invocation of the muse of epic poetry, Calliope, followed by a roll call of classical heroes, who are as nothing when compared with Arthur:

> since Arthur's glory exceeds that of Achilles by as much as Achilles' glory outstrips that of Thersites. The author of the Aeneid would have preferred Arthur's praises, which are worthy of the Maeonian bard, to the story of old Anchises, weighty Lucan would have passed over Caesar's doings, and ancient Thebes would have lacked eternal fame, if only Arthur's deeds had preceded these poets.[51]

Arthur competes and outdoes the great classical martial heroes, just as the poet seeks to outdo his own poetic models: Virgil's *Aeneid*, Statius' *Thebaid*, Lucan's *De bello civili* and, above all, Walter of Châtillon's *Alexandreid*. The debt owed to Walter of Châtillon is the greatest but never acknowledged: he was not ancient so there was nothing to be gained from trumpeting his name. The relentless classicization occasionally affects content as well as style. For example, while the games during the Whitsuntide Feast in *HRB* are recognizably medieval (some knights fight in a tournament, watched by their lady-loves, while others compete in archery, stone-throwing, and dice), those in the *Gesta* are a curious mixture of the classical and the medieval, with knights choosing between athletics, combat training, wrestling, dice, and chariot racing. Are these Arthur's Whitsuntide Festivities or Aeneas' Funeral Games?

The ponderous display of book learning is an unattractive aspect of the *Gesta*. Surprisingly, however, erudition combines with the poet's lively belief in Arthur's possible survival. Mordred, for example, is condemned not just for treachery but also for being stupid enough to think that he can annihilate Arthur, 'of whom all the people of the Antipodes are frightened, and to whom according to Merlin – if we are to believe him – the road to death is closed'.[52] When on the battlefield at Camlann the combatants are dead and Arthur himself has been 'mortally' wounded, the king stays on his feet: 'King Arthur, to whom the door of death is believed to be closed, still lives.'[53] Towards the end of Book IX, he hands the crown to Constantine, sails (under his own steam, it appears) to a paradisal island, and there makes his way to the court of the king of Avalon. The king's daughter, a beautiful nymph skilled in the art of medicine, heals him and 'keeps his cured limbs for herself' (*sanati membra reseruat / Ipsa sibi*). So the lucky King and Nymph live together, 'if it is permissible to believe it' (*si credere fas est*, IX.317). The phrasing remains derivative to the end (Wright adduces *Alexandreid*, IV.313, '*si credere fas est*'); but it is interesting to see that what is dressed up in second-hand Latin is the folk belief that Arthur lives on and will return to free the British from their oppressors. The explanation for the poet's faith in Arthur's return is that he was himself a proud Briton, as his rallying cry to his compatriots shows:

> I write this entirely for the British, so that, mindful of their ancient homeland, their hereditary rights, the exile of their fathers, and their own shame, they may strive with voice and prayer to restore the kingdom, which the English enemy now occupies, to their jurisdiction as before; and so that the treacherous possessor does not lay claim to our farms and his case gain strength through the passage of time.[54]

'British' could mean 'Welsh' or 'Breton', but since the work is dedicated to Cadioc (elected bishop of Vannes in 1235), the poet – whether William of Rennes or someone else – must have been a Breton.

It is no coincidence that the second eccentric adaptation of *HRB*, the *De vera historia de morte Arthuri*, also originates from Celtic lands, in this case Wales. The earliest two surviving witnesses (London, Gray's Inn, MS 7, *c.*1340, and *Chronicon monasterii de Hales* in London, BL Cotton Cleopatra D. III, *c.*1314, containing an abbreviated version) are from the early fourteenth century and have connections with the Cistercian House of Aberconwy in Gwynedd, North Wales.[55] The story itself also has some Celtic touches.[56] *De vera historia* picks up the history of Arthur after the final battle of Camlann. As the king is resting, a mysterious young man, armed with a poisoned spear, stabs him. Arthur asks to be taken to the isle of Avalon (here located in Gwynnedd), makes his final confession in the presence of the archbishop of London and the bishops of Bangor and Llandaff (Dubricius, archbishop of St David's, being temporarily indisposed). Arthur's corpse, embalmed, is taken to 'a certain small abbey dedicated to the Virgin Mary', but is too large to enter by the door: it is left outside on a bier, while inside the abbey the prelates perform a requiem service. A terrifying storm breaks out, and the abbey is enveloped by mist. By the time the air clears and the bishops return to the bier, the king's body is gone, though some say the bishops found a tomb, already sealed and solidly enclosed in one of the abbey's recesses.

Many of the additions in *De vera historia* (Arthur's confession, his last rites, the requiem mass) are of a religious nature and seem inspired by the desire to give Arthur a good end. The mysterious disappearance of Arthur's body, on the other hand, seems to be a back-formation designed to explain the present uncertainty about Arthur's death: 'great doubt concerning the truth arose among them . . . and even up to the present the place where King Arthur was to find his rest is guarded by clouds of unknowing'.[57] But what I think *De vera historia* most wants to say is that the abbey where Arthur wanted to be buried (and perhaps lies) is not Glastonbury but Aberconwy.[58] This would explain why Avalon is relocated to Gwynedd, and why the chapel to which Arthur is brought is 'dedicated to the honour of Holy Mary of God, the perpetual Virgin Mary', as was the Abbey at Aberconwy. This hypothesis would also give added point to the title: 'The *true* history' (as distinct from the false Glastonbury myth). Whatever the case may be, the chronicler of *De vera historia*, unlike the Glastonbury monks, was too committed to the 'Breton hope' to show us a corpse. Possibly, 'Arthur's tomb' can be found in a chapel in Gwynedd, but if so, the tomb was found already sealed: what, if anything, lies inside remains for ever mysterious.

III: Latin Arthurian Historiography at the End of the Middle Ages: 1350–1500

The vogue for universal histories lasted well into the Renaissance. Scotland's answer to Higden's *Polychronicon* was John of Fordun's *Chronica Gentis Scotorum* (*c*.1384) and its derivative, Walter Bower's *Scotichronicon* (1447).[59] Both combated the English foundation myth by propagating a myth that was just as fantastical but redounded to the greater glory of Scotland. According to Geoffrey's *HRB*, the Scots were descended from the Picts and the Irish. Ireland had been colonized by Partholaym, the leader of a group of exiles from Spain – hence the similarity between *Hiberia* (Spain) and *Hibernia* (Ireland). Partholaym and his companions had been sailing the seas in search of a land in which to settle, and the British king Gurguint Barbtruc had given them Ireland, which was then uninhabited. This particular 'history' suited the English Crown and was used throughout the period to justify English dominion over Scotland and Ireland.[60] John of Fordun and Walter Bowers countered Geoffrey's story with a different foundation myth: Scotland owes its name to the daughter of King Pharao of Egypt (named Scota) who married Gaithelos, a Greek prince who had fled his native country. The two migrate to Spain and their son, Hyber, colonizes an island that still carries his name (Hibernia). The Scottish characterization of King Arthur, the alleged conqueror of Scotland and Ireland, also puts the English in their place. Arthur was quite simply an illegitimate child (begotten out of wedlock), in contrast to his virtuous sister Anna who married Loth (a Scottish consul and lord of Lothian). As *HRB* confirms, she gave birth to two children. Since these children, Gawain and Mordred, were begotten in holy matrimony and Arthur was not, the crown really belonged to the former. So Mordred was well within his rights to rise up against Arthur as he did.

Obviously, this anti-English line on Mordred's rebellion did not go down well beyond the border, and within Scotland, too, many writers remained loyal to King Arthur.[61] In England, the model of history continued to follow *HRB*, often as mediated through Higden, though two trends become more pronounced towards the end of the Middle Ages. The first is the influence of Arthurian romances on the modelling of history; the second is the growing antiquarian interest in local history.

The local histories, which I shall consider first, require an adjustment in our expectations of the political relevance of the Arthurian legend. *HRB* obviously portrayed Arthur as a national hero, but it is a mistake to think that the ideological value of the Arthurian myth was solely a matter of *national* politics. For medieval historians, to think of Arthur as King of Britain also meant to imagine the role he might have played in the history of one's local town or city. Nicholas Cantelupe and John Rous (or Ross) were two fifteenth-century Englishmen who did just that.

Nicholas Cantelupe was at the time of his death (1441) prior of the Carmelite house of Northampton.[62] Earlier he had been a student in Cambridge, and it is probably in his student days that he wrote a history of Cambridge University: *Historiola de antiquitate et origine almae et immaculatae Universitatis Cantebrigiae*.[63] Its aim was to claim for Cambridge a more ancient origin than its rival, Oxford. Nicholas's case rested on the linguistic coincidence that Cambridge, Latin *Cantabrigia*, sounds like the region of Northern Spain called *Cantabria*. This suggested that Spaniards must have founded Cambridge, and the aforesaid episode of the Spanish refugee Partholaym in *HRB* helped to explain how. What Geoffrey of Monmouth had failed to mention, however, was that Partholaym had a brother, Cantebrus, heir of the Spanish state Cantabria. Cantebrus founded Cambridge, which was named after him, and then invited over his former teachers in Athens, Anaximander and Anaxagoras. Thus the University is founded, in the memorable year *anno a mundi creacione* 4321. After Greek and Roman times, Cambridge flourishes under some excellent lecturers such as Bede, John Scotus and Aldhelm.

King Arthur, too, contributes to Cambridge's success. In the year 529 Arthur appoints Kynoc[64] as Proctor of Cambridge University, and two years later he grants Cambridge a royal charter exempting the institution from royal taxes:

> This charter is written AD 531, on the seventh of April, in the city of London.
>
> And to give it great authority, King Arthur sent this charter to Kynot, the Proctor of the schools of the aforesaid city, through his nephew Gawain, renowned for his virtue.[65]

The charter is conveyed to Cambridge by Gawain, who is also employed as Arthur's messenger in *HRB* (where he delivers Arthur's challenge to Lucius Hiberius). Mordred's betrayal, however, does great damage to the University:

> But alas! After the death of the famous King Arthur, Cambridge, the city that was full of people, the mother of virtues, is widowed from her doctors because of the envy of warriors, the plundering of books, and the destruction of enemies. Thus the heinous Ambrones, the Picts and Saxons, whom that traitor Mordred had invited, destroy alike the Christ-loving students and the citizens of Cambridge with sword and fire, as wolves destroy sheep.[66]

The destruction of Cambridge is likened to that of ancient Jerusalem, lamented by the prophet Jeremiah in unmistakably similar words – 'Quomodo sedet sola *civitas plena populo! Facta est quasi vidua* domina gentium' (Lamentationes 1.1) – except that Nicholas has given contextual relevance to the image: 'facta est quasi vidua *a doctoribus*'. Happily, the University is restored to its former glory under King Ethelbert of Kent, and the privileges granted by Arthur are confirmed in further charters by King Cadwallader and Pope Sergius I, dated AD 689. In its own day, Nicholas' *Historiola* was a popular work (surviving in at least ten manuscripts and even inspiring a poem by John Lydgate), and all the evidence we have suggests that early readers took it seriously. Copies of Arthur's charter can be found in the University's official archives right up to the seventeenth century.

John Rous was a historian in Cantelupe's mould. Unlike Cantelupe, however, he had been a student at Oxford and was in later life a chantry priest at Guy's cliff (named after Guy of Warwick) just outside Warwick.[67] His local attachments to Oxford and Warwick explain some of his embellishments of *HRB* in his *Historia regum Angliae* (*c*.1486).[68] With regard to Oxford, John Rous rehearses a myth linking the history of Oxford University with that of a town west of Oxford named Cricklade, also spelt *Grekelade* in medieval documents. This last spelling suggested the false etymology 'load of Greeks', which in turn raised the question of how this load of Greeks ended up in Cricklade. To that question *HRB* held the answer. According to *HRB*, the Trojan leader Brutus had fled with Aeneas to Italy, and thence to Greece, where he discovered amongst the population many descendants of King Priam of Troy. With these Greeks Brutus had set forth on a westward journey, finally arriving in Britain, to which he gave his name. The Greeks (with various philosophers in tow) then founded Cricklade, and some time later Cricklade College transferred to Oxford (formerly called Memre or Bellesitus, and founded by Brutus' great-great-grandson, Mempric). In short, Oxford University was really much older than Cambridge.

The city of Warwick, too, is given an ancient history. Inspired by Higden, who had (not unreasonably) hailed the Roman city of Chester as another 'City of Legions', Rous insists that there had been several 'Cities of the Legion': Caerleon-on-Usk in Wales, Chester, and last but not least Warwick. The latter had been founded by Guithelin (who in *HRB* rules Britain after Gurguint Barbtruc), which explains why Warwick was once known as Caer-*leon* (< Guthe-*linus*). All this is confirmed by the authority of Gildas, who according to Rous was 'in his days the most erudite and respected of men and the principal chaplain of the great King Arthur'.[69] St Dubricius had been bishop at Warwick, and had built the chapel at Guy's cliff, where Guy of Warwick retired at the end of his chivalric career. During the political turmoil of Vortigern's rule, Dubricius fled from his beloved Warwick to his native Wales, became bishop of Llandaff and then archbishop of Caerleon-on-Usk, where of course he crowned Arthur. Rous gives as his source for this information David Llewellyn, treasurer of Llandaff Cathedral.[70] Arthur liberated Britain from the yoke of the Romans, and instituted the Round Table, choosing as one its knights Arthal (= Artgualchar, Earl of Warwick, briefly mentioned in *HRB* in the list of noblemen attending Arthur's Whitsuntide Feast). As in *HRB*, Arthur is said to have died in 542, but, thanks to some historians of Glastonbury Abbey, where Arthur lies buried, Rous is able to supply the exact date: 21 May.[71] Rous's final words about Arthur have a measured air that will not, by this stage, convince the modern reader: he had indeed been a great conqueror, but quite how many lands he had actually conquered is impossible to say.[72] The history closes with opportunistic praise of Henry VII, whose son, Arthur, Prince of Wales, promises to be another great King Arthur.

Devotion to the English Crown is clearly one motive behind Rous's *Historia regum Angliae*; local pride in Oxford and Warwick is another; but over and above these is Rous's fidelity to a model of history that can reconcile *HRB* with knowledge garnered from other sources. In this spirit, Rous introduces the Round Table, which, though absent in *HRB*, was ever-present in the romances, and hardened into fact when it was introduced first into the chronicle tradition (originally by Wace in his *Brut*, *c*.1155) and then into physical reality as the Winchester Round Table (probably commissioned by Edward I). Other authorities absorbed into Rous's history are the *Travels* of John Mandeville (hailed by Rous as an 'English knight and Doctor of Civil Law in the reign of Edward III'[73]) and a Treatise on Giants (perhaps derived from *De origine gigantum*[74]), both of which establish to Rous's satisfaction that there were indeed giants in days of old. Rous also uses John Hardyng's *Chronicle* (*c*.1460), which he quotes, for example, on the subject of Brutus' coat-of-arms and the foundation of a university by King Bladud in the town of Stamford, which 'as Merlion doth sey, / Had scholars full of great habilite'.[75]

One of the sources to be gradually absorbed into Latin historiography was French Arthurian romance. This phenomenon is of considerable interest, since it suggests that at least some medieval writers did not make the conceptual distinction – Latin chronicle is 'history' and vernacular romance is 'fiction' – that governs modern criticism of medieval Arthurian literature. In the English language, John Hardyng incorporates a summary of the Grail Quest in his fifteenth-century account of Arthur's reign. Scholars have looked for political contexts as a way of explaining Hardyng's use of the *Queste del saint graal*,[76] but his inclusion of romance material seems less remarkable in light of the French and Latin tradition, which had amalgamated romance and chronicle in comparable ways.[77] For example, a continuator of Robert of Avesbury's *Historia de gestis mirabilibus Edwardi III* traced Arthur's descent back to Joseph of Arimathea, and enlarged Loth's and Anna's progeny by adding Agravain, Gaheres and Gahereth.[78] This continuator must have read the Vulgate Cycle and thought it was history.

As a final example of the model-building that makes the Latin chronicle tradition so rewarding, I would mention Giovanni Boccaccio's *De casibus virorum illustrium* (translated as the *Fall of Princes* by John Lydgate, via Laurent de Premierfait's French translation). Boccaccio's Arthurian section begins with a rapid summary of Arthur's conquests, after which follows the foundation of the Round Table:

> Then so that their valour would not be attenuated by leisure, on the advice of Merlin the prophet, who flourished during that period of time, Arthur ordained what the English call the Round Table, to which he summoned, as if to a great feast, all those from amongst his nobility whom he knew to be excellent in arms and in morals.[79]

The 'official' explanation of the Round Table, given by Wace, is that Arthur founded it to create equality between the barons and so put an end to their arguments about precedence, but Boccaccio knew the French prose romances in which the invention of the Round Table is credited to Merlin. The influence of the romances is clearly confirmed by the code of chivalry which all knights of the Round Table swear to uphold:

> Thus all were bound by a supreme law not to lay aside one's arms, and to seek strange adventures, to protect the rights of the weak when called upon, to violate no one and not to harm each other, to fight for the welfare of one's companions, to lay down life for the fatherland, to seek nothing for oneself apart from honour, never on any account to break faith, to protect religion most assiduously, and to show hospitality to all.[80]

From romance we then return to chronicle summary. Arthur fights the Romans but has to abandon his campaign to deal with Mordred. That moment produces a breathless climax as Arthur pursues Mordred to the death:

> And when Arthur saw Mordred rushing about with renewed vigour and almost winning victory with his valour, he laid aside his fatherly affection, took his lance, and with the full force of his fresh horse rushed to meet Mordred as he was coming towards him, piercing the chest of the miserable wretch completely. But truly, not with impunity, for when the young man, struck down by deadly pain, had summoned all his remaining strength he struck the approaching king on the head with outstretched sword in such a way that the sword, with the helmet giving no protection, sank into the brain. The king then wheeled around on his horse; when he wrenched his lance from the dying man's chest, the wound is said to have been so wide that the setting sun could penetrate it with its rays. So Mordred died and ended his ill-starred presumption and life. But the king, feeling the end of his days, immediately jumped off his horse, boarded a ship, and, dying, ordered himself to be taken to the isle of Avalon.[81]

Behind this clearly lies the description of Arthur's death from the Vulgate *Mort Artu*:

> He was holding a thick strong lance, and he spurred on his hose as fast as it would gallop. Mordred, realizing that the king's only intention was to kill him, did not refuse battle but turned his head towards him; and the king, who was coming with all his strength, struck him so violently that he broke the links on his coat of mail and put the blade of his lance through his body. The story tells that when Arthur wrenched out the lance, a ray of sunlight passed through the wound so clearly that Girflet saw it. The local people said that this had been a sign of Our Lord's anger. When Mordred saw he was so badly injured, he was sure his wound was mortal; and he struck King Arthur so violently on the helmet that nothing could save him from feeling the sword in his skull.[82]

Thus Boccaccio weaves together romance and chronicle material. In turn, an Anglo-Latin chronicler (*c*.1400) followed Boccaccio's example and integrated Boccaccio's narrative into a fuller account of Arthur's reign, [83] mainly derived from Higden's *Polychronicon*. His ingenious compilation, *Cronicon de origine et rebus gestis Britanniae et Angliae*, survives in a late fifteenth-century manuscript, Oxford, MS Magdalen College, Lat. 72; it has never been edited and few people now read it.[84]

No doubt many other fascinating Latin Arthurian chronicles lie waiting to be rescued from obscurity, their neglect justifiable only by our own anachronistic expectations of what good 'histories' should be. By medieval standards, the Latin chroniclers we have considered wrote history as it should be written. To recall C. S. Lewis, 'A Model must be built which will get everything in without a clash; and it can only do this only by becoming intricate, by mediating its unity through a great, and finely ordered multiplicity.'

Notes

[1] P. G. Walsh and M. J. Kennedy (ed. and trans.), *The History of English Affairs: Book I* (Warminster, 1988). Quotations and translations will be from this edition unless otherwise indicated. For an edition and translation of the whole work see Richard Howlett (ed.), *Chronicles of the Reigns of Stephen, Henry*

II, and Richard I, vol. 1, RS 82 (London, 1884) and Joseph Stevenson (trans.), *The Church Historians of England* (London, 1956), vol. 4.

[2] See on this point Siân Echard, *Arthurian Narrative in the Latin Tradition* (Cambridge, 1998), pp. 78–9.

[3] William of Newburgh, *Historia rerum Anglicarum*, p. 30.

[4] William of Newburgh, *Historia rerum Anglicarum*, p. 30: 'porro ad ea quae vel ante ipsum vel in diebus ejus evenerunt taliter sua, quod utique facile poterat, temperavit figmenta ut congruam possent interpretationem recipere.' I have adapted Walsh and Kennedy's translation of this passage in order to provide a more literal one.

[5] William of Newburgh, *Historia rerum Anglicarum*, p. 32: 'ut ad Britonem illum in veritate spectare videatur quod Augusto Romano a poeta nobili adulator dicitur: "tibi serviet ultima Thule"'.

[6] For instance, as Alexander is begotten out of wedlock by Nectanebus, who sleeps with Olympia after assuming the shape of a dragon, so Arthur is conceived out of wedlock by Uther Pendragon, who sleeps with Ygerna after assuming the shape of her husband Gorlois.

[7] Henry of Huntingdon, *Historia Anglorum*, ed. and trans. Diana E. Greenway (Oxford, 1996). Quotations are from this edition. In the final colophon of *HRB*, Geoffrey himself refers to Henry of Huntingdon's history

[8] Robert Huntington Fletcher, *The Arthurian Material in the Chronicles, especially those of Great Britain and France* (Boston, 1906), p. 120.

[9] Neil Wright, 'The place of Henry of Huntingdon's *Epistola ad Warinum* in the text-history of Geoffrey of Monmouth's *Historia regum Britannie*: a preliminary investigation', in Gillian Jondorf and D. N. Dumville (eds), *France and the British Isles in the Middle Ages and Renaissance: Essays in Memory of Ruth Morgan* (Woodbridge, 1991), pp. 71–114.

[10] C. S. Lewis, *The Discarded Image: An Introduction to Medieval and Renaissance Literature* (Cambridge, 1964), p. 11.

[11] *Geoffrey of Monmouth: The History of the Kings of Britain. An Edition and Translation of the De gestis Britonum (Historia Regum Britanniae)*, ed. and trans. Michael J. Reeve and Neil Wright (Woodbridge, 2007), ch. 178: 'Set et inclitus ille rex Arturus letaliter uulneratus est; qui illinc ad sananda uulnera sua in insulam Auallonis euectus Constantino cognato suo et filio Cadoris ducis Cornubiae diadema Britanniae concessit anno ab incarnatione Domini .dxlii..'

[12] *HRB*, ch. 112: 'exitus eius dubius erit.'

[13] *HRB*, ch. 205: 'antequam tempus illud uenisset quod Merlinus Arturo prophetauerat'.

[14] Henry of Huntingdon, *Historia Anglorum*, p. 580 (trans. p. 581): 'Cumque insequeretur eum usque in Cornubiam cum paucis incidit super eum inter multos. Cumque se non posse reuerti uideret, dixit, "Vendamus socii mortes nostras. Ego enim iam caput nepotis et proditoris mei gladio auferam. Post quod mori delicisiosum est." Dixit. Et gladio per aciem uiam sibi parans in medio suorum Modredum galea arripuit, et collum loricatum uelut stipulam gladio resecauit. Inter eundem tamen et in ipso actu tot uulnera recepit quod et ipse procubuit. Mortuum tamen fuisse Britones parentes tui negant. Et eum uenturum sollempniter expectant.'

[15] See Wright, 'Place of Henry of Huntingdon's *Epistola*'.

[16] Two important correctives to the older view that Gerald had no truck with *HRB* are Julia Crick, 'The British past and the Welsh future: Gerald of Wales, Geoffrey of Monmouth and Arthur of Britain', *Celtica*, 23 (1999), 60–75, and Barbara Lynn McCauley, '"Giraldus "Silvester" of Wales and his *Prophetic History of Ireland*: Merlin's role in the *Expugnatio Hibernica*', *Quondam et Futurus*, 3–4 (1993), 41–62.

[17] The *Journey Through Wales* is Gerald's account of his tour of Wales to preach the crusade in 1188. There is an edition in vol. VI of *Giraldi Cambrensis Opera* (henceforth *Opera*), ed. J. S. Brewer, J. F. Dimock and G. F Warner, RS 21, 8 vols (London 1861–91), and a translation by Lewis Thorpe, *The Journey through Wales/The Description of Wales* (Harmondsworth, 1978).

[18] Gerald of Wales, *Itinerarium Kambrie* in *Opera*,VI, I.5: 'Contigit aliquando, spiritibus immundis nimis eidem insultantibus, ut Evangelium Johannis ejus in gremio poneretur: qui statim tanquam aves evolantes, omnes penitus evanuerunt. Quo sublato postmodum, et Historia a Galfrido Arthuro tractata, experiendi causa, loco ejusdem subrogata, non solum corpori ipsius toti, sed etiam libro superposito, longe solito crebrius et taediosius insederunt.' The translation is from Thorpe, *Journey*, p. 117.

[19] That the Gospel of St John was thought to be especially effective as demon-repellent is shown by Gerald's own *Gemma Ecclesiastica* (ed. *Opera,* II, I.48): 'Quia medicina est et phantasma fugat, praecipue Johannis initium' (It [i.e. the New Testament] is good medicine for the laity and drives away ghosts, especially the beginning of the gospel according to John) (trans. John J. Hagen, *Gerald of Wales: The Jewel of the Church* (Leiden, 1979), p. 99).

[20] Ed. and trans. A. B. Scott and F. X. Martin, *Expugnatio Hibernica: The Conquest of Ireland* (Dublin, 1978). The work tells the history of how Ireland was conquered, first by Gerald's own relatives, then by Henry II and Prince John. The text survives in two versions: the earliest, *c.*1189, dedicated to Count Richard, the second, datable ante 1218, entitled *Expugnatio Hibernica.*

[21] See Robert Bartlett, *Gerald of Wales: 1146–1223* (Oxford, 1982), pp. 63–4 and Ad Putter, 'Gerald of Wales and the prophet Merlin', *Anglo-Norman Studies*, 31 (2009), 90–103.

[22] *Itinerarium Kambrie*, in *Opera*, VI, II.8: 'Erant enim Merlini duo; iste qui et Ambrosius dictus est, quia binomius fuerat, et sub rege Vortigerno prophetizavit, ab incubo genitus, et apud Kaermerdyn inventus; unde et ab ipso ibidem invento denominata est Kaermerdyn, id est, urbs Merlini; alter vero de Albania oriundus, qui et Celidonius dictus est, a Celidonia silva in qua prophetizavit, et Silvester, quia cum inter acies bellicas constitutus monstrum horribile nimis in aera suspiciendo prospiceret, dementire coepit, et ad silvam transfugiendo silvestrem usque ad obitum vitam perduxit. Hic autem Merlinus tempore Arthuri fuit, et longe plenius et apertius quam alter prophetasse perhibetur.' Thorpe (trans.), *Journey*, pp. 193–4. The association of Merlin with Carmarthen is due to the folk etymology of Carmarthen < *caer* (town) + *Myrrdin* (Merlin).

[23] *Itinerarium Kambrie*, in *Opera* VI, II.2: 'Unde et libros egregios, quos de gestis Arthuri, et gentis suae laudibus, multos scripserat, audita fratris sui nece, omnes, ut asserunt, in mare projecit.' Thorpe (trans.), *Journey*, p. 259.

[24] *Itinerarium Kambrie*, in *Opera,* VI, II.2: 'Cujus rei causa, nihil de tanto principe in scriptis authenticis expressum invenies.'

[25] Christopher Brooke, 'The archbishops of St Davids, Llandaff and Caerleon-on-Usk', in N. K. Chadwick et al. (eds), *Studies in the Early British Church* (Cambridge, 1958), pp. 201–42.

[26] *HRB*, ch. 112: 'Delebitur iterum religio, et transmutacio primarum sedium fiet. Dignitas Lundoniae adornabit Doroberniam, et pastor Eboracensis septimus in Armorico regno frequentabitur. Meneuia pallio Vrbis Legionum induetur . . .'

[27] *HRB*, chs 156–8: 'Cum igitur sollempnitas Pentecostes aduenire inciperet, post tantum triumphum maxima laeticia fluctuans Arturus affectauit curiam ilico tenere regnique diadema capiti suo imponere . . . Venerunt ergo . . . trium etiam metropolitanarum sedium archipraesules, Lundoniensis uidelicet atque Eboracensis nec non et ex Vrbe Legionum Dubricius. Hic Britanniae primus et apostolicae sedis legatus . . . Beatus igitur Dubricius, in heremiticam uitam anhelans, sese ab archiepiscopali sede deposuit. In cuius loco sacratur Dauid auunculus Regis . . . In loco uero sancti Samsonis Dalensis archipraesulis destinatur Teliaus illustris presbiter Landauiae.'

[28] As suggested by Christopher Brooke, 'Geoffrey of Monmouth as historian', in C. N. L. Brooke et al. (eds), *Church and Government in the Middle Ages* (Cambridge, 1976), pp. 77–91.

[29] Various passages from Gerald's works pertaining to this episode have been collected and translated by H. E. Butler, *The Autobiography of Giraldus Cambrensis* (London, 1937), reissued with a guide to further reading by John Gillingham (Woodbridge, 2005), pp. 182–8.

[30] *De jure et statu Menevensis ecclesiae*, *Opera,* III, pp. 170–1: 'Sicque ordinatum a viris sanctis praedictis duobus fuerat, ut in occidentali insulae parte, quae et nunc adulterino vocabulo Wallia dicitur, proprie vero Kambria, a Kambro Bruti filio dicta, urbs Legionum metropolis fuerat, xii. suffrageneos

habens . . . et archiepiscopo sedis ejusdem Dubricio Davidi honorem cedente, et eodem Davide postea procurante, sedes metropolitica usque Meneviam est translata, quod a vate nostro Merlino longe fuerat in hunc modum ante praedictum: "Menevia pallio urbis Legionum induetur." Habuimus autem apud Meneviam urbis Legionum archiepiscopos successive xxv., quorum primus fuit Sanctus David, ultimus vero Sanctus Sampson, qui ingruente per Walliam icteritia clade in Armoricam Galliae Britanniam navigio se transtulit cum pallio nostro' (my translation). *De jure* (*c.*1218) is Gerald's fullest account of his campaign to restore St David's to metropolitan status.

[31] *De Invectionibus*, ed. W. S. Davies, *Y Cymmrodor*, xxx (London, 1920), p. 167.

[32] *De Jure*, pp. 166–7: 'respondit Giraldus, exponens ei quomodo per ultimum archiepiscopum Menevensem Sampsonem nomine, fugientem cladem ictericiam et ob hoc in Armoricam Britanniam transfretantem, metropolitica dignitas evanuit . . . Quo audito, papa respondit: "Quinimmo Eboracensis, ut fertur, fuerat archiepiscopus Sampson ille Dolensis." Ad quod Giraldus: "Immo quod noster fuerit et non aliunde Sampson ille, salva, pater, reverentia vestra, Dolenses etiam historiae contestantur . . . Eborancensis autem aequivocatio decepit, quoniam hoc eodem nomime quidam eorum archiepiscopus nuncupatus extiterat.'

[33] I refer to the facsimile edition (Graz, 1964) of Vincent's *Speculum* as printed by the Benedictines of Douai (Douai, 1624), 4 vols, III, pp. 799–801.

[34] W. P. Gerritsen gives a lucid account of the textual history of Vincent's Arthurian section in 'L'épisode de la guerre contre les Romains dans *La mort artu* néerlandaise', in *Mélanges de langue et de la littérature du Moyen Âge et de la Renaissance offerts à Jean Frappier* (Geneva, 1970), 2 vols, I, pp. 337–49. There is no full modern edition of the interpolated passages in Sigebert's chronicle. My quotations from Sigebert are taken from Gerritsen, with one correction (*omnia* for *omnis* – see n. 37) that is required by sense and confirmed by the printed edition by Jehan Petit (Paris, 1513), p. 28. Translations are mine.

[35] 'Nam si fidem narrationi illius historiae praebeamus, huic loco inserendi actus celeberrimi regis, qui post patrem suum Utherpendragon regnum Britanniae adeptus est. Sed quia in aliis historiis nullam de eo mentionem invenimus, et haec ipsa Britonum historia supputationem annorum quibus Arturus et multi alii regnaverunt vel aperte non dicit, vel omnis tacet, nec dubia pro veris affirmamus, nec historicam narrationem, quae nuper de Britannico in Latinum translata est, lectori subtrahimus.'

[36] The reason why later chroniclers knew the dates of popes and Roman emperors better than Geoffrey is that they had at their disposal a new research tool, the chronological table correlating reigns of popes and emperors. The Ourcamp interpolator was one of the first chroniclers to take advantage of this resource. See Anna-Dorothee v. den Brincken, 'Zur Herkunft und Gestalt der Martins-Chroniken', *Deutsches Archiv fur Erforschung des Mittelalters*, 37 (1981), 694–735 (704).

[37] 'Porro haec omni[a] ut supradiximus nullam fidei authorem videntur habere si cum caeteris historiis conferantur.'

[38] E.g., the Dutch poet Jacob van Maerlant translated Vincent's account of Arthur as part of his *Spiegel Historiael*: see Gerritsen, 'L'épisode'. In Latin, Vincent's most important follower is Martin of Troppau (Martinus Polonus), who in turn inspired the French Arthurian chronicler Jean d'Outremeuse. See Richard Trachsler, *Clôtures du cycle Arthurien* (Geneva, 1996), p. 267, and W.-V. Jkas, 'Martinus Polonus' *Chronicle of the Popes and Emperors*: a medieval bestseller and its neglected influence on medieval English chroniclers', *English Historical Review*, 116 (2001), 327–41.

[39] Ed. Henry Richards Luard, RS 95 (London, 1890), 3 vols. Quotations are taken from the translation by C. D. Yonge, *Matthew of Westminster: The Flowers of History* (London, 1853), 2 vols. For more discussion of the universal chronicle tradition in England with particular reference to Glastonbury, see the essay by Edward Donald Kennedy in this volume.

[40] *FH* I, p. 261: 'Boetius, exilio fatigatus, a [Theodoro] Gothorum rege perimitur. Eodem anno nunciatum est Arthuro, Scotos atque Pictos in urbe Aldclud Hoelum regem obsedisse . . .'

[41] *FH* I, p. 266: 'Sanctus Benedictus, secundum quosdam, ab hoc saeculo migravit ad Christum. Rex quoque Arthurus, partes Gallicanas suae ditioni subdere cupiens, parato navigio, Modredo nepoti suo custodiam totius Britanniae cum uxore sua commisit.'

[42] *FH* I, p. 265: 'Erat autem tunc Walwanius filius praedicti Loth, xii. annorum juvenis, Vigilio papae traditus ad nutriendum, a quo etiam [et] militiae cingulum accepit.'

[43] *FH* I, p. 269: 'occultavit se rex moribundus, ne casui tanto insultarent inimici amicique confusi molestarentur; unde, quoniam de morte Arthuri vel ejus sepultura nihil referunt historiae, gens Britonum ipsum adhuc vivere prae magnitudine dilectionis contendunt.'

[44] Both have been edited by Churchill Babington and J. R. Lumby, *Polychronicon Ranulphi Higden*, RS 41 (London, 1865–86), 9 vols. The most detailed study is John Taylor, *The Universal Chronicle of Ranulf Higden* (Oxford, 1966).

[45] Higden, *Polychronicon* V, p. 339.

[46] Higden, *Polychronicon* V, p. 336: 'sed fortassis mos est cuique nationi aliquem de suis laudibus attollere excessivis . . . Quod saepe contingit, sicut dicit Josephus, aut propter historiae decorem, aut propter legentium delectationem, aut ad proprii sanguinis extaltationem.'

[47] Higden, *Polychronicon* V, p. 330: '*Henricus, libro secundo*. Hoc anno . . . regnum West Saxonum incepit sub Cerdico et Kynrico filio suo.'

[48] Some manuscripts of the *Polychronicon* read *In chronicis Dunensis* ('In chronicles of Devon'). 'Devon' was often used to refer to Cornwall.

[49] Higden, *Polychronicon*: 'In quibusdam chronicis, legitur quod Cerdicus cum Arthuro saepius confligens, si semel vinceretur, alia vice acrior surrexit ad pugnam. Tandem Arthurus extaediatus, post vicesimum sextum annum adventus Cerdici, fidelitate sibi jurata, dedit ei Hampshiram et Somersetam, quam partem vocavit Westsexam.'

[50] See Neil Wright (ed. and trans.), *Gesta regum Britanniae* (Cambridge, 1991); also Rosemary Morris, 'The *Gesta regum Britanniae* of William of Rennes: an Arthurian epic?', *Arthurian Literature*, 6 (1986), 60–123.

[51] *Gesta regum Britannie*, VII.17–24:

. . . quia quantis fortis Achilles
Tersitem excedit, tantis prefertur Achilli
Laudibus Arturus. Cuius preconia uatis
Meonii condigna modis Eneidos auctor
Hystorie ueteris Anchise preposuisset,
Lucanusque grauis tacuisset Cesaris actus
Et ueteres Thebe caruissent perpete fama,
Si precessissent Arturi gesta poetas.

[52] *Gesta regum Britannie* IX.238–40:

. . . quem totus obhorret
Antipodum populus, cui morti clausa propheta
Merlino testante uia est, si credimus illi?

[53] *Gesta regum Britannie* IX.292–3: 'Uiuo rege tamen, cui mortis ianua clausa / Creditur, Arturo.'

[54] *Gesta regum Britannie* X.492–8:

Solis hec scribo Britannis,
Ut memores ueteris patrie iurisque paterni
Exiliique patrum propiique pudoris, anhelent
Uocibus et uotis et regnum restituatur
Antiquo iuri, quod possidet Anglicus hostis;
Neue male fidei posessor predia nostra
Prescribat sumatque bonas a tempore causas.

[55] Michael Lapidge's *editio princeps* (with translation) is based on these two manuscripts: 'An edition of *De vera historia de morte Arthuri*', *Arthurian Literature*, 1 (1981), 79–93. Several manuscripts have

been discovered since. See Lapidge, 'Additional manuscript evidence for *De vera historia de morte Arthuri*', *Arthurian Literature*, 2 (1982), 163–8 and Richard Barber, 'The manuscripts of the *Vera historia de morte Arthuri*', *Arthurian Literature*, 6 (1986), 163–4. Barber discusses manuscripts of *HRB* in which Geoffrey's paragraph on Arthur's death has been replaced by *De vera historia.*

[56] See Echard, *Arthurian Narrative*, pp. 81–2.

[57] 'inter eos magna uersatur ambiguitas . . . necnon adhuc presenti tempore [tenebris tenetur] ignorancie ubi rex Arthurus locus refrigerii sit sortitus.' The Gray's Inn MS reads 'tenebras cenantur'. Lapidge emended to 'tenebrae cernuntur' , before discovering MS Cotton Titus A. XIX (T) with its reading 'tenebris tenentur' (see Lapidge, 'Additional manuscript evidence'). The T reading is still problematic. Lapidge manages to make some sense of it, translating '(they) are held by shadows of ignorance (as to) where King Arthur was destined to find his place of rest', but needs to emend *locus* to *locum* in the process. My emendation gives better sense.

[58] An alternative hypothesis is that the author did not know of the Glastonbury exhumation or wrote his history before it (Echard, *Arthurian Narrative*, p. 81, n. 35).

[59] See John of Fordun, *Chronicle of the Scottish Nation*, trans. F. J. H. Skene and ed. W. F. H. Skene, Historians of Scotland, 4 (Edinburgh, 1872), and Walter Bower, *Scotichronicon*, ed. D. E. R. Watt et al. (Aberdeen, 1987–97), 9 vols. For recent discussion see Rhiannon Purdie and Nicola Royan (eds), *The Scots and Medieval Arthurian Legend* (Cambridge, 2005), especially the chapter by Juliette Wood, 'Where does Britain end: the reception of Geoffrey of Monmouth in Scotland and Wales', pp. 9–24.

[60] Gerald of Wales built his case that Henry II was the rightful overlord of Ireland on *HRB*, and Edward I and Edward III did the same with Scotland. On the Irish case see Gerald of Wales, *The History and Topography of Ireland*, trans. J. O'Meara, (Harmondsworth, 1982), p. 99; on the Scottish, see Bower, *Scotichronicon*, vol. VI, pp. 133–89 and Susan Kelly, 'The Arthurian material in the *Scotichronicon* of Walter Bower', *Anglia*, 97 (1979), 431–8.

[61] See Flora Alexander, 'Late medieval Scottish attitudes to the figure of King Arthur', *Anglia*, 73 (1975), 28–34.

[62] The following paragraphs draw on my article, 'King Arthur at Oxbridge: Geoffrey of Monmouth and Cambridge's Arthurian foundation myth', *Medium Aevum*, 72 (2003), 63–81. See also Alfred Hiatt, 'Forgery at the University of Cambridge', *New Medieval Literatures*, 3 (1999), 95–118, repr. in Hiatt, *The Making of Medieval Forgeries* (London, 2004).

[63] In *Thomae Sprotti Chronica*, ed. T. Hearne (Oxford, 1719), pp. 221–80. All references will be to Hearne's edition. Translations are my own. The only published translation is by Richard Parker, *History and Antiquities of the University of Cambridge* (London, 1721?), pp. 1–18.

[64] Perhaps read 'Kynot', who in *HRB* is promoted *ad altiorem dignitatem*, by which Geoffrey meant the archbishopric of Caerleon (*HRB*, p. 254).

[65] Cantelupe, *Historiola*, in *Thomae Sprotti Chronica*, p. 269: 'Scripta autem est cartula anno ab incarnacione Domini 531, septimo Aprilis in civitate Londoniensi. Et pro ampliori firmitate rex Arthurus transmisit cartulam praedictam Kynoto, rectori scolarium civitatis praedictae, per suum nepotem Walwanum probitate clarum.'

[66] Cantelupe, *Historiola*, in *Thomae Sprotti Chronica*, p. 269: 'Sed heu! civitas plena populo, mater virtutum, Cantebrigia post mortem incliti regis Arthuri bellancium invidiis, librorum direpcionibus, et hostium depraedacionibus facta est quasi vidua a doctoribus. Unde nefandi Ambrones, Picti & Saxones, quos proditor ille Modredus invitaverat, Christicolas studentes pariter & cives Cantebrigiae gladiis & flammis, ut lupi oves, exterminant.'

[67] On Rous's life and works see Nicholas Orme's entry in the *Oxford Dictionary of National Biography* (Oxford, 2004).

[68] John Rous, *Historia regum Angliae*, ed. Thomas Hearne (Oxford, 1716; 2nd edn, 1745). Quotations are from the second edition.

[69] Rous, *Historia regum Angliae*, p. 26, '. . . Gildam, virum diebus suis literatissimum et moribus excellenter pollentem magni regis Arturi praecipuum capellanum'.

[70] Rous, *Historia regum Angliae*, p. 45.

[71] Rous, *Historia regum Angliae*, p. 65.

[72] Rous, *Historia regum Angliae*, p. 159.

[73] Rous, *Historia regum Angliae*, p. 16.

[74] Ed. James P. Carley and Julia Crick, 'Constructing Albion's past: an annotated edition of *De Origine Gigantum*', *Arthurian Literature*, 13 (1995), 41–114.

[75] Rous, *Historia regum Angliae*, pp. 17–20.

[76] See Richard Moll, *Before Malory: Reading Arthur in Later Medieval England* (Toronto, 2003), p. 175.

[77] For French precedents see Trachsler, *Clôtures*, pp. 262–313.

[78] See Fletcher, *Arthurian Material*, p. 189.

[79] 'Ne ocio virtus marcesceret (ut fertur) Merlini vatis ea tempestate florentis consilio tabulam quam rotundam Angli vocitant ordinabat. Ad quam quasi ad conuiuium celebre quoscunque ex suis nobilioribus armis et moribus novit egregios convocauit.' Boccaccio's Arthurian section is cited from the edition by Henry Bergen in *Lydgate's Fall of Princes*, EETS e.s. 121–4 (London, 1924–7), 4 vols, IV, pp. 327–34. The English translations are my own.

[80] Boccaccio, *De casibus*: 'Fuit quippe omnibus lex praeccipua arma non ponere, monstruosa exquirere, ius debilium vocatos totis viribus defensare, violare neminem, se inuicem non laedere, pro salute amicorum pugnare, pro patria vitam exponere, sibi praeter honorem nil quaerere, fidem nullam ob causam infringere, religionem diligentissime colere, hospitalitatem quibuscunque pro facultatibus exhibere.'

[81] Boccaccio, *De casibus*: 'Quod cum . . . Arthurus videretque Modredum quasi renovatis viribus discurrentem, et fere sua virtute victoriam occupantem, deposita adfectione patria lancea sumta toto recentis equi impetu in venientem irruit, eiusque miserrimi pectus lancea tota transfodit. Verum non impune. Nam iuuenis letali dolore percitus quum se totum in vires collegisset extremas, propinquantis Regis erecto gladio caput adeo percussit, vt, non resistente galea ad cerebrum usque descenderet. Rex vero transuectus equo, dum lanceam ex pectore moribundi traheret aiunt adeo ampliatum vulnus ut cadens iam sol illud radiis penetraret. Modredus igitur illico decidens finem sumsit infaustae praesumtionis et vitae. Rex autem, iam dierum extremum sentiens, continuo prosiluit ex equo, nauimque conscendens iussit se moriturum transferri in insulam Auallonis.'

[82] *La Mort le roi Artu*, ed. Jean Frappier (Geneva, 1954), para. 190: 'Il tint un glaive gros et fort, et lesse corre tant comme il pot del cheval trere; et Mordrés, qui bien connoist que li rois ne bee fors a li ocirre, nel refusa pas, einz li adresce la teste del cheval, et li rois, qui li vient de toute sa force, le fiert si durement qu'il li ront les mailles del hauberc et li met par mi le cors le fer de son glaive; et l'estoire dit que après l'estordre del glaive passa par mi la plaie uns rais de soleill si apertement que Girflet le vit, dont cil del païs distrent que ce avoit esté sygnes de corrouz de Nostre Seigneur. Quant Mordrés se vit si navré, si pense bien qu'il est navrez a mort; si fiert le roi Artu si durement el hiaume que riens nel garantist qu'il ne li face sentir l'espee jusqu'au test.' The translation is by James Cable, *The Death of Arthur* (Harmondsworth, 1971), p. 220.

[83] Daniela Delcorno Branca has pointed out the English chronicler's debt to Boccaccio in '"De Arturo Britonum rege": Boccaccio fra storiografia e romanzo', *Studi sul Boccaccio*, 19 (1990), 151–90 (179, n. 63).

[84] As far as I am aware the only recent brief mention of it (apart from Delcorno Branca: see n. 83) is by Edward Donald Kennedy, 'Generic intertextuality in the English *Alliterative Morte Arthure*: the Italian connection', in Norris J. Lacy, ed., *Intertextuality in Medieval Arthurian Literature* (New York, 1996), pp. 41–56.

6

GLASTONBURY

Edward Donald Kennedy

In the Middle Ages Glastonbury was surrounded by marshes that made it seem like an island, and Welsh tradition may have long associated it with Avalon, the Celtic otherworld to which King Arthur was taken for the healing of his wounds. Arthur had been associated with Glastonbury at least as early as *c.*1150 when the monks at the abbey commissioned Caradoc of Llancarfan to write a *Vita* of St Gildas in which Arthur rescued Guenevere when she was held captive there by the king of Somerset.[1] The Arthurian associations became better known when in 1191 monks at the abbey discovered what were supposedly the bodies of Arthur and Guenevere. Shortly thereafter, in the first decade of the thirteenth century, the first redaction of the French prose Grail romance *Perlesvaus* appears to have been composed there: a colophon in two of the manuscripts says that its Latin source was found in the Isle of Avalon in a holy religious house (*une sainte meson de religion*); and at one point in the romance, Lancelot visits Guenevere's tomb at Avalon, an apparent allusion to the discovery of her body there in 1191.[2] By the mid-thirteenth century some at the abbey were claiming that Joseph of Arimathea, who in the Bible had provided the tomb for Christ's body and who in the French Vulgate *L'Estoire del saint graal* had brought the Grail to Britain, had established a church there in apostolic times and was buried at some unknown spot there.[3] Moreover, according to John of Glastonbury's fourteenth-century *Cronica sive antiquitates Glastoniensis ecclesie*, Arthur was descended from the family of Joseph through his mother Igerne, a genealogy that would be repeated in anonymous comments added to the end of a manuscript of Robert of Avesbury's mid-fourteenth-century chronicle *Historia de mirabilibus gestis Edwardi III*.[4]

The association of both Arthur and Joseph with the abbey was encouraged at different periods by monks at Glastonbury and perhaps more significantly by English kings, notably Henry II and Edward I, who in the twelfth and thirteenth centuries were interested in Arthur's relation to Glastonbury, and Henry V, who in the fifteenth century was also interested in Joseph's association with it. There were contrasts too between popular and scholarly acceptance of their association with the abbey: the scholars who wrote the chronicles accepted Arthur's burial at the abbey more readily than they accepted Joseph's association with it. In contrast, much popular sentiment reflected the belief that Arthur had never died but accepted Joseph's establishment of a church at Glastonbury and his bringing the Grail there. Joseph's activities in Britain were ignored by most who wrote the chronicles, the most notable exception being the scholar(s) who wrote one of the chronicles known as a Latin *Brut*, which had fairly wide circulation and which appears to have been written as much to present Lancastrian propaganda as to present a history of Britain.

The discovery at Glastonbury in 1191 of what was claimed to be Arthur's tomb was a significant event. Throughout much of the Middle Ages people debated whether Arthur had ever lived, with those on the Continent frequently dismissing the stories about him as fictitious and probably most in Brittany and in England believing that he had been a great king of the Britons. Even among those who believed that he lived, however, there was debate over whether he had ever died. Orally circulated legends maintained that he had been taken to Avalon for the healing of his wounds and that he would some day return to restore people of Briton descent to power. William of Malmesbury, writing in his *Gesta regum Anglorum* in 1125, believed that Arthur had once lived but that he should be the subject of 'veraces historiae' (reliable history) rather than the 'fallaces fabulae' (false tales) spread by the people of Brittany. William had to admit, however, that the tomb of Arthur had never been found and that old tales still predicted his return.[5] About ten years later Geoffrey of Monmouth's *Historia regum Britannie* (*c.*1136/8), supposedly a translation into Latin prose of a previously unknown ancient book written in the Briton language, seemed to many to fulfil William of Malmesbury's hope that Arthur would be remembered in a reliable history.

Through Geoffrey's *Historia*, discussed elsewhere in this book,[6] Arthur's conquest of much of the western world became known throughout Europe, and the book appears to have been accepted by most in England as authentic. Geoffrey had endeavored to make his account of Arthur seem plausible, with even Arthur's killing of the giant of Mont Saint Michel seeming not too far-fetched to an audience familiar with the story of David and Goliath and with Merlin's deeds being those of an engineer and a physician rather than those of a wizard.[7] An implausibility remained, however, for Geoffrey incorporated into his account the implication that Arthur had never died; in the *Historia*, in the year 542, Arthur, although described as being mortally wounded, is nevertheless taken to the isle of Avalon for the healing of his wounds. This conclusion did nothing to solve a problem expressed earlier by William of Malmesbury: the tomb of Arthur was still nowhere to be seen and the Bretons would still talk of his return.

Arthur, Geoffrey says, went to Avalon, and since Avalon had been associated with Glastonbury, it was a logical place for Arthur's body to have been discovered. Gerald of Wales, in a work on kingship known as *De principis instructione*, written *c.*1193/5, shortly after the discovery of Arthur's tomb, includes the following account of Glastonbury:

> What is now known as Glastonbury used in ancient times to be called the Isle of Avalon. It is virtually an island, for it is completely surrounded by marshlands. In Welsh it is called 'Ynys Avallon', which means the Island of Apples . . . After the Battle of Camlan, a noblewoman called Morgan,

> who was the ruler and patroness of these parts as well as being a close blood-relation of King Arthur, carried him off to the island now known as Glastonbury, so that his wounds could be cared for. Years ago the district had also been called 'Ynis Gutrin' in Welsh, that is the Island of Glass, and from these words the invading Saxons later coined the place-name Glastingebury.[8]

Thus Giraldus gives a place in Celtic myth a geographical location, and drawing upon either Celtic tradition or Geoffrey's *Vita Merlini* (rather than the *Historia*) brings Morgan le Fay into the story.[9] The island of Avalon to which Morgan le Fay took Arthur to heal his wounds was Glastonbury. Even those unfamiliar with Giraldus' account would have identified Glastonbury as Avalon after Arthur's body was discovered there.[10]

A monastery had been located at Glastonbury probably as early as the seventh century.[11] Although before the Norman conquest it had allegedly been the wealthiest monastery in England, it had fallen on hard times after 1066 since the Normans did not have much interest in monasteries that claimed to be burial grounds for Anglo-Saxon saints. Moreover, during the early post-Conquest period it had also had weak abbots and its estates had become impoverished. It fell on even harder times on 25 May 1184 when the church and monastery were destroyed by fire, after which it needed funds to rebuild its abbey.[12] One way for a monastery to increase its wealth was to become a place that pilgrims would visit; and during the twelfth and thirteenth centuries many monasteries, not just Glastonbury, rewrote their histories, exaggerating their antiquity in order to encourage pilgrims to visit and patrons to make contributions.[13]

The monks at Glastonbury had been fortunate in the late twelfth century because Henry II had been interested in their abbey and, concerned about its financial state, had given it considerable support.[14] Thanks to the king, the monks had done well with raising funds to rebuild the abbey destroyed by the fire, but in July 1189, before much reconstruction had been completed, Henry II died. His successor, Richard I, although apparently interested in Arthurian legends,[15] turned his attention to raising money for a crusade to the Holy Land rather than for Glastonbury. Nobles followed his lead and stopped contributing to the abbey.[16] The monks needed another source of funds.

The monks discovered the bodies of Arthur and Guenevere in the grounds of their monastery in 1191, two years after Henry II's death. Gerald of Wales presents the earliest account of the discovery in his *De principis instructione*: their grave was identified by an inscribed leaden cross, which Giraldus himself had seen.[17] The sixteenth-century antiquarian John Leland also saw this cross,[18] and the late sixteenth- to early seventeenth-century antiquarian William Camden published its inscription in the 1590 edition of his *Britannia,* and then a drawing of the cross in the 1607 edition. The cross, no longer extant, was apparently last seen in the early nineteenth century when Sharon Turner in the third edition of his *History of the Anglo-Saxons* (1820) reported it was in the hands of the chancellor of Wells Cathedral.[19] Although the phrasing of the inscription of the cross varies in different accounts, the one given on Camden's illustration is: 'Hic iacet sepultus inclitus rex arturus in insula avalonia'

(Here lies buried the renowned King Arthur in the island Avalon).[20] The cross, whose length scholars have estimated to have been from 6⅞ inches to a foot,[21] must have looked quite ancient to people in the twelfth century. Judging from the illustration in Camden's *Britannia*, its lettering, although not of the fifth or sixth centuries, was of a style used in the tenth century rather than the twelfth. As C. A. Ralegh Radford has speculated, the cross could have been created in the tenth century, for at that time graves at the abbey had been dug up and raised, and it is possible that a tenth-century cross was made to replace an original monolith possibly destroyed when the graves were disturbed.[22]

On the other hand, it could have been a twelfth-century forgery. The monks probably would not have known what fifth-century letters looked liked since few manuscripts survived from that period, but a tenth-century style of lettering would have looked sufficiently old in the twelfth century. They would have had access to tenth-century documents whose style they could have imitated. Both Aelred Watkin and Stephen Morland find the antiquity of the cross suspect since the adjective 'inclitus' appears to have been first used to describe Arthur in Geoffrey of Monmouth's *Historia*.[23] Thus the lead cross could be a twelfth-century attempt to produce an object that looked as if it belonged to an earlier period.

Some, even in the Middle Ages, suspected that Henry II had suggested that the monks look for Arthur's body. In his *De principis instructione*, Giraldus Cambrensis writes that before his death Henry II told the monks that a Welsh bard had said that Arthur's body could be found at Glastonbury and that Henry suggested that the monks look for Arthur's tomb. [24] Henry would have had reason to be interested in the Arthurian legend. Besides the apparent popularity of stories associated with Arthur at Henry's court,[25] Henry's problems governing the Welsh would have been reason enough for him to be interested. Many Welsh anticipated Arthur's return from Avalon and expected him to lead them once again to power. Henry may have wanted to eliminate the hope that Arthur would return by proving that he was dead. William of Malmesbury had said that the location of Arthur's tomb was unknown and that the British looked for his return; it would therefore surely have been helpful if a grave were discovered, and for that reason Henry may have asked the monks at Glastonbury to dig around and see what they could find.

Eighty-seven years after Glastonbury became known as the burial place of King Arthur, it received further publicity in 1278 when Edward I and his queen had the bodies moved to the front of the great altar of the abbey. That is the spot that is marked by a plaque today at Glastonbury Abbey. Edward, like Henry, was trying to impose English rule on the Welsh and wanted to emphasize that Arthur was dead and therefore unable to lead them back to power.[26] Moreover, he had another reason to be interested in the Arthurian legends: according to Geoffrey of Monmouth, Arthur had conquered Scotland, and Arthur's control of that country was one of the bases for Edward's claim to England's having hegemony over it.

The discovery of the tomb permitted the scholars who wrote chronicles to modify Geoffrey's *Historia* with information that had not been available to him. This addition was a significant exception to their usual way of incorporating Geoffrey's work into their accounts. Although they often condensed or summarized the *Historia* or expanded it through the addition of speeches for the characters, for the most part they did not make major changes in the plot of Geoffrey's Arthurian story and repeated it for at least the next 350 years. This would have been due to the English chroniclers' desire to preserve Geoffrey's story as history. Their view of King Arthur was different from that of chroniclers on the Continent, who tended to dismiss Geoffrey's account as fiction. Being conquered by the British was generally not a part of French historical tradition except for chronicles produced in Brittany, and similarly Italians, such as Boccaccio, found it difficult to believe that the British had conquered the Romans.[27] Although some in England, such as William of Newburgh and Ranulph Higden, dismissed Geoffrey's *Historia* as an insult to the honorable field of history, most English chroniclers seem to have accepted it as historically true;[28] and while French writers of the prose romances freely intermingled romance and chronicle elements, in England most chroniclers kept Geoffrey's account free of influence from romances and generally did not modify the basic events of the account.[29] Some, however, must have found Arthur's disappearance to Avalon, to use a modern critical term, 'fictive' to say the least. This event belonged among the fables of the Bretons that William of Malmesbury had said were circulating, and it must have been an embarrassment to those who were presenting the story as historically true. The discovery of his body at Glastonbury would have been a godsend.

Many of the chroniclers who wrote in the vernacular and in Latin thus emended Geoffrey's account by adding the information that Arthur had been buried at Glastonbury. An early sign of the wish to modify Geoffrey's conclusion to his story of Arthur occurs in the first adaptation of an Arthurian chronicle into English, Laȝamon's *Brut*. This work has been dated between 1189 and 1216,[30] and there is a good chance that this writer who lived in western England, not too far from Glastonbury and who, he says, traveled far to gather evidence for his book, knew of the discovery of Arthur's tomb. Laȝamon concludes his Arthurian account with Arthur's being taken to Avalon, but he modifies a statement in his primary source, Wace's *Roman de Brut*: Wace had said that the Britons believe that Arthur is still in Avalon 'awaited by the Britons, as they say and believe, and will return and may live again'; people will always doubt whether Arthur is alive or dead.[31] Laȝamon's version is significantly different: 'But while wes an witeȝe Mærlin ihate; / he bodede mid worde – his quides weoren soðe – / þat an Arður sculde ȝete cum Anglen to fulste'.[32] [Once there was a wise man named Merlin; he said – and his words were true – that an Arthur will yet come to help the English.] Laȝamon's words suggest a possible change in attitude toward the legend of Arthur's return: Laȝamon does not say 'Arthur will return' but 'an Arthur'. The significance of the statement lies in its implicit acknowledgment that Arthur is dead but that someday another man as great as Arthur – another Arthur – will arise to restore his people to power. The other significant feature of those final words is that, according to La3amon, the people 'an Arthur' will help are the English, not the Britons or Welsh.[33] His statement points toward the English appropriation of the Arthurian legend.[34]

Other chroniclers writing in both English and in Latin went further than La3amon in emending Geoffrey's account and wrote that Arthur was buried in Glastonbury. The metrical chronicle attributed to Robert of Gloucester (*c.*1300), for example, is the earliest chronicle written in English to incorporate Geoffrey's account of the British kings into the whole history of England. This chronicle points out that Arthur's bones were found at Glastonbury and they lie in a fine tomb there. Arthur, Robert asserts, was 'in cornwaile to deþe . . . was ydo' [killed in Cornwall].[35] Similarly, Castleford's Chronicle says that after receiving deadly wounds in his final battle against Mordred, 'he went, alls for a quile, / To duel in Auolones hile, / þarin for to warisse his wondes' [he went for a while to linger in Avalon's hill to care for his wounds] but adds 'certes, he lifede bot schort stondes' [certainly he lived but a short time] and was buried with great honor at Glastonbury.[36] Although both of Robert Mannyng's Anglo-Norman sources, the chronicles of Wace and Pierre Langtoft, tell of Arthur's survival in Avalon, Mannyng says that Arthur 'was born tille Auiloun' but 'he was so wonded þat him burd die' [he was taken to Avalon but he was so wounded that he had to die] .[37] Some English chronicles like the fourteenth-century *Short Metrical Chronicle* and the revised Yorkist version of the fifteenth-century metrical chronicle of John Hardyng do not even mention Avalon but simply say that Arthur was buried at Glastonbury.

The vernacular chronicles were intended to reach a generally unlearned audience. The discovery of Arthur's tomb would have seemed even more important to the chroniclers who wrote in Latin, the language of historical truth and scholarship. In fact, the story of Arthur's return probably suggested to some of the clerics writing the chronicles uncomfortable analogies with the story of Christ. Thus it is not surprising to find that many Latin chroniclers, even while accepting most of Geoffrey's history, changed Geoffrey's conclusion by saying that Arthur was buried at Glastonbury. The early part of one of the chronicles entitled *Flores historiarum*, now attributed to Matthew Paris, rationalizes Arthur's disappearance by saying that he went for the healing of his wounds to the isle of Avalon, 'which is now called Glastonbury' [quae nunc Glastonia dicitur]; the dying king kept himself out of sight so that his enemies might not gloat and his friends not grieve. Because of this, the Britons maintain he is alive. The chronicle later adds that Arthur's bones were discovered at Glastonbury.[38] Others, like the fourteenth-century chronicler Thomas Sprott, simply say that Arthur died. The anonymous *Eulogium historiarum* follows Geoffrey's account with some modifications from La3amon and the French Prose *Brut*, but then, contrary to all three sources, announces that Arthur was not just wounded but was dead and buried in a tomb like any mortal and tells of the discovery of the tomb at Glastonbury during the reign of Richard I. He cites the inscription on the tomb as 'Hic jacet inclytus rex

Arthurus a Mordredo proditore occisus'. There are similar accounts in the chronicles of Joannes Historici, Ranulph Higden, Richard of Cirencester, Ralph of Coggeshall, and Adam of Domerham.[39] The Scots, as might be expected, tended to be critical of Geoffrey of Monmouth since he had presented Arthur as conqueror of Scotland. They do not follow Geoffrey's account closely, but two major ones, the fifteenth-century chronicle of Walter Bower and the early sixteenth-century chronicle of John Major, say that Arthur is buried at Glastonbury.[40]

Even after the discovery of the tomb, however, accounts of his being taken to Avalon continue to circulate in a number of chronicles. Chronicles, such as the Anglo-Norman chronicle of Pierre Langtoft and the Latin chronicles of Ralph Diceto and Gervase of Canterbury continued to tell of Arthur's journey to Avalon and said nothing about his burial at Glastonbury. The most notable chronicles to suggest Arthur's survival in Avalon were the Anglo-Norman and English versions of the Prose *Brut*, the most popular secular work produced in England in the Middle Ages. The Prose *Brut* covered the history of the island from its legendary founding throughout the Middle Ages, with continuations added to cover fairly recent times. The Anglo-Norman versions, first written in the late thirteenth century, survive in over fifty manuscripts, and only the oldest version has recently been published.[41] It was translated at least twice into English, the first version appearing at about 1400, and it survives in at least 175 English manuscripts.[42] Most people in England in the later Middle Ages who knew anything about King Arthur got this information from some version of the Prose *Brut*. In this work, Arthur becomes more of a Christian king fighting the pagans than he was in Geoffrey's account, but for the most part the chronicle's account of British history follows Geoffrey closely. As in Geoffrey's *Historia*, Arthur is unlike the other kings in the chronicle, because it is uncertain that he dies: as Tamar Drukker points out, 'when he dies he seems to be spirited away . . . his body is never found and he has neither tomb nor shrine'.[43] This popular chronicle continued to tell of Arthur's being taken to Avalon and repeats Wace's statement that people 'weten nouȝ wheþer þat he leueþ or is dede'. It would have reinforced for many the legend of Arthur's survival and future return.[44]

Much evidence attests to the refusal of many to believe that Arthur had died and their rejection of the archaeological discovery at Glastonbury. Stories of his being alive circulated orally, of his living in a fairy palace, for example, on Mount Etna, in a hollow hill in England, near Mont de Chat in Savoy, on an island in the Mediterranean, in the depths of the sea, on the shores of the Red Sea, in India, and in a paradise in the Far East.[45] Gerald of Wales, in his *Speculum ecclesie*, a work written twenty-five years after his earlier reference to the discovery of Arthur's tomb in his *De principis instructione*, tells of his death again, this time saying that Morgan buried the corpse in a churchyard on the Isle of Avalon, which he identifies as Glastonia, but the credulous Britons invented the story of his being taken to Avalon to have his wounds healed, and as a result they really expect him to come back, just as the Jews expect their Messiah to return.[46] Although Robert of Gloucester tells of Arthur's tomb at Glastonbury, he also says that the Britons and Cornish still believe that Arthur will return; and Robert Mannyng, while maintaining that Arthur was dead, reports that the Britons refuse to believe this and 'loude lie' [loudly lie] in proclaiming that he is alive.[47] The *Flores historiarum* also says that the Britons believe that he is still alive.[48] In the early fifteenth century, John Lydgate laments Arthur's death in *Fall of Princes*, but reports that the Britons believe he is living in a fairy land and will return to reign in Britain.[49] Sir Thomas Malory, while telling us at the end of his *Morte Darthur* that Arthur is buried 'in a chapell beside Glassyngbyry', nevertheless adds that many believe that Arthur 'shall com agayne' and says that there is written on his tomb 'Hic iacet Arthurus, Rex quondam Rexque futurus' [Here lies Arthur, the once and future king],[50] an inscription whose variant appears in the short chronicle *Arthur* as well as the Scottish chronicles of Walter Bower and John Major.[51] Thus while there was probably general scholarly acceptance of the discovery of Arthur's tomb, there was considerable popular rejection of it.[52]

Valerie Lagorio's article 'The evolving legend of St Joseph of Arimathea' discusses the impact that the legend of Joseph of Arimathea had upon English literature and history.[53] The legend seems to have originated in a romance about the early history of the Grail written by Robert de Boron in the late twelfth century. Although Robert, writing in verse, would have intended the work as a fiction that, along with its continuations, presented the chivalry of the Round Table corresponding to the society of Christ and his disciples,[54] it began to be taken seriously as history by some in the thirteenth and fourteenth centuries, particularly after Robert's account had been developed into the long romance, *L'Estoire del saint graal*, which served as the introductory romance of the Vulgate Cycle.[55] The first appearance of the story of Joseph written in English was the verse Joseph of Arimathea, now dated *c.*1400. Described by David A. Lawton as a 'homiletic romance',[56] it was apparently written independently of the Glastonbury tradition. The *Estoire* was translated into English *c.*1425 by Harry Lovelich, the skinner of London.[57] Neither of these works seems to have circulated widely. The legend of Joseph was, as Lagorio points out, a 'slowly' evolving legend, that reached its height in the fifteenth and sixteenth centuries,[58] and it continued into modern times when pilgrims would visit Glastonbury Abbey and worship at the spot where an ancient Christian church had supposedly been built. In early versions of the legend, Joseph's visit occurred in AD 63 or 64; but by the fifteenth century, it occurred much earlier, in AD 31, thus making Britain one of the first nations to have been visited by Christian missionaries. Glastonbury considered itself Roma Secunda.[59]

As James Carley and Valerie Lagorio have pointed out, there have been a number of attempts to explain why the story of Joseph of Arimathea did not generate as much interest as the discovery of Arthur's tomb: the abbey's financial and political security was greater in the thirteenth century than it had been in the late twelfth and so there was no urgent economic reason for publicizing the legend of Joseph. The abbot from 1342–75 seems to have had no interest in the story of Joseph or in the Arthurian legends, and it was not until the late fourteenth century that John Chinnock, abbot from 1375–1420, began to exploit the story of the story of Joseph.[60] Chinnock didn't know where to excavate for Joseph's bones, so decided to rededicate a decayed chapel full of unidentified bones to the saint.[61] Chinnock's interest led to the legend's being presented before four church councils, those of Pisa (1409), Constance (1417), Pavia-Siena (1424) and Basel (1434), at which it was argued that the church in Britain had an antiquity on a par with that of the traditional four-nation division of Italia, Germania, Gallia, and Hispania.[62] That the councils took no action on the matter and did not decide whether the story should be considered true or not indicates that there was considerable doubt among scholars of the church on the matter. The Glastonbury monks may have been troubled too by the unorthodox nature of the Grail story, its associations with the world of romance rather than with sacred Scripture. Moreover, as Charles T. Wood points out, in light of Joseph's role in the crucifixion, the monks may have had religious scruples about exploiting the story.[63]

Although the discovery of Arthur's body at Glastonbury had been widely accepted by the chroniclers, the story of Joseph of Arimathea's establishing a church there was not. While Lagorio persuasively argues for the importance of the legend, she could find little about Joseph of Arimathea in the English chronicles outside of those produced at Glastonbury abbey. Most chronicles repeated Geoffrey's account, also found in Bede, of the first missionaries, Faganus and Duvianus sent by Pope Eleutherius during the reign of the British King Lucius in the second century.[64] The story of Joseph's arrival at Glastonbury first occurs in a late twelfth- or thirteenth-century redaction of William of Malmesbury's *De antiquitate Glastoniensis ecclesiae* that William had originally written *c.*1130. William had said that a wattle church had been built at Glastonbury by missionaries sent by Pope Eleutherius in AD 166, the approximate time when, according to Bede and Geoffrey of Monmouth, the Britons were Christianized. William added, with skepticism, that some said it was actually built by disciples of Christ.[65] Probably sometime in the early thirteenth century, interpolations were added to William's account that indicated that St Philip appointed Joseph of Arimathea to be head of twelve disciples that he sent to Britain from the Continent. The angel Gabriel instructed them to build a church in honor of the Virgin Mary.[66] The church died out, however and was later restored during the reign of King Lucius by Eleutherius's missionaries. The redactor added later in the opening chapter allusions to Arthur, Gawain, Lancelot, Galahad and the Holy Grail,[67] which were derived from the early thirteenth-century French Vulgate prose romances *Estoire del saint graal*, the *Lancelot*, and the *Queste del saint graal*. Later John of Glastonbury, in his *Cronica sive antiquitates Glastoniensis ecclesie*, probably written in the 1340s,[68] included material from the *Estoire* in his history of the Abbey and, like the interpolator of William of Malmesbury's history, mentions the quest for the Grail in King Arthur's time.[69] John did not say that Joseph had brought the Grail, with its fictive associations with romance, to Britain, but rather two vessels (*fascula* [sic]), one containing the sweat and the other containing the blood of Christ,[70] relics that might be sanctioned by the church. Joseph's vessel containing the blood of Christ, however, could easily be associated with the Grail, since in the *Estoire* the Grail was a vessel (*escüele*, or a dish, not a cup or chalice) containing the blood of Christ. The identification of the two objects is implied when John later refers to the quest in King Arthur's time as the 'quest for the vessel which is *there* called the Holy Grail [emphasis mine]'.[71] Others made the identification more explicit. Malory, for example, wrote at the conclusion to his book of Tristram: 'Here folowyth the noble tale off the Sankegreall, whyche called ys the holy vessel and the sygnfycacion of blyssed bloode off Oure Lorde Jesu Cryste, whyche was brought into thys londe by Joseph off Aramathye'.[72] This was information not in Malory's source, the Vulgate *Queste del saint graal*, since the Grail there was associated with the body of Christ rather than the blood. Malory's statement reflects what must have been popular interpretation of the nature of one of the vessels that Joseph had brought with him, or the statement could reflect the influence of another of his sources, the *Perlesvaus*, which on its opening page identifies the Grail as a vessel containing the blood of Christ that was in the keeping of Joseph of Arimathea.

Although John of Glastonbury's account of Joseph became a source at the end of the fifteenth century for Capgrave's saint's life of St Joseph, which appeared in his the third and final edition of *Nova legenda Angliae*,[73] the only other references to the story in chronicles that Lagorio found was a fifteenth-century one sentence interpolation into a manuscript of Robert of Gloucester's chronicle that referred to Joseph of Arimathea having lived at Glastonbury in Christ's day and the fifteenth-century verse chronicle of John Hardyng.[74] There were, however, several others.

Most of these are interpolations into individual manuscripts, like the one Lagorio cited in the manuscript of Robert of Gloucester's chronicle. One is a brief reference in the anonymous *Chronicon Angliæ Petriburgense*, under the year 1367, that notes 'The bodies of Joseph of Arimathea and his companions were found at Glastonbury'.[75] Another is an addition to one manuscript of the previously mentioned *Flores historiarum* of Matthew Paris, Lambeth Palace 1106: it is a paragraph inserted between the years AD 73 and 74 [sic] and repeats John of Glastonbury's account of Joseph's having brought to the isle of Avalon two *vascula* containing the blood and sweat of Christ.[76] Another reference is found in Lambeth Palace MS 84, a manuscript of the English Prose *Brut*, compiled in the late fifteenth century. This manuscript, as Lister Matheson has shown, incorporates into the English Prose *Brut* material from the Arthurian prose romances as well as from Ranulph Higden's *Polychronicon*, saints' legends, and the Constance and Havelok stories.[77] The Arthurian material that was added comes ultimately from the Vulgate *Estoire* and *Merlin* (and possibly directly from their Middle English translations).[78] The *Brut* in Lambeth MS 84 tells of Arthur's journey to Avalon, but also indicates that although the Britons hope that Arthur will return, he died and was buried at Glastonbury. It also says that Joseph was buried at Glastonbury.[79] Another is an annotation written in the margin of the English prose *Brut* in Oxford, Bodleian, MS Hatton 50 indicating that in the year AD 63 Joseph and eleven other Christians arrived at Glastonbury and built a chapel there and that they were buried there.[80] These are interpolations added to single manuscripts and would have had limited circulation.

The story would have received wider circulation in the *Eulogium historiarum*, a mid-fourteenth century universal chronicle, which survives in five manuscripts and was probably written at Malmesbury Abbey in Wiltshire. As mentioned above, it is one of the chronicles that, while following Geoffrey of Monmouth fairly closely, nevertheless tells of the discovery of Arthur's tomb at Glastonbury. It is unusual in that it also gives a brief account of Joseph's establishing a church there.[81] Antonia Gransden suggests that the author, who refers to Ranulph Higden as the 'besotted monk of Chester', hoped to write a work that would compete with the *Polychronicon*, although he nevertheless used it as a source.[82] A desire to complete with Higden's work could account for both the reference to Joseph and the use of Geoffrey of Monmouth's *Historia*, which Keeler estimates takes up about fifteen percent of the whole *Eulogium*.[83] Higden does not mention Joseph's arrival at Glastonbury and had largely ignored Geoffrey because he questioned his book's veracity. The author of the *Eulogium* probably included this information in order to provide better coverage of this period than Higden had. He would, in all likelihood, have found the information about Joseph in the previously-mentioned interpolated version of the history of Glastonbury Abbey by the *Eulogium* author's great predecessor at Malmesbury, William.

Probably more significant, however, is a chronicle known as the Latin *Brut,* which, judging from the number of surviving manuscripts as well as a translation into English, had a wider circulation than the *Eulogium*. The term Latin *Brut* is misleading because scholars have used it to refer to several different chronicles. Of the twenty-four manuscripts that have been classified as Latin *Brut*s, eight represent five different chronicles that do not mention the story of Joseph's coming to Glastonbury.[84] The remaining sixteen manuscripts, however, represent one chronicle. The complete, or almost complete, chronicle survives in ten of them. In its entirety the Latin prose *Brut* begins with the legendary founding of Albion or Britain and ends, like a number of English *Bruts*, with the murder of James I of Scotland in 1436/7.

Charles Lethbridge Kingsford divided this chronicle into two groups, depending upon whether or not the chronicle included a long or short version of the life of Henry V. Of the sixteen manuscripts, probably six have the long life of Henry, and there may have been a seventh manuscript of this version destroyed in the Cottonian fire of 1731.[85] Nine have the shorter life of Henry V.[86] The version with the longer life of Henry the V was translated into an as yet unedited English chronicle, *The New*

Croniclys compendyusly idrawn of the Gestys of the Kynges of England, which survives in three manuscripts.[87] It was, moreover, a source for one version of the English prose *Brut* (formerly known as *Davies's Chronicle*), which survives in two manuscripts. Unlike most versions of the English Prose *Brut*, these briefly mention Joseph's establishing a church at Glastonbury.[88] The Latin *Brut* has never been edited except for Hearne's edition of the Brut/universal chronicle in Bodleian Rawlinson C.234 and Kingsford's edition of parts concerning the fifteenth century,[89] and since little had been written on it when Lagorio published her article, it is not surprising that she missed it. Following John of Glastonbury's account, it indicates that Joseph and other missionaries came to Britain in AD 63 at St Philip's bidding. King Arveragus gave them 'xii hydys of ground yn þe yle of Auallo þat nowe ys ycallyd Glastenbery' and 'by þe monycyoun of Seynt Michael þe archangyll þey beldyd a cherche yn the worschypp of owr Lady makynge þe wallys of wytthis.' They 'conuertyd to Crystyn faythe meny folke of dyuerse nacyouns and yn þe same place they beþ beryed'. Joseph moreover is 'beryed by þe forseyd cherche wythe ij fyollys full of blody swette of owr Lord þe which he brow3te with hym from þe holy lond'.[90] Shortly after this the chronicle reports that King Lucius was baptized by Pope Eleutherius's missionaries and was the first Christian king of Britain, thus making the chronicle somewhat consistent with Geoffrey of Monmouth's version.

The Latin *Brut* and its English translation are much shorter than most versions of the English Prose *Brut*. Its account of Arthur, for example, reads like a summary of the story in the English *Brut*.[91] The Latin *Brut* is in part drawn from material in the Anglo-Norman and English *Brut*s but also includes considerable information not in them. Besides including an account of Joseph of Arimathea at Glastonbury and indicating that Arthur was buried at Glastonbury rather than taken to Avalon, it includes other details as well.[92] It can be considered an original compilation, covering the same period as the vernacular *Brut*s but possibly intended as a chronicle that, because it was written in Latin, might have more authority than the vernacular ones. Moreover, its reference to Arthur's being buried at Glastonbury would probably have made it seem more authentic than the vernacular *Brut*s with their accounts of Arthur's being taken to Avalon. Its opening line in some manuscripts proclaim it to be the 'nova cronica de gestis regum Anglorum', and this was the title given to its English translation, the *New Croniclys*, perhaps suggesting that it was intended as a revision and a substitution for the Anglo-Norman and English *Brut* chronicles then in circulation.

As noted above, the Latin *Brut* influenced at least one of the versions of the English *Brut*, the one once known as *Davies's Chronicle*. William Marx, in his recent edition of this version of the English *Brut*, notes the Latin *Brut*'s influence on its account of the life of Henry V and suggests that the Latin *Brut* was a vehicle for Lancastrian propaganda.[93] Although Antonia Gransden believes that chronicles were not generally used in England for purposes of government propaganda since the monks who wrote them were usually independent, she writes that there were exceptions in times of crisis.[94]

Although she does not discuss the Latin *Brut*, it could well be one of those exceptions, written at a time Henry VI was still young and without much experience ruling. The version with the longer life of Henry V was a source for the *Vita Henrici Quinti*, the propaganda piece honoring Henry that Titus Livius Frulovisi wrote sometime between March 1437 and 1438 for Henry's brother, Humphrey, Duke of Gloucester.[95] Moreover, one of the Latin manuscripts with the shorter life, Rawlinson C. 398, was, according to Kingsford, prepared shortly after 1437 for Sir John Fortescue, who in 1442 was appointed Henry VI's Chief Justice of the King's Bench.[96] Thus versions with the shorter and the longer lives of Henry V had Lancastrian associations and both appeared shortly after the concluding date of the chronicle, 1437.

The Lancastrian bias of the Latin *Brut* could account for the inclusion of the story of Joseph's establishing a church at Glastonbury. As James Carley has shown, Henry V was interested in the church council of Constance (1417) at which the story of Joseph's evangelization of Britain was used to argue for the enhancement of England's status as a Christian nation, and at least by 1421 Henry had become interested in finding evidence that Joseph was buried at Glastonbury. He had heard that in 1419 the monks had begun to search for Joseph's body in their cemetery (and may have possibly commissioned the dig himself), and he let them know that he wished to know the results. The response the king received, Carley observes, was 'remarkably restrained', possibly because the monastery might have wished to prepare for 'a major revelation at a later date, on the occasion perhaps of a royal visitation', somewhat like the occasion of the reburial of Arthur's body in 1278 when Edward I visited Glastonbury. However, this was precluded by Henry's death in 1422. Nevertheless at the Council of Siena (1424), the English representative Richard Fleming claimed that Joseph's tomb had been discovered at Glastonbury, identified by a lead plaque, recalling, Carley observes, the leaden cross found at Arthur's tomb. However, by the time of the Council of Basel (1434), the claim of the discovery had been dropped, and the English representative simply refers to the ancient books at Glastonbury for information about Joseph.[97] Nonetheless, the story must have continued to interest Lancastrians since these versions of the Latin *Brut* were written shortly after the death of James I of Scotland in 1437/8, fifteenth years after the death of Henry V but just three after the last council in which Joseph's mission to Glastonbury was alluded to. And, in fact, late in the century, the antiquarian William Worcestre, writing *c.*1478, tells of visiting Glastonbury, where in one place in the churchyard King Arthur's bones are buried and in a different direction Joseph of Arimathea lies buried.[98]

Two manuscripts of the Latin *Brut* omit the early section and give only the history from 1377 (Trinity R.7.13, Harley 3906). Julian M. Luxford has discussed the two that present the history from 1377. He doesn't believe that either Trinity R.7.13 or Harley 3906 should be considered prose *Brut*s since their coverage of years prior to 1377 is different from that of this Latin *Brut*.[99] The two manuscripts Luxford discusses include continuations produced at the Benedictine abbey of Sherborne in Dorset, and Luxford believes that the multiple copies offer 'evidence of the interest that Sherborne's monks had in the history of their institution, and its place in a broader historical spectrum'.[100] The early parts of these manuscripts for history prior to 1377 are derived primarily from Geoffrey of Monmouth and Higden's *Polychronicon* rather than from the Latin *Brut*.[101] These manuscripts do not give the account of Joseph of Arimathea, and the section derived from the Latin *Brut* presents an abbreviated life of Henry V. In light of Gransden's remarks about the general independence of monks, those at Sherborne may have rejected the early part of the manuscript if they recognized it as a work pushing a Lancastrian agenda. The later section, moreover, is the version with an abbreviated account of the life of Henry V, which would give it less importance as a piece of Lancastrian propaganda. They may also have rejected the Joseph of Arimathea story because it reflected a rival abbey's propaganda.

One of the few chronicles that Lagorio found that included the story of Joseph and Glastonbury was that of John Hardyng. Hardyng wrote two versions of his chronicle, one in 1457 for the Lancastrian king Henry VI, and another one, completed at about 1465 intended first for Richard Duke of York and after Richard's death for Edward IV.[102] The story of Joseph and Glastonbury was included in both versions, and Hardyng's source for this may have been this Latin *Brut* or the *Eulogium*. Hardyng's chronicle is anti-Scottish and was intended in part to encourage Henry VI (and later Edward IV) to conquer Scotland, and the story of Joseph was probably included to enhance Britain's prestige and to counter Scotland's claims to eminence as a Christian nation because it had been converted by the miraculous appearance of St Andrew's relics on its shores.[103] However, Hardyng was originally writing his chronicle for the Lancastrians, and it is possible that he drew upon the story too because its authenticity would have been supported by the appearance less than twenty years earlier of the story in a Latin chronicle probably being disseminated as Lancastrian propaganda.

Most medieval chroniclers had little interest in the story of Joseph of Arimathea. Aside from the two histories of Glastonbury Abbey, the references in chronicles amount to brief references in five MSS – one in a manuscript of Robert of Gloucester's chronicle, one in the *Chronicon Angliæ Petriburgense*, one in the Lambeth Palace manuscript of Matthew Paris's *Flores historiarum*, one in the Lambeth Palace MS 84 of the English Prose *Brut*, and one in Bodleian, Hatton MS 50 – and five works – the universal chronicle *Eulogium historiarum*, a Latin *Brut*, its translation *The New Croniclys*, the Davies's *Chronicle* version of the English *Brut* that used the Latin *Brut* and the *Eulogium* as sources, and Hardyng's *Chronicle*. The last four appear to have been produced as Lancastrian propaganda.

The story of Joseph would not have been added to many of the chronicles for a number of reasons. One would be that the distinction between Arthurian history and Arthurian romance could account for the chroniclers' reluctance to admit the story of

Joseph into their accounts. Wood's speculation about why the monks at Glastonbury may not have publicized the story may also have held true for other clerics who wrote chronicles: they too may have had scruples about including an unauthenticated story about a man so closely associated with the Passion of Christ. The story of the discovery of Arthur's body, which circulated a little over fifty years after Geoffrey of Monmouth's account, provided, as mentioned earlier, what must have seemed like much needed closure to Geoffrey's account of Arthur sailing off to Avalon. The story of Joseph, in contrast, was late in developing, and it developed at a time – after the mid-fourteenth century – when the facts as stated by Geoffrey, particularly the conversion of the Britons to Christianity in the second century, had had about two hundred more years to be established and fixed in readers' minds. Moreover, the story of Joseph was evolving at a time – the late fourteenth and fifteenth centuries – when the history that Geoffrey had so firmly established was unraveling for some who were having doubts about the truth of the Arthurian story as well of the rest of his chronicle. As Caxton explains in his preface to *Morte Darthur*, 'dyvers men holde oppynyon that there was no suche Arthur and that alle suche bookes as been maad of hym ben but fayned and fables, bycause that somme cronycles make of hym no mencyon ne remember hym noothynge, ne of his knyghtes'.[104] This would not have been the time for those who were trying to keep the Arthurian history alive to add new material that was tainted by its association with Arthurian romance.

The story of Joseph was, however, one that many in England believed and that was a part of popular culture involving English patriotism and pride over its preeminence as a Christian nation. This popularity appears to have grown in the early sixteenth century judging from the fact that there were three editions of the story of Joseph published then: Wynkyn de Worde's *Life of Joseph of Arimathy* (n.d.), Richard's Pynson's *De Sancto Joseph ab Arimathia* in the *Kalendre of the New Legende of Englande* (1516) and his verse *Lyfe of Joseph of Armathia* (1520).[105] The early printers would not have produced these editions if they had not believed there were a good many people interested in purchasing them. Moreover, the story was retained in the second, Yorkist version of Hardyng's chronicle, which survives in twelve manuscripts and three fragments and of which Grafton published two editions in 1543. The story also appeared in 1577 in Holinshed's popular *Historie of England* as well as in the 1587 version completed by others after Holinshed's death:

> That one Iosephus preached here in England, in the time of the Apostles, his sepulchre yet in Aualon, now called Glessenburg or Glastenburie, an epitaph affixed therevnto is proofe sufficient. Howbeit, sith these things are not of competent force to persuade all men, I will ad in few, what I haue read elsewhere of his arriuall here. First of all therefore you shall note that he came ouer into Britaine, about the 64. after Christ, when the persecution began vnder Nero, at which time Philip and diuers of the godlie being in France (whether [sic] he came with other christians, after they had sowed the word of God in Scythia, by the space of 9. yeares) seuered themselues in sunder, to make the better shift for their owne safegard, and yet not otherwise than by their flight, the gospell might haue due furtherance. Hereby then it came to passe, that the said Philip vpon good deliberation did

> send Iosephus ouer, and with him Simon Zelotes to preach vnto the Britons, and minister the sacraments there according to the rites of the churches of Asia and Greece, from whence they came not long before vnto the countrie of the Galles.[106]

Although the version of the English Prose *Brut* that was published thirteen times between 1480 and 1528 ignored the story of Joseph,[107] the *Brut* became less significant later in the century, replaced by works like Hardyng's *Chronicle* (two editions in 1543) and Holinshed's (1577, 1587). By this time the story would have become important not just because it enhanced England's preeminence as a Christian nation but also because it helped justify the break with the Roman Catholic Church by emphasizing the antiquity of the British Church.

The two Glastonbury stories of Arthur and Joseph appealed to different types of readers. A great many medieval chroniclers readily accepted the discovery of Arthur's body, but many other people refused to believe the story and thought, as Malory says, that Arthur would some day return. On the other hand, the story of Joseph and the Grail seems to have been popularly accepted but rejected by the scholars who wrote the chronicles. The most notable exception is the version of the Latin *Brut* written (or revised) to publicize the life of Henry V, for it included the story of Joseph in which Henry had been interested. It was a chronicle written not long after the European councils before which the evangelization of Britain had been argued, and it was written or revised by an author with a particularly Lancastrian axe to grind. It would have been an attempt to give the story of Joseph authenticity by incorporating it into a Latin chronicle, not just of Glastonbury Abbey, like that of John of Glastonbury, but of the whole history of Britain and England. Hardyng's use of the story was also politically motivated. Thus the most significant exceptions to the chroniclers' rejection of the story of Joseph were products of political propaganda, and its acceptance by Holinshed in his *Historie* of 1577 and by those who published the 1587 version can be attributed to similar motives. The works of Hardyng and Holinshed, of course, belong to the popular, vernacular tradition, not the learned Latin tradition. The acceptance or rejection of the two great Glastonbury discoveries depended to a great extent upon whether one was referring to a popular approach to a story or a scholarly one; and the scholars, in their general rejection of both the legend of Arthur's survival and Joseph of Arimathea's evangelization of Britain, were, as is often the case, out of touch with popular sentiment.

Notes

[1] C. A. Ralegh Radford, 'Glastonbury Abbey', in Geoffrey Ashe, Leslie Alcock, C. A. Ralegh Radford, Philip Rahtz and Jill Racy (eds), *The Quest for Arthur's Britain* (London, 1968), p. 120; Siân Echard, *Arthurian Narrative in the Latin Tradition* (Cambridge, 1998), pp. 122–3.

[2] *Le haut livre du graal/ Perlesvaus*, ed. W.A. Nitze and T. A. Jenkins, 2 vols (Chicago, 1932–7), I.409, 317–18.

[3] Two basic studies of these legends are J. Armitage Robinson, *Two Glastonbury Legends* (Cambridge, 1926) and R. F. Treharne, *The Glastonbury Legends* (London, 1967). Also for an account by one who apparently accepted the legend of Joseph as true, see the book by a vicar of Glastonbury, Lionel Smithett Lewis, *St. Joseph of Arimathea at Glastonbury,* 7th edn (Cambridge, 1955).

[4] John of Glastonbury, *The Chronicle of Glastonbury Abbey: An Edition, Translation and Study of John of Glastonbury's 'Cronica sive antiquitates Glastoniensis ecclesie'*, ed. James P. Carley, trans. David Townsend (Woodbridge, 1985), p. 55; Robert Huntington Fletcher, *The Arthurian Material in the Chronicles* (1906), 2nd edn (New York, 1966), p. 189. Arthur's descent from Joseph is given in genealogical form in Lewis, *St. Joseph of Arimathea*, p. 159.

[5] William of Malmesbury, *Gesta regum Anglorum*, ed. R. A. B. Mynors, R. M. Thompson and M. Winterbottom, 2 vols (Oxford, 1998), I.27, 521.

[6] Also see Siân Echard, *Latin Tradition*, pp. 31–67 and Robert W. Hanning, *The Vision of History in Early Britain: From Gildas to Geoffrey of Monmouth* (New York, 1966).

[7] Merlin, for example, moves Stonehenge from Ireland to Salisbury plain with ropes and hawsers, and he gives Uther Pendragon drugs to change his appearance to that of Igerne's husband, the Duke of Cornwall.

[8] Giraldus Cambrensis, *De principis instructione liber*, ed. George F. Warner, in *Giraldi Cambrensis opera*, RS 21, vol. 8 (London, 1891), p. 128: 'Quae nunc autem Glastonia dicitur, antiquitus insula Avallonia dicebatur. Est enim quasi insula tota paludibus obsita, unde dicta est Britannice Inis Avallon, id est, *insula pomifera* . . . Unde et Morganis, nobilis matrona et patrium illarum dominatrix atque patrona, necnon et Arthuro regi sanguine propinqua, post bellum de Kemelen Arthurum ad sanandum ejusdem vulnera in insulam quae nunc Glastonia dicitur deportavit. Dicta quoque quondam Britannice Inis gutrin fuerat, hoc est, *insula vitrea*; ex quo vocabulo supervenientes postea Saxones locum illum *Glastingeburi* vocitabant.' The translation is from Gerald of Wales, *The Journey through Wales/The Description of Wales*, trans. Lewis Thorpe (Harmondsworth, 1978), Appendix 3: 'Gerald of Wales and King Arthur', p. 283. For a recent discussion of Giraldus' Arthurian comments, see Siân Echard, *Latin Tradition*, cited in n. 1.

[9] Morgan is not on the boat that takes Arthur to Avalon in the *Historia*, but in Geoffrey's later Latin poem, the *Vita Merlini*, she welcomes Arthur to Avalon. See Geoffrey of Monmouth, *Life of Merlin/Vita Merlini*, ed. and trans. Basil Clarke (Cardiff, 1973), p. 103.

[10] See John Scott (ed. and trans.), *The Early History of Glastonbury: An Edition, Translation and Study of William of Malmesbury's 'De antiquitate Glastonie ecclesie'* (Woodbridge, 1981), p. 34.

[11] Antonia Gransden, 'The growth of the Glastonbury traditions and legends in the twelfth century', in *Glastonbury Abbey and the Arthurian Tradition*, ed. James P. Carley (Cambridge, 2001), p. 37, reprint of article originally published in *Journal of Ecclesiastical History*, 27 (1976), 337–58.

[12] Ibid., pp. 30–1; Scott, *Early History of Glastonbury*, pp. 1–2.

[13] Scott, *Early History of Glastonbury*, pp. 27–8.

[14] Gransden, 'Growth of the Glastonbury traditions', pp. 48–9.

[15] Shortly after the discovery of Arthur's tomb, Richard gave Tancred of Sicily Arthur's sword Excalibur as a gift. See E. M. R. Ditmas, 'The cult of Arthurian relics', *Folklore*, 75 (1964), 27.

[16] Treharne, *Glastonbury Legends*, pp. 100–1.

[17] Giraldus, *De principis instructione*, p. 127; Gerald of Wales, *Journey through Wales*, trans. Thorpe, pp. 281–2.

[18] See T. D. Kendrick, *British Antiquity* (London, 1950; reprint 1970), pp. 96–8. For a full discussion of the attitudes of early modern antiquaries to Britain's Arthurian past, see the contribution by James Carley in this volume.

[19] Sharon Turner, *History of the Anglo Saxons*, 3rd edn, 3 vols (London, 1820), I.276, n. 43, cited in Robinson, *Two Glastonbury Legends*, p. 59.

[20] For some variants see Michelle P. Brown and James P. Carley, 'A fifteenth-century revision of the Glastonbury epitaph to King Arthur', in *Glastonbury Abbey and the Arthurian Tradition*, ed. Carley, pp. 193–203, originally published in *Arthurian Literature*, 12 (1993), 173–7.

[21] Philip Rahtz and Lorna Watts, *Glastonbury: Myth and Legend* (1993; reprinted Stroud, 2003), pp. 58–9; Kendrick, *British Antiquity*, p. 98

[22] Radford, 'Glastonbury Abbey', p. 137.

[23] Watkin, 'The Glastonbury Legends', in *Glastonbury Abbey and the Arthurian Tradition*, ed. Carley, p. 20, originally a lecture given at St Andrews University in the 1950s, published in *Arthurian Literature*, 15 (1997), 77–91; Rahtz and Watts, *Glastonbury Abbey*, p. 59 indicate that Stephen Morland points this out as well but do not give a source.

[24] Giraldus, *De principis*, pp. 127–8, trans. in Gerald of Wales, *Journey through Wales*, pp. 282–3; Scott, *Early History of Glastonbury*, p. 29; Carley (ed.), *Chronicle of Glastonbury Abbey*, pp. xlix–l; Robinson, *Two Glastonbury Legends*, pp. 8–17; Treherne, *Glastonbury Legends*, pp. 105–6; Gransden, 'Growth of the Glastonbury Traditions', pp. 48–9.

[25] Wace's Anglo-Norman verse adaptation of Geoffrey of Monmouth's *Historia* had been written for Henry's wife Eleanor of Aquitaine. Other Anglo-Norman Arthurian writers associated with Henry's court include Marie de France, some of whose work has affinity with Arthurian legends, and Thomas of Britain who wrote a version of the Tristan story. Chrétien de Troyes may have written his first Arthurian romance, *Erec and Enide*, for Henry's court and appears to have had Henry's England in mind when writing his second romance *Cligès* (Chrétien de Troyes, *Arthurian Romances*, trans. William Kibler and Carleton W. Carroll (London, 1991), pp. 5–7).

[26] Gransden, 'Growth of the Glastonbury Traditions', p. 49.

[27] Most of the chronicles written in French that tell of the Arthurian story were produced in England and are Anglo-Norman or were produced in Brittany or Flanders. See Fletcher, *The Arthurian Material in the Chronicles*, pp. 209–35 and my 'Arthurian material' in *Encyclopedia of the Medieval Chronicle*, gen. ed. Graeme Dunphy (Leiden, 2010), vol. 1, pp. 114–18. Boccaccio tells the story of Arthur (drawn from a chronicle and the French Vulgate *Mort Artu*) in his *De casibus virorum illustrium*, but dismisses the story as a fable and says, 'We do not recognize the evidence of his greatness and his fate as worthy of credence.' He adds that Arthur 'was carried off to Avalon, and there death relieved him from his misery', but 'many Britons think that he is not dead but held in a secret place'. See *The Fates of Illustrious Men*, trans. Lewis Brewer Hall (New York, 1965), pp. 214–15, 218. Boccaccio's account of Arthur was known in England by the late fourteenth century as evidenced by its incorporation into a chronicle of British/English history found in Oxford, Magdalen College Lat. 72, ff. 23v–25r. See my 'Generic intertextuality in the English alliterative *Morte Arthure*: the Italian connection', in *Text and Intertext in Medieval Arthurian Literature*, ed. Norris J. Lacy (New York, 1996), pp. 49–51. Ad Putter discusses Boccaccio's *De casibus* in his contribution to this volume.

[28] Alfred of Beverley, one of the earliest chroniclers to incorporate a summary of Geoffrey's *Historia* into his own chronicle, did wonder why no one outside Britain seemed to know of Arthur's conquest of Europe. See Kendrick, *British Antiquity*, p. 12.

[29] Notable exceptions are the fourteenth-century chronicler Robert Mannyng and the fifteenth-century chronicler John Hardyng. Mannyng, while not adding new adventures from romances to his adaptation of Geoffrey's account, nevertheless explains that Arthur's adventures in the verse romances took place during a nine-year period of peace and those in the prose romances during the several years Arthur was ruling in France. Hardyng added details from the French Vulgate *Queste del saint graal* and *Mort Artu*, including his own version of Galahad's Grail Quest. See Ad Putter, 'Finding time for romance: mediaeval Arthurian literary history', *Medium Aevum*, 63 (1994), 1–16; Lesley Johnson, 'Robert Mannyng's history of Arthurian literature', in Ian Wood and G. A. Loud (eds), *Church and Chronicle in the Middle Ages* (London, 1991), pp. 129–47; my 'John Hardyng and the Holy Grail', *Arthurian Literature*, 8 (1989), 185–206; Felicity Riddy, 'Glastonbury, Joseph of Arimathea and the grail in John Hardyng's *Chronicle*', in Lesley Abrams and James P. Carley (eds), *The Archaeology and History of Glastonbury Abbey*

(Woodbridge, 1991), pp. 317–31. Both of the latter are reprinted in *Glastonbury Abbey and the Arthurian Tradition*, ed. Carley, pp. 249–84.

[30] Françoise Le Saux, *La3amon's Brut: The Poem and Its Sources* (Cambridge, 1989), pp. 9–10.

[31] 'Encore i est, Bretun l'atendent, / Si cum il dient e entendent; / De la vendra, encor puet vivre', lines 13279–81, Wace's *Roman de Brut: A Text and Translation*, trans. Judith Weiss (Exeter, 1999), pp. 332–4.

[32] *Selections from La3amon's 'Brut'*, ed. G. L. Brook (Oxford, 1963), lines 4088–90.

[33] The scribe of one of the two surviving manuscripts of La3amon's chronicle, Cotton Otho C. xiii, substituted 'Bruttes' for 'Anglen' there. The other manuscript, Cotton Caligula A. ix, is usually considered earlier, and it is more likely that La3amon meant 'Anglen', that he was expressing interest in the plight of the English, who were now a conquered people, and was saying in effect that a great leader would some day come to help them just as Arthur had helped the Britons. In the fifteenth century when Edward IV and Henry VII tried to strengthen their weak claims to the English throne, they hoped to enhance their popularity by emphasizing their Welsh ancestry and to suggest fulfilment of the prophecy of giving the English, not the Welsh, a new King Arthur, with Henry VII even naming his oldest son Arthur with the hope of fulfilling a prophecy that we can see beginning with La3amon: 'an Arthur' will again lead the English people.

[34] The English came to think of Arthur as an English king, not a British one. Sir Thomas Malory describes Arthur's father Uther Pendragon as 'kynge of all Englond', and the people who rebel against Arthur are his English, not his British, subjects. See *The Works of Sir Thomas Malory*, ed. Eugène Vinaver, rev. P. J. C. Field, 3 vols (Oxford, 1990), I.7, III.1229.

[35] Robert of Gloucester, *The Metrical Chronicle*, ed. William Aldus Wright, RS 86, 2 vols (London, 1887), I.324, line 4596.

[36] *Castleford's Chronicle or the Boke of Brut*, ed. Caroline D. Eckhardt, EETS os 305, 306 (1996), II.647, lines 23956–89.

[37] Robert Manning of Brunne, *The Chronicle*, ed. Idelle Sullens (Binghamton, NY, 1996), lines 13724, 13735.

[38] Laura Keeler, *Geoffrey of Monmouth and the Late Latin Chroniclers 1300–1500* (Berkeley, 1946). *Flores historiarum*, ed. H. R. Luard, RS 95, 3 vols (London, 1890), II.106. Luard had not realized that this chronicle was written by Matthew Paris but attributes it to a Matthew of Westminster. This *Flores historiarum* is different from the earlier *Flores historiarum* by Roger of Wendover. Both were written at St Alban's.

[39] Keeler, *Geoffrey of Monmouth*, pp. 16, 36, 13, 38; *Eulogium historiarum*, ed. Frank Scott Hayden, RS 9, 3 vols (London, 1858–63), II.363, *Polychronicon Ranulphi Higden monachi Cestrensis*, ed. Churchill Babington and Joseph Rawson Lumby, RS 41, 9 vols. (London, 1865–86), V.332–3; Ralph of Coggeshall, *Chronicon Anglicanum*, ed. Joseph Stevenson, RS 66 (London, 1875), p. 36; Adam of Domerham, *Historia de rebus gestis Glasoniensibus*, ed. T. Hearne (Oxford, 1727), p. 43.

[40] Walter Bower, *Scoticronicon*, gen. ed. D. E. R. Watt, 9 vols (Aberdeen, 1987–98), II.69 (Bk 3, ch. 26); John Major, *A History of Greater Britain as well England as Scotland*, trans. Archibald Constable (Edinburgh, 1892), p. 85.

[41] *The Oldest Anglo-Norman Prose 'Brut' Chronicle*, ed. and trans. Julia Marvin (Woodbridge, 2006).

[42] The numbers vary depending on what one classifies as a Prose *Brut*. I classified as separate chronicles some that Matheson describes as 'peculiar' versions of the *Brut*. See the lists in my *Chronicles and Other Historical Writing*, vol. 8 of *A Manual of the Writings in Middle English*, gen. ed. Albert E. Hartung (New Haven, 1989), pp. 2818–21, and Lister Matheson, *The Prose 'Brut': The Development of a Middle English Chronicle* (Tempe, AZ, 1998), pp. xxi–xxxiii. I missed Brogyntyn 8 (Porkington), on deposit at the National Library of Wales, which Matheson includes, and the Bristol chronicle that I had classified as a summary of a *Brut*. After the publication of both of our books, another *Brut* manuscript was listed at a Sotheby sale, 22 June 2004 (listed as an unlocated manuscript in Matheson, p. xxxii, no. 5). This manuscript is now in the Rauner Special Collections Library at Dartmouth College. See Elizabeth J. Bryan, 'Rauner Codex MS 003183: the Beeleigh Abbey Brut at Dartmouth College', *Journal of the Early Books Society*, 12 (2009), 207–43.

[43] See Tamar Drukker, 'King, crusader, knight: the composite Arthur of the Middle English prose *Brut*', *Arthurian Literature*, 20 (2003), 172.

[44] *The Brut or the Chronicles of England*, ed. Friedrich W. D. Brie, EETS os 131, 136 (1906, 1908), I.90.

[45] See Richard Cavendish, *King Arthur and the Grail* (London, 1978), pp. 37–8.

[46] Giraldus, *Speculum ecclesiae*, ed. J. S. Brewer in *Opera*, IV.49; Gerald of Wales, *The Journey through Wales*, p. 286.

[47] Robert of Gloucester, *Metrical Chronicle*, lines 4589–95, I.324; Mannyng, *Chronicle*, lines 13719–24.

[48] Keeler, *Geoffrey of Monmouth*, p. 6.

[49] *Lydgate's Fall of Princes*, ed. Henry Bergen, Pt. 3, EETS es 123 (1924), VIII.3109–15, p. 910.

[50] Malory, *Works*, III.1242.

[51] See the discussion by John Withrington, 'The Arthurian epitaph in Malory's *Morte Darthur*', in *Glastonbury Abbey and the Arthurian Tradition*, ed. Carley, pp. 211–47, reprinted from *Arthurian Literature*, 7 (1987), 103–44.

[52] Geoffrey's account of Arthur's being taken to Avalon entered into romance accounts of the death of Arthur, but the romances also tell of Arthur's burial as well. In one of Malory's sources, the French prose *Mort Artu*, for example, Arthur is taken away on the boat to Avalon; however, it is reported afterward that ladies bring his body to be buried at the Black Chapel, which in the two English adaptations, the stanzaic *Morte Arthur* and Malory's *Morte Darthur*, becomes the chapel at Glastonbury. Malory, as mentioned earlier, tells of the Latin inscription on Arthur's tomb at Glastonbury that predicts his return. Although all four of the alliterative *Morte Arthure*'s chronicle sources mention the journey to Avalon, this work simply says that Arthur is buried at Glastonbury.

[53] Lagorio, 'The evolving legend of St Joseph of Arimathea', in *Glastonbury Abbey and the Arthurian Tradition*, ed. Carley, pp. 55–81. It was originally published in *Speculum*, 46 (1971), 209–31.

[54] Of the verse romances usually attributed to Robert de Boron, only the *Joseph of Arimathie* and a 502-line fragment of a Merlin romance survive. *Le Roman de l'Estoire dou Graal*, ed. William A. Nitze (Paris, 1971) is an edition of both. These romances are thought to have been rewritten in prose along with another romance, an account of Perceval's Grail quest to which was added a short account of the death of King Arthur, adapted from a chronicle (where Arthur is 'borne to Avalon, telling his people to wait for him, for he would return'). There is no reference to his burial at Glastonbury. See Nigel Bryant, trans., *Merlin and the Grail: Joseph of Arimathea, Merlin, Perceval* (Cambridge, 2001), p. 171. Although there has been speculation about the authorship of the *Perceval* and its concluding account of Arthur's death, the romances together represent an early brief cyclic Arthurian account beginning with the early history of the Grail and ending with the death of Arthur. Linda Gowans has argued that Robert wrote just the prose version of the Joseph and that the other verse and prose romances were written by later authors ('What did Robert de Boron really write?', in *Arthurian Studies in Honour of P. J. C. Field*, ed. Bonnie Wheeler (Cambridge, 2004), pp. 15–28).

[55] Robert W. Hanning, 'Arthurian evangelists: the language of truth in thirteenth-century French prose romances', *Philological Quarterly*, 64 (1985), 347–65.

[56] David A. Lawton, ed., *Joseph of Arimathea: A Critical Edition* (New York, 1983), p. xiii. Also see W. W. Skeat, ed., *Joseph of Arimathie*, EETS, os 44 (1871).

[57] *The History of the Holy Grail*, ed. F. J. Furnivall, EETS es 20 (1874), 24 (1875), 28 (1877), 30 (1878), 95 (1905), ed. Dorothy Kempe.

[58] Lagorio, 'Evolving legend', p. 55.

[59] Ibid., 69–70; Kendrick, *British Antiquity*, p.16.

[60] Carley, *Chronicle of Glastonbury Abbey*, p. xxviii.

[61] James Carley, 'A grave event: Henry V, Glastonbury Abbey, and Joseph of Arimathea's bones', in *Glastonbury Abbey and the Arthurian Tradition*, ed. Carley, pp. 288–9, originally published in Martin B. Shichtman and James P. Carley (eds), *Culture and the King: The Social Implications of the Arthurian Legend* (Albany, 1994), pp. 129–48.

[62] Carley, 'Grave Event', ibid., p. 290; Lagorio 'Evolving Legend', in ibid., p. 68–72.

[63] Charles T. Wood, 'Fraud and its consequences: Savaric of Bath and the reform of Glastonbury', in *The Archaeology and History of Glastonbury Abbey*, ed. Abrams and Carley, p. 282.

[64] Geoffrey of Monmouth, *History of the Kings of Britain*, trans. Lewis Thorpe (Harmondsworth, 1966), p. 124 (Bk 4, ch. 19); Bede, *Ecclesiastical History of the English People*, trans. Leo Sherley-Price, rev. R. E. Latham (London, 1990), p. 49 (Bk 1, ch. 4).

[65] Scott, *Early History of Glastonbury,* p. 1.

[66] Robinson, *Two Glastonbury Legends*, p. 28; Scott, *Early History of Glastonbury*, pp. 43–6.

[67] Scott, *Early History of Glastonbury,* pp. 46–7.

[68] Carley (ed.), *Chronicle of Glastonbury Abbey*, p. xxx.

[69] On John's use of romance material, see Echard, *Latin Tradition*, pp. 123–30.

[70] *Chronicle of Glastonbury Abbey*, ed. Carley, pp. 52–5.

[71] Ibid., pp. 52–3: 'in inquisione vasis quod ibi vocant Sanctum Graal'.

[72] Malory, *Works*, II.845–6.

[73] Lagorio, 'Evolving legend', in *Glastonbury Abbey and the Arthurian Tradition*, ed. Carley, p. 77.

[74] Ibid., p. 73.

[75] *Chronicon Angliæ Petriburgense*, ed. J. A. Giles, Caxton Society, II (1845; repr. New York, 1967), p. 173: 'Inventa sunt corpora Joseph ab Arimathæa, sociorumque eius, apud Glastoniam.' Robinson cites this as a comment by an anonymous East Anglian chronicler (*Two Glastonbury Legends*, pp. 64–5). I am indebted to Dr Sarah Peverley, the University of Liverpool, for identifying the chronicle.

[76] *Flores historiarum*, I.127. The interpolation is on fol. 10b of the Lambeth Palace manuscript. I am indebted to Dr Peverley for this reference.

[77] Lister M. Matheson, 'The Arthurian stories of Lambeth Palace Library MS 84', *Arthurian Literature*, 5 (1985), 70–91.

[78] Matheson, 'Lambeth', *passim*.

[79] Ibid., pp. 73–5, 89–91.

[80] Tamar Drukker, '"I read therefore I write": readers' marginalia in some *Brut* manuscripts', *Trivium*, 36 (2006), 97–130, 107.

[81] *Eulogium historiarum*, I.157 (Bk 2, ch. 3) I am indebted to Dr Peverley for calling my attention to this reference to Joseph. For more discussion of the Arthurian portions of the *Eulogium* and *Flores historiarum*, see the essays by Julia Crick and Ad Putter in this volume.

[82] Antonia Gransden, *Historical Writing in England II* (Ithaca, NY, 1982), p. 104. The *Eulogium* did not have quite the success of the *Polychronicon*, which survives in at least 115 Latin manuscripts, 18 manuscripts and fragments of Trevisa's translation, another complete fifteenth-century English translation, and several other partial English translations as well as the fifteenth-century editions of Trevisa's translation published by Caxton (1482) and Wynkyn de Worde (1495). See John Taylor, *The Universal Chronicle of Ranulf Higden* (Oxford, 1966), pp. 152–9, and Edward Donald Kennedy, *Chronicles and Other Historical Writing*, vol. 8 of *A Manual of the Writings in Middle English*, ed. Albert Hartung (New Haven, 1989), pp. 2656–3, 2677–8, 2866–78, 2890–1.

[83] Keeler, *Geoffrey*, p. 35.

[84] One of these chronicles is found in British Library, Harley 941 and simply represents the 'Syrian' version of the Albina story which was sometimes used as a prologue to Brut chronicles; a second, British Library, Cotton Galba E. vii consists of only a fifteenth-century 'Greek' version of the Albina prologue interpolated into a fourteenth-century manuscript of the *Eulogium historiarum*; a third chronicle, in Oxford, Magdalen College, MS 200; London, Lambeth Palace, MS 99; and British Library, Cotton Julius B. iii covers British/English history from its origins to the Conquest with continuations to 1372 in the latter two manuscripts; a fourth chronicle, in Durham, Dean and Chapter Library, MS B. ii 35 and Cotton Vitellius A. xx; and the fifth, the Wigmore Abbey MS, in the University of Chicago's Library, MS 224.

[85] London, British Library, Lansdowne 212, and Harley 3884 (two extracts; not a complete *Brut*); Oxford, Bodleian, MSS Rawlinson B 169; Oxford, St. John's College, MS 78; Cambridge, Corpus Christi

College, MS 311 and possibly Gonville and Caius College, MS 72, said in the College's manuscript catalogue to be a copy of CCC MS 311. Cotton Vitellius D. xii, which was destroyed in the Cottonian fire in 1731, may have belonged to this group as well.

[86] Oxford, Bodleian, MSS B 195, and C 398; London, British Library, MS Cotton Domitian iv; London, College of Arms, MS Arundel 5, and Huntington HM 48570. The latter has not been included in previous lists of Latin *Brut* MSS, the most recent being that of Matheson, *Prose 'Brut'*, pp. xx–xxi. It is almost identical to Cotton Domitian iv, and neither has the story of Joseph's coming to Glastonbury. Rawlinson B.147 has a short life of Henry V but, in the words of Kingsford, also 'has some peculiarities' (Kingsford, *Historical Literature*, p. 311). Bodleian, Rawlinson C 234, is a Latin *Brut* combined with a universal chronicle; it has a short life of Henry V but is fuller for the years 1415–21 (ibid., p. 311). Thomas Hearne published this as the Godstow chronicle in an appendix to his 1716 edition of William Roper's life of Thomas More (see n. 89 below). Two others, Cambridge, Trinity College, MS R 7 13 and London, BL, Harley 3906, present the shorter version of the life of Henry V but follow the *Brut* only for 1377–1437 and thus do not have the account of Joseph of Arimathea. Huntington Library MS HM 19960, a historical miscellany, includes material for 1399–1437 drawn from the Latin version with the abbreviated life of Henry V. The early part of this manuscript is drawn from a number of sources, but includes an early section of the Latin *Brut* that tells of Joseph's visit as well (fol. 41v) which is identical to the account in Rawlinson C.398.

[87] Holkham Hall 669; Columbia University Plimpton 261; and Bodleian Ashmole 791. For discussion of this chronicle see my *Chronicles and Other Historical Writing*, pp. 2638–40, 2833, and Matheson, *Prose 'Brut'*, pp. 302–6. Matheson points out that I incorrectly described this chronicle as having the short form of the life of Henry V rather than the long (Matheson, *Prose 'Brut,'* p. 46, n. 115).

[88] See Lister M. Matheson, *The Prose 'Brut': The Development of a Middle English Chronicle* (Tempe, AZ, 1998), pp. 287–94 (Bodleian Lyell 34 (Davies's Chronicle) and National Library of Wales MS 21608), and William Marx (ed.), *An English Chronicle 1377–1461: A New Edition* (Woodbridge, 2003), pp. lx–lxxiii, who discusses the influence of this Latin *Brut* upon the later part of this chronicle. However, Marx argues elsewhere that the source for the story of Joseph in this chronicle was the *Eulogium historiarum*. See his 'Aberystwyth, National Library of Wales, MS 21608 and the Middle English Prose *Brut*', *Journal of the Early Book Society*, 1 (1997), 1–16. I am indebted to Dr Peverley for the reference to this article.

[89] *Anonymi Chronicon Godstovianum*, in Thomas Hearne, *Guilielmi Roperi vita D. Thomae Mori equitis aurati* (1716), pp. 180–246; Charles Lethbridge Kingsford, *English Historical Literature in the Fifteenth Century* (Oxford, 1913), pp. 310–37.

[90] Holkam Hall MS 669, pp. 29–30. This is a close translation of the Latin. Cf. the Latin *Brut* in Bodleian, Rawlinson C. 398, fols. 8v–9r: in AD 63: 'duodecim discipuli venerunt in Britanniam . . . quorum primus fuit Joseph ab Armathia . . . Quibus rex Aruiragus . . . duodecim hidas terre contulit in insula Auallonis que nunc dicitur Glastonia quo loco ecclesiam in honore beate virginus per admonicionem sancti Michaeli archangeli de vitorquatis muros facientes construxerunt . . . Joseph vero ab Armathia ibidem supultus est iuxta dictam ecclesiam cum duabis fialis pleins de sudore Christi sanguineo quas secum de terra sancta attulerat.'

[91] The accounts of Arthur in Cotton Domitian iv and Huntington HM 48570 are somewhat longer than in the other manuscripts but are still much shorter than in the Anglo-Norman and English prose *Brut*s.

[92] These include Arthur's slaying Mordred in their final battle, which came ultimately from the French Vulgate *Mort Artu*, Richard II's being starved to death, and details about the assassination of James I of Scotland not found in the English Prose *Brut*.

[93] Marx (ed.), *An English Chronicle 1377–1461*, p. lxxiii. For more discussion of the propagandistic deployment of Arthurian material, particularly in the early modern period, see James Carley's essay in this volume.

[94] Antonia Gransden, 'Propaganda in English medieval historiography', *Journal of Medieval History*, 1 (1975), 363–81.

[95] Kingsford, *Historical Literature*, pp. 52–3, 127–31.

[96] See Charles Plummer's edition of Sir John Fortescue, *The Governance of England* (Oxford, 1885), pp. 45–6, 180–1; Kingsford, *Historical Literature*, p. 310.

[97] Carley, 'Grave event', pp. 293–6.

[98] William Worcestre, *Itineraries*, ed. John H. Harvey (Oxford, 1969), pp. 298–9: 'in linea bifurcata iacet Josephus ab Arimathia.' Dr Peverley sent me this reference.

[99] Julian M. Luxford, 'A previously unlisted manuscript of the Latin *Brut* chronicle with Sherborne Continuation', *Medium Ævum*, 71 (2002), 289. Luxford was the first to note that Trinity R.7.13 belongs to this group of Latin *Brut* chronicles (although, since they omit the earlier legendary material, he does not think they should be described as Latin *Brut*s).

[100] Ibid., p. 286.

[101] Ibid., p. 289.

[102] The first version has not yet been edited in its entirety but Sarah Peverley and James Simpson are preparing an edition. Richard Grafton published two editions of the second version in 1543, and Henry Ellis published an edition in 1812.

[103] See my 'John Hardyng and the Holy Grail', in Carley, *Glastonbury Abbey and the Arthurian Tradition*, pp. 249–68.

[104] Malory, *Works,* I.cxliv

[105] All three are published in W. W. Skeat's edition of the fourteenth-century verse account, *Joseph of Arimathie*, EETS, os 44 (1871; reprint New York, 1969), pp. 25–52.

[106] *Holinshed's Chronicles of England, Scotland and Ireland*, ed. Henry Ellis, 6 vols (London, 1807–8), I.40. See James Carley's essay in this volume for a thorough discussion of the learned, as distinct from the more popular, response to Arthur in the early modern period.

[107] See my *Chronicles and Other Historical Writing*, p. 2821.

7

ARTHURIAN LATIN ROMANCE

Elizabeth Archibald

It is often assumed that Latin was the language choice for serious writing in the Middle Ages, that medieval romance was regarded as frivolous entertainment suited to the vernacular, and thus that the inevitable language choice for romance writers in France was French, and in post-Conquest Britain Anglo-Norman or English. It is also assumed that most churchmen, who formed the majority of those literate in Latin, were hostile to the Arthurian legend, or at least to frivolous Arthurian fables as opposed to serious 'history'. William of Malmesbury, dismissing the legend of Arthur's eventual return, wrote that Arthur deserved better than the *nugae Britonum* (the foolish tales of the Britons), and *fallaces fabulae* (deceitful fables): he should be celebrated in *veraces historiae* (truthful histories), for his political achievements.[1] Ailred of Rievaulx describes a novice monk confessing how he had wept over tales of Arthur but remained dry-eyed when hearing religious readings and sermons.[2] But there was in fact an eager audience for Arthurian adventures of a not entirely 'historical' kind written in Latin. William of Newburgh dismissed Geoffrey of Monmouth's account of Arthur as British fables, attacking him for inappropriately presenting this rubbish in Latin. Yet Geoffrey's British history, which not only describes Arthur's reign but also his conception through Merlin's magic, was an immediate best-seller; it survives in over 250 copies, and was translated and adapted throughout the Middle Ages.[3] Readers of Geoffrey in Latin were presumably also the target audience for Arthurian romances in Latin which chose to develop the fables rather than the political history. Echard comments that 'many Latin writers, in many genres, revelled in the Arthurian story every bit as much as Geoffrey did', and notes that some writers of Latin Arthurian texts may in fact have been the authors of vernacular romances too.[4]

In this essay I shall consider four very different Latin Arthurian romances or romance episodes which raise many questions about writers, audiences and expectations in the multilingual medieval world, where Latin was not usually a mother tongue: *De ortu Waluuanii nepotis Arturi* (*The Rise/Origins of Gawain Nephew of Arthur*) and *Historia Meriadoci* (*The History of Meriadoc*), *Narratio de Arthuro rege Britanniae et rege Gorlagon lycanthropo* (*The Story of King Arthur of Britain and King Gorlagon the Werewolf*), and the quest for the sparrowhawk in Book II of Andreas Capellanus' *De amore* (*On Love* – also known as *The Art of Courtly Love*).[5] There is scholarly debate about the date and authorship of all these texts, and this uncertainty makes discussion of them problematic. If they are products of the mid- to late twelfth century, as Echard argues, some at least may be linked to the Angevin court where, as she has shown, there was great interest in narrative and the theme of good kingship, and a delight in satire and wit.[6] There also seems to have been an awareness at court that the new developments in vernacular literature were proving very popular, and providing competition. Michael Clanchy remarks that Walter Map's *De nugis curialium* 'was a flashy attempt to make modern Latin literature attractive' (though, as John Gillingham has pointed out, it is striking that Map did not include any Arthurian tale).[7] If the texts under discussion are twelfth-century, they represent an early phase in the evolution of the romance genre and Arthurian romance in particular, and so may be quite innovative; if they are thirteenth- or fourteenth-century, they can be read as comment on a popular and established form of narrative with distinctive and characteristic motifs. But in either case, they offer striking versions of Arthurian themes, and raise questions about authors and audiences, and about literary cross-fertilization in a multilingual culture. I shall be focusing here mainly on the Arthurian issues.

The *De ortu* and *Historia Meriadoci* are preserved together in an early fourteenth-century manuscript, London BL Cotton Faustina B. vi; the other texts in the manuscript are not romances, but include annals, papal letters, and other ecclesiastical notices (there is another copy of the *Historia* in Oxford Bodleian Library MS Rawlinson B 149, late fourteenth to early fifteenth century). The two romances were known to the sixteenth-century bibliophile John Bale, who ascribed them both to Robert of Torigni, a Benedictine monk who was prior and librarian at Le Bec and abbot of Mont Saint Michel (*c.*1110–86). Modern critics generally agree that they are by the same author, but estimates of their date of composition vary from the mid-twelfth century to the thirteenth and even the fourteenth century, on the basis of arguments ranging from fashions in armour to the possible authorship of Ranulph Higden.[8] Both narratives concern the adventures of a young knight winning his spurs. Meriadoc is on the periphery of the Arthurian world; his stay at Arthur's court leads to one of many adventures, and not the conclusive one. Gawain is Arthur's long-lost nephew, and so his coming-of-age story has stronger resonances and links with other Arthurian texts. In both texts, Arthur comes in for some criticism.

The *De ortu* uses the popular framework of the Fair Unknown motif to allow the foundling hero Gawain both to prove and to discover himself.

> At Arthur's court King Loth of Norway falls in love with Anna, sister of Arthur; she bears him a son in secret, and gives the baby to merchants to take far away, with money, jewels, an elaborately worked cloak (*pallium*), a ring belonging to Arthur, and a sealed document giving the baby's name, Gawain, and his parentage. When the merchants anchor near Narbonne and go ashore, a poor fisherman, Viamundus, and his wife steal the baby with the money and tokens. Hiding their new riches, they raise the child in poverty but after seven years go on pilgrimage to Rome to start a new life. Rome has been ravaged by barbarians, and the emperor is rebuilding the city. Viamundus lives splendidly and is generous, and everyone admires both him and his son. On his deathbed, Viamundus confesses to the pope and emperor how he gained his wealth, and identifies his 'son' as Arthur's nephew, asking that the boy (who is known as *Puer sine nomine* or Boy without a Name) be sent back to Britain when he grows up. When he is fifteen, he is knighted by the emperor, and acquires a red tunic to wear over armour which gives him his next name, *Miles cum tunica armature* (Knight of the Surcoat).

War breaks out between the Christians in Jerusalem and the Persians, and Gawain claims a boon from the emperor, to fight a duel against the Persian champion. His ship is blown by a storm to the island home of Milocrates, who has abducted the emperor's niece. When Gawain and some companions go hunting and attack local foresters who challenge them, Milocrates plans revenge. Gawain kills a huge boar *en route* to the city; he enters in disguise, and is able to overhear his enemy's plans. He is taken to meet the abducted queen, who begs for his help. Gawain defeats the huge enemy champion, sets fire to the city, restores the queen to her husband, wins a sea battle in which Greek fire (a sort of proto-napalm) is used against his side, and returns in triumph to Rome, where the emperor rewards him. Gawain hears of the fame of Arthur's court and asks permission to go there. The emperor agrees and gives him all that was found with him by Viamundus, forbidding him to look in the chest containing the proof of his parentage till he meets Arthur.

Arthur is at Caerleon. Gawain arrives at nearby Usk at nightfall as a storm breaks. Queen Gwendoloena, a sorceress, tells Arthur as they lie in bed that a knight who cannot be defeated has come to Usk. When she is asleep, Arthur creeps out with Kay to challenge the unknown knight at a ford. The king is very rude to Gawain, who knocks both Arthur and Kay into the water. Arthur returns home soaked and lies to the queen about what has happened, though she sees through his story. When Gawain arrives, Arthur reads his documents and is amazed and delighted to discover his nephew, but orders that the young man should not be told the truth. He is dismissive to Gawain, telling him to prove himself worthy of a place at court. A suitable adventure arises at once: a damsel is being besieged by a pagan king in the Castle of Maidens, so they all hurry north. Arthur is nervous, as he has been defeated before by this king; eventually he flees to avoid disaster. Gawain mocks him, and defeats the pagan forces single-handed. When he brings the king's head to court, Arthur reveals his name and parentage, and Gawain is reunited with his delighted parents.

The most recent editor of *De ortu*, Mildred Leake Day, makes a strong case for composition in the third quarter of the twelfth century by Robert of Torigni. He is known to have written several chronicles, and to have been an early reader of Geoffrey of Monmouth, whose influence is evident in *De ortu*.[9] In Geoffrey too Gawain is the son of Loth and is raised at Rome, though he is legitimate and is sent at the age of twelve by his father to the pope (rather than the emperor as in Geoffrey;[10] but he does not have a series of independent adventures in the Middle East and the Mediterranean, his identity is not a mystery, and nothing is said about his return to Arthur's court. Once grown up, Geoffrey's Gawain is always at Arthur's side. The story of his clandestine birth and exposure seems to have been circulating by the end of the twelfth century, however, for it appears in the French prose Arthurian romance *Perlesvaus* (first half of the thirteenth century) and in a verse fragment known as *Les Enfances Gauvain* (*c*.1230); the *De ortu* may represent an early example of this trend, or may be drawing on various versions.[11] Clandestine birth is often associated with heroes, in both classical and post-classical texts (Perseus, Alexander, Arthur himself); in medieval romance it is frequently linked with the Fair Unknown theme.[12]

De ortu offers a fascinating mixture of 'history', epic and romance (the latter is particularly evident in the opening and final sections). It contains many learned classical allusions and digressions, most famously the account of how to make Greek fire, which combines fantastic magical ingredients with more scientific details; the boar hunt includes echoes of Meleager's hunt in Ovid's *Metamorphoses*; and two sets of Latin verses are included in the account of the fighting on Milocrates' island. Clearly this text is aimed at a learned audience – but equally clearly, the author was quite familiar with Arthurian adventure stories as well as with Geoffrey's pseudo-history. In the final phase of the story, Gawain's comic night combat with Arthur and Kay is a parody of a popular romance motif, the knight guarding a ford and challenging all comers to battle. The summons to rescue a maiden besieged in her own castle by an unwelcome suitor is also a common romance theme. The surprise here is that Arthur is presented as so incompetent, knocked into the ford, mocked by his queen, and then fleeing in fear from an enemy who has frequently defeated him. This characterization mixes the inadequate *roi fainéant* of early French romance and the king outdone by saints of Welsh hagiography.[13] Nevertheless, his court is Gawain's final destination, and his acknowledgement as 'Arthur's nephew' is the last stage of his quest for glory. Bruce, an early editor, notes that Robert of Torigni died in 1186, and argues that 'it would be astonishing to find a romance of this period combining so many Arthurian commonplaces, even if we assumed it was written towards the end of his life.'[14] But there is considerable evidence that Arthurian motifs and conventions made famous by Chrétien de Troyes (though perhaps already known earlier in oral tradition) were rapidly disseminated and exploited, for instance in Marie de France's Arthurian lay *Lanval* (1170s–80s) and Renaut de Beaujeu's *Bel Inconnu* (*c.*1185).

In support of his theory of thirteenth-century composition, Bruce noted some possible parallels with the Prose *Tristan* (1230–5), in the form of names borrowed from early French history.[15] Another possible influence is the very popular Alexander romances, notably in the episode where Gawain enters Milocrates' city and councils in disguise: Alexander visits both Darius and Queen Candace in disguise, though in both cases he is eventually recognized.[16] Alexander's adventures showcase his brilliance both in military strategy and in fighting; love is not a major theme.[17] The same might be said of Gawain in *De ortu*, who is neither inspired nor rewarded by love. Another possible analogue is the equally popular story of Apollonius of Tyre, which also includes Latin verse (in the storm scene and the final riddle scene), and shows little interest in the psychology of love.[18] Gawain's combat with a giant and freeing of an abducted queen might be seen as a more decorous version of Arthur's fight with the rapist Giant of Mont Saint Michel in Geoffrey, with a happier outcome for the victim.[19]

Echard and Day both see a mixture of comedy and seriousness in *De ortu*. The story begins and ends in Britain, where the long-lost Gawain must be reintegrated into his birth family and take his place at his uncle's court, but much of the comedy is aimed at Arthur. Most of Gawain's adventures take place in the greater Roman Empire, including his combat in Jerusalem. The recognizable Arthurian conventions are found at the beginning and the end only, and there are some curious twists, including the characterization of Arthur and his queen. The story ends with a tantalizing disclaimer:

> What other outstanding exploits fall to the share of Gawain, he who desires to know must demand by request or payment from one who knows. Realizing that just as it is more decisive to take part

in a battle than to record a battle, even so it is more difficult to compose a history in eloquent style than it is to relate it orally [perhaps rather 'spread it around'] in the words of common speech.[20]

Is this a hint that it is unusual for this writer to narrate an Arthurian romance? Does it suggest that the writing of an Arthurian romance is unusual in itself, whether in Latin or the vernacular? It certainly shifts the focus from the plot to the writer, who seems to be fishing for compliments here, as well as differentiating himself from vernacular writers (or minstrels).

There is no final comment at the end of the *Historia Meriadoci*, but it begins with a prologue which suggests that the extant text is based on a much longer version (this is of course a common medieval conceit and does not necessarily mean that such a source actually existed):

The prologue by R. introduces the history of Meriadoc, king of Cambria. Because I consider Meriadoc's chivalrous deeds and distinguished career worthy of remembrance, I have decided to write his story. The old text is embellished with tales of such prowess and such excellence that if I plodded through each episode one by one I should turn its sweetness into surfeit. Therefore, taking into account the benefit of my readers, I set out to confine it to a concise style, knowing that a pithy discourse that makes sense is worth more than a rambling tale empty of meaning.[21]

It is striking that R (which could stand for Robert) expects to be read rather than heard (*legentium igitur consulens utilitati*). The tone and style seem quite similar to the epilogue to *De Ortu*, and as in *De Ortu*, the story proper begins with Uther rather than Arthur as king, and with Britain divided into three separate kingdoms. Arthur is thus not the paramount lord, but one of several kings.

When the king of Cambria dies, he is succeeded by his sons, Caradoc (as the main king) and Griffin. Griffin has Caradoc killed and usurps the throne. He plots to have Caradoc's twin children, Meriadoc and Orwen, killed too, but they are rescued by their foster-parents Ivor and Morwen. They all live in the forest for five years, till Orwen is abducted by Urien, who subsequently marries her, and Meriadoc by Kay, who takes him to Arthur's court. Within a few years Ivor and Morwen are reunited with the children, who are anxious for vengeance against their uncle. They appeal to Arthur, who besieges Griffin and has him tried and beheaded.

Meriadoc is made King of Cambria, but is keen to win his spurs. He champions Arthur against the Black Knight, who claims ownership of the Black Forest, and defeats his opponent after thirty-eight of Arthur's knights had failed. He restores the forest to the Black Knight, and the same scenario is repeated when he fights the Red and White Knights. Meriadoc then sets out to serve the emperor of the Alemanni, whose daughter had been abducted by Gundebald, king of the Land from Which No One Returns. Soon he is in charge of all the emperor's mercenaries. He defeats Gundebald's invading army, and then finds himself with his men on a plain where a huge castle has mysteriously appeared. Inside he dines with a beautiful lady (possibly Fortuna) who tells him she knows him; no one else in the castle speaks. Meriadoc and his men flee, overcome with panic; they find another mysterious castle, where Meriadoc behaves very boorishly. They then rejoin the emperor's forces and defeat the army of Gundebald's brother.

Meriadoc is determined to rescue the emperor's daughter; at her urging he succeeds in entering incognito the castle where she is held, and kills the gatekeeper as she watches. The princess has been left in charge of the castle; following her advice, Meriadoc defeats Gundebald in a battle by a quicksand, and Gundebald's men offer him the throne, agreeing to surrender to the emperor as long as the princess marries Meriadoc. Meanwhile the king of Gaul invades the emperor's lands, and the emperor, forced to agree a treaty which includes the marriage of his daughter to the King, plots to entrap Meriadoc. Pretending to arrange the wedding, the emperor allows Meriadoc to visit his daughter, but then announces publicly that she is pregnant and Meriadoc must be punished. The princess is horrified; the king of Gaul, learning of the pregnancy, breaks off the engagement and annuls the treaty; the war begins again. Meriadoc escapes from a tower, borrows armour and a horse, and kills the emperor. The king, having heard of Meriadoc's prowess, gives him the princess along with great estates, and Meriadoc has a son.

The *Historia Meriadoci* survives in two copies, one in the same manuscript as the *De ortu* (fourteenth century), and the other in the manuscript containing *Arthur and Gorlagon* (late fourteenth to early fifteenth century).[22] There are sufficient similarities in style between the *Historia* and *De ortu* to have persuaded the few critics who have discussed them that they are by the same author, but they also differ in numerous respects. While the *De ortu* is in many ways a typical Fair Unknown story, the *Historia* seems to combine motifs from various types of romance in an unusual arrangement. The opening section describing the attempt to assassinate Meriadoc and his sister by their wicked and usurping uncle, their miraculous rescue, their subsequent abductions, and their reunion, is reminiscent of Anglo-Norman and later Middle English romances such as *Haveloc* and *Horn* (though the elaborate method of cooking employed by Ivor in the wilderness seems to be added, like the Greek fire episode in *De ortu*, to show off arcane technical knowledge). But whereas these episodes of family betrayal, separation and reunion constitute a complete romance elsewhere, in *Meriadoc* they represent only the *hors d'oeuvre*. There are other examples of separated families in which the lost children are twins or triplets (*Lai le Freine*, *La Belle Hélène de Constantinople*, *Octavian*, *Sir Isumbras*, *Valentine and Orson*); but I know no other example of twin brother and sister. They are not babies when they are abducted, and Orwen is a remarkably compliant abductee – we are told that she herself alerts Urien when she reaches *nubilem etatem* (marriageable age).[23] It is unusual for parents (or in this case foster-parents) to search for their lost children; and here they are found very quickly and easily, within a couple of years. So the recognition scenes are unproblematic, and the family reunion comes very early in the story.

We hear no more of Orwen after this; it is indeed the history of Meriadoc. Arthur helps them to take vengeance on their wicked uncle Griffin, who is defeated and beheaded within two pages. But Meriadoc turns down his rightful throne and sets out to prove himself as a knight in a series of judicial duels against the Black, Red and White Knights. All three adversaries claim that Arthur has treated them unjustly; the chivalric context is expanded to include frequent references to law. When Meriadoc returns to court after defeating the Black Knight, he tells Arthur that he has won the case for him;[24] he then rebukes the king at some length for his unjust behaviour, claiming that his main concern has been to save a noble man from being destroyed by the king's legal action.[25] Legal terminology is frequently used in this section; after defeating all three knights and resolving their disputes, Meriadoc seeks out the country which is 'undergoing the judicial ordeal of war'.[26] The rest of the narrative focuses on continental wars. Meriadoc never returns to Britain, and it is striking that when he infiltrates Gundebald's city, he describes himself and his companions as serving the king of Britannia without naming Arthur, which seems rather contemptuous.[27] Judith Weiss points out that in Wace's *Roman de Brut*, breaches of *dreit* are frequently mentioned in critical comment on Arthur's invasion of France; she makes a brief reference to the treatment of Arthur in the *Historia Meriadoci* and also *De ortu* (both of which she dates to the late twelfth century) as examples of 'the age's equivocal attitudes to the exercise of supreme power'.[28]

Meriadoc distinguishes himself on the continent through both his cunning and his prowess, but it is striking that the princess he wants to rescue is given a major role, and a lot of power. In these two romances, abductors treat their victims with great respect, it seems, and the ladies are given considerable freedom compared with better-known abductees such as Guinevere. However, the writer of the *Historia Meriadoci* treats love more pragmatically than romantically. The abducted princess (who has no name) corresponds secretly with Meriadoc, having heard of his prowess; curiously, in the absence of her abductor she is 'the acting administrator of the city',[29] and so is able to entertain Meriadoc for three days, and give him detailed instructions about how to defeat Gundebald and liberate her. We are not told that she is in love with him, nor he with her, though once she is freed and back in her father's city, spies report to the emperor that when Meriadoc and the princess are alone together, they embrace passionately. The story ends with their marriage, but love has been a very minor factor in Meriadoc's adventures, as have his dealings with Arthur.

Love is the *raison d'être* of *De amore* (*On Love*), a Latin treatise attributed to one Andreas Capellanus, which is problematic in every way, and not least in its Arthurian episode.[30] It is usually dated to the late twelfth century, and the author is linked to Marie de Champagne, daughter of Eleanor of Aquitaine (both mother and daughter commissioned literary works). Marie is one of the ladies (all historical) named in *De Amore* as arbiters in cases of love; Andreas is described in the manuscripts as a royal chaplain, and an Andreas, apparently a priest, witnessed several documents in Champagne in the 1180s. C. S. Lewis based his influential interpretation of 'courtly love' on the first two books of the *De Amore*, in which romantic love is defined and analysed, hypothetical problems in love are debated, and seduction techniques outlined for the benefit of a young friend called Walter who has recently fallen in love.[31] The third book, however, is a savage denunciation of women and of all worldly passion, which inevitably leads to damnation: love should be focused on Christ alone. Scholars have been much exercised by how to make sense of the contradictory arguments contained in this tantalizing text. If it was written for the court of Marie as a study of the newly popular literary theme of passionate love, what is the purpose of the third book with its hardline rejection of love? If it was written to promote the love of God, why spend so much time on elaborate accounts of yearning and wooing? The medieval reception of the text does not help us; in the late thirteenth century one reader thought it hilariously funny, but the bishop of Paris condemned it in 1277. Walsh falls back on the lame argument that Andreas unaccountably changed his plan for unknown reasons. However, Peter Dronke has raised serious questions about previous assessments of Andreas and the *De amore.* He argues that Andreas may well be a pseudonym; that the book was written in the early thirteenth century in a university context, for a clerical audience; and that it is an example of 'high-spirited casuistry'.[32]

The Arthurian episode is just as problematic as the rest of the text. It is entitled '*De regulis amoris*' (The Rules of Love), and forms the final chapter (8) of Book II, after a series of 'judgements on love' in which hypothetical cases are resolved by great ladies such as Eleanor and Marie.

> A nameless British knight must win his lady's love by fetching a sparrowhawk from a golden perch in Arthur's court. After receiving directions from a passing damsel in a forest, he defeats a knight guarding a bridge and arrives in a wonderful park containing a circular palace, outside which are tables laid with food and drink. Seeing no one there, and unable to enter the palace, he helps himself, whereupon a giant porter arrives, demanding to know who presumes to eat the king's food. The knight replies that the king should be generous and make his food available to all. He defeats the porter in battle and obtains the gauntlet he needs to acquire the hawk. He then rides to another splendid palace where he finds Arthur on a golden throne surrounded by countless knights and ladies. He greets Arthur, but is answered by the knights assigned to defend the hawk, who challenge him. He defeats one in battle and takes the hawk, and with it two dogs and also a scroll chained to the perch; when he enquires about the scroll, he is told, apparently by the knights, as no speaker is specified: 'This is the scroll on which are inscribed the rules of love, which the king of love himself announced to lovers with his own lips. You must bear this off and inform lovers of the rules, if you wish to take back the hawk without a struggle.'[33]
>
> The knight returns to the forest and reports to the damsel, who kisses him thirty-one times and tells him that she will be waiting whenever he returns alone, then sends him back to Britain, where his lady grants him her love and disseminates the rules to all lovers.[34]

The thirty-one rules focus on love rather than marriage. They are consistent with the behaviour of lovers in French romances such as Chrétien's *Lancelot*, but can hardly be intended as serious guides to behaviour, any more than the preceding 'court cases'. The association of these rules with Arthur is also problematic. They are found at his court – but the nameless protagonist has little difficulty in taking away the sparrowhawk with which they are associated. If the plan is to spread the word about the rules of love, it seems a clumsy one, and it is hard to see what kudos is gained by their association with Arthur; they hint at Guinevere's affair with Lancelot, though neither is mentioned. No Arthurian character is named apart from the king, and he never speaks. Echard has noted that the glittering, silent tableau of the Arthurian court is reminiscent of Celtic otherworld scenes, though no other example is connected with Arthur; the writer also seems to know other romances in which the sparrowhawk quest is linked to the winning of a bride, such as Chrétien's *Erec*.[35] It is not clear where Arthur's court is situated in Andreas: the British knight returns to Britain at the end, so the forest seems to be a continental one such as Wace's Broceliande. More worryingly, Arthur's behaviour is questioned when the porter rebukes the knight for eating uninvited at Arthur's table; the king's lack of generosity (a crucial chivalric virtue) and the inability of his knights to protect the sparrowhawk suggest that this court, in spite of its rich appearance, is not the centre of courtly life and standards, even if the god of love has left his rules there.

Two other factors contribute to the problematization of this episode. One is that a set of rules for lovers has already appeared in *De amore* in a dialogue between a nobleman and a noblewoman in Book One.[36] The nobleman threatens the reluctant noblewoman with a story about what happens to women who refuse to love, the motif known as the Purgatory of Cruel Beauties: the god of love's entourage includes a group of beautiful women wretchedly dressed in animal skins and riding on emaciated horses, one of whom explains that they must suffer terrible torments for having rejected love. The god of love instructs the nobleman to warn women of this punishment, and gives him a list of twelve precepts. The god adds that more rules can be found 'in the book addressed to Walter', a meta-fictional joke. The result of this story is that the noblewoman decides to look for a worthy lover.

To use the rules of love motif twice in one text is to risk making the second episode seem bathetic; Dronke calls it 'an ironic anticlimax'.[37] The first episode focuses on women, in both the framing debate and the lurid account of the suffering of women who reject love, which brings about the desired change of heart. In the second episode, the protagonist's lover is only seen at the end, and very little is said about their relationship. The sparrowhawk adventure of the British knight is eclipsed by the transmission of the rules, which were not part of his original quest (and the helpful damsel seems to offer herself as an alternative lover). Dronke reads the episode as 'an exuberant parody of an Arthurian romance', but it ends abruptly, with little emphasis on the happy outcome of the love story; it seems too two-dimensional to grip the imagination, especially if one compares it with an indisputably 'exuberant parody' such as Guillaume le Clerc's *Fergus*, which is filled with comic echoes of Chrétien.[38] The second problematic factor is that the Arthurian episode is the last section of the second book, and thus marks the point of transition to the misogynist vitriol of the diatribe against love in Book Three. This curious finale might be taken as a *reductio ad absurdum* of the treatise on romantic love.[39] Here as in the other Latin Arthurian texts under discussion we find Arthur's court presented ambiguously, as a place of some splendour but also of inertia or injustice of some kind. As in the *Historia Meriadoci*, the focus is not on Arthur, who is damned with faint praise, but on a protagonist who comes to the court only briefly; the knight in *De Amore* is a Briton, but does not seem to be an actual or would-be subject of Arthur's.

The *Narratio de Arthuro rege Britanniae et rege Gorlagon lycanthropo* (hereafter *Arthur and Gorlagon*) is the opposite of Andreas' Arthurian adventure, and of *De ortu* and the *Historia Meriadoci* too, in the sense that Arthur begins as the protagonist – but here too he is not presented in a positive light. He goes on a quest, but it is caused by his ineptitude, and he spends most of it listening to a story whose moral, and relevance, are left unclear in the abrupt ending.

At the Pentecost feast, Arthur embraces his queen so passionately that she blushes, and asks why. When he says that he loves her so much, and is sure that she loves him, she tells him that he understands nothing about *ingenium mentemque femine* (the mind or nature of woman). He swears to find out, and not to touch food before he does so. He rides off with Kay and Gawain, and three days later they arrive at the court of the wise king Gorgol. The king invites Arthur to dismount and eat with him; Arthur explains his quest, and eventually, with great reluctance, joins the king at dinner. Gorgol says he cannot answer the question, and directs Arthur to his brother Gorleil. Here too he is eventually persuaded to dismount and eat, and again the king cannot answer the question and sends Arthur to a third brother, Gorlagon. Here Arthur absolutely refuses to dismount and eat, though he allows his men to do so. Gorlagon begins the story of the Wolf.

A worthy king keeps a sapling with magic properties enclosed in a private garden: he would be turned into a wolf if someone struck him on the head with it and said a certain phrase. His beautiful wife, who loves a neighbouring prince, extracts the secret and turns her husband into a wolf, but mistakes the magic phrase so that he has the mind of a man, not a wolf. She marries her lover, who becomes ruler. The wolf hides in the forest, mates and has cubs, and hopes for revenge. He and his family kill the queen's children by her lover, and then her brothers; the wolf's mate and cubs are trapped. The wolf and his companions ravage several countries; in the third, the king hunts for him, but the wolf appears and bows down to the king. The king takes the wolf home with him. When he goes on a journey, he entrusts the wolf to his queen, who is having an affair with the seneschal. They make love in front of the wolf, who is chained in the royal bedroom. He attacks the seneschal, half-killing him. The queen pretends that her lover was unsuccessfully defending her child, which was eaten; she then hides the child. When the king returns, the queen tells her false story, but the wolf greets the king joyfully, and leads him to the place where the child is hidden. The seneschal confesses, and the king has the lovers executed; he frees the wolf, and follows him to his native land. He captures the false queen and her lover; the sapling is found, and the wolf restored to human shape. The lover is executed and the queen punished.

The story is over, but Arthur has another question: who is the miserable-looking woman sitting opposite Gorlagon, who kisses a bloody head in a dish before her whenever Gorlagon kisses his wife? Gorlagon reveals that she is the faithless first wife and the bloody head is that of her dead lover; he himself was the werewolf, and the two kings who helped him were his brothers, whom Arthur has just met. Arthur dismounts and eats at last, and next day he rides home.

This tantalizing story survives in only one fourteenth-century manuscript which also contains the *Historia Meriadoci*, and a possible link between them is the marginalizing of a not entirely admirable Arthur. Critics agree that *Arthur and Gorlagon* is heavily influenced by (if not translated from) Celtic sources; Echard comments that 'it hardly matters if the author was a Welshman, when it is so clear that he knew Welsh forms and methods.'[40] Phrases are repeated word for word, for instance each time that Arthur arrives at a castle and refuses to eat. Echard reads it as a playful parody, though she comments that it is impossible to know whether the Latin is parodying Welsh storytelling conventions, or whether 'the original Welsh text was a parody along the line of *Culwch* or *Rhonabwy*'.[41] Certainly Arthur is introduced only to be sidelined once he embarks on his quest, and presented as rather ridiculous. The kings speak very briskly to him: Gorgol reproaches him for his rude entry on horseback, and says his foolish quest has diminished his reputation as a wise man, and Gorlagon is very dismissive at the end of his story. This is not a heroic quest, and Arthur does not return to court with any glory.

There are a number of other medieval stories about werewolves with treacherous wives, and several include Arthur: in *Biclarel*, a version of the better known *Bisclavret* of Marie de France, and *Melion*, another French lay, Arthur acts as benefactor and is involved in the werewolf's restoration to human shape.[42] But as Hopkins points out, only in *Arthur and Gorlagon* does the werewolf tell his own story, with Arthur for audience. In the Latin narrative, the story ends very abruptly when the faithless wife has been pointed out to Arthur. Arthur goes home, marvelling at the story he has heard.[43] We hear nothing of what he has learned, or what he says to Guinevere. Kay and Gawain set out on the quest with him, but they are never mentioned again. Has the Arthurian opening been grafted onto an existing werewolf story?[44] If so, is this meant to be a pointer to the disasters to come for Arthur? Is Guinevere's comment that he doesn't understand women an oblique and ironic allusion to her later adultery? One might then interpret the story as a misogynistic and fatalistic commentary on Arthur's fall: he learns that women are dangerous, but does not take action to control his queen.

There is an interestingly analogous episode in *Die Wrake von Raguisel* in the Dutch *Lancelot Compilation*, apparently taken from a French source, though it does not appear in the extant *La Vengeance Raguidel*.[45] Gawain asks Guinevere what women want (because he has just been told that his beloved Ydeine has a promiscuous reputation); the queen replies that no one can possibly know the answer to his question, but he is determined to ride off on a quest for the truth. He stays with a dwarf king with magical powers, who keeps his wife locked up and passes food to her through a hole in the wall because she has had an affair with a servant. The king tells Gawain that this answers the question about women's thoughts on love; the quest is over. Encouraged by the king, Gawain then tests Ydeine by disguising himself; in a precursor of *Così fan tutte*, he succeeds in obtaining from her a ring he had previously given her, and shames her into good behaviour. These stories seem to be related to fourteenth- and fifteenth-century narratives such as Chaucer's *Wife of Bath's Tale* and the anonymous *Wedding of Sir Gawain and Dame Ragnell*, though this plot is not always connected to the Arthurian world, and as Day points out, in the English stories 'a woman's choice is honored, not condemned'.[46] If *Arthur and Gorlagon* is a twelfth-century text, it would be a very early example of this tale-type; if it is later, it would reflect the popularity of this misogynistic theme. It is striking that though the Dutch version omits the werewolf, it does emphasize a punitive ritual involving food. Echard suggests that *Arthur and Gorlagon* might have been particularly appropriate as after-dinner entertainment, and notes that the provision and consumption of food is frequently exploited in the story, both in oaths and as a means of coercion.[47] Is this at least in part a reference to the dangers of carnal appetites, and could there be a connection here between eating and knowledge, punning on the two meanings of the Latin verb *sapere*, to taste and to know?[48]

The four Latin texts discussed here are all as problematic as they are intriguing. We might read them very differently if we were confident of when they were written: are they early witnesses to the evolution of the Arthurian legend, or later witnesses to the popularity of certain characterizations and motifs? Composition in Latin indicates that they are aimed at an elite and largely ecclesiastical audience; would such an audience be less likely to subscribe to the idealization of the Arthurian world, or is *Arthur and Gorlagon* adapted from an equally non-idealistic Welsh source? Even if these texts could be securely dated in the twelfth century, there is still critical disagreement about the status of Arthur at this time. Gillingham, noting Walter Map's striking omission of Arthur, argues that he only became an accepted model of kingship at the very end of the twelfth century; this might suggest an early date for the Latin Arthurian romances, in which his role is far from model. Simon Meecham-Jones notes that as a resistance fighter against 'colonial aggression', Arthur was a dangerous model of British sovereignty, and that this led to 'a curiously carping, and often unheroic, depiction of the figure of Arthur'.[49] He continues:

> It was in Latin discourse, rather than Welsh or British tradition, that the myth of Arthur as national redeemer had developed – to serve the ideological neuroses of a usurping cultural tradition, and the Romances display many of the inconsistencies and anxieties inherent in this melting together of ideas from unrelated discourses.

The four texts discussed here seem to represent such 'inconsistencies and anxieties' and a 'melting together of ideas from unrelated discourses': Arthur's court is still a magnet for young warriors, but it is also one that they may criticize, and leave behind in search of further adventure, and its association with love is far from straightforward. Arthur himself is not always successful in his wars and quests, and can be criticized, even mocked, with impunity by established kings, by young knights beginning their careers, and by his own wife. The writers of these stories were certainly interested in Arthur, but it cannot be said of them that 'they revelled in the Arthurian story every bit as much as Geoffrey did'.[50]

Notes

[1] I use the translations of Siân Echard in '"Hic est Artur": reading Latin and reading Arthur', in Alan Lupack (ed.), *New Directions in Arthurian Studies* (Cambridge, 2002), pp. 49–67 (pp. 49–50).

[2] Quoted by R. S. Loomis in 'The oral diffusion', in R. S. Loomis (ed.), *Arthurian Literature in the Middle Ages: A Collaborative History* (Oxford, 1959), pp. 52–63, p. 59.

[3] The most recent edition is by Michael Reeve, with translation by Neil Wright (Woodbridge, 2007); see also the translation by Lewis Thorpe (Harmondsworth, 1966).

[4] Echard, '"Hic est Artur"', pp. 52 and 64. See Ad Putter's comments in this volume on the *Vera historia*, in which an elaborated version of Arthur's death at the hands of a mysterious youth seems to reflect Celtic traditions, though the revelation of the empty tomb is clearly based on the Resurrection.

[5] References to *De ortu*, *Historia Meriadoci* and *Arthur and Gorlagon* will be taken from the recent editions with translation by Mildred Leake Day in *Latin Arthurian Literature* (Cambridge, 2005). See also Philippe Walter (ed.), *Arthur, Gauvain et Mériadoc. Récits arthuriens latins du XIIIe siècle* (Grenoble, 2007), which includes facing French translations; I am grateful to Dr Carolyne Larrington for drawing my attention to this collection, which also includes the *Vera historia de morte Arthuri*.

[6] Siân Echard, *Arthurian Narrative in the Latin Tradition* (Cambridge, 1998), p. 18.

[7] M. T. Clanchy, *From Memory to Written Record: England 1066–1307*, 2nd edn. (1979; Oxford, 1993), p. 204; John Gillingham, 'The cultivation of history, legend and courtesy at the court of Henry II', in Ruth Kennedy and Simon Meecham-Jones (eds), *Writers of the Reign of Henry II: Twelve Essays* (New York and Basingstoke, 2006), pp. 25–52 (see p. 37).

[8] For a survey of critical views see Mildred Leake Day's introduction to *Latin Arthurian Literature*, pp. 2–11.

[9] References to Geoffrey's *Historia* are to the edition of Reeve, and to the Penguin translation by Thorpe (see n. 3 above).

[10] Geoffrey of Monmouth, *HRB* ix.11; Reeve, pp. 205, 241–3; Thorpe p. 223.

[11] *Perlesvaus: Le Haut Livre du Graal*, ed. W. A. Nitze and T. A. Jenkins, 2 vols (Chicago, 1932–7); 'Les Enfances Gauvain, fragment d'un poème perdu', ed. Paul Meyer, *Romania* 39 (1910), 1–32. See also Keith Busby, *Gauvain in Old French Literature* (Amsterdam, 1980).

[12] See Otto Rank, *The Myth of the Birth of the Hero*, trans. F. Robbins and S. E. Jelliffe (New York, 1957); Raymond H. Thompson, 'Gawain against Arthur: the impact of a mythological pattern upon Arthurian tradition in accounts of the birth of Gawain', *Folklore*, 85 (1974), 113–21, repr. in Raymond H. Thompson and Keith Busby (eds), *Gawain: A Casebook* (New York and London, 2006), pp. 209–16; Elizabeth Archibald, 'Comedy and tragedy in some Arthurian recognition scenes', *Arthurian Literature*, 19 (2003), 1–16; and *Enfances arturiennes*, ed. C. Ferlampin-Acher and D. Hüe (Orleans, 2006).

[13] On French Arthurian romance see Glyn S. Burgess and Karen Pratt (eds), *The Arthur of the French: The Arthurian Legend in Medieval French and Occitan Literature* (Cardiff, 2006). On Arthur in hagiography see Oliver J. Padel, *Arthur in Medieval Welsh Literature* (Cardiff, 2000), pp. 37–46, as well as the essay by Andrew Breeze in this volume.

[14] *Historia Meriadoci and De ortu Walwanii: Two Latin Arthurian Romances of the XIIIth Century*, ed. J. D. Bruce (Baltimore, 1913), p. xii.

[15] Bruce, *Historia Meriadoci*, p. xxi.

[16] See *The Greek Alexander Romance*, II.13–15 and III.19–22, trans. Richard Stoneman (London, 1991), pp. 100–4 and 136–41.

[17] Alexander material was often included in manuscripts also containing texts of Geoffrey of Monmouth; see Julia Crick, *The Historia regum Britannie of Geoffrey of Monmouth, IV: Dissemination and Reception in the Later Middle Ages* (Cambridge, 1991), p. 22.

[18] The Latin verse in the *De ortu* appears at p. 70, lines 24–6 (Miles poaching on Milocrates' island), and p. 82, lines 24–31 (the battle against Milocrates). See *Historia Apollonii*, chs 11 and 41–3, ed. and trans. Elizabeth Archibald in *Apollonius of Tyre: Medieval and Renaissance Themes and Variations* (Cambridge, 1991), pp. 122 and 160-–6.

[19] See Geoffrey, *Historia*, Bk 10, ed. Reeve, pp. 224–8; trans. Thorpe, pp. 237–41.

[20] *De ortu*, p. 120: 'Cetera que uirtutum Waluuanii secuntur insignia qui scire desiderat; a sciente prece uel precio exigat. Sciens quod sicut discriminosius est bellum inire quam bellum referre; sic operosius sit composito eloquencie stilo historiam exarare quam uulgari propalare sermone'; trans. Day, p. 121.

[21] *Historia Meriadoci*, p. 122: 'Incipit prologus R. in *Historia Meriadoci regis Kambrie*. Memoratu dignam dignum duxi exarare historiam, cuius textus tantarum probitatum tantique leporis decoratur titulis, ut si singula seriatim percurrerem, faui dulcorem in fastidium uerterem. Legentium igitur consulens utilitati, illam compendioso perstringere stilo statui, sciens quod maioris sit precii breuis cum sensu oracio, quam multiflua racione uacans locucio'; trans. Day, p. 123.

[22] The second manuscript, Bodleian Rawlinson MS B 149, also contains the stories of Apollonius of Tyre and of Alexander (the *De preliis*); a compiler might well have thought it appropriate to add an Arthurian story to this group of very popular adventure narratives.

[23] *Historia Meriadoci*, pp. 140–1.

[24] *Historia Meriadoci*, pp. 156–7: 'causam decreui'.

[25] *Historia Meriadoci*, pp. 158–9: 'ne suo iure nobilem uirem contigat destitui'.

[26] *Historia Meriadoci*, pp. 160–1: 'quenam terrarum regio bellorum subiaceret legibus'.

[27] *Historia Meriadoci*, pp. 184–5: 'ex Britonibus originem ducimus, regi Britannie diu militauimus'.

[28] Judith Weiss, 'Arthur, emperors, and antichrists: the formation of the Arthurian biography', in *Writers of the Reign of Henry II*, ed. Kennedy and Meecham-Jones, pp. 239–48 (see pp. 243–4).

[29] *Historia Meriadoci*, pp. 186–7: 'ut domina urbi presidet'.

[30] References are to the edition and translation of P. G. Walsh, *Andreas Capellanus on Love* (London, 1982). For a recent survey of critical interpretations see the 'Introduction' in Kathleen Andersen-Wyman, *Andreas Capellanus on Love?* (Basingstoke, 2007), pp. 18–25.

[31] C. S. Lewis, 'Courtly love', ch. 1 in *The Allegory of Love* (London, 1936), pp. 1–43.

[32] Peter Dronke, 'Andreas Capellanus', *Journal of Medieval Latin*, 4 (1994), 51–63 (the quotation is taken from p. 57); see also Neil Cartlidge, *Medieval Marriage: Literary Approaches, 1100–1300* (Cambridge, 1997), pp. 24–32.

[33] Andreas Capellanus, *De Amore*, p. 280: 'Haec est [enim] chartula, in qua regulae scribuntur amoris, quas ipse amoris rex ore proprio amatoribus edidit. Hanc te asportare oportet et regulas amantibus indicare, si pacificum volueris accipitrem reportare.'

[34] In Walsh's translation there are fourteen kisses, but thirty-one seems correct, as there are thirty-one rules of love.

[35] Echard, *Arthurian Narrative*, pp. 120–1. See also Alfred Karnein, *Amor est passio: Untersuchungen zum nicht-höfischen Liebesdiskurs des Mittelalters* (Trieste, 1997), pp. 168–75, and Beate Schmolke-Hasselman, '"Accipiter et chirotheca". Die Artusepisode des Andreas Capellanus – eine Liebesallegorie?' *Germanisch-romanisch Monatsschrift*, n.F. 32.4 (1982), 387–417.

[36] See *De amore*, ed. Walsh, pp. 96–121.

[37] Dronke, 'Andreas Capellanus', p. 58.

[38] *The Romance of Fergus*, ed. Lincoln Frescoln (Philadelphia, 1983); trans. D. D. R. Owen, *Fergus of Galloway, Knight of King Arthur* (London, 1991).

[39] Dronke, 'Andreas Capellanus', p. 58.

[40] Echard, *Arthurian Narrative*, pp. 204–13 (p. 205). See also G. L. Kittredge's edition and discussion '*Arthur and Gorlagon*: versions of the werewolf's tale', *Harvard Studies and Notes in Philology and Literature*, 8 (1903), 140–275, and Amanda Hopkins, 'Why Arthur at all? The dubious Arthuricity of *Arthur and Gorlagon*', *Arthurian Literature*, 26 (2009), 77–95.

[41] Echard, *Arthurian Narrative*, p. 214.

[42] For an overview of this material with useful bibliography see Hopkins, 'Why Arthur?'. Caroline Walker Bynum refers to a 'werewolf renaissance of the twelfth century': Bynum, 'Metamorphosis or Gerald and the werewolf', ch. 2 of *Metamorphosis and Identity* (New York, 2005), pp. 77–111 (p. 94).

[43] *Arthur and Gorlagon*, ed. Kittredge, pp. 234–5: 'valde miratus'.

[44] Walter suggests that Gorlagon is an avatar of Merlin, and that Arthur's quest parallels the Grail quest and Percival's questions: see his Introduction to *Arthur, Gauvain*, pp. 13–14.

[45] *Dutch Romances*, vol. III: *Five Interpolated Romances from the Lancelot Compilation*, lines 1475–1890, ed. David F. Johnson and Geert H. M. Claassens (Cambridge, 2003), pp. 112–32; this episode is preceded by a version of the mantle chastity test.

[46] Mildred Leake Day, 'Arthur's werewolf: horror and comedy in four languages' (unpublished conference paper), p. 3; I am grateful to Dr Day for sending me a copy of her paper.

[47] Echard, *Arthurian Narrative*, p. 210; see also Walter, 'Introduction' to *Arthur, Gauvain*, p. 13, on Arthur's refusal to eat.

[48] Jill Mann, discussing a reference in Langland's *Piers Plowman* to Adam and Eve (B.xv.61–7), remarks that 'the image of eating is actually *contained* in the desire to know', and that *sapere* 'means first to taste and only secondly to know'; see 'Eating and drinking in *Piers Plowman*', *Essays and Studies*, 32 (1979), 26–43 (pp. 40–1; emphasis hers).

[49] Gillingham, 'The cultivation of history', pp. 37–8; Simon Meecham-Jones, 'Introduction' to *Writers of the Reign of Henry II*, ed. Kennedy and Meecham-Jones, pp. 1–24 (see p. 17).

[50] See Echard's comment cited at the beginning of this essay: '"Hic est Artur"', p. 4.

Section Four
After the Middle Ages

> I am not unsensible that I expose myself to the Censures of some Persons, by publishing this Translation of a Book, which they think had better been suppressed and buried in Oblivion, as being at present generally exploded for a groundless and fabulous Story, such as our modern Historians think not worthy relating, or at least mention with Contempt.[1]

In 1718, Aaron Thompson published the first complete English translation of Geoffrey of Monmouth's *Historia regum Britannie*. He preceded his translation with a lengthy introduction in which he defended the Brutus foundation story; by contrast, he touched on the question of Arthur's historicity only briefly. Thompson's defence of Geoffrey and Brutus alike is, by the early eighteenth century, decidedly unusual, but from the vantage point of this collection, we may see it as the last remnant of a long tradition of scholarly, historical response to the foundation myths promulgated by the Latin writers represented in these pages. The final section of *The Arthur of Medieval Latin Literature* consists of one long essay that takes us out of the Middle Ages and into the early modern period. James Carley's exploration of how Tudor antiquaries responded to the stories of Brutus and Arthur – how these stories were deployed as part of a new national myth-building – reminds us once again of the range of uses to which Latin Arthurian material could be put. As Carley shows us how these Renaissance schoolmen deployed and refashioned the medieval Latin material according to their own interests and for their own ends, we see how it is that Arthur became 'rex quondam rexque futurus'. However 'groundless and fabulous' the story, it continued to fascinate all manner of readers, and if this was a spurious history, it nevertheless played its part in the 'real thing'.

SE

Note

[1] Aaron Thompson, *The British History, Translated in English From the Latin of Jeffrey of Monmouth* (London, 1718), p. vi.

8

ARTHUR AND THE ANTIQUARIES[1]

James P. Carley

Preface

In 1485 William Caxton's 'edited' version of Thomas Malory's rambling Arthuriad was printed under the title of *Le Morte Darthur* and the following year Henry VII, first of the so-called Tudor dynasty, named his son after this ancient British king and hero. By the mid sixteenth century, however, enthusiasm for Arthur seems to have waned considerably and Roger Ascham, tutor and Latin secretary to Elizabeth, would dismiss *Le Morte Darthur* – and by extension the Arthurian cycle as a whole – as papistical nonsense.[2] Notwithstanding William Caxton's prefatory affirmation of Arthur's historical reality, vouchsafed by tangible evidence dotted throughout the English landscape, Ascham viewed Malory's account as fictional as well as morally repugnant, certainly nothing to take at face value. Nevertheless, during Elizabeth's reign John Dee cited Arthur's conquests as a precedent and indeed legal justification for imperial claims by the English Crown, and in the 1580s Edmund Spenser began work on *The Faerie Queene*, in which Prince Arthur was portrayed as the embodiment of magnificence, that Aristotelian virtue so prized by Renaissance monarchs.

How then was Arthur viewed in the sixteenth century? Was his historical status well and truly demolished by the end of Henry VIII's reign and did he resurface *merely* as a literary figure under Elizabeth? Or did the efforts of the antiquaries, John Leland in particular, convince the scholarly, and more importantly political, community that he did live and conquer much of Europe some thousand years previously. Opinion on the topic is divided.

Introduction

In an influential article Sidney Anglo argued that the 'British History' as most comprehensively articulated in Geoffrey of Monmouth's *Historia regum Britannie* (*c.*1138) had a brief vogue at the beginning of Henry VII's reign, but that by the time of Henry VIII 'the material had been replaced by other, more congenial, themes – notably that of the union of York and Lancaster and that of Henry as a great warrior prince. So that the Early Tudor use of the *British History* should be regarded not as a continuous and expanding cult but, less dramatically, as an early efflorescence and subsequent decline.'[3] More recently, David Carlson has observed that the humanist poems in praise of Prince Arthur's birth pointedly downplayed the historical resonances of his name and replaced 'the medieval fiction of Arthurian heritage and authority with antique fictions, the Roman triumph, Vergilian messianism and the Golden Age, and the Homeric council of the gods, in effect denying the political value of the Arthur myth, even perhaps seeming to knock the prop of Arthurian ancestry out from under Henry's somewhat shaky authority'.[4] Carlson concludes that this was a result of the new humanist historiography and that 'Arthur was perhaps already generally regarded as an historically negligible figure in educated, courtly circles by 1486'.[5] Although he continued to appear in bourgeois entertainments it was not until the reign of Elizabeth that Arthur re-emerged in courtly circles, but now as a literary topos. In this latter context, moreover, belief in his historicity, which had in any case been 'reduced to its present levels by the beginning of the seventeenth century', did not matter one way or another.[6] Likewise Joseph M. Levine has postulated that the sixteenth century saw a new distinction between fact and fiction and as a result 'not only Geoffrey of Monmouth and the medieval romances but Arthur's seal, floating traditions, gravestones at Glastonbury, even the Round Table itself – were equally untenable'.[7] Henceforth history and fiction would be seen as different disciplines with different aims.

To some degree Anglo was reacting to earlier historians who (mistakenly in his opinion) believed 'that the Tudor period witnessed an unprecedented burst of enthusiasm for the *British History* now verified by the fulfilment of the Cadwallader prophecy; that there was a continuous and officially-encouraged cult of King Arthur; and that the Tudors adopted the *red dragon of Cadwallader* as a symbol of their descent from the last British king'.[8] Although Anglo did not cite him by name—he singled out Charles Bowie Millican and E. A. Greenlaw – Richard Koebner provided an important example of this position. Koebner maintained not only that the medieval royal cult of Arthur and his ancestor Constantine increased with Henry VII's accession – a king whose dynasty 'was hailed almost officially as the embodiment of the mythical hero coming into his own' – but also that it played a role in Henry VIII's 'Great Matter', that is his attempt to rid himself of his first wife, Catherine of Aragon.[9] In the last few years some scholars have been returning to a modified, and perhaps slightly less strident, version of this position, influenced in particular by David Starkey who has argued that Arthur provided a consciously invoked model in Henry VIII's reign. Caxton's Malory, in Starkey's view, provided 'an atmosphere which Henry and his intimates not only breathed but whose heady fumes affected their behaviour and beliefs as well. The result is to rescue the Arthurian tradition from the sidelines, where Sidney Anglo's work has shunted it, and to place it once more at the centre of the early Tudor polity.'[10]

Martin Biddle has shown, moreover, just how fully Arthur figured in the iconography surrounding Henry VIII's dealings with the Holy Roman Emperor Charles V in the early 1520s.[11] Indeed, it is possible that the newly refurbished Round Table viewed by the two men at Winchester in June 1522 (in which Arthur bore a remarkable resemblance to Henry), had been repainted for this occasion, although it is more likely that the refurbishment occurred in 1516. If the latter is the case it was simply a matter of adding verse, no longer legible, on the wall below the table at the time of Charles's visit: 'Carolus Henricus uiuant defensor uterque / Henricus fidei Carolus ecclesiae.'[12]

More generally Patrick Collinson has observed that during the humanist revival it was the political dimension rather than strict fact that determined attitudes toward the past, as well as acceptance of what we would consider to be dubious sources:

> the best critics were often the greatest forgers, and vice versa. Their truths were not quite the same thing as ours . . . The capacity to examine evidence critically was not an invention of something called the Renaissance (Geoffrey of Monmouth had severe critics in his own time) still less equivalent to more modern critical capacities. But the motives which determined its application to particular questions were not always those of disinterested scholarship.[13]

The attitude of the antiquaries and poets toward the historical Arthur cannot, in other words, be considered in isolation, but must be seen in the context of political and religious currents in the country as a whole.

I

Thomas Wolsey's inability to persuade Pope Clement VII to dissolve Henry's marriage to Catherine of Aragon ultimately led to his downfall in 1529 and also to a reformulation of royal strategy. The ensuing rejection of the pope's authority in national matters was forcefully articulated in the Act in Restraint of Appeals to Rome of April 1533, where it was declared that 'this realm of England is an empire.'[14] As the Act clearly articulated, the king henceforth had full power to determine 'all causes, matters, debates and contentions happening to occur, insurge or begin within the limits thereof [his kingdom], without restraint or provocation to any foreign princes or potentates of the world'.[15] This provocative claim had been prefigured in a statement made to the imperial ambassador Eustace Chapuys by Charles Brandon, Duke of Suffolk, in September 1530 that 'the King was absolute both as Emperor and Pope in his own kingdom'.[16] In a letter Chapuys wrote to Charles V he recounted how Thomas Howard, Duke of Norfolk, told him on 12 January 1531 (two days after the king received 'some very injurious mandates' from Rome that 'did not please him much'):

> that the Popes in former times had tried to usurp authority, and that the people would not suffer it, – still less would they do so now; that the King had a right of empire in his kingdom, and recognised no superior; that there had been an Englishman who had conquered Rome, to wit, Brennus; that Constantine reigned here, and the mother of Constantine was English &c. . . . the Duke said he had lately shown the ambassadors of France the seal on the tomb (le sceau ou la sepulture) of King Arthur – I [i.e. Chapuys] did not know of whom he spoke – in which there was a writing, which I would see in a bill of parchment, which he took out of his purse, saying that he had had it copied out for me. This bill contained only the words 'Patricius Arcturus, Brittaniae, Galliae, Germaniae, Daciae Imperator'. I said I was sorry he was not also called Emperor of Asia . . . and if from this he

> argued that they might still make conquests like the said Arthur, let him consider what had become of the Assyrians, Macedonians, Persians, &c.[17]

As Chapuys chose to interpret it, two concepts of *imperator* were merged in the evocation of Arthur that is, both the ruler's right of sovereignty within his own territory and the right of conquest. The claim was thus both jurisdictional and territorial.[18] Although Norfolk may have been invoking only the first concept on this occasion, both certainly would be deployed by English historians and antiquaries in their discussions of Arthur throughout the century.[19]

The figure of *Arthurus imperator* was not specifically invoked in the 1533 Act in spite of the reference to 'divers sundry old authentic histories and chronicles' which could be cited to show that 'this realm of England is an empire, and so hath been accepted in the world, governed by one supreme head and king having the dignity and royal estate of the imperial crown of the same'.[20] Nevertheless, as J. J. Scarisbrick has observed:

> [Thomas] Cromwell's preamble cut out this knotted pleading [found in earlier drafts and discussions] and, not only pushed the case onto rather different grounds, but set England's autonomy on one foundation only, that of secular national history . . . It was to the world of Arthur and Constantine and Geoffrey of Monmouth, therefore, that, rather hesitantly and cryptically, appeal was made. All else had gone.[21]

In early summer 1533, almost immediately after the coronation of Anne Boleyn, for which event he had prepared verses, John Leland, armed with some sort of 'gratius commission', set out on his first set of travels throughout England to examine monastic houses and record the contents of their libraries. It was almost certainly Cromwell, under whose patronage he was operating, who was responsible for the commission. Modelling himself on the efforts of the learned abbot of Spanheim Johann Tritheim (1462–1516), Leland was already envisaging a comprehensive bio-bibliographical dictionary of British writers, *De uiris illustribus*, records of whose writings he hoped to find in the recesses of the monastic libraries.[22] Just over a month before he left London, as we have seen, 'divers sundry old authentic histories and chronicles' had been cited to buttress Henry's imperial claims and there is no doubt that he had his eye out for precisely these sorts of materials.[23] Accounts of Arthur's reign were at the forefront of his mind and Glastonbury Abbey, where Arthur's tomb was still to be found, was one of his first destinations. It proved to be a storehouse of treasures, containing writings by William of Malmesbury, Gerald of Wales, Geoffrey of Monmouth, fragments from the poetry of Melkin the Bard, and 'charta quadam rotunda de laudibus Arthuri'.[24]

Like earlier writers Leland acknowledged that it was not easy to disentangle fact from fiction when dealing with Arthur. He was well aware that although Gildas's *De excidio et conquestu Britannie,* the only written source for the relevant period, described the siege of 'Mons Badonicus' Gildas did not mention Arthur by name. This was (and continues to be) a sticking point. The Italian humanist and long-time English resident Polydore Vergil had produced an edition of the *De excidio c.*1526–7 using a manuscript he himself had acquired and which he had collated with one lent him by Cuthbert Tunstall.[25] It is possible that in producing this edition Vergil was laying the groundwork for his future attack on Geoffrey of Monmouth's glorification of Arthur.[26] Leland, on the other hand, would maintain in his *De uiris illustribus* that although the 'fragmentary short history' printed by Vergil was no doubt 'the work of Gildas' the text had become corrupted over the course of time.[27] One of his goals in 1533 was to find more reliable manuscripts hidden in the monastic libraries, but he was disappointed in his quest: 'I was positive that I would find something, if not at Winchester then at Glastonbury, where, as it turned out, I did not discover so much as a stray leaf' (Quaesiui tamen diligentia quanta potui maxima, et spes fere certa erat, si non Ventae saltem Glessoburgi aliquid inuenirem. At euenit ut ne pagellam quidem offenderim). Admitting defeat, he concluded his chapter on Gildas with the observation that 'So far I have found nothing else about the works of Gildas' (Praeterea de Gildae libris hactenus nihil). As he would point out later, however, Gildas was only just born the year the battle of Mons Badonicus took place and even if he did not mention Arthur in the Ur-*De excidio* this did not prove that the British hero never lived.[28]

In 1534 the Act of Supremacy was passed in which, as befitted his imperial claims, Henry was accorded the title of 'the only supreme head in earth of the Church of England, called Anglicana Ecclesia'. The break with Rome was thus complete and the risk of Henry's excommunication real. That same year Leland travelled through East Anglia and up into Yorkshire and beyond, examining library collections, and came across a copy of pseudo-Nennius' *Historia Brittonum* at Jervaulx Abbey:

> Among these [ancient manuscripts in the library] one presented itself to me with this inscription: 'Nennius on the origin of Britain' . . . I learned from this book that some would-be learned monk had done for Nennius what someone has also done for the history of Gildas, namely, inundated the whole work with extravagant lies, old wives' tales, and prodigious barbarity. Thus it finally came about that instead of the real Nennius some kind of fictitious and ill-equipped trifler emerged.[29]

Because he realized that Nennius was one of the earliest witnesses to Arthur, Leland subsequently collated this manuscript with two others and

> pieced together the history of the text, although it is not free from corruption. It contains much about the origin of the Britons and their genealogies and cities; then about Arthur and the Saxon usurpation . . . Four hundred years ago Henry of Huntingdon came across Nennius's history, although he did not know his name; this is especially clear in the place where he names Arthur's valiant battles.[30]

Ultimately, then, the *Historia Brittonum* (as he restored it) provided a pivotal witness as far as Leland was concerned and vindicated Arthur's historicity in the face of problems with Gildas's surviving text.[31]

In 1534 Polydore Vergil's *Anglica historia* (in a version carrying down to 1509) was printed by Johannes Bebel in Basel. Vergil had begun work on this history not long after his arrival in England in 1502. Soon afterwards, in 1508, the *editio princeps* of Geoffrey of Monmouth's *Historia regum Britannie* was printed in Paris, and in Vergil's original text, completed in 1512–13, the description of Arthur was conceived primarily as a corrective to Geoffrey's excesses:

> After Uther Pendragon was poisoned, his son Arthur succeeded him . . . But he is above all worthy to be remembered by posterity because he is said to have been a strong cultivator of piety, and a lover of the Christian religion. He is said to have defeated three of the leaders of the Saxons in war, and to have imposed a tax on those Saxons; likewise to have reduced Scotland and the islands surrounding Britain to sovereignty; and in like manner to have conquered the Romans near Paris with his troops; also to have laid waste to Gaul and subjected it to himself, and to have slain a great many giants in battle. At last, when he wished to wage war on the city of Rome, he was turned aside from the journey which he had begun by civil discord and he killed his nephew Mordred who had gained control of the kingdom through tyranny in his absence and, wounded himself in that battle, died. Afterwards his body was committed for burial to the monastery at Glastonbury, which he had enriched with many and very large donations. I have narrated these things shortly in order not to neglect my intended brevity, particularly since Geoffrey has written many things about Arthur most effusively, whom I gladly allow to have more faith in these sorts of deeds.[32]

For the most part this is a summary of Part 7 of the *Historia regum Britannie*. Geoffrey, however, was vague about the place of Arthur's burial, stating only that he had been 'carried off to the Isle of Avalon, so that his wounds might be attended to'.[33] By the end of the twelfth century Avalon had been identified with Glastonbury and Vergil picked up on this amplification to Geoffrey's account without making any comment about its reliability.[34]

Why did Vergil wait some twenty years before seeing his work into print and why did it appear exactly when it did? Koebner suggests that his rejection of the Arthurian tradition and his attack on Geoffrey of Monmouth offended Henry and that the king refused to accept the original dedication.[35] Hay argues that a revised version was substantially completed between 1521 and *c*.1524, but that its publication was probably delayed because of the evolving crisis over Henry's first marriage.[36] Koebner too would place the revisions to the early 1520s. Like Hay he believed that it was the printing of Gildas which allowed Vergil to put forth such a strong 'anti-Arthurian position'.[37] Because Henry's concern with the imperial crown in the 1530s made the *Anglica historia* a welcome text, by this reading, and since Vergil had revised his original manuscript to emphasize the precedents for Henry's imperial status and in particular the Constantinian link he was able to stick to his humanist principles on the question of Arthur in the printed edition. Koebner envisaged a very close collaboration between author and Henry's 'henchmen', arguing that in return for supporting Henry's imperial pretensions Vergil was 'permitted to clear his scholarly conscience' and maintain his humanist principles of historiography. Stewart Mottram has also argued that the publication of the *Anglica historia* in 1534 was officially sanctioned and indeed he gives the king himself full credit as the motivating factor: 'It was no coincidence, however, that Henry chose eventually to publish Vergil's chronicle at a time coincident with the 1533 Appeals Act, for if the *Anglica historia* dismisses aspects of the Arthurian legend, it on the other hand enthusiastically affirms the historicity of Norfolk's assertion that "Constantine reigned here, and the mother of Constantine was English".'[38]

According to a letter he wrote to Erasmus on 19 June 1532, Vergil had recently been recalled to Italy. As Vergil explained to Erasmus, Bebel, who had printed most of his books, was visiting England and the two men had met: 'Bebel was recently amongst us and he diligently troubled himself about my business; I told him about my plans and how I have been called back to Italy.'[39] Presumably by 'my business' Vergil meant the printing of the *Anglica historia*.[40] Shrewdly, he had added imperial references – minor word changes or small additions – to his earlier text to suit the current political situation, but it was by no means rewritten in the early 1530s as a piece of Henrician propaganda and was not treated as such by Thomas Cromwell or Henry's other advisers. The final impetus to print, in other words, seems to have come from his meeting with Bebel rather than pressure from the king or his advisers.

In 1529, the same year in which he went to France on government business, presumably relating to the king's divorce, John Rastell published his *The Pastime of People*. As Vergil had done, Rastell summarized Geoffrey's account of Arthur which, as he observed, was 'gretly dyscordant' from that of other medieval writers.[41] He also pointed out that one of the principal pieces of evidence used to prove Arthur's existence was the seal found at Westminster which he considered to be 'faynyd of late'. He gave several reasons for his scepticism, including the fact that Westminster was not founded until after Arthur's supposed reign. In the end Rastell stated that he would neither affirm or deny this story (and presumably the legend as a whole) but that he would 'let every man be at his lyberte to beleve ther in what he lyste'.[42] Given that Norfolk would make so much of the wax seal in 1531 it seems somewhat surprising that Rastell was not challenged on this point when the book first appeared.[43]

Rastell's treatment of the story of Arthur would certainly have appealed to Vergil and it may even have inspired the principal modification to his earlier account of Arthur in his printed edition:

> At this time Uther departed this life, and was succeeded by his son Arthur, who was indeed such a man that, had he lived longer, he would have finally restored the British state, which was all but ruined. Because of the powers of his body and the virtues of his mind, posterity has published the same kind of things about him as are in our days still recounted among the Italians about Roland, the nephew of Charlemagne by his sister. For even now the common folk praise Arthur to the skies, for thrice he overwhelmed Saxon captains in war, gained possession over Scotland and the neighboring islands, defeated the Romans with their general (a certain Lucius) in the territory of Paris, laid waste to Gaul, and finally bested some giants in a fight. It is related that in the end, while he was wanting to visit Rome, he was recalled from this journey by domestic seditions, that he killed his nephew Mordred, who in his absence had gained control of the kingdom as a tyrant, but that he himself received a wound in this fight and died. A few years ago a magnificent tomb for Arthur was erected in the monastery of Glastonbury, that posterity might understand that he was worthy of all ornaments, since [in] Arthur's day that monastery had not yet been founded.[44]

Like Rastell, then, Vergil now used the supposed early date of Arthur's *floruit* to contradict the putative physical remains associated with him, in this case his tomb with its famous inscribed cross at Glastonbury rather than the seal at Westminster. It was, moreover, Vergil's scepticism about the Glastonbury burial – the discovery of which remains a key piece of evidence in the post-Galfridian accounts of Arthur's historicity – that most upset Vergil's contemporaries.[45] Leland was one of the first to react, observing:

> Nevertheless, so that [Polydore] may not seem to be alone in having sense, he does place [Arthur] among the kings in his history, more to pay lip-service to the custom of our race than because he believes it in his heart. This will be readily apparent from the passage, among others, in which he pokes merry and witty fun, or so he thinks, at Arthur's tomb, which is at Glastonbury in Somerset.
>
> (Quanquam, ne solus sapere uideretur, eum inter reges in sua historia ponit, potius ut genti nostrae morem gerat quam quod tale quicquam ex animo scribat, id quod facile apparet cum ex aliis locis tum etiam ex illo ubi lepide et festiue, ut sibi uidetur, in eius sepulchrum, quod est Glessoburgi Smertarum, iocatur.)[46]

Most modern scholars concur with Leland's view that Vergil was sceptical about Arthur's very existence even if he did not state this openly. By Hay's reckoning, for example, Vergil 'expressed himself in terms so scathingly critical that it was clear that he completely disbelieved the story [of Arthur's reign]'.[47] Is this, however, actually the case? As early as the twelfth century William of Malmesbury had affirmed that:

> This [warlike] Arthur [who aided Ambrosius] is the hero of many wild tales among the Britons even in our own day, but assuredly deserves to be the subject of reliable history rather than of false and dreaming fable; for he was long the mainstay of his falling country, rousing to battle the broken spirit of his countrymen, and at length at the siege of Mount Badon, relying on the image of our Lord's Mother which he had fastened upon his arms, he attacked nine hundred of the enemy single-handed, and routed them with incredible slaughter.[48]

Vergil has, in fact, modelled himself on William and the first part of his account is closely similar to William's, perhaps even containing verbal echoes. His point of view is, moreover, paralleled by that of other contemporary antiquaries such as Leland's friend John Twyne, the Canterbury antiquary (*c.*1505–81), who recounted that:

> I should be ashamed to pass over the name of Arthur entirely in silence. He was truly a noble and vigorous youth, a spirited champion of his country, as our native histories tell us, but he was a far lesser figure than is depicted in the writings of Geoffrey. I had rather that so great and pious a prince, and so well-deserving of his country, had not been propped up with such extravagent lies and dull-witted frivolity . . . Arthur has acquired distinction enough on his own account; he does not need fictitious encomia. In peace his justice shall long be borne on the lips of men, in war shall his virtue be praised.
>
> (Verum Arthuri nomen prorsus silentio praeterire, piaculum duxero. Fuit ille quidem uere nobilis iuuenis, strenuus et animosus patriae propugnator, quemadmodum domestica nobis tradunt monumenta, sed Galfredi scriptis multo impar. Nollem equidem tantum tamque pium principem, et tam bene de patria meritum, tam portentosis mendaciis, tamque frigidis nugamentis fulciri . . . Arthurus se ipse satis exornat, nec eget fictitiis encomiis, sed feretur linguis hominum quadiu in pace iusticia, et in bello uirtus laudabitur.)[49]

For both Vergil and Twyne, as for others earlier and later, it was Geoffrey of Monmouth rather than Arthur himself who was being dismissed when they cast doubt on the 'British history'.[50]

The *Anglica historia* did not bring Vergil any tangible benefits in England and there is no indication that it made any impact in the court circles with which he was supposedly connected. There is evidence, however, that it circulated in England soon after its issue, and Leland's reaction, which was almost immediate, is characteristic.[51] In 1535, as in the two previous years, Leland spent part of the year examining monastic libraries, but he also began to compose a preliminary draft of *De uiris illustribus*. Although Leland was by nature a notorious procrastinator, the *Anglica historia* spurred him into action and he planned by means of his bio-bibliographical dictionary to show just how faulty the research of the Italian scholar had been. In a series of passages, many later expunged, he attacked Vergil, sometimes in vituperative language, on a number of specific issues – ancient Latin names and their modern equivalents, lack of profound knowledge of English antiquities and, in particular, unacknowledged borrowings from medieval historians.

Leland's defence of Geoffrey was crucial to his view of the British past and he devoted an extremely long chapter to Geoffrey in the first draft of *De uiris illustribus*. Much was subsequently deleted and only found its way into print when Thomas Hearne published it 'ex autographo' in 1715 under the title *Codrus, Siue Laus & Defensio Gallofridi Arturii Monumetensis contra Polydorum Vergilium*.[52] That this chapter was originally written in response to Vergil is clear; why it was later removed from its original context and incorporated the *Assertio Arturii* is less obvious.

The final session of the Reformation Parliament assembled in February 1536 and by 18 March both Commons and Lords had passed a bill for the dissolution of monastic houses with an annual income of less than £200, the Act for the Suppression of the Lesser Monasteries. There was some discontent and reaction to the first wave of dissolutions, especially on a popular level, and this culminated in the Lincolnshire uprising in October 1536.[53] In May 1536 Thomas Cromwell had summoned the young humanist scholar and budding propagandist Richard Morison back to England from Padua to form part of his secretariat. Written in great haste Morison's *Lamentation in whiche is Shewed what Ruyne and Destruction Cometh of Seditious Rebellyon* was a response, printed anonymously late in 1536, to the October events. The sequel, the longer *Remedy for Sedition*, also anonymously printed in 1536, was directed specifically to those involved in the Pilgrimage. Stewart Mottram has argued that in *A Lamentation* Morison adopted a new approach to replace the Arthurian motif used by earlier Henrician writers:

> Writing to appease rebels who had demanded that Henry put a stop to the dissolution of religious houses in Lincolnshire and elsewhere in England, Morison was only too well aware that the use of Arthurian precedent in existing Royal Supremacy propaganda had failed to adequately popularize Henry's pretensions to empire in the English Church. In the *Lamentation*, Morison responds to these shortfalls in the rhetoric of empire, and he does so by ventriloquizing his own support for Tudor empire in the person of mother England.[54]

In reaction to the so-called Exeter Conspiracy of 1538 Morison composed his *An Invective agenste the Great and Detestable Vice, Treason* (London, 1539). Printed later in the same year was his *Exhortation to Styrre up All Englishemen to the Defence of their Country*, which was a response to very real fears of invasion by continental forces stirred up by 'the cankered and venomous serpent Paul, bishop of Rome.'[55] Leland dealt with the same crisis in his *Antiphilarchia* (not completed until after mid-1541), which answered the attack against Henry found in Albertus Pighius' *Hierarchiae ecclesiasticae assertio* of 1538. It was almost certainly a commissioned work to the degree that it had, like the earlier letter from the king admitting him to the monastic houses, Cromwell's strong backing.

Leland had ceased work on *De uiris illustribus* late in 1536 or in 1537 and did not return to the manuscript in a serious way until 1543. The reasons why he turned to other concerns for some six years are complex, a response perhaps to Henry's hardening attitudes towards monastic life as a result of the Pilgrimage of Grace rather than Leland's own vaunted desire to see and record as much of the countryside as possible after having read about it in the manuscripts he had examined:

> Wherfore after that I had perpendid the honest and profitable studies of these historiographies, I was totally enflammid with a love to see thoroughly al those partes of this your opulente and ample reaulme, that I had redde of yn the aforesaid writers: yn so muche that al my other occupations intermittid I have so travelid yn yowr dominions booth by the se costes and the midle partes, sparing nother labor nor costes, by the space of *these vi. yeres paste* [italics mine], that there is almoste nother cape, nor bay, haven, creke or peere, river or confluence of rivers, breches, waschis, lakes, meres, fenny waters, montaynes, valleis, mores, hethes, forestes, chases, wooddes, cities, burges, castelles, principale manor placis, monasteries, and colleges, but I have seene them; and notid yn so doing a hole worlde of thinges very memorable.[56]

In 1543 he set about filling in new information, adding entries, and deleting material he now planned to use elsewhere. Many of his criticisms of Vergil were removed at this time. The following year his *Assertio inclytissimi Arturii regis Britanniae* appeared in print.[57] Leland included in it information contained in the so-called *Codrus* and he also expanded considerably based on further reading, travels and discoveries. As he explained in the dedicatory letter to Henry VIII, he saw it as his task to defend Arthur against the aspersions of medieval historians such as William of Newburgh as well as modern detractors like Polydore Vergil. Leland's intention was to bring all the available evidence together in one place:

> Therefore in order the whole world might hereafter know how great and how splendid the fame of Arthur formerly was, I shall not be reluctant to write in clear order a full account of his whole life and what ancient authors thought about him.[58]

But for what purpose? If, as Mottram and others have argued, the Arthurian debate was by now rendered otiose, 'the rhetoric of empire [replaced] with a rhetoric of nationhood' in the person of Mother England, why did Leland bring out the *Assertio Arturii* in 1544? Was he merely indulging in an antiquarian whim or is there a context for this?[59]

II

In 1513, when the Scots declared war on England, Henry retaliated by claiming suzerainty over the northern kingdom.[60] Likewise in 1522, when the army of John Stuart, Duke of Albany, was assembled to invade the North of England, Thomas Wolsey presented the imperial ambassador evidence to show that Scotland owed homage to England.[61] This same position was taken up considerably more forcefully when Henry VIII declared war on Scotland in 1542 and issued *A declaration conteyning the iust causes and consyderations of this present warre with the Scottis wherin alsoo appereth the trew & right title the Kinges Most Royall Maiesty hath to the soverayntie of Scotland.*[62] As its title suggests, Henry's treatise was divided into two parts, the first a defence of the war, the second an assertion of England's imperial rights over Scotland from the very earliest times, based on the evidence of historical writings. In the second section Henry appealed, as he had done in the Act in Restraint of Appeals, to precedent – 'dedes, wordes, actes and writings' – to establish 'that the kynges of Scottes have always knowleged the kynges of Englande superior lordes of the realme of Scotlande, and have done homage and fealtie for the same'.[63] Histories which, as he pronounced, 'be called witnesses of tymes, the lyghte of trueth, and the lyfe of memory, and fynally the convenient way and meane, wherby thinges of antiquitee may be brought to mens knowlege', proved that from the first division of the kingdom after Brutus' death England received homage from Scotland and Wales.[64] After a brief discussion of Brutus and his sons Henry passed over 'the deathe of kynge Humbre, the actes of Dunwald king of this realme, the division of Belin and Brene, the victories of king Arthure' (no doubt because they were so well known not because they were irrelevant) and began his full account

> at the yere of our lord, DCCCC, which is, DCXLII, yeres by past, a tyme of sufficient auncientie, from whiche we shall make speciall declaration and evidence of the execution of our right and title of superioritie evermore contynued and preserved hytherto.[65]

After having worked his way forward reign by reign up to Henry VI he noted that Edward IV died as he was preparing for war with Scotland, but that neither the usurper Richard III nor his own father had demanded the legitimate homage. Nor had he himself done so, but this did not, nevertheless, entail 'the losse of any right'.

It has been asserted that Leland was the true author of this tract.[66] Is there, in fact, any tangible evidence to substantiate this claim? Over a number of years Leland's disciple and fellow bio-bibliographer John Bale (1495–1563) kept a notebook in which he recorded the names of British authors, titles of their works, and sources for the information.[67] It contains a list of books 'Ex bibliotheca Anglorum regis' compiled *c.*1548 which includes 'Leylandus de titulo regis ad Scotiam'.[68] Among individual authors Bale gave the following *fons* for his information about Walter of Guisborough's chronicle of the times of Edward III: 'Ex opere Lelandi de iure regis'.[69] He recorded in this same notebook a hitherto unpublished list of 'Autores citati a Ioanne Lelando, in opere de iure Anglorum regis ad Scotie regnum' which shows he must have examined the tract at some length, presumably while it was in the royal library.[70] Bale also listed this work, along with an incipit, in a separate entry for Leland in the *Index*: 'De titulo regis ad Scotiam, li. i: "Lucis natura talis est, quod".'[71] No treatise with this incipit – and this might well be Bale's own translation from English – is known to have survived and one must presume it has been lost.[72] Leland's own notebooks contain a short treatise in English with the heading 'How England should have homage and feaulty of Scotlande'.[73] It begins with an account of Brutus and his sons, followed by 'Dunwald . . . Beline and Brene, king Arthur'. After Arthur it jumps – as did Henry's *A declaration* – to the reign of Edward the Confessor, where it is noted that 'Edward King of Englande, Sun to King Alured, had under his Dominion, and Obedience, the Kinges of Scottes, of Humbre, and Stregtle Waleis, as it apperith in Chronicles written by Mariane a Scote, Roger Hoveden, and Willyam of Malmesbyri'. The rest of the text consists of entries by year or by ruler: the last two are January 1420 (1421 N.S.) for the homage of James I to Henry VI at Windsor, and Februrary 1423 (1424 N.S.) for the marriage of James to Joan, daughter of John Beaufort, Marquess of Dorset and of Somerset.[74]

William Harrison, who had access to Leland's manuscripts, perhaps including some that are now lost, cited Leland extensively in his 'Description of Britain' published in 1577 as part of Holinshed's *Chronicles*.[75] The sixteenth chapter of the first book contains an examination of why 'the sovereigntie of the whole Islande remained still to the prince of Lhoegres and his posteritie after him', citing among other authorities the book written by Leland on the topic for Henry VIII. Harrison described it as follows:

> The tytle also that Lelande giveth his booke, which I have had written with his owne hand, beginneth in this maner: 'These remembraunces following are found in Chronicles authorized, remaining in divers monasteries both in Englande and Scotlande, by which it is evidently knowne and shewed, that the kings of England have had, and now ought to have the sovereigntie over all Scotland, with the homage and fealtie of the kings there reigning from time to time, &c.'[76]

This is, in fact, a quote with minor variations from the text in Leland's notebooks – from which Harrison no doubt copied it – and in what follows most of Leland's account is incorporated into Harrison's narrative, including the section on Arthur.[77] Harrison thus considered this treatise, unattributed in the manuscript, to have been composed by Leland himself rather than copied by him and to have been dedicated to Henry.

Although Leland's text does not contain a declaration of war, it does bear a strong resemblance to the second part of Henry's treatise. They both cover the same materials monarch by monarch, and they are both closely similar in the information they contain for large sections. There are many verbal echoes if not direct quotations.[78] What seems almost certainly the case, then, is that the text found in Leland's notebooks formed the basis for the second part of the *A declaration*.[79] To this extent Leland was indeed the progenitor if not the actual author of the text circulating in Henry's name, a text which set out to provide a more or less unbroken historical line for English overlordship of Scotland.

In the *Assertio Arturii* Leland himself cited a 'Libellus de imperio Britannorum, & Anglorum in Scottos beneficiarios', giving it as a source for the information that Hoel (cousin to King Arthur) defeated the Scots at York and that Arthur made Augustellus 'regulus' over them.[80] The reference was almost certainly to his own English treatise (or the Latin version thereof), in which it is stated that 'the saide King Arture, holding his Royal Fest at Cairleon, had there al the Kinges, that were Subjectes on to hym, emong the which Augusel, the said King of Scottes, did his due Service for the Realm of Scotland, and bare King Artures Swerd afore hym'.[81] For Leland, as for Henry, there was a strong link between overlordship of Scotland and Arthur himself. This, then, gives an explanation for the appearance of the *Assertio Arturii* in 1544, at a point when the Scots had reneged on the Treaty of Greenwich of 1543, which would have brought about union between the two countries, and when Edward Seymour was leading new invasions into Scotland.

In a concluding set of verses to the *Assertio Arturii* Leland saluted Henry in the following terms:

> With a sagacious voice the most learned Widow
> Compared Edward the Black Prince with Hector's triumphs,
> And the poet made known the immortal worth of his achievement.
> The noble impulse of an honest spirit inspired by this
> Commands me to extoll the fame of Henry the Great
> And indeed to join one with many conquerors.
> Amongst whom the distinguished hero Arthur stands out,
> Who often vanquished the Caledonian Scots and the proud
> French through the power of war which he had inflicted.
> Henry by far the most lofty in greater things,
> Surpassed these deeds, the happy victor called the Eighth.
> Edinburgh fell. Boulogne was crushed
> And the bountiful father of his country, and also second Arthur,
> Deliverer from the wickedness that had been committed,
> Returned to his people.
> Now the most sad image of death is present to the conquered
> And the Scots and Morini summon their inauspicous fates.
>
> (Contulit Hectoreis arguta uoce triumphis
> Eduerdum Viduus doctissimus ille Nigellum,
> Et facti pretium tulit immortale poeta.
> Impetus hinc crescens animi generosus honesti,
> Me iubet Henrici titulos extollere magni,
> Et conferre quidem multis uictoribus unum.
> Inter quos praestans Arturius eminet heros,
> Saepe Caledonios qui Scottos, quique superbos
> Perdomuit Gallos indicti fulmine belli.
> Praestitit haec eadem, longe & maiora supremus

> Henricus, felix Octaui nomine uictor.
> Castra puellarum cecidere. Bononia fracta est
> Adque suos rediit patriae pater almus, et idem
> Commissi sceleris uindex Arturius alter.
> Nunc superest uictis tristissima mortis imago,
> Et sua fata uocant Scotti, Morinique sinistra.)[82]

Arthur's story, as this encomium make clear, provided one of the culminating moments of England's overlordship of Scotland and it also emphasizes the close parallel between Henry and his illustrious ancestor, especially in his conquests.[83] It is in this context of Henry as 'Arturius rediuiuus' that Vergil's or even William's restrained evocation of Arthur as a *local* hero who died before he could fulfil his potential is shown to be wanting. It was the rejection by these historians of Geoffrey's imperial Arthur, conqueror of Scotland and France, not just the historical Arthur *per se*, that was at the heart of the matter.[84] From the very beginning, as Leland observed, Arthur's kingdom included more than England alone: 'The history of Brittaine affirmeth that Arthure began his Raigne over the Islandes of this kingdome in the xv. yeare of his age, and was crowned of Dubritius Bishop of the City of Caerlegion vpon Vske in Wales.'[85] And, as the 'libellus de imperio Britannorum, & Anglorum in Scottos beneficiarios' made clear, Arthur quelled the Scots when they attempted to deny his sovereignty. Likewise Arthur formed part of a continuity of rulers that stretched far back and which included Rome itself among its conquests:

> Were not those Brittaines valiant and coragious persons? Againe, what were they when Bellinus & Brennus added the Romane Empyre vnto their victories? what were they in the daies of Constantine the Emperor, & sonne of Helen sometime heere Queene? what were they in the raigne of Aurelius Ambrosius Anno, post Christ. 466. whom also Paule the Deacon extolleth with praises? And to conclude what fellowes were they in the daies of our famous Arthure?[86]

Writing in the years just after the Dissolution, when so many records had been destroyed, so much historical knowledge lost for ever, Leland was acutely sensitive to the manner in which manuscripts documenting the past could disappear. By his reckoning the present situation may well have been paralleled by the destruction unleashed when the Saxons overwhelmed the British.[87] Unlike the Saxons, the British had maintained a pure form of Christianity and had rejected the Roman Church; in so doing they incurred the wrath of the pope who, in turn, exercised every means possible to keep the Saxons under his wicked jurisdiction (*imperium*) and who was cursed for this by the Britons. Craftily, the Roman pontiff then turned Saxon against Briton and no Saxon writer henceforth would praise the British. Silence about Arthur the Briton could therefore ultimately be interpreted as part of a campaign of repression on the part of the papacy and Leland's recovery of this hero was, among other things, a vindication of Henry's break with Rome.[88]

III

In the early years of Elizabeth's reign William Cecil (later Lord Burghley) envisaged a united Protestant Britain, but Elizabeth herself 'remained unmoved by the claim to feudal superiority over Scotland which had so excited her father and which Cecil was not slow to resurrect'.[89] Arthur's name once again became linked with empire in the 1570s, however, both in a more modern sense and the earlier one deployed by Henry in his break with Rome and in his negotiations with the Scots. In this context, of course, upholding Arthur's historicity was crucial.

John Dee (1527–1608), the Elizabethan antiquary and magus, saw an extraordinary precedent in the heroic exploits of Arthur – after whom he named his eldest son – and tried to influence Elizabethan policy in radical ways based on them. Two of his works, one printed and one left in manuscript, examine Elizabeth's imperial claims in detail. The printed book, his *General and Rare Memorials Pertayning to the Perfect Arte of Navigation* (*STC* 6459; London, 1577), which focuses upon Edgar as father of the English Navy, has been much analysed,[90] but the manuscript, *Brytanici imperii limites*, which devotes considerable space to Arthur, and which can be seen as an occult key to the *General and Rare Memorials* , has only recently come to light.[91]

In the *Limites* Dee claimed to have gone back *ad fontes* in good humanist manner.[92] He specifically maintained that he had not plundered 'secondary sources' such as the Arthurian tracts of Leland and Prise:

> Your Majestie may perceive that I borrow heere no parcell either of Mr *Leyland* or of Sir John Ap *Rhese* knight ther notable *Arthurien* pamphletes wherwith to make heere some shew answerable to Kinge Arthur his due commendations.[93]

In spite of his disclaimers, however, most of his evidence had already been deployed by these earlier writers.[94] Ultimately, Dee's most authoritative source for the Arthurian period was Geoffrey of Monmouth and he claimed, implausibly, that he had seen the lost British source 'translated' by Geoffrey.[95] He stated, moreover, that many other monuments of antiquity recounting the same events had survived, in spite of the machinations of Polydore Vergil who had tried to suppress the evidence they presented by burning 'a whole carte load almost'.[96] Among other authorities, Dee cited Edward's letter to Boniface and related documents, Thomas Walsingham (not used by Leland), and Henry's *A declaration conteyning the iust causes and consyderations of this present warre with the Scottis*. He concluded that 'From these and other premises it is clearly agreed, and recognized as the case, that the foresaid kingdom of Scotland both actually and by right fully belongs to us.'[97]

Dee's chief addition to the accounts of Leland and Prise (he believed he was related to the latter) derived from a letter sent him by the cartographer Gerard Mercator (1512–94) concerning the adventures of Jacobus Cnoyen of Herzogenbusch. A fourteenth-century traveller, Cnoyen had apparently seen a *Gesta Arthurii* and had met at the Norwegian court a priest from Greenland. This priest knew an Oxford Franciscan who was the author of the *Inuentio fortunatae*, a lost treatise describing the north polar regions.[98] These documents proved authoritatively in Dee's opinion that King Arthur had discovered and colonized lands in the North Atlantic and therefore 'That all these Northern Iles and Septentrional Parts are lawfully appropriated to the Crown of this Brytish Impire.'[99]

Dee's considerable emphasis on the Scottish question in his discussion of 'this Incomparable Brytish Empire', so Armitage has argued

> owed something to the ideological heritage of the Rough Wooing, as his vision of the British empire included an English claim to 'the Lawfull Possession as well as the Proprietie of the Supremacy over *Scotland*' . . . This was still a British empire founded on England's terms, an Anglo-British composite monarchy, extending the borders of the recently expanded Anglo-Welsh state to incorporate the surrounding isles and kingdoms as 'British'.[100]

There was, however, another factor, one which Dee articulated most clearly in a later treatise, now BL MS Royal 7 C. xvi, fols. 158–66, addressed in 1597 to Sir Edward Dyer (who had been the dedicatee of the manuscript version of the *Memorials*) and entitled 'Thalattokratia Brettaniki or British Sea-Sovereignty'.[101]In the 'Thalattokratia Bretanniki' Dee observed that Scotland's position opposite those northern parts colonized by Arthur meant that England had 'Limits Absolute' (that is total jurisdiction) to the ocean separating the two regions, since both areas were subject to the queen. More specifically, he referred Dyer to the significance of the arguments put forth in the *Limites* concerning Elizabeth's sovereignty over Scotland.[102] Dee had observed in the *Limites* that Norway faced Scotland on the west and that Arthur had conquered Norway, citing 'De iure et de appendiciis corone regni Britannie' (in his translation) to the effect that

> in those times King Arthur made petition to the Lord Pope and to the Roman curia, that Norway be confirmed in perpetuity to the British crown in augmentation of this kingdom: and the said Arthur called it the vault of Britain.[103]

Since, however, Norway had not remained under the jurisdiction of the English monarch, he was willing, at least for the time being, to concede a Limit Respective, that is a divided control over the sea.

In terms of Elizabeth's sovereignty over the whole island, in terms of her claims in North America, in terms of Europe, then, Arthur was crucial to Dee's arguments. Ultimately, however, it was the European context that mattered most when he wrote the *Limites*. Unlike the *Memorials*, the *Limites* included the Spanish Netherlands in Arthur's conquests.[104] By right of descent from Arthur, moreover, Elizabeth could claim even greater parts of Europe.[105] The *Limites* was composed under the patronage of Robert Dudley, Earl of Leicester. Leicester, who was aware of Elizabeth's respect for Dee, wished at this particular juncture to thwart the Catholic party at court who were attempting to promote the Anjou match. It was probably he who arranged for Dee to bring a copy to the court which was at Norwich in August in 1578. Dee's prayer that Elizabeth be granted life until

> all the westerne and northen partes of your mightie British Impier maie completlie be rediscovered, recovered, and trivmphantlie enioyed, but till also your easterlie and southerlie disdaynfull vassalles and tributaries will in very lovinge wise render such homage and arrerages unto your Majestie as by reason conscience and lawe they ought to doo

would, Leicester believed, encourage Elizabeth to support his aggressive policies in the Netherlands.[106] Dee's own thoughts during this period, however, were considerably more apocalyptic than Leicester's. Basing himself on the historical/astrological divisions posited by Johann Tritheim in his *De septem secundeis* (completed in 1508 and dedicated to the Habsburg Emperor Maximilian I; pr.1515) and on astrological signs Dee believed that he was witnessing the propitious time for Elizabeth to pursue her 'iust Arthurien clayme and title Imperiall'. Under the auspicious influence of Venus, he posited, 'The Preeminence and Priviledge by God, and Nature, Appropriat to this British Monarch is Incredible' for the attainment of an 'Incredible Politicall Mystery and will be for yet awhile'. The mystery was no less than Elizabeth's identification as the Last Reforming Emperor who would unify Christendom.[107]

Although Leicester's plans failed and although the *Limites* did not influence government policy,[108] Dee was once again summoned to the court two years later, in October 1580, to discuss Elizabeth's Arthurian 'Title Royall, to many forraign Countryes, kingdomes, and provinces'.[109] On this occasion, however, Burghley, who had a deep familiarity with genealogical matters, disputed his claims. Later that year, moreover, Leicester shifted his support to an alliance with Anjou and soon severed his ties with Dee.[110] Dee himself left for Europe in 1583 in the company of his notorious scryer Edward Kelley and did not return until November 1589. For the next few years he attempted to recoup his finances by jockeying for various appointments, without much success, but in February 1596 he took up the wardenship of the collegiate church at Manchester. It was from Manchester that he wrote the 'Thalattokratia Brettaniki' at Dyer's request, but, as Parry has argued, 'in historical terms the treatise proved meaningless . . . Political expediency had trumped traditional theories of *mare liberum*.[111]

IV

In the years leading up to Elizabeth's death, when it became more and more clear that James VI would succeed her, the Scots showed themselves disturbed by the idea of a united Britain, so crucial to Leland and Dee's thought, in which they might be 'subalterne' to England.[112] When James first came to the throne he was prepared to consider the possibility of a multiple monarchy, but soon retreated to the position articulated by Henry's *A declaration* and taken up by Dee in the *Limites* of a single imperium. In the final analysis, however, as Mason has observed, 'when James gloried in his Constantinian and even Arthurian inheritance, he [no doubt] understood it to mean something different from Elizabeth's understanding of it: expansive, perhaps even transoceanic, rather than insular and introverted'.[113]

Edmund Spenser had obtained a place in Leicester's household in 1579 and in 1580, the year he began work on *The Faerie Queene*, he was made secretary to Lord Grey of Wilton, who had been appointed lord lieutenant of Ireland through Leicester's patronage. As we have seen, Leland's *Assertio* was translated into English by Richard Robinson and printed by John Wolfe in 1582.[114] It was addressed to Lord Grey, to Sir Henry Sidney, Leicester's brother-in-law,[115] and Sir Thomas Smythe (1522–91), 'customer' of the port of London, and a client of Leicester's.[116] The dedications situate the text within the Leicester orbit and the material would have had resonances for Leicester himself. It also gives a good indication of how Arthur was perceived by the middling sort of Englishman in the years leading up to the publication of *The Faerie Queene*. Like Dee, Robinson had no doubt about the historicity of Arthur, the 'renoumed auncestor' of King Henry VIII. He praised Leland as the culmination of a long successions of scholars who had asserted and glorified the historical Arthur,[117] and himself added further information from more recent antiquaries, Stephan Batman (*c.*1542–84), chaplain to Archbishop Parker, John Stow (1524/5–1605), historian of the City of London, and William Camden (1551–1623), the sixth edition of whose *Britannia* (1607) contains an engraving of the lost cross from Arthur's tomb at Glastonbury. In spite of the antiquarian and historical nature of the tract itself, nevertheless, Robinson's own view of Arthur, as his preface makes clear, was primarily a moral and religious one.[118] In 1543, by Robinson's account, Henry VIII granted a charter to the Worshipful Society of Archers of London, an organization that modelled itself on King Arthur and his Round Table.[119] Through his patronage Henry

> not onely . . . imitated the examplers of godly K. David for his Israelites as before, and of that noble Emperour Leo in ouerthrowing idolatrie, and exalting archerie maugre the mallice of that Romane Antichrist, and all his members: but also invincibly maintayned the praiseworthie practize of this shooting in peace & wars by the examples of his princly progenitors.[120]

It was to foster this society and through it to advance the Universal Church of Christ so that

> with the shaftes of his mouth or worde and gospell of peace may pearce throughout the worlde to the advancement of his glory which shal sit on the raineboe in his maiestie to iudge all Nations',

that Robinson undertook his translation.[121]

The following year Robinson's *The auncient order, societie, and unitie laudable, of Prince Authure, and his knightly armory of the Round Table With a threefold assertion frendly in favour and furtherance of English archery at this day* appeared, also published by Wolfe, and dedicated to Smythe. In his prefatory letter Robinson affirmed that the Round Table was a religious as well as military organization, ordained by the Lord of Lords and King of Kings. The text contains a detailed explanation of the significance of the Round Table:

> I say therfore that the Rounde Table was one ordenance and institution which King Arthure of great Britayne made and ordained . . . And it was on this maner made to defend the Island of Malogres within the said Kingdome of Great Brittaine. By this ordenance ought & were bound to come & assist him once in the year at ye feast of Whytsontyde all travayling Knights, and theare to enranck themselves at the sayd table, and were set downe in great honour and reverence, feasting in the presence and Companie of the saide King Arthure. And moreover, every Knight of this order was bound to rehearse and recon up all his feates of armes, valyant actes and conquestes which they had exployted, by the labour and travaill of their Bodyes for the honour of Nobility, and estate of Knighthood and as well for the honour of their Ladyes as for other purposes tending unto al honour and glory: In such sort that they all, and every of them so aspired to that estate, that they mightely amplified the said Round Table, whereby the nomber of them was very great.[122]

What is emphasized, then, is the moral dimension of the Round Table: it provides a model of behaviour towards which the present generation can aspire and thus each member of the Elizabethan Society took the name, and thereby the attributes, of one of the knights of Arthur's court. The initials of the individual who incarnated this knight's virtues flanked the fifty-eight shields of the original Arthurian knights. It appears that Spenser's old headmaster, Richard Mulcaster, was a member of the Society[123] and in Robinson's description of its workings we certainly get a prefiguration of the way in which Spenser would treat Arthur through the colouring of 'historicall fiction' as 'the image of a brave knight, perfected in the twelve private morall vertues'.[124] As Leland's river poem the *Cygnea cantio* was transformed in Spenser's *Prothalamion*,[125] so too does his Arthurianism as reflected in *A Learned and True Assertion of the Original Life, Actes, and Death of the Most Noble Prince Arthure, King of Great Britaine* take on a new and different life in *The Faerie Queene*.

Notes

1 Various people have read drafts of this essay and have commented on it. I thank them here: William Connell, Julia Crick, Igor Djordjevic, Siân Echard, Felicity Heal, Glyn Parry, Philip Schwyzer, William Sherman, and Jennifer Summit. I have also profited from C. S. L. Davies's 'Information, Disinformation, and Political Knowledge under Henry VII and early Henry VIII' which he kindly showed me in advance of publication.

2 Later in the century Thomas Bowes railed against 'the Legend of lies, *Huon of Burdeaux*, *King Arthur*, with the rest of that rabble': see *The Second Part of the French Academie* (London, 1594), sig. B4r.

3 'The *British History* in early Tudor propaganda', *Bulletin of the John Rylands Library,* 44 (1961–2), 17–48 (p. 40); see also his *Spectacle, Pageantry, and Early Tudor Policy* (Oxford, 1969).

4 'King Arthur and court poems for the birth of Arthur Tudor in 1486', *Humanistica Lovaniensia,* 36 (1987), 147–83 (p. 155).

5 Ibid., p. 164.

6 Ibid., p. 163.

7 See *Humanism and History: Origins of Modern English Historiography* (Ithaca and London, 1987), p. 49.

[8] ‘The *British History* in early Tudor propaganda’, p. 19.

[9] ‘“The Imperial Crown of this Realm”: Henry VIII, Constantine the Great and Polydore Vergil’, *Bulletin of the Institute of Historical Research,* 26 (1953), 29–52 (p. 31).

[10] See ‘King Henry and King Arthur’, *Arthurian Literature*, 16 (1998), pp. 171–96 (pp. 173–4).

[11] See his ‘The painting of the Table’, in *King Arthur's Round Table: An Archaeological Investigation*, ed. Martin Biddle (Woodbridge, 2000), pp. 425–73 (pp. 450–63). Concerning the London pageants in 1522 see ibid., pp. 425–8.

[12] ‘The painting of the Table’, esp. pp. 472–3.

[13] ‘John Foxe as historian’, in *John Foxe's Book of Martyrs On Line Variorum Edition*, Introductory essays.

[14] Apart from Koebner see Walter Ullmann, ‘This Realm of England is an Empire’, *JEH*, 30 (1979), 175–203; John Guy, ‘Thomas Cromwell and the intellectual origins of the Henrician revolution’, in *Reassessing the Henrician Age: Humanism, Politics and Reform 1500–1550*, ed. Alistair Fox and John Guy (Oxford, 1986), pp. 151–78; Dale Hoak, ‘The iconography of the Crown Imperial’, in *Tudor Political Culture*, ed. Dale Hoak (Cambridge, 1995), pp. 54–103.

[15] *The Tudor Constitution: Documents and Commentary*, ed. G. R. Elton, 2nd edn (Cambridge, 1982), p. 353.

[16] *Cal. State Papers: Spanish*, IV.i, 734 (no. 445).

[17] *LP* V.20 (1531–2), 45. See also Graham Nicholson, ‘The Act of Appeals and the English Reformation’, in *Law and Government under the Tudors: Essays Presented to Sir Geoffrey Elton on His Retirement*, ed. Claire Cross, David Loades and J. J. Scarisbrick (Cambridge, 1988), pp. 19–30, at pp. 23–5. The seal (on which see below) was not, in fact, kept at Glastonbury where Arthur's body was found but rather at Westminster. Norfolk owned a copy of the world chronicle of Guillaume de Nangis (d.1300) which he subsequently presented to the king. It contains a section on King Arthur, including his victories against the Romans, and there is a marginal note by his secretary, ‘Nota de fine Arturi’. I thank Dan Williman for this reference.

[18] See David Armitage, ‘Making the empire British: Scotland in the Atlantic world 1542–1707’, *Past and* Present, 155 (May 1997), 34–63. As Armitage has pointed out, ‘The Scottish Parliament claimed in 1469 that James III had “ful Jurisdictioune and fre Impire within his Realme”, thereby ante-dating the Henrician parliament's assertion that the “realm of England is an empire” by more than sixty years’ (p. 38).

[19] Stewart Mottram has maintained that Chapuys misunderstood Norfolk's meaning. He also observed that as early as 1517 Cuthbert Tunstall, at that time Master of the Rolls and vice-chancellor, upheld ‘England as an empire in recognition of the political autonomy of its sovereign’ (‘Reading the rhetoric of nationhood in two Reformation pamphlets by Richard Morison and Nichola Bodrugan’, *Renaissance Studies*, 19 (2005), 523–40 (pp. 530, 535)).

[20] Koebner suggests that the vagueness occurs because Henry had become aware ‘that it was unwise to make Constantine's Church settlement a point of public argument’ (p.43). He also points out that the wording of the Act had been modified to remove the ‘phrase which made the Imperial Crown and its jurisdiction in spiritual matters appear to be the customary law of the land’ (p. 44). See also Ullmann, ‘“This Realm of England is an Empire”’, p. 203, who notes that ‘Henry's “imperial crown” formally signalled the rebirth and the appropriation of late Roman governmental principles in a contemporary, native guise.’

[21] *Henry VIII* (London, 1968), p. 314. On the earlier draft of the bill of annates with its strong invocation of ‘the imperial crown of this realm’ see G. W. Bernard, *The King's Reformation: Henry VIII and the Remaking of the English Church* (New Haven and London, 2005), pp. 56–7. As Bernard has pointed out, the draft corresponds closely to the arguments put forward to a group of great men by the Duke of Norfolk in February 1532. In March 1532 the Supplication against the Ordinaries had maintained that canon law and ecclesiastical courts diminished Henry's imperial jurisdiction. Geoffrey's Arthur, it should

be noted, refused to pay tribute to Rome and thus confirmed England as a sovereign rather than a vassal nation.

[22] See John Leland. *De uiris illustribus / On Famous Men*, ed. James P. Carley with the assistance of Caroline Brett (Toronto and Oxford, 2010).

[23] On 5 September, 1533 – just two days before the birth of Elizabeth – Norfolk wrote from Greenwich to Thomas Cranmer, archbishop of Canterbury, requesting in the name of the king all books and writings in Cranmer's custody concerning Henry's 'great cause'. In his response Cranmer explained that these had been delivered to Cromwell. (See *LP* 6.1078.) Cromwell was presumably building up his arsenal of learned materials in preparation for a backlash to the Act and the birth of the new royal heir, who at this date was presumed to be a boy.

[24] See *English Benedictine Libraries: The Shorter Catalogues*, ed. R. Sharpe *et al.* (Corpus of British Medieval Library Catalogues, 4; London, 1996), B44.

[25] On the date and probable publication in Antwerp see Dennis E. Rhodes, 'The first edition of Gildas', *The Library*, 6th ser., 1 (1979), 355–60.

[26] See *The Anglica Historia of Polydore Vergil A.D. 1485–1537*, ed. and trans. Denys Hay, Camden Series, 74 (1950), p. xiii; also his *Polydore Vergil: Renaissance Historian and Man of Letters* (Oxford, 1952), p. 30.

[27] *De uiris illustribus*, ed. Carley, c. 32. See also Leland's comments on Gildas in his *Assertio inclytissimi Arturii regis Britanniae* (London, 1544): 'Gildas a Polidoro aeditus, fragmentum in dubie Gildae ueteris, sed mancum, luxatum, & mutilum' (*Gildas* his historie is published abroade of *Polidorus*, undoubtedlie a fragment of the old *Gildas*, but it is lame, out of order, and maimed). In what follows I quote, for the most part, Leland's *Assertio* in the translation by Richard Robinson, as *A learned and true assertion of the original, life, actes, and death of the most noble, valiant, and renoumed Prince Arthure, King of great Brittaine* (London, 1582). My page references are to the edition by William Edward Mead, in *The Famous Historie of Chinon of England*, ed. Christopher Middleton (EETS, OS 165; 1925), pp. 140, 79.

[28] 'Gildas nullam prorsus Arturii mentionem facit: ergo non fuit. Arguta plane collectio, qualis & haec. Gildas non meminit Aruiragi, Lucii, aut Constantini Magni, proinde non fuerunt. O nouum dialectices acumen' (*Gildas* makes no mention at all of *Arthure*: *Ergo* he was nevere living. Undoubtedly a subtile gathering, such a one as this is: *Gildas* remembreth not *Arviragus*, *Lucius*, or *Constantine* the greate, and therefore they were not living. O straunge force of Logicke!) (*Assertio*, pp. 140, 79). On the problems posed by Gildas's ignorance of Lucius and the importance of Nennius' reference to him see Felicity Heal, 'What can King Lucius do for you? The Reformation and the early British Church', *English Historical Review*, 120 (2005), 593–614 (p. 595).

[29] *De uiris illustribus*, ed. Carley, c. 47: 'Inter quae unum se mihi obtulit cum hac inscriptione: "Nennius de origine Britanniae" . . . hunc ego ex illa lectione fructum coepi, ut deprehenderim sciolum aliquem monachum id in Nennii gratiam, quod quidam etiam in Gildae historia fecit, praestitisse, nempe totum opus splendidis mendaciis, anilibus fabulis, et prodigiosa barbarie confudisse. Ita tandem euenit ut pro uero Nennio emerserit nescio quis ficticius et subornatus nugator.'

[30] 'inuenta tandem duo, multo cum labore, exemplaria plane antiquissima, ex quibus deprehendi non incorruptam autoris historiam. Multa illic de Britannorum origine et genealogiis ac urbibus; tum de Arturio et Saxonum tyrannide . . . Inciderat Henricus Venantodunensis quadringentis abhinc annis in Nennii historiam, sed nomine ignotam; id quod eo maxime liquet loco quo fortia Arturii bella recitat.'

[31] Leland's friend Sir John Prise, on whom see below, believed that the *Historia Brittonum* was written by Gildas, and Leland pointed out that he was inaccurate in this supposition: see *Assertio*, pp. 100, 22. For Prise, as Daniel Huws has observed ('Gildas Prisei', *The National Library of Wales Journal,* 17 (1971–2), 314–20 at p. 314), the *Historia Brittonum* was 'the cornerstone of his arguments, the proof that the core of the British History existed long before Geoffrey of Monmouth got to work'.

[32] 'Vtherium Pendraconem ueneno necatum Arthurus filius insecutus est . . . Sed inprimis dignus est, cuius memoria clara sit ad posteros, quod uehemens fuisse dicitur cultor pietatis, religionisque

Christianae amator. Hic fertur tres Saxonum duces bello superasse, ipsisque Saxonibus uectigal imposuisse, item Scotiam ac circumiacentes Britanniae insulas in ditionem redegisse, Romanos itidem prope Parisium armis uicisse, Galliam quoque ferro et flamma deuastasse, sibique subegisse, Gigantes simul plures pugnando trucidasse, ac ad postremum dum uellet urbem Romam bello petere, domesticis seditionibus ab incoepto itinere auersus Mordredum nepotem qui regnum per tyrannidem in eius absentia occupauerat, interfecisse, et in eo certamine ipse uulneratus cecidisse. Corpus postea in coenobio Glasconiense sepulturae demandatum est, quod ille multis ac amplissimis ditauerat donariis. Haec paucis perstrinximus, ne propositam breuitatem omitteremus, cum praesertim Gaufredus multa effusissime de Arthuro litteris mandauerit, cui plus fidei quam nobis super huiusmodi gestis rebus haberi facile patimur.' The Latin text is quoted in Hay, p. 199. See also p. 187 on a passage later omitted in the printed text to the effect that 'the need to give material from Geoffrey of Monmouth arises from the publication of an edition by the greedy Paris printers.'

[33] Vergil would, of course, have been aware of William of Malmesbury's statement: 'Sed Arturis sepulchrum nusquam uisitur, unde antiquitas neniarum adhuc eum uenturum fabulatur' (Arthur's grave, however, is nowhere to be found, whence come the traditional old wives' tales that he may yet return). See *Gesta regum Anglorum*, ed. and trans. R. A. B. Mynors, R. M. Thomson and M. Winterbottom, 2 vols (Oxford, 1998), I.520–1.

[34] On this identification see my 'Introduction' to *Glastonbury Abbey and the Arthurian Tradition* (Cambridge, 2001), pp. 1–11, at pp. 1–4.

[35] Koebner, 'The Imperial Crown', pp. 35–6. See also Mottram, 'Reading the rhetoric of nationhood', p. 537: 'Vergil had completed his original manuscript in 1513, but Henry had seen fit to prohibit its publication during the interim period. This prohibition was related to Vergil's refusal in the *Anglica Historia* to accept the historicity of the Arthurian legend that Norfolk would later use to uphold Henry's pretensions to empire in the English Church.'

[36] *Polydore Vergil*, p. 82. Henry's concerns over the legitimacy of his marriage to his brother's widow date to approximately 1527.

[37] Koebner, 'The Imperial Crown', p. 36.

[38] 'Reading the rhetoric of nationhood', p. 537.

[39] 'Fuit nuper nobiscum Bibelius, qui rem meam nauiter curauit; illum docui de rebus meis et quemadmodum reuocor in Italiam': *Opus epistolarum Des. Erasmi Roterodami*, ed P. S. Allen *et al.*, 12 vols (Oxford, 1906–58), X.2662.

[40] Certainly this is how William J. Connell inteprets it in *ODNB*.

[41] Sig. Ciiir. Rastell signalled out Bede and William of Malmesbury among these writers.

[42] Sig. Ciiiv.

[43] It seems likely, however, that Leland was reacting to Rastell when he discussed the seal at such length in a deleted passage in c. 161 of *De uiris illustribus*: 'The [visible] side bears a truly heroic effigy of Arthur himself. He sits, robed in royal purple, on a semicircle which looks to me like a rainbow. He wears a crown on his head and carries a sceptre ornamented with a lily in his right hand. In his left he holds an orb, in the middle of which rises the cross, the symbol of a Christian prince' (Altera effigiem refert ipsius Arturii plane heroicam. Sed et etenim regali indutus purpura super semicirculum, qualis nobis apparet pluuius arcus. Capite coronam gestat dextraque sceptrum, lilii ornamento insigne. Leua autem tenet orbem, in cuius medio crux eminet, Christiani principis indicium) (*De uiris illustribus*, ed. Carley, pp. 314–15). In the *Assertio Arturii* Leland speculated that the seal had been transported from Glastonbury to Westminster by Henry II, thus answering Rastell's dismissal of it as a fake on the grounds of the later foundation date of Westminster. He therefore maintained: 'Neither surely is there any thing apparant, (that I doe knowe of) which more evidently approveth that *Arthure* was living, then the same Seale doth' (Nec certe, quod ego sciam, extat quicquam quod luculentius ipso sigillo comprobet Arturium fuisse) (*Assertio*, pp. 41, 113–14). Writing in the late 1540s Elis Gruffydd, on the other hand, paraphrased Rastell's account of the seal and concluded that it was probably a forgery: see Ceridwen Lloyd-Morgan,

'Welsh tradition in Calais: Elis Gruffydd and his biography of King Arthur', in *The Fortunes of King Arthur*, ed Norris J. Lacy (Cambridge, 2005), pp. 77–91 (p. 90).

[44] Book III. c. 13: 'Vtherius per idem tempus e uita migrauit, cui successit filius Arthurus, uir profecto talis qui, si diutius uixisset, rem prope perditam suis omnino Britannis tandem aliquando restituisset. De hoc propter ingentes pariter corporis uires atque animi uirtutes posteritas ea ferme praedicauit quae de Rolando Caroli Magni ex sorore nepote memoria nostra apud Italos decantatur, tametsi ille in flore iuuentutis periit. Quippe etiam nunc uulgus mirandis fert ad coelum laudibus Arthurum, quod tres bello superasset Saxonum duces, quod Scotiam cum uicinis insulis in suam potestatem redegisset, quod Romanos in agro Parisiorum cum quodam Lucio eorum duce deleuisset, Galliamque deuastasset, ac demum gigantes homines ualentes pugnando occidisset. Hic ad extremum tot bellorum uictor fertur, dum uellet urbem Romam bello petere, domesticis seditionibus ab incoepto itinere reuocatus, Morderedum nepotem, qui regnum per tyrannidem in eius absentia occupauerat, interfecisse, et in eo certamine ipse uulneratus cecidisse. Abhinc item paucos annos positum fuit Arthuro in Glasconiensi coenobia sepulchrum opere magnificum, quo posteri intelligerent illum omnibus ornamentis dignum fuisse, quando Arthuri tempore coenobium illud nondum erat conditum.' The text and translation come from the hypertext edition by Dana F. Sutton: see www.philological.bham.ac.uk/polverg/3lat.html #13; 3eng.html#13.

[45] On monuments to Arthur at Glastonbury Abbey see Michelle P. Brown and James P. Carley, 'A fifteenth-century revision of the Glastonbury epitaph to King Arthur', in *Glastonbury Abbey and the Arthurian Tradition*, pp. 193–204. In *A chronycle with a genealogie declaryng that the Brittons and Welshemen are linealiye dyscended from Brute* (London, 1547), sig. c.iiiiv Arthur Kelton referred to an otherwise unattested cross with letters of gold commemorating Arthur found at Glastonbury *c*.1538/9. Kelton's treatise was directed against Vergil and on sig. c.viiv. 'To Master Polldorus' appears in the margin beside a stanza that reads: 'Recante your fayned fantasie / Confesse your faulte, all is untrewe / Make some excuse, with honestie / Affirme the slepe, was in your iye / Feble with watche, hevy was your hed / Ye wist not well, what ye wrote or said.' On Kelton see my 'Glastonbury, the Grail-Bearer and the sixteenth-century antiquaries', in *The Grail, the Quest and the World of Arthur*, ed. Norris J. Lacy (Cambridge, 2008), pp. 156–72 (pp. 167–8).

[46] *De uiris illustribus*, ed. Carley, pp. 312–13.

[47] *Polydore Vergil*, p. 158.

[48] *Gesta regum Anglorum*, ed. and trans. Mynors *et al.*, I. 26–7: 'Hic est [bellicosus] Artur de quo Britonum nugae hodieque delirant, dignus plane quem non fallaces somniarent fabulae sed ueraces predicarent historiae, quippe qui labantem patriam diu sustinuerit infractasque ciuium mentes ad bellum acuerit, postremo in obsessione Badonici montis, fretus imagine Dominicae matris quam armis suis insuerat, nongentos hostium solus adorsus incredibili cede profligarit.'

[49] *De rebus Albionicis, Britannicis, atque Anglicis commentariorum libri duo*, c. 79. I quote from the forthcoming edition and translation by James Hankins and I am very grateful to him for providing me with this material in advance of publication. Although this work was not printed until after Twyne's death (it appeared in 1590), it was probably first drafted in the 1530s. Twyne's son Thomas translated Humphrey Llwyd's *Commentarioli Britannicae descriptionis fragmentum* (1568), as *The Breviary of Britayne* (1573). In this text Llwyd saluted King Arthur, 'whose everlastynge renowme, and moste noble deedes: our freende Mayster *Leland*, hath set foorthe, and made more apparant by infinite testimonies, and moste weightie argumentes agaynst the gnarrynge, and doggysh mouthe, and hatred more then ever was *Vatinians* of *Polydorus Vrbine*' (fols 91v–92r).

[50] Nevertheless, as Mottram states ('Reading the rhetoric of nationhood', pp. 537–8), Geoffrey had become so deeply associated with Arthur that 'By undermining Geoffrey's treatment of King Arthur, Vergil undermines the historicity of the Arthurian legend that Norfolk had used to uphold Henry's imperialist pretensions before the Imperial ambassador, Eustace Chapuys.'

[51] For a much earlier account of my thoughts on this topic, focusing almost entirely on the *Assertio Arturii*, see 'Polydore Vergil and John Leland on King Arthur: the battle of the books', in *King Arthur: A Casebook*, ed. Edward Donald Kennedy (New York and London, 1996), pp. 185–204.

[52] See *De rebus Britannicis collectanea*, ed. Thomas Hearne, 2nd edn, 6 vols (Oxford, 1774), V.2–10. Subsequent scholars, including Thomas Kendrick (in *British Antiquity* (London, 1950), pp. 85–6), have assumed that this 'angry pamphlet' was originally intended as a separate text which would be more fully elucidated in the *Assertio Arturii.*

[53] On the spread of this uprising, the so-called Pilgrimage of Grace, see most recently Bernard, *The King's Reformation*, pp. 293–404.

[54] 'Reading the rhetoric of nationhood', p. 536.

[55] See Bernard, *The King's Reformation*, p. 456.

[56] Top. gen. C.III, pp. 284–5.

[57] The presentation copy on vellum to Henry VIII survives in the British Library: see my *The Libraries of King Henry VIII* (London, 2000), H2.929.

[58] *Assertio*, p. 94: 'Quare ut orbis uniuersus post hac intelligat quanta, & quam praeclara Arturii fama olim fuerit, non grauabor uel uniuersam eius uitam, et quid ueteres de eo senserint autores, lucido quodam ordine perscribere.' (The translation is mine.)

[59] In 'Henry VIII and King David', in *Early Tudor England: Proceedings of the 1987 Harlaxton Symposium,* ed. Daniel Williams (Woodbridge, 1989), pp. 183–205 (p. 191) Pamela Tudor-Craig has stated that by the time Leland produced the *Assertio Arturii* in 1543 (*sic*) 'Henry VIII had virtually lost interest in the subject.'

[60] See Gervase Phillips, 'Henry VIII and Scotland', *History Review,* 55 (September 2006), 15–20; also R. A. Mason, 'This realm of Scotland is an empire? Imperial ideas and iconography in early Renaissance Scotland', in *Church, Chronicle and Learning in Medieval and Early Renaissance Scotland*, ed. B. E. Crawford (Edinburgh, 1999), 73–91. As Mason has observed elsewhere ('Scotland, Elizabethan England and the idea of Britain', *Transactions of the Royal Historical Society*, 14 (2004), 279–93 (p. 282, n. 10)), the third child of James IV and Margaret Tudor was called Arthur (1509–10), no doubt after his dead uncle, but the naming must also have been 'indicative of the Stewart king's British ambitions'. James V's second son, Arthur, was born in April 1541, shortly before Henry VIII's planned meeting with James in York, a meeting at which James did not appear.

[61] See Phillips, 'Henry VIII and Scotland', p. 17.

[62] *RSTC* 9179: There is a modern edition in *The Complaynt of Scotland*, ed. James A. H. Murray, EETS ES 17–18 (1872–3), pp. 192–206. In 1536 Convocation declared England to be 'an imperial see of itself'. In both 1536 and 1543 there were Acts of Union with Wales and in 1541 Henry had assumed kingship of Ireland. Through these strategies it would appear, as Phillips has suggested ('Henry VIII and Scotland', p. 18), that Henry (or more probably Cromwell) was attempting to make the king 'Rex et Imperator' (A. F. Pollard's term) of all the British peoples. See also Armitage, 'Making the Empire British', p. 39. On the *Declaration* see Clare Kellar, *Scotland, England, and the Reformation 1534–61* (Oxford, 2003), pp. 73–7.

[63] Sig Biiiir. Alan MacColl has stated that *A declaration* 'is the last gasp of the tradition in which the legends could be read as having legal authority. Defences of Arthur and Brutus continued to pour from the presses, and British and Arthurian themes still played a prominent part in Elizabethan pageant and ceremony, but something had irrevocably changed.' (See 'King Arthur and the making of an English Britain' in *History Today*, 49.3 (March 1999),7–13.) In fact, the same arguments were taken up after Edward Seymour, Duke of Somerset's successful invasion of Scotland by Nicholas Bodrugan in his *An Epitome of the title that the Kynges Maiestie of Englande, hath to the souereigntie of Scotlande* (1548): see Mottram, 'Reading the rhetoric of nationhood', pp. 524, 538–40. In this treatise Bodrugun paid deference to the Seymour family, observing that 'Eldulph de Samour . . . in the tyme of Kyng Aurelie Ambrose slew Hengest the Saxon . . . by whiche noble service like as this Realme was delivered from the tyrany of Saxons, and restored to the whole Empire & name of greate Briteigne' (sig. aiiir–v). Arthur himself is credited with having subdued the rebellious Scots and having 'made one Angusian his kynseman kyng of Scottes, Vrian kyng of Islande, & Murefrence kyng of Orknay, he made one Pyramium Archbishop of Yorke, whose auctoritie extended through all Scotlande' (sig. d.ir). In his *An Exhortacion to the Scottes*

(1547) James Henrisoun (or Harryson) cited Henry's 1542 tract. For these and other similar writings see E. J. Devereux, 'Empty tuns and unfruitful grafts: Richard Grafton's historical publications', *Sixteenth Century Journal,* 21 (1990), 33–56 (p. 41); Mason, 'Scotland, Elizabethan England and the idea of Britain', p. 284; Kellar, *Scotland, England, and the Reformation*, pp. 104–5, 108; also Peter Barber, 'Putting Musselburgh on the map: two recently-discovered cartographic documents from the "Rough Wooing"', in *Mappæ antiquæ: liber amicorum Günter Schilder*, ed. Paula van Gestel-van het Schip and Peter van der Krogt ('t Goy-Houten, 2007), pp. 327–38 (p. 330).

[64] Sig. Biiiiv.

[65] Sig. C.ir. Henry thus began with the reign of Edward the Confessor. As Felicity Heal has pointed out ('What can King Lucius do for you?', pp. 598–600), the *Leges Edwardi Confessoris* contained the putative letter of Pope Eleutherius to King Lucius which could be used to 'bolster the royal claim to jurisdictional power in the divorce crisis' (p. 599). William Lambard printed the *Leges* in his *Archaionomia* in 1568: see Heal, pp. 598, 603. See also John Carmi Parsons, 'The second exhumation of King Arthur's remains at Glastonbury, 19 April, 1278', in *Glastonbury Abbey and the Arthurian Tradition*, pp. 179–83, at pp. 180–1, on 'De iure et de appendiciis corone regni Britannie' found in the *Leges Edwardi boni regis*: this section contained an account of Arthur and emphasized 'the right of the Crown of England to rule the ancient British imperium'.

[66] See, for example, Sir Thomas Craig, *De hominio disputatio adversus eos qui Scotiam feudum ligium Angliae, regemque Scotorum eo nomine hominium Anglo debere asserunt*, written before 1602, and translated by George Ridpath as *Scotland's soveraignty asserted; being a dispute concerning homage, against those who maintain that Scotland is a feu, or fee-liege of England, and that therefore the king of Scots owes homage to the king of England* (Edinburgh, 1695), p. 9. Craig (1538?–1608) was a lawyer and jurist, deeply concerned in the years before Elizabeth's death to establish the hereditary right of kings (in particular James VI's claim to the English throne) and the ancient independence of the Scottish kingdom. Subsequent references are to Ridpath's translation.

[67] *Index Britanniae scriptorum*, ed. R. L. Poole and M. Bateson (Oxford, 1902; repr. with introduction by C. Brett and J. P. Carley, Cambridge 1990).

[68] See *The Libraries of King Henry VIII*, H4.62 (p. 259).

[69] *Index Britanniae scriptorum*, p. 105. This text, misattributed to Walter, was edited by Thomas Hearne in *De gestis regis Edwardi III* in *Walteri Hemingford . . . Historia de rebus gestis Edvardi I* (Oxford, 1731), II.267–386. Bale's annotations are found in the copy in Oxford, Magdalen College, MS lat. 53.

[70] Oxford, Bodleian Library, MS Selden supra 64, fol. 190v.

[71] *Index Britanniae scriptorum*, p. 226. An incipit almost inevitably indicates that Bale had actually seen the text in question.

[72] A number of books in Henry's libraries subsequently disappeared. The incipit for *A declaration* reads: 'Beyng nowe enforced to the warre, which we have always hitherto so moch abhorred and fled'.

[73] Printed in *De rebus Britannicis collectanea,* III.2–10.

[74] Henry VI was born on 6 December 1421 and succeeded his father to the throne in September 1422, and so Leland's date for James's homage must be incorrect. *A declaration* gives 1423 for the homage, but does not allude to the marriage which took place on 12 February 1524.

[75] See Oliver Harris, '"Motheaten, mouldye, and rotten": the early custodial history and dissemination of John Leland's manuscript remains', *Bodleian Library Record*, 18/5 (2005), 460–501 (pp. 471–2, 475).

[76] *Holinshed's Chronicles. England, Scotland and Ireland*, ed. Sir Henry Ellis, 6 vols (London 1807–8), I.196. Ellis's text was based on the 1587 edition, but he normally indicated where these were additions to the 1577 edition.

[77] On Harrison's borrowings from Leland see my '"one in our time that curiously serched out old antiquities": William Harrison on John Leland', in *The Holinshed Handbook*, ed. Ian Archer, Felicity Heal,and Paulina Kewes (Oxford, forthcoming).

[78] Although Henry's text refers, as I have mentioned, to subsequent events, the historical precedents conclude, like Leland's, with James I's homage to Henry VI at Windsor. This is a crucial event, of course, because it was the last occasion on which there was an oath of homage. Much later John Dee, on whom see below, would argue that Elizabeth should require similar homage from James VI and he even prepared a version of the oath of homage as it appeared in *A declaration*: see William H. Sherman, *John Dee: The Politics of Reading and Writing in the English Renaissance* (Amherst, 1995), p. 197. The only difference between the two versions is that Dee added 'France and Ireland' after 'England'.

[79] No doubt Leland also composed a second more formal treatise naming the historical authorities on which he based his arguments: it is this latter text that Bale would have seen and from which he listed authors and texts.

[80] *Assertio*, pp. 99, 21–2.

[81] *De rebus Britannicis collectanea,* III.3. Presumably it is the title that formed the inspiration for Bale's attribution of a second Scottish text to Leland in his *Scriptorum Illustrium Maioris Britanniae Catalogus* (2 vols; Basel, 1557–9, I.672): 'De imperio Anglorum in Scotos, Lib.i: "Giraldus in institutione princip."' Immediately following 'How England should have Homage and Feaulty of Scotland' in the *Collectanea* there is a series of excerpts from medieval historians, containing information on Brutus and his sons, Brennus, Constantine, Arthur, Glastonbury, the English imperium, and Scotland's fealty to England. The first excerpt is 'Ex prima distinctione libri Syluestri Giraldi de institutione principis' – hence Bale's incipit.

[82] *Assertio*, p. 147. On Robert Widow's lost verses on the Black Prince see *De uiris illustribus*, ed. Carley, pp. 814–15. Edward Seymour captured Edinburgh in May 1544 and Boulogne fell on 18 September. The verses, not included in the later translation by Richard Robinson, must have been written therefore just before the *Assertio* went to press.

[83] Likewise in 1543 Richard Grafton brought out an edition of John Hardyng's chronicle which he dedicated to the Duke of Norfolk who had led the invasion of Scotland late in 1542: see Devereux, 'Empty tuns and unfruitful grafts', pp. 35–8. As Grafton observed in his dedication, Hardyng 'Serched out of chronicles, bothe late an olde / All that ever by the same hath bee tolde / How from the beginnyng, Scotlande dooth reigne / Under kynges of Englande, as their sovereigne'. On Hardyng's use of the Arthur story in general see Edward Donald Kennedy 'John Hardyng and the Holy Grail', in *Glastonbury Abbey and the Arthurian Tradition*, pp. 249–68; also Alfred Hiatt, *The Making of Medieval Forgeries* (London, 2004), pp. 112–35.

[84] At the beginning of the seventeenth century, Craig took an even more strident position on Arthur than William and Vergil had done when he wished to uphold the tradition of Scotland's independence from England and questioned his very existence (*Scotland's Soveraignty Asserted*, pp. 109–10).

[85] *Assertio*, pp. 99, 20: 'Britannica adfirmat historia Arturium insulis regni decimo quinto aetatis suae anno initiatum fuisse a Dubritio vrbis Legionum episcopo.'

[86] *Assertio*, pp. 141, 80–1: 'Nunquid non [Britanni] fortes fuere? Quid etiam quando Bellinus, & Brennus Romanum imperium suis addidere uictoriis? Quid Helenae nostrae filii Imperatoris tempore Constantini? Quid Aurelii Ambrosii regno, quem & laudibus Paulus Diaconus effert? Et Arturii nostri famosi tempore quanti fuere?' (Note Robinson's embellishments in his somewhat loose translation.)

[87] *Assertio*, pp. 143, 85.

[88] On this topic see also Mason, 'Scotland, England and the idea of Britain', p. 285, who points out that 'By the late 1540s, the first Christian emperor [Constantine] had become a symbolic precedent for an empire that was explicitly British – or, perhaps more accurately, Anglo-British – as well as emphatically Protestant.' In the reign of Elizabeth, on the other hand, Archbishop Matthew Parker used primarily Saxon materials in his justification of the Anglican Church: see Benedict Scott Robinson, '"Darke speech": Matthew Parker and the reforming of history', *Sixteenth Century Journal*, 29 (1998), 1061–83.

[89] Mason, 'Scotland, England and the idea of Britain', p. 287. On the background to Cecil's Scottish claims see Stephen Alford, *The Early Elizabethan Polity: William Cecil and the British Succession Crisis, 1558–1569* (Cambridge, 1998), pp. 43–52.

[90] Although Arthur's deeds are not enumerated in the *General and Rare Memorials*, Dee does have a marginal note beside a passage concerning Edgar's rights of empire as they were laid out in a foundation charter granted to Worcester Cathedral: 'Note now our Ancient Limits, by this Saxon King Possessed. But the Brytish Arthur had enlarged them much farder before his dayes: As by good Records, and Forein Testimonies, in an other place is declared' (*General and Rare Memorials*, p. 58).

[91] See *John Dee. The Limits of the British Empire*, ed. Ken MacMillan with Jennifer Abeles (Westport, CT and London, 2004). The documents making up this text were composed in 1577/8, but the surviving copy (now BL, Add. MS 59,681), was not transcribed until 1593 under Dee's supervision. For a perceptive study, to which I am much indebted, see Glyn Parry, 'John Dee and the Elizabethan British Empire in its European context', *The Historical Journal*, 49 (2006), 643–75.

[92] Like earlier scholars Dee realized that there had been exaggeration in the accounts of Arthur throughout the centuries; as a result 'overbould writters' have 'both confounded the truth with their untruthes, and also have made the truth yt selfe to be doubted of or the les regarded for the aboundance of their fables, glosinges, vntruthes, and impossibilities incerted in the true historie of Kinge Arthure his life and actes' (*The Limits of the British Empire*, ed. MacMillan, p. 53).

[93] *The Limits of the British Empire*, ed. MacMillan, p. 55. Dee's annotated copy of the *Assertio Arturii* is now Oxford, Christ Church, Wb.5.13(1). Prise (1502/3–1555), on whom see N. R. Ker, 'Sir John Prise', in his *Books, Collectors and Libraries*, ed. Andrew G. Watson (London and Rounceverte, 1985), pp. 471–96, completed a draft of his *Historiae Brytannicae defensio* before 1545. It was not, however, pubished until 1573. Using the evidence of medieval manuscripts, including those in Welsh, his aim was 'to present a reasoned argument dealing . . . with four areas of contention: first, the credibility and antiquity of the Galfridian tradition; second the name "Britain" and "British" (this opens up the whole matter of the Brutus legend); third, the stories connected with Brennus (or Brennius), one of the sons of Dunvallo Molmutius; and fourth (and at great length) Geoffrey's account of King Arthur': see Ceri Davies, 'Two Welsh Renaissance Latinists: Sir John Prise of Brecon and Dr John Davies of Mallwyd', in *Britannia Latina: Latin in the Culture of Great Britain from the Middle Ages to the Twentieth Century*, ed. Charles Burnett and Nicholas Mann (London and Turin, 2005), pp. 129–44 (p. 132); also Philip Schwyzer, *Literature, Nationalism, and Memory in Early Modern England and Wales* (Cambridge, 2004), pp. 85–9. In his 'An historicall and legall discourse upon this case following taken out of the 26 of Ass. p. 60', William Fleetword (*c.*1525–94) observed that Leland, Prise and Sir Brian Tuke had argued that 'Polidore is not stauncht in all his discourses.' He also added Humphrey Llwyd to this list of those who pointed out Polydore's 'manifest errors': see J. D. Alsop, 'William Fleetwood and Elizabethan Historical scholarship', *Sixteenth Century Journal*, 25 (1994), 155–76 (p. 167).

[94] As Dee did point out, nevertheless, they had not quoted Roger Howden's observation that Richard the Lion Heart had given Caliburn to Tancred of Sicily, whose daughter had been promised in marriage to Richard's nephew Arthur. (On this episode see E. M. R. Ditmas, 'The cult of Arthurian relics', *Folklore*, 75/1 (1964), 19–33 (pp. 26–7). Ditmas makes a 'guess' that 'when the monks of Glastonbury notified King Richard of the discovery of the grave of Arthur, they sent at the same time an ancient sword as a fitting gift to the warrior king' (p. 27).) Dee also quoted Arthurian precedent from the 'lawes of good King Edward, which William the Bastard later confirmed' concerning 'the Rights and Appurtenances of the British Crown' (*The Limits of the British Empire*, ed. MacMillan, pp. 56–8). His copy of the 1543 edition of Hardyng's chronicle has been signed and dated (Joannes Dee 1574); it contains emphatic underlining in the stanza mentioning Arthur's conquest of 'Denmarke, Friselande, Gotelande, & Norway /Iselande, Greneland, Thisle of Man & Orkynay'. Formerly owned by the fifth Earl of Rosebery, it was sold by Sothebys in 2009. (I thank William Sherman for drawing my attention to this book and for examining it for me.)

[95] See *The Limits of the British Empire*, ed. MacMillan, p. 61.

[96] *The Limits of the British Empire*, ed. MacMillan, p. 62. Dee's acknowledged source for this attack on Vergil was John Caius, *De antiquitate Cantabrigiensis academiae* (London, 1568), pp. 70–1. Dee also

took on John Mair and Hector Boece. As a Scot, so Dee suggested, Boece would also have liked to have expunged records of Arthur's foreign conquests, but he was prevented from doing so because so many were to be found (ibid., p. 62).

[97] *The Limits of the British Empire*, ed. MacMillan, p. 82. See also the 'Additions', pp. 105–14, where Robert of Avesbury is mentioned. Dee attributed great significance to Arthur's arms – they showed the three crowns of Scotland, Wales and England – maintaining that they 'were appropriated to the "enheritable Monarchy of Loegre" from the time of Brutus': see Peter French, *John Dee: The World of an Elizabethan Magus* (London, 1972), pp. 193–4.

[98] See *The Limits of the British Empire*, ed. MacMillan, pp. 21–2, 83–7; also E. G. R. Taylor, 'A letter dated 1577 from Mercator to John Dee', *Imago Mundi*, 13 (1956), 56–68. On the putative identity of the Franciscan as Hugh of Ireland see Taylor, pp. 67–8; also Richard Sharpe, *A Handlist of the Latin Writers of Great Britain and Ireland before 1540* (Turnhout, 1997), p. 186. See as well the *ODNB* entry for Nicholas Lynn.

[99] Taylor, 'A letter dated 1577', p. 56. In the notes accompanying a map of the western hemisphere which he presented to Queen Elizabeth on 3 October 1580 (now BL MS Cotton Augustus I.i.1) Dee described Arthur's exploits: he 'not only Conquered Iseland, Groenland, and all the Northern Iles cumpassing unto Russia, But even unto the North Pole (in manner) did extend his Jurisdiction: And sent Colonies thither, and into all the Isles betwene Scotland and Iseland, whereby yt is probable that the late named Friseland Iland is of the Brytish ancient Discovery and possession: And allso seeing Groenland beyond Groenland did receive their inhabitants by Arthur, yt is credible that the famous Iland Estotiland was by his folke possessed' (quoted in French, *John Dee*, p. 197).

[100] 'Making the Empire British', p. 41.

[101] See Sherman, *John Dee*, pp. 192–200; also Parry, 'John Dee and the Elizabethan British Empire', p. 661.

[102] See Sherman, *John Dee*, p. 250, n. 164.

[103] *The Limits of the British Empire*, ed. MacMillan, p. 57. This statement is preceded by a more general outline of Arthur's conquests in this part of the world: 'he vigorously subjugated the whole of Scantia, now called Norway, and all the islands beyond Scantia, viz. Iceland and Greenland, which are dependencies of Norway, and Snechorda and Scotland and Gotland and Dacia, Semeland, Winlandia, Curlandia, Row, Femelandia, Wirelandia, Flanders, Cherrela, Lapland, and all the other lands and islands of the eastern ocean, as far as Russia (seeing that he established the eastern limit of the British Empire at Lippe) and many other islands beyond Scantia, right up to the farthest north, which are among the dependencies of Scantia, now called Norway.' See also ibid., p. 64, where he pointed out that Arthur installed Loth as king of Norway. For Lambard's Latin original from which this material is derived see *Archaionomia*, fols 137v–138r. In *Scotland's Soveraignty Asserted,* pp. 121–2, Craig referred with contempt to the *Archaionomia* and observed tartly that 'There are some of those Countries, *viz. Island* and *Greenland*, which are known to Sailers, the Soveraignty of which no Body envies *Arthur*, they are so very disagreeable to Mankind. Nor did we ever see any Men from those parts, either eminent for their Actions, instructed in Learning, or indeed scarce Christians, the Country being full of Apparitions, Ghosts, Hobgoblins and Fairies: and therefore 'tis not without reason, that I am brought to think him the Prince of the Ghosts, and feign'd on purpose to frighten Children into their good Behaviour, or to terrify the Minds of weak Men. As for the other Countries, *Snechorda*, *Gutlandia*, *Semelandia*, *Winlandia*, *Wirelandia*, and *Cherrela*, which are no where to be met with, and whose Names were never heard of, they are fittest for *Arthur*; that this new and fictitious King should reign and govern in these new and fictitious-Territories, according to his own Will and Pleasure; so that he be but kept out of *Britain*, and not made use of as a Bugbear to frighten timorous Men.' Craig and his fellow sceptics did not, however, convince everybody, and the eminent lawyer and scholar John Selden (1584–1654) would list these conquests, citing Geoffrey and Lambard, in his *Mare clausum*, written in 1619 and published in 1635.

[104] As Parry has pointed out 'Dee thus extended into the distant past Elizabeth's genealogical claims to the Netherlands pressed upon the 1576 parliament' ('John Dee and the Elizabethan British Empire', p. 662).

[105] See ibid., p. 655.

[106] *The Limits of the British Empire*, ed. MacMillan, pp. 99–100.

[107] See Parry, 'John Dee and the Elizabethan British Empire', p. 653; also p. 649. On Dee's earlier support for Habsburg imperial pretensions see ibid., pp. 651–2.

[108] As Sir Roy Strong has observed, nevertheless, in 1579 'there appears the first of a long series of portraits of Elizabeth which introduce a heavy overlay of imperial pretensions stemming from maritime power and from a reassertion of dominion based on the descent of the House of Tudor from the imperial stock of Troy and on the conquests of King Arthur' (*The Tudor and Stuart Monarchy: Pageantry, Painting, Iconography*, 3 vols (Woodbridge, 1995–8), II.11).

[109] Quoted in Parry, 'John Dee and the Elizabethan British Empire', p. 669.

[110] In spite of the changed political situation in which Arthur's European conquests no longer seemed so crucial, however, Leicester continued to identify himself with his illustrious ancestor – as he had done at Kenilworth in 1575 – and made use of Arthurian iconography in his triumphal entry into the Netherlands in 1586: see Parry, 'John Dee and the Elizabethan British Empire', pp. 661–2.

[111] 'John Dee and the Elizabethan British Empire', p. 675.

[112] See Mason, 'Scotland, England and the idea of Britain', pp. 292–3. This is the context, moreover, in which one must read *Scotland's Soveraignty Asserted*.

[113] Mason, 'Scotland, England and the idea of Britain', p. 293.

[114] Robert Chester's *Love's martyr, or, Rosalins complaint* (*RSTC* 5119; London, 1601) incorporates large sections of Robinson's translation into its rambling poetic structure.

[115] The Welsh antiquary David Powell was associated with Sidney, who would employ him as his personal chaplain, and in 1584 his *The Historie of Cambria, now called Wales*, appeared in print, based on Welsh materials (including Madoc's discovery of America) translated by Humphrey Llwyd. Sidney was also the dedicatee of his *Pontici Virunii viri doctissimi Britannicae historiae*, which included Gerald of Wales's *Itinerarium Cambriae* and his *Descriptio Cambriae* (1585).

[116] On the 'benevolence' given in return to Robinson by these individuals see George McGill Vogt, 'Richard Robinson's *Eupolemia* (1603)', *Studies in Philology*, 21 (1924), 629–48 (p. 635).

[117] These included 'learned Gildas, William of Malmsbury, Nennius, Diuionenses, Graius, Iosephus, Geoffrey of Munmuth, Siluester Giraldus, &c.' (*Assertion*, p. 7).

[118] A great deal has been written on the relationship between history and literature in this period. Perhaps most useful in the context of this paper is Charlotte Artese, 'King Arthur in America: making space in history for *The Faerie Queene* and John Dee's *Brytanici Imperii Limites*', *Journal of Medieval and Early Modern Studies*, 33 (2003), 125–41, and the references cited therein.

[119] The most thorough discussion of this society remains Charles Bowie Millican, 'Spenser and the Arthurian legend', *Review of English Studies*, 6 (1930), 167–74.

[120] *Assertion*, p. 8.

[121] *Assertion*, p. 9.

[122] Sig. I 2v.

[123] See Millican, 'Spenser and the Arthurian legend', pp. 167–8, 171.

[124] Likewise Richard Harvey's *Philadelphus, or, A Defence of Brutes, and the Brutans History* (1593), written as a response to George Buchanan's *Rerum Scoticarum historia* (1582), provided moral reflections on the British history, including Arthur. On Spenser's use of history, see John E. Curran Jr., 'Spenser and the historical revolution: Briton Moniments and the problem of Roman Britain', CLIO, 25 (1996), 273–92. In 'Monuments and ruins: Spenser and the problem of the English library' (*ELH*, 70.1 (2003), 1–34, at pp. 13–15) Jennifer Summit has argued that as a result of new reading practices and, in particular, the rejection of the medieval theories of allegoresis 'the story of Arthur, in order to be preserved, needed to be proven true' (p. 14). She maintains, moreover, that in his casting away of

trifles and retaining the true accounts 'Leland produces a *modus legendi* for the post-Reformation library' (p. 15).

[125] See my 'John Leland's *Cygnea cantio*: a neglected Tudor river poem', *Humanistica Lovaniensia*, 32 (1983), 225–41, at 240.

BIBLIOGRAPHY

Abbreviations

AC	*Annales Cambrie*
ALMA	*Arthurian Literature in the Middle Ages*
DEB	*De excidio et conquestu Britannie*
ELH	*English Literary History*
EETS	Early English Text Society
FH	*Flores historiarum*
HB	*Historia Brittonum*
HE	*Historia ecclesiastica gentis Anglorum*
HRB	*Historia regum Britannie*
ODNB	*Oxford Dictionary of National Biography*
RS	Rolls Series
VM	*Vita Merlini*

Editions and Translations of Latin and English Texts Cited

This is not a complete list of all primary material cited in the essays in this collection. Instead, it is intended to be a guide to the most significant and/or readily accessible editions and translations of the major texts discussed in the essays. Some editions of historical importance, now superseded, have been included in the research bibliography below, as they remain of interest or importance for the critical tradition. For more detailed bibliographic references, readers should consult the notes for each individual essay.

Annales Monastici, ed. Henry Richards Luard, RS 36, 4 vols and index (London,1864–9).

Bale, John. *Index Britanniae scriptorum*, ed. R. L. Poole and M. Bateson (Oxford, 1902; repr. with introduction by C. Brett and J. P. Carley, Cambridge 1990).

Bede. *Bede's Ecclesiastical History of the English Church and People*, ed. Bertram Colgrave and Roger A. B. Mynors (Oxford, 1969).

——. *Ecclesiastical History of the English People*, trans. Leo Sherley-Price, rev. R. E. Latham (London, 1968).

Bek, Thomas. *Castleford's Chronicle or the Boke of Brut*, ed. Caroline D. Eckhardt, EETS os 305, 306 (1996).

Boccaccio, Giovanni. *The Fates of Illustrious Men*, trans. Louis Brewer Hall (New York, 1965).

Bower, Walter. *Scotichronicon*, gen. ed. D. E. R. Watt, 9 vols (Aberdeen, 1987–98).

The Brut or the Chronicles of England, ed. Friedrich W. D. Brie, EETS os 131, 136 (1906, 1908).

Caesarius of Heisterbach. *The Dialogue on Miracles: Caesarius of Heisterbach (1220–1235)*, trans. H. von E. Scott and C. C. Swinton Bland, 2 vols (London, 1929).

Capellanus, Andreas. *Andreas Capellanus on Love*, ed. and trans. P. G. Walsh (London, 1982).

Chronicles of the Reigns of Stephen, Henry II and Richard I, ed. Richard Howlett, RS 82, 4 vols (London, 1884–9).

Chronicon Angliæ Petriburgense, ed. J. A. Giles, Caxton Society II (1845; reprint New York, 1967).

An English Chronicle 1377–1461: A New Edition, ed. William Marx (Woodbridge, 2003).

Eulogium (historiarum siue temporis): Chronicon ab orbe condito usque ad annum domini M.ccc. lxvi a monacho quodam Malmesburiensi exaratum, ed. Frank Scott Haydon, RS 9, 3 vols (London, 1858–63).

Fortescue, Sir John. *The Governance of England,* ed. Charles Plummer (Oxford, 1885).

Geoffrey of Monmouth. *Geoffrey of Monmouth: The History of the Kings of Britain. An Edition and Translation of the De gestis Britonum (Historia regum Britanniae)*, ed. and trans. Michael J. Reeve and Neil Wright (Woodbridge, 2007).

——. *The Historia regum Britannie of Geoffrey of Monmouth I: Bern, Burgerbibliothek, MS. 568*, ed. Neil Wright (Woodbridge, 1984).

——. *The Historia regum Britannie of Geoffrey of Monmouth II: The First Variant Version:A Critical Edition*, ed. Neil Wright (Woodbridge, 1988).

——. *The History of the Kings of Britain*, trans. Michael Faletra (Peterborough, 2008).

——. *Life of Merlin: Geoffrey of Monmouth, Vita Merlini*, ed. and trans. Basil Clarke (Cardiff, 1973).

Gerald of Wales. *The Autobiography of Giraldus Cambrensis*, sel. and trans. H. E. Butler (London, 1937); reissue ed. John Gillingham (Woodbridge, 2005).

——. *Expugnatio hibernica: The Conquest of Ireland by Giraldus Cambrensis*, ed. and trans. A. B. Scott and F. X. Martin (Dublin, 1978).

——. *The Jewel of the Church: A Translation of Gemma Ecclesiastica by Giraldus Cambrensis*, trans. John J. Hagen (Leiden, 1979).

——. *Giraldi Cambrensis opera*, ed. J. S. Brewer, J. F. Dimock and G. F. Warner, RS 21, 8 vols (London 1861–91).

——. *The History and Topography of Ireland*, trans. J. O'Meara (Harmondsworth, 1982).

——. *The Journey through Wales / The Description of Wales*, trans. Lewis Thorpe. (Harmondsworth, 1978).

Gervase of Tilbury. *Otia imperialia: Recreation for an Emperor*, ed. and trans. S. E. Banks and J. W. Binns (Oxford, 2002).

Gildas. *The Ruin of Britain and Other Works*, ed. Michael Winterbottom (London, 1978).

Henry of Huntingdon. *Historia Anglorum*, ed. and tr. Diana E. Greenway (Oxford, 1996).

Higden, Ranulf. *Polychronicon Ranulphi Higden monachi Cestrensis*, ed. Churchill Babington and J. R. Lumby, RS 41, 9 vols (London, 1865–86).

Historia Brittonum. Nennius: British History and the Welsh Annals, ed. and trans. John Morris (London, 1980).

Historia Brittonum iii: The 'Vatican' Recension, ed. David N. Dumville (Cambridge, 1985).

Holinshed, Raphael. *Holinshed's Chronicles of England, Scotland and Ireland*, ed. Henry Ellis. 6 vols (London, 1807–8).

Joachim of Fiore. *De prophetia ignota. Eine frühe Schrift Joachims von Fiore*, ed. Matthias Kaup, Monumenta Germaniae Historica Studien und Texte 19 (Hanover, 1998).

John of Fordun. *John of Fordun's Chronicle of the Scottish Nation*, trans. F. J. H. Skene and ed. W. F. H. Skene, Historians of Scotland 4 (Edinburgh, 1872).

John of Glastonbury. *The Chronicle of Glastonbury Abbey: An Edition, Translation and Study of John of Glastonbury's Cronica, sive, Antiquitates Glastoniensis Ecclesie*, ed. James P. Carley, trans. David Townsend (Woodbridge, 1985).

John of Salisbury. *Frivolities of Courtiers and Footprints of Philosophers, being a translation of the First, Second, and Third Books and Selections from the Seventh, and Eighth Books of the Policraticus of John of Salisbury*, trans. Joseph B. Pike (New York, 1972).

——. *Ioannis Saresberiensis Policraticus I–IV* , ed. K. S. B. Keats-Rohan (Turnhout, 1993).

Latin Arthurian Literature, ed. and trans. Mildred Leake Day (Cambridge, 2005). Includes *De ortu Waluuanii*, *Historia Meriadoci*, *Arthur and Gorlagon* and the Arthurian episode from the *Draco Normannicus*.

Le Neve, John. *Fasti ecclesiae Anglicanae 1066–1300, VII: Bath and Wells*, ed. D. E. Greenway (London, 2001).

Lives of the British Saints, ed. Sabine Baring-Gould and John Fisher, 4 vols (London, 1907–13).

Mannyng, Robert. *The Chronicle*, ed. Idelle Sullens (Binghamton, NY, 1996).

Matthew of Westminster. *Flores historiarum*, ed. Henry Richards Luard, RS 95, 3 vols (London, 1890).

——. *Matthew of Westminster: The Flowers of History*, trans. C. D. Younge (London, 1894), 2 vols.

Paris, Matthew. *Matthaei Parisiensis monachi Sancti Albani, Chronica majora*, ed. Henry Richards Luard, RS 57, 6 vols + index (London, 1872–83).

Passiones vitaeque sanctorum aevi Merovingici cum supplemento et appendice, Scriptores rerum Merovingicarum VII, ed. Bruno Krusch and Wilhelm Levison (Hanover, 1920), pp. 225–83.

Peter of Blois. *De inuectiua,* Patrologia Latina, ed. Jacques-Paul Migne, 221 vols (Paris, 1844–65).

Pierre de Langtoft. *The Chronicle of Pierre de Langtoft*, ed. Thomas Wright, RS 47, 2 vols (London, 1866–8).

Ralph de Diceto. *Radulfi de Diceto decani Lundoniensis opera historica: The Historical Works of Master Ralph de Diceto, Dean of London*, ed. William Stubbs, RS 68, 2 vols (London, 1876).

Ralph of Coggeshall. *Radulphi de Coggeshall Chronicon Anglicanum*, ed. Joseph Stevenson, RS 66 (London, 1875).

Robert of Gloucester. *The Metrical Chronicle*, ed. William Aldus Wright, RS 86, 2 vols (London, 1887).

Roger of Howden. *Chronica Magistri Rogeri de Houedene,* ed. William Stubbs, RS 51, 4 vols (London, 1868–71).

Vergil, Polydore. *The Anglica historia of Polydore Vergil A.D. 1485–1537*, ed. and trans. Denys Hay, Camden Series 74 (1950).

Vitae sanctorum Britanniae et genealogiae, ed. A. W. Wade-Evans (Cardiff, 1944).

Vitalis, Ordericus. *The Ecclesiastical History of Orderic Vitalis*, ed. and trans. Marjorie Chibnall, 6 vols (Oxford, 1969–80).

William of Malmesbury, *Gesta regum Anglorum*, ed. and trans. R. A. B. Mynors, R. M. Thomson and M. Winterbottom, 2 vols (Oxford, 1998).

——. *The Early History of Glastonbury: An Edition, Translation and Study of William of Malmesbury's De antiquitate Glastonie ecclesie*, ed. and trans. John Scott (Woodbridge, 1981).

William of Newburgh. *The History of English Affairs: Book I*, ed. and trans. P. G. Walsh and M. J. Kennedy (Warminster, 1988).

William of Rennes. *Gesta regum Britannie*, ed. and trans. Neil Wright (Woodbridge, 1991).

Research Bibliography

This is a list of selected surveys and general studies dealing with the Latin texts discussed in this collection. In general, I have not listed articles unless these are overviews, or of some particular historical importance (a good deal of the early, foundational work on medieval Latin literature appeared in article form). There are many further, more specific studies in the notes to each individual essay. Note that when an edited volume contains more than one essay of potential interest, only the collection is listed, rather than the individual contributions; again, the notes to individual essays are more specific. Some editions of historical importance, now superseded, have also been included, as they remain of interest or importance for the critical tradition.

Abrams, Lesley and James P. Carley (eds). *The Archaeology and History of Glastonbury Abbey* (Woodbridge, 1991).

Andersen-Wyman, Kathleen. *Andreas Capellanus on Love?* (Basingstoke, 2007).

Ascensio, Gloria Torres. *Los orígenes de la literatura artúrica* (Barcelona, 2003).

Barber, Richard. 'The *Vera historia de morte Arthuri* and its place in Arthurian tradition', *Arthurian Literature*, 1 (1981), 62–77.

Barron, W. R. J. (ed.). *The Arthur of the English: The Arthurian Legend in Medieval English Life and Literature* (Cardiff, 1999).

Bartlett, Robert. *Gerald of Wales, 1146–1223* (Oxford, 1982).

Bromwich, Rachel, A. O. H. Jarman and Brynley F. Roberts (eds). *The Arthur of the Welsh: the Arthurian legend in medieval Welsh literature* (Cardiff, 1991).

Brooke, Christopher N. L. 'Geoffrey of Monmouth as a historian', in C. N. L. Brooke et al. (eds), *Church and Government in the Middle Ages* (Cambridge, 1976), pp. 77–91.

Bruce, J. Douglas (ed.). *Historia Meriadoci and De Ortu Waluuanii: Two Arthurian Romances of the XIIIth Century in Latin Prose* (Baltimore, 1913).

Brugger, Ernst. 'Zu *Historia Meriadoci* und *De Ortu Walwanii*', *Zeitschrift für französische Sprache und Literatur*, 46 (1923), 247–80, 406–40.

Carley, James P. *Glastonbury Abbey* (Woodbridge, 1988).

——, ed. *Glastonbury Abbey and the Arthurian Tradition* (Cambridge, 2001).

——, and Julia Crick, 'Constructing Albion's past: an annotated edition of *De origine gigantum*', *Arthurian Literature*, 13 (1995), 41–114.

Chambers, E. K. *Arthur of Britain* (London, 1927).

Colligan, Francis. *Historiography of Geoffrey of Monmouth* (Berkeley, 1941).

Coote, Lesley A. *Prophecy and Public Affairs in Later Medieval England* (Woodbridge, 2000).

Crick, Julia C. 'Geoffrey of Monmouth, prophecy and history', *Journal of Medieval History*, 18 (1992), 357–71.

——. *The Historia regum Britannie of Geoffrey of Monmouth, III: A Summary Catalogue of the Manuscripts* (Woodbridge, 1989).

——. *The Historia regum Britannie of Geoffrey of Monmouth, IV: Dissemination and Reception in the Later Middle Ages* (Woodbridge, 1991).

Curley, Michael J. *Geoffrey of Monmouth* (New York, 1994).

Doble, G. H. *Lives of the Welsh Saints*, ed. D. Simon Evans (Cardiff, 1971).

Dronke, Peter. 'Andreas Capellanus', *Journal of Medieval Latin*, 4 (1994), 51–63.

Dumville, David N. *Histories and Pseudo-Histories of the Insular Middle Ages* (Aldershot, 1990).

Echard, Siân. *Arthurian Narrative in the Latin Tradition* (Cambridge, 1998).

——. '"Hic est Artur": reading Latin and reading Arthur', in Alan Lupack (ed.), *New Directions in Arthurian Studies* (Cambridge, 2002), pp. 49–67.

Eckhardt, Caroline D. *The Prophetia Merlini of Geoffrey of Monmouth: A Fifteenth-Century English Commentary* (Cambridge MA, 1982).

Faral, Edmond. *La Légende Arthurienne. Études et documents*, 3 vols (Paris, 1929).

Field, P. J. C. 'Nennius and his history', *Studia Celtica*, 30 (1996), 159–65.

Finke, Laurie A., and Martin B. Shichtman. *King Arthur and the Myth of History* (Gainesville, 2004).

Fletcher, Robert Huntington. *The Arthurian Material in the Chronicles, especially those of Great Britain and France* (Boston, 1906).

Gransden, Antonia. *Historical Writing in England c.550 to c.1307* (London, 1974).

Griscom, Acton (ed.). *The Historia regum Britanniae of Geoffrey of Monmouth* (London, 1929).

Hammer, Jacob (ed.). *Historia regum Britanniae. A Variant Version edited from Manuscripts* (Cambridge, MA, 1951).

Hanning, Robert W. *The Vision of History in Early Britain: From Gildas to Geoffrey of Monmouth* (New York, 1966).

Hay, Denys. *Polydore Vergil: Renaissance Historian and Man of Letters* (Oxford, 1952).

Henken, Elissa. *Traditions of the Welsh Saints* (Cambridge, 1987).

Higham, Nicholas J. *King Arthur: Myth-Making and History* (London, 2002).

Hughes, Kathleen. 'The Welsh Latin chronicles: *Annales Cambriae* and related texts', *Proceedings of the British Academy*, 59 (1973), 233–58.

Hutson, Arthur. *British Personal Names in the Historia regum Britanniae* (Berkeley, 1940).

Ingham, Patricia Clare. *Sovereign Fantasies: Arthurian Romance and the Making of Britain* (Philadelphia, 2001).

Jackson, Kenneth H. 'Nennius and the twenty-eight cities of Britain', *Antiquity,* 12 (1938), 44–55.

——. 'Once again Arthur's battles', *Modern Philology*, 43 (1945), 44–57.

Jones, Ernest van Beurden. *Geoffrey of Monmouth, 1640–1800* (Berkeley, 1944).

Jones, Thomas. 'The early evolution of the legend of Arthur', *Nottingham Medieval Studies*, 8 (1964), 3–21.

Keeler, Laura. *Geoffrey of Monmouth and the Late Latin Chroniclers, 1300–1500* (Berkeley, 1946).

Kelly, Susan. 'The Arthurian material in the *Scotichronicon* of Walter Bower', *Anglia*, 97 (1979), 431–8.

Kendrick, T. D. *British Antiquity* (London, 1950; repr. 1970).

Kennedy, Edward Donald. *Chronicles and Other Historical Writing*, vol. 8 of Albert E. Hartung (ed.), *A Manual of the Writings in Middle English* (New Haven, 1989).

Kennedy, Ruth, and Simon Meecham-Jones (eds). *Writers of the Reign of Henry II: Twelve Essays* (New York and Basingstoke, 2006).

Kittredge, G. L. '*Arthur and Gorlagon*': versions of the werewolf's tale', *Harvard Studies and Notes in Philology and Literature*, 8 (1903), 140–275.

Krappe, A. Haggerty. 'Arthur and Gorlagon', *Speculum*, 8 (1933), 209–22.

Lagorio, Valerie M., and Mildred Leake Day (eds). *King Arthur through the Ages* (New York, 1990).

Lapidge, Michael. 'An edition of the *Vera historia de morte Arthuri*', *Arthurian Literature*, 1 (1981), 79–93.

Leckie, R. William. *The Passage of Dominion: Geoffrey of Monmouth and the Periodization of Insular History in the Twelfth Century* (Toronto, 1981).

Loomis, C. Grant. 'King Arthur and the saints', *Speculum*, 8 (1933), 478–82.

Loomis, R. S. (ed.). *Arthurian Literature in the Middle Ages: A Collaborative History* (Oxford, 1959).

Malone, K. 'Artorius', *Modern Philology*, 22 (1925), 367–74.

Miller, Molly. *The Saints of Gwynedd* (Woodbridge, 1979).

Moll, Richard. *Before Malory: Reading Arthur in Later Medieval England* (Toronto, 2003).

Morris, John. *The Age of Arthur: a history of the British Isles from 350 to 650* (London, 1973).

Morris, Rosemary. 'The *Gesta regum Britanniae* of William of Rennes: an Arthurian epic?' *Arthurian Literature*, 6 (1986), 60–123.

Nitze, William A. 'Geoffrey of Monmouth's King Arthur', *Speculum*, 2 (1927), 317–21.

Padel, Oliver J. *Arthur in Medieval Welsh Literature* (Cardiff, 2000).

——. 'Geoffrey of Monmouth and the development of the Merlin legend', *Cambrian Medieval Celtic Studies*, 51 (2006), 37–65.

Pähler, Heinrich. *Strukturuntersuchungen zur Historia regum Britanniae des Geoffrey of Monmouth* (Bonn, 1958).

Parry, John Jay (ed. and trans.). *The Vita Merlini* (Urbana, 1925).

Pigott, Stuart. 'The sources of Geoffrey of Monmouth', *Antiquity*, 15 (1941), 269–86, 305–19.

Rahtz, Philip and Lorna Watts. *Glastonbury: Myth and Archaeology* (1993; repr. Stroud, Gloucestershire, 2003).

Rhodes, Dennis E. 'The first edition of Gildas', *The Library*, 6th ser. 1 (1979), 355–60.

Rigg, A. G. *A History of Anglo-Latin Literature 1066–1422* (Cambridge, 1992).

Schirmer, Walter F. *Die frühen Darstellungen des Arthurstoffes* (Cologne, 1958).

Tatlock, J. S. P. 'Geoffrey and King Arthur in *Normannicus Draco*', *Modern Philology*, 31 (1933), 1–18.

——. 'Geoffrey of Monmouth's *Vita Merlini*', *Speculum*, 18 (1943), 265–87.

——. *The Legendary History of Britain: Geoffrey of Monmouth's Historia regum Britanniae and its Early Vernacular Versions* (Berkeley, 1950).

Taylor, John. *The Universal Chronicle of Ranulf Higden* (Oxford, 1966).
Thomson, Rodney. *William of Malmesbury* (Woodbridge, 1987).
Tolhurst, Fiona, ed. *Arthuriana*, 8 (1998): special issue on *Theoretical Approaches to Geoffrey of Monmouth*.
Tolstoy, Nikolai, 'Geoffrey of Monmouth and the Merlin legend', *Arthurian Literature*, 25 (2008), 1–42.
Treharne, R. F. *The Glastonbury Legends: Joseph of Arimathea, the Holy Grail and King Arthur* (London, 1967).
Warren, Michelle R. *History on the Edge: Excalibur and the Borders of Britain, 1100–1300* (Minneapolis, 2000).
Zumthor, Paul. *Merlin le prophète. Un thème de la littérature polémique de l'historiographie et des romans* (Lausanne, 1943).

INDEX OF MANUSCRIPTS

Aberystwyth
NLW Brogyntyn MS 8 127 n.42
NLW MS 21608 130 n.88
Avranches
Bibliothèque Municipale Codex no. 162 23 n.42
Cambridge
Corpus Christi College, MS 26 79 n.45
Corpus Christi College, MS 139 22 n.2
Corpus Christi College, MS 311 129 n.85
Gonville and Caius College, MS 72 129 n.85
Trinity College, MS R.7.13 121, 130 n.86, 131 n.99
University Library, MS Peterborough E.648 74
Chartres
MS 98 23 n.40
Chicago
University of Chicago Library, MS 224 129 n.85
Dartmouth College
Rauner Codex MS 003183 127 n.42
Durham
Dean and Chapter Library, MS B. ii 35 129 n.82
Edinburgh
National Library of Scotland, MS Adv. 18.4.5 77 n.11
Exeter
Cathedral Library, MS 3514 74, 81 n.66
Holkham
Holkham Hall, MS 669, 130 n.87, 130 n.90
London
BL Additional MS 59681 175 n.91
BL MS Cotton Augustus I.i.1 176 n.99
BL MS Cotton Caligula A. ix 127 n.33
BL MS Cotton Claudius B. vii 78 n.35
BL MS Cotton Cleopatra D. iii 97
BL MS Cotton Domitian iv 130 nn.86 and 91
BL MS Cotton Faustina B. vi 133
BL MS Cotton Galba E. vii 129 n.82
BL MS Cotton Julius B. iii 129 n.82
BL MS Cotton Otho C. xiii 127 n.33
BL MS Cotton Titus A. xix 107 n.57
BL MS Cotton Titus D. xxii 29
BL MS Cotton Vespasian A. xiv 26, 29, 32, 37
BL MS Cotton Vitellius A. xx 129 n.82
BL MS Cotton Vitellius D. xii 129 n.85
BL Harley MS 941 129 n.82
BL Harley MS 3859 22 n.5, 23 n.40
BL Harley MS 3884 129
BL Harley MS 3906 121, 130 n.86
BL Lansdowne MS 212 129 n.85
BL MS Royal 4 D. viii 82 n.80
BL MS Royal 7 C. xvi 164
BL MS Royal 8 D. iii 82 n.79
BL MS Royal 14 C. ii 79 n.46
College of Arms, MS Arundel 5 130 n.86
Gray's Inn, MS 7 97, 107 n.57
Lambeth Palace MS 81 118–19, 122
Lambeth Palace MS 99 129 n.82
Lambeth Palace MS 1106 118, 122
New York
Columbia University Library, Plimpton MS 261 130 n.87
Oxford
Bodleian Library, MS Ashmole 791 130 n.87
Bodleian Library, MS Bodley B 195 130 n.86
Bodleian Library, MS Bodley C 398 130 n.86
Bodleian Library, MS Digby 154 82 n.79
Bodleian Library, MS Selden supra 64 173 n.70
Bodleian Library, MS Hatton 50 119, 122
Bodleian Library, MS Lyell 34 130 n.88
Bodleian Library, MS Rawlinson B 147 130 n.86
Bodleian Library, MS Rawlinson B 149 133, 144 n.22
Bodleian Library, MS Rawlinson B 169 129 n.85
Bodleian Library, MS Rawlinson C 234 120, 130 n.86
Bodleian Library, MS Rawlinson C 398 121, 130 n.86, 130 n.90
Magdalen College, MS lat. 53 173 n.69
Magdalen College, MS lat. 72 102, 126 n.27
Magdalen College, MS 200 129 n.82
St John's College, MS 78 129 n.85
New York
Columbia University, MS Plimpton 266 77 n.6
Paris
BnF MS lat. 6232 81 n.66

San Marino
Huntington Library, Huntington MS HM 19960 130 n.86
Huntington Library, Huntington MS HM 48570 130 nn.86 and 91

Vatican
Biblioteca apostolica Vaticana, MS Ottoboni lat. 1474 79 n.37

GENERAL INDEX

Abed, Julien 63 n.38, 78 n.32
Aberconwy, abbey 83, 97
Adam of Domerham 115
Adelard of Bath 75
Aelfsige Hunlafing 18
Aeneas 48, 61 n.21, 96, 100
Agravain 101
Aided Óenfir Aífe 17
Ailred of Rievaulx 132
Alan of Brittany 72
Alanus ab Insulis (Alain de Lille)
Explanatio in prophetiam Merlini Ambrosii 70, 74
Albina (foundation myth) 49, 119, 129 n.84
see also De origine gigantum; *Des grantz geanz*
Alcock, Leslie 25 n.74, 32, 33
Aldhelm 99
Alexander, bishop of Lincoln 51, 69
Alexander III, pope 72–3
Alexander, Flora 107 n.60
Alexander the Great 86, 103 n.6, 134
Alexander romances 135, 144 nn.17 and 22
Alford, Stephen 174 n.89
Alfred of Beverley 126 n.28
Alliterative *Morte Arthure* 128 n.52
Alsop, J. D. 175 n.93
Alwalton 18
Ambrosius Aurelianus *see* Aurelius
Anaxagoras 99
Anaximander 99
Andelys 85
Andersen-Wyman, Kathleen 145 n.30
Andrew, saint 122
Angevins 2, 132
see also Eleanor of Aquitaine; Henry I; Henry II
Anglesey 9
Anglo–Saxon Chronicle 86
Anglo, Sidney 149, 150
Anjou 165
see also Angevins
Anna, sister of Arthur 98, 101
Annales Cambrie 7, 16, 18–21, 32
Arthur in 19–21, 32
Sources 18–21
Annals of Worcester 80 n.47
Apollonius of Tyre 135, 144 nn.18 and 22
Archibald, Elizabeth 144 n.12
Arberth 36
Armagh 16
Armitage, David 164, 172 n.62
Arnulf, bishop of Lisieux 69, 72
Artese, Charlotte 177 n.118
Arthal (Artgualchar, earl of Warwick) 100
Arthur
Amr (son) 17
Arms 176 n.97
As Christian leader 13–15, 32, 55, 115
As Joshua figure 14–15
As potential rapist 7, 27, 36–8
As tyrant 28, 33–4, 36
Battle of Camlann 19, 20, 29, 96, 97, 110
Battle of Mount Badon 7, 12, 14–17, 20, 93, 152, 153, 156
Battles 16–17, 86
Cabal (dog) 17
Caliburn 54–5, 93, 125 n.15, 175 n.94
Chair 26, 29
Compared to Alexander the Great 86, 103 n.6
see also Alexander romances
Conception 45, 54, 87, 98, 103 n.6, 132
Conquests: Europe 55, 86, 92, 95, 100, 101, 110, 126 n.28, 149, 154–5, 161–2, 164–5, 175 nn.94 and 96, 176 nn.99 and 103, 177 nn.108 and 110
see also Arthur: Roman wars
Conquests: Scotland 98, 107 n.60, 112, 115, 154–5, 161–2, 164, 176 n.97
Death 50, 58, 59, 83, 94, 96–7, 104 n.55, 155
see also Arthur: Return myth; Arthur: tomb
Excalibur *see* Arthur: Caliburn
Fights giant of Mont St Michel 48, 56–7, 110, 135, 155
Historicity 11, 18, 22 n.4, 49, 89, 93, 95, 147, 150–57, 163, 166, 170 n.35, 171 n.50, 174 nn.84, 92 and 93, 176 n.103
see also Geoffrey of Monmouth: reception
Kills Gildas's brother Huail 27, 29–34, 38, 89
Oven 26, 29, 37

Return myth 14, 31, 39, 58, 87, 94, 96, 110, 112, 113–16
see also Arthur: death; Arthur: tomb
Roman wars 45, 56, 57–8, 86, 102, 154–5, 162, 168 nn.17 and 21
Round Table 100–1, 116, 150–1, 166–7
Seal 155, 168 n.17, 170 n.43
Tomb 59, 97, 109–16, 119, 121, 123–4, 125 n.15, 128 n.52, 151–2, 155–6, 166, 175 n.94
see also Glastonbury
Tomb cross 111–12
Arthur and Gorlagon 3, 132, 137, 140–3
Arthur, prince of Wales 100
Arveragus, king 120
Ascensio, Gloria Torres 35, 37
Ascham, Roger 149
Ashe, Geoffrey 60 n.3
Astrology 75
see also prophecy
Athens 99
Augustellus 161
Augustine
De civitate Dei 74
Aurelius 11, 20, 172 n.63
In *HRB* 50–1, 54
Avalon 94, 96–7, 109–11, 114–15, 118, 123, 154
In *HRB* 58–9, 83, 128 n.52
see also Glastonbury

Badon *see* Arthur: Battle of Mount Badon
Bakhtin, Mikhail 1
Balaam, prophet 74
Baldwin, John W. 76 n.5
Bale, John 74, 133, 159–60, 173 nn.69 and 71, 174 n.79
Scriptorum Illustrium Maioris Britanniae Catalogus 174 n.81
Bangor 19, 89, 97
Bannog 29
Barber, Peter 173 n.63
Barber, Richard 107 n.55
Baring-Gould, Sabine 26–7
Barlow, Frank 80 n.49
Bartlett, Robert 104 n.21
Basel 153
Baswell, Christopher 62 n.30
Bath 50
Batman, Stephan 166
Bayless, Martha 4 n.5
Beaufort, John, marquess of Dorset and Somerset 160
Bebel, Johannes 153, 155
Bec 68, 86, 133
Becket, Thomas 69, 70–2, 75, 80 nn.49, 52 and 56
Bede 2, 10–14, 16–18, 23 n.32, 51, 85, 87, 99, 117, 170 n.41
Chronica majora 20
Historia ecclesiastica gentis anglorum 10
Bedwyr (Bedevere) 7, 28–9
In Welsh saints' lives 27, 33, 35–6
In *HRB* 45, 56–8
Bel inconnu see Renaut de Beaujeu
Belinus 159–60
In *HRB* 49–50
Belshazzar, king 73
Beornwulf, king 19
Bernard, G. W. 168 n.21, 171 n.53
Bernau, Anke 62 n.30
Biclarel 142
Biddle, Martin 150–1
Bisclavret see Marie de France
Black Death 67, 77 n.6
Blacker, Jean 63 n.38, 73, 77 n.6, 79 n.41, 81 n.69
Bladud 50, 101
Blodeuedd 37
Boccaccio, Giovanni 101–2, 113
De casibus virorum illustrium 101, 126 n.27
Bodmin 26, 29, 32
Bodrugan, Nicholas
An Epitome of the title that the Kynges Maiestie of Englande, hath to the souereigntie of Scotlande 172 n.63
Boece, Hector 176 n.96
Boethius
Consolation of Philosophy 94
Boleyn, Anne 152
Boniface, pope 163
Boudet, Jean-Patrice 81 nn.71, 72 and 75
Boulogne 174 n.82
Bower, Walter 115–16
Scotichronicon 98
Bowes, Thomas 167 n.2
Branca, Daniela Delcorno 108 n.83
Brandon, Charles, duke of Suffolk 151
Brandt, William M. 60 n.13
Brecon 27, 37
Breeze, Andrew 3, 7
Brennius 159–60, 174 n.81, 175 n.93
In *HRB* 49
Breton hagiography 26–7, 30, 34–5, 37–8
see also Goeznovius
Breton hope 58, 66 n.67, 97, 110, 113
see also Arthur: return myth
Bretons 29, 31, 61 n.16, 72, 88, 97, 110, 113
Britain 9, 10–15, 19, 29, 33, 35–7, 45–50, 55–6, 58, 67, 69–70, 85, 87, 90–4, 98, 100, 109–10, 116–18, 121–4, 126 n.28, 132–3, 135–6, 138–9, 154, 160, 163–5, 176 n.103

Foundation myth: Albina 49, 119, 129 n.84
Foundation myth: Brutus 2, 17, 47, 60 n.5, 91, 115, 119, 147, 175 n.93, 177 n.108
Britons (British) 2, 7, 9–12, 14–16–19, 22 n.15, 32, 45–6, 50–4, 58, 63 n.35, 67–8, 85–7, 89, 94, 96, 110, 113–16, 124, 126 n.27, 127 nn.33 and 34, 132, 140, 153, 156, 162
see also Arthur: return myth
Brittany 31–2, 35, 39, 67, 72, 80 n.48, 110, 113, 126 n.27
Bromwich, Rachel 24 n.53, 29, 33–5
Brooke, Christopher 31, 60 n.12, 62 n.26, 65 n.59, 80 nn.49 and 56, 104 nn.25 and 28
Brown, Michelle P. 126 n.20, 171 n.44
Brychan 7, 27, 31
Bruce, J. D. 135
Brutus 2, 17, 61 n.21, 67, 91, 100–1, 159–60, 174 n.81
Founds Britain 2, 60 n.5, 115, 147, 175 n.93, 177 n.108
In *HRB* 45, 47, 49–50, 55, 100
Bryan, Elizabeth J. 127 n.42
Bryant, Nigel 128 n.54
Buchanan, George
Rerum Scoticarum historia 177 n.124
Burgess, Glynn 144 n.13
Busby, Keith 144 n.11
Butler, H. E. 104 n.29
Bynum, Caroline Walker 145 n.42

Cadioc, bishop of Vannes 97
Cadog, saint 7, 26, 31–2, 36, 39
Life 7, 26–7, 30, 33–5, 37–8, 61 n.17
Altercation with Arthur 26–7, 34, 36
Cadwallader *see* Caedwallon
Cadwy 28
Caedwallon (Caedwalla), king 11, 68, 76, 176 n.1, 99
In *HRB* 45, 58, 67, 87, 150
Caerleon 27, 56, 65 n.59, 88, 90, 100, 107 n.64, 161–2
Caesarius of Heisterbach 2–3, 70
Cai (Kay) 28–9, 135, 142
In Welsh saints' lives 27, 33, 35–6
In *HRB* 45, 57–8
Caiaphas, high priest 74
Caius, John
De antiquitate Cantabridgiensis academiae 175 n.96
Cambridge 98–100
Camden, William 166
Britannia 111–12, 166
Camelford 29
see also Arthur: Battle of Camlann
Camlann *see* Arthur: Battle of Camlann
Cantabria 99
Cantebrus 99
Cantelupe, Nicholas
Historia de antiquitate et origine almae et immaculatae Universitatis Cantebrigiae 98–9
Canterbury 89–91
Capellanus, Andreas 138
De amore 132, 138–40
Capgrave, John
Nova legenda Angliae 118
Caradog of Llancarfan 26–30, 32, 34–9, 89, 109
see also Cadog: *Life*; Gildas: *Lives*
Carannog, saint 26–8, 31, 32, 34–7
Arthur steals his altar 26, 28, 36
Kills a dragon 26, 38
Tames a giant snake 28
Carey, Hilary M. 76 n.5, 77 n.8, 81 n.75
Carhampton 28
Carley, James P. 3, 34, 49, 62 n.28, 116, 121, 126 n.20, 170 n.34, 171 nn.44 and 51, 173 n.77, 178 n.125
Carlson, David 149–50
Carmarthen 104 n.22
Carn Gafallt 17
Carno, battle of 18
Cartlidge, Neil 145 n.32
Castleford's Chronicle 114
Catherine of Aragon 150–1
Cavendish, Richard 128 n.45
Caw of Pictland 29
Caxton, William 123, 129 n.82, 149–50
Cecil, William, lord Burghley 163, 165, 174 n.89
Cei *see* Cai
Cenydd, saint 35
Ceolwulf, king 10
Ceredigion 18, 28, 33, 34, 37
Cerdic, king of Wessex 95
Chadwick, H. M. and N. K. 24 n.52
Chambers, Edmund 27
Champagne 138
Chapuys, Eustace 151–2, 168 n.19, 171 n.50
Charles V, holy Roman emperor 150–1
Charles-Edwards, Thomas 22 n.4
Chartres 73
Chaucer, Geoffrey
The Wife of Bath's Tale 142
Chester 94, 100
Chester, Robert
Love's martyr, or, Rosalins complaint 177 n.114
Chinnock, John 117
Chrétien de Troyes 30, 45, 126 n.25, 135, 140
Cligès 126 n.25
Erec et Enide 126 n.25, 139
Lancelot 139

Chronica majora see Bede
Chronicle of Clonmacnoise 18
Chronicon Angliae Petriburgense 118, 122
Chronicon monasterii de Hales 97
Clanchy, Michael T. 4 n.4, 4 n.6, 133
Clarke, Basil 64 n.40
Cligès see Chrétien de Troyes
Clement VII, pope 151
Cnoyen, Jacobus 163
Coenwulf, king 10
Coleman, Janet 60 n.13
Collinson, Patrick 151
Conan II, duke of Brittany 80 n.48
Connell, William J. 170 n.40
Constance 118
Constans 51
Constantine, emperor 150–5, 162, 165 n.28, 174 nn.81 and 88
Constantinus, king 51
Constantine, king, son of Cador 58, 87, 96
Constantius
  Vita Germani 16, 23 n.25
Cooper, Helen 62 n.30
Coote, Lesley A. 76 n.3, 77 nn.6 and 14, 81 n.76
Corineus 47
  Fight with Gogmagog 48, 56–7
Cornish people 29–31, 37, 116
Cornwall 9, 28–30, 39, 106 n.48, 114
  Origin of name in *HRB* 47–8
Cotts, John D. 80 n.57
Council of Basel 117, 121
Council of Clarendon 80 n.52
Council of Constance 117, 121
Council of Pavia–Siena 117, 121
Council of Pisa 117
Coventry 75
Craig, Sir Thomas 174 n.84, 176 n.103
  De hominio disputatio adversus eos qui Scotiam feudum ligium Angliae… 173 n.66
Cranmer, Thomas, archbishop 169 n.23
Crantock 28
Crawford, T. D. 61 n.16
Crick, Julia 3, 43, 44, 46, 49, 62 n.28, 63 n.38, 77 n.6, 78 n.17, 78 n.25, 79 n.38, 103 n.16
Cricklade 100
Crockern Tor 29
Cronicon de origine et rebus gestis Britanniae et Angliae 102
Cromwell, Thomas 152, 155, 157–8, 169 n.23, 172 n.62
Culhwch and Olwen 17, 30, 33, 35
Cunedda, king 31
  In *HB* 10–11
Curley, Michael J. 60 n.8, 64 n.40, 77 n.16, 78 nn.21 and 30, 79 n.37
Curran, John E., Jr. 177 n.124
Cybi, saint 31

Daniel of the Bangors 19
Daniel, prophet 69, 73
Dark, Ken 36
David, saint 33
Davies, Ceri 35, 175 n.93
Davies, Pennar 31
Davies, R. R. 77 n.14
Davies, Wendy 34
Davies's Chronicle 120, 122, 130 n.88
Day, Mildred Leake 66 n.67, 134, 135, 142, 144 n.9
Dee, John 149, 163–6, 174 n.78, 175 nn.91–4 and 96, 176 nn.97 and 99, 177 n.107
  Brytanici imperii limites 163–5
  General and Rare Memorials Pertayning to the Perfect Arte of Navigation 163–4, 175 n.90
Deheubarth 18
De casibus virorum illustrium see Boccaccio, Giovanni
De origine gigantum 49, 101
De ortu Waluuanii 3, 132–8, 140
  Authorship 134
  Sources and analogues 134–5
De Sancto Joseph ab Arimathia 123
Des grantz geanz 49
Devereux, E. J. 173 n.63
Devon 30, 39
Die Wrake von Raguisel 142
Dinas Emrys 11
Ditmas, E. M. R. 125 n.15, 175 n.94
Doble, G. H. 32
Donatus 35
d'Outremeuse, Jean 105 n.38
Dover Priory 75
Draco Normannicus see Étienne de Rouen
Dronke, Peter 139, 140
Drukker, Tamar 115, 128 n.43
Dubricius, bishop 55, 100, 162
Dudley, Robert, earl of Leicester 164–6, 177 n.110
Dumville, David 22 nn.2 and 4–5; 23 n.26, 24 n.64, 25 nn.67 and 69, 37, 76 n.1
Dunster 28
Dunvallo Molmutius (Dunwald) 50, 55, 159–60, 175 n.93
Duvianus 90, 117
Dyer, Sir Edward 164, 165
Dyfed 18, 20, 38, 39
Dyfrig, saint 35

Eadred, king 18
Ecgfrith, king 16
Echard, Siân 4 n.2, 5 n.15, 35–6, 38, 62 n.26, 63 n.35, 64 n.50, 103 n.2, 107 nn.56 and 58, 124 n.1, 125 nn.6 and 8, 132–3, 135, 139, 141, 142
Eckhardt, Caroline D. 76 n.6, 77 nn.9 and 15, 79 nn.42 and 43, 81 n.73
Edgar, king 163, 175 n.90
Edinburgh 174 n.82
Edward I, king 77 n.13, 101, 107 n.60, 109, 112, 121, 163
Edward II, king 67
Edward III, king 107 n.60, 159
Edward IV, king 122, 127 n.33, 159
Edward the Black Prince 174 n.82
Edward the Confessor 160, 173 n.65
Edwin, king 11
Efflam, saint 26, 30, 35, 38, 39
Egberht, king 10
Egbert, archbishop of York 12
Eleanor of Aquitaine 126 n.25, 138–9
Eleutherius, pope 117, 120, 173 n.65
Elizabeth I, queen 149, 163–6, 169 n.23, 173 n.66, 174 n.88, 176 n.99, 177 n.108
Elliott-Binns, L. E. 29
Ellis, Henry 131 n.102, 173 n.76
England 9–10, 29, 46, 62 n.30, 70–2, 77 nn.14 and 15, 85, 89, 93, 98, 105 n.39, 110, 112–15, 120–1, 123–4, 126 n.27, 151–3, 154, 155, 157–60, 162, 164–5, 169 n.21, 172 n.62, 173 nn.65 and 66, 174 n.81, 176 n.97
Erasmus, Desiderius 155
Erec et Enide see Chrétien de Troyes
Estoire del saint graal 116–18
Ethelbert, king 99
Étienne de Rouen
  Draco Normannicus 66 n.67, 70
Eulogium historiarum 71, 79 n.43, 114–15, 119, 122, 129 nn.82 and 84
Evans, Simon 35
Evans, Ruth 62 n.27
Everard, J. A. 80 n.48
Exeter 26, 32
Expert, David 63 n.38
Ezekiel, prophet 73

Faganus 90, 117
Fair Unknown motif 133–4, 137
Faletra, Michael 61 n.16, 66 n.67
Faral, Edmond 22 n.5, 25 n.65, 28–30
Field, P. J. C. 22 n.2
Finke, Laurie A. 60 n.13
Fionn mac Cumhaill 35
Fisher, John 26–7
Flanders 126 n.27
Fleetwood, William 175 n.93
Fleischman, Suzanne 60 n.12
Fletcher, Robert Huntington 78 n.31, 85, 108 n.78, 126 n.27
Flint, Valerie I. J. 62 n.26, 65 n.59
Flores historiarum 71, 73–4, 79 n.43, 93– 5, 114, 116, 118, 127 n.38
Foliot, Gilbert, bishop 69
Fortescue, Sir John 121
Four Branches of the Mabinogi 30, 33, 36–9
  Pwyll 36
France 56, 70, 76 n.5, 77 n.15, 81 n.66, 138, 155, 162
Frederick I Barbarossa, holy Roman emperor 70
French, Peter 176 n.97
French, Roger 81 n.71
Frulovisi, Titus Livius 121
Fulton, Helen 77 n.6

Gaheres 101
Gahereth 101
Gaimar 68
Galahad 117, 114, 126 n.29; *see also* Grail
Gamber, river 17
Ganieda 39, 52, 53, 57, 59
Garman, saint 11, 16
Gaul 56
Gawain 98–9, 117, 142
  In *HRB* 45, 57
  In *De ortu Waluuanii* 133–6
Gawain-poet 46
Geoffrey of Monmouth 1, 2, 3, 20, 29–2, 34–8, 43–4, 45–66, 134–5, 152, 153, 156–7, 162, 163, 171 n.50, 177 n 117
  Biography 46
  Ethnicity 2, 46, 47
  Historia regum Britannie 1, 3, 35, 43, 45, 59, 67, 68, 71, 83, 85–100, 107 n.60, 110, 113–15, 117, 119, 121, 123, 128 n.52, 132, 147, 149–50, 154
    Ancient British book 1, 45–6, 59, 92, 163
    Arthur in 54–9, 83, 112
    Arthur's Whitsun court 56, 90, 96, 100, 161
    Arthur's fight with giant of Mont Saint Michel 57, 135
    Arthur's Roman wars 56–8, 92
    Eponymous lore 47, 48, 50
    Giant's Ring (Stonehenge) 54
    Massacre at Mount Ambrius 54
    Modesty topos 1, 4 n.8, 51, 58–9
    Prophecies in 3, 51, 53–4, 58–9, 67, 69–71, 86, 90, 150
    Reception 1–2, 3, 45–7, 49, 68, 74–5, 85–6, 92

Style 48, 50, 53, 56–9
Title 4 n.15, 49
Use of Welsh material 46, 59
See also Arthur: death, Arthur: historicity
Prophetia Merlini 43, 51–2, 54, 58, 67–82, 88
Vita Merlini 43, 52–3, 57, 59, 69, 111, 125 n.9
Gerald of Wales (Giraldus Cambrensis) 3, 69, 70, 73, 80 nn.52 and 53, 86–91, 107 n.60, 152
De jure 105 n.30
De principis instructione 110–12, 115
Descriptio Cambriae (*Description of Wales*) 89, 103 n.17, 177 n.115
Gemma Ecclesiastica 104 n.19
Itinerarium Cambriae (*Journey through Wales*) 88, 177 n.115
Speculum ecclesie 115
Vaticinalis Historia (*Conquest of Ireland*) 88
Germanus, saint 16
In *HB* 11, 13, 18
Germany 70
Gerritsen, W. P. 105 nn.34 and 38
Gervase of Canterbury 115
Gervase of Tilbury 74
Gildas 2, 7, 9–11, 14, 16, 18, 22 n.15, 23 n.32, 26–7, 31–2, 51, 85, 100, 177 n.117
Death of, in *AC* 19
De excidio et conquestu Britannie 7, 9, 89, 152–4, 169 n.28
Ambrosius 16
Britons as Israelites 9–10
Saxons as God's punishment 9–10
Lives 26–30, 32, 34–6, 39, 89, 109
Arthur kills Huail 27, 29–34, 38, 89
Gillingham, John 62 n.26, 104 n.29, 133, 143
Giraldus Cambrensis *see* Gerald of Wales
Glamorgan 28, 32, 34, 36, 37, 39
Glastonbury 3, 30, 34, 36, 38, 49, 83, 94, 97, 100, 107 n.58, 109–31, 152, 154, 155–6, 166, 168 n.17, 170 n.43, 171 n.44, 174 n.81
see also Arthur: tomb
Godfrey of Viterbo 70
Pantheon 2
Goewin 37
Goeznovius, saint 26, 30, 35, 37, 39
Gogmagog 48–9, 56–7
see also Corineus
Gorlois 103 n.6
see also Ygerna
Gowans, Linda 128 n.54
Grabowski, K. 24 n.64
Grafton, Richard 123, 131 n.102, 174 n.83
Grail 3, 101, 109, 114, 116–18, 124, 126 n.29, 128 n.54, 145 n.44
see also Galahad, Joseph of Arimathea, Perceval
Gransden, Antonia 4 n.8, 60 n.13, 119, 120, 122
Greek fire 134, 137
Green, Thomas 24 n.61
Greenland 163
Greenlaw, E. A. 150
Greenway, D. E. 80 n.58
Greenwich 169 n.23
Grey, lord, of Wilton 166
Gruffydd, Elis 32, 170 n.43
Guenevere (Guinevere) 111, 139, 142
Abduction of 30, 36, 109, 138
In Caradog's *Life* of Gildas 30, 34, 36, 38
In *HRB* 45
Guillaume de Nangis 168 n.17
Guillaume le Breton 70
Guillaume le Clerc
Fergus 140
Guithelin 100
Gurguint Barbtruc 98, 100
Guy, John 168 n.14
Guy of Warwick 99
Guy's Cliff 99
Gwladus 7, 27, 36–8
Gwynedd 9, 10, 18, 19, 38, 39, 97
Gwynllyw 7, 27, 29, 31–2, 36–7

Hammer, Jacob 70, 79 n.35, 81 n.66
Hankins, James 171 n.49
Hanning, Robert 53, 62 n.26, 125 n.6
Hardyng, John 122–3, 114, 126 n.29
Chronicle 101, 114, 124, 174 n.83, 175 n.94
Harris, Oliver 173 n.75
Harrison, William 160, 173 n.77
Harvey, Richard
Philadelphus, or, A Defence of Brutes, and the Brutans History 177 n.124
Haveloc (Havelok) 118, 137
Hay, Denys 154, 156, 169 n.26, 170 n.32
Haycock, M. E. 77 n.16
Heal, Felicity 169 n.28, 173 n.65
Hearne, Thomas 120, 130 n.86, 157, 173 n.69
Henderson, Charles 29
Heng, Geraldine 65 n.53
Hengist (Hengest) 12, 68, 172 n.63
In *HRB* 51, 54
Henken, Elissa 34
Henrisoun, James
An Exhortacion to the Scottes 172 n.63
Henry I, king 67, 71, 89
Henry II, king 70–3, 75, 88, 104 n.20, 107 n.60, 109, 111–12, 126 n.25, 170 n.43
Henry V, king 109, 119–22, 124, 130 nn.86 and 88
Henry VI, king 121–2, 159–60, 173 n.74, 174 n.78
Henry VII, king 100, 127 n.33, 149, 150, 159

Henry VIII, king 149–54, 158–63, 165–6, 170 nn.35 and 36, 171 n.50, 172 nn.57, 60 and 62, 173 nn.65 and 72
  A declaration conteyning the iust causes and considerations of this present warre with the Scottis 159–61, 173 nn.63, 72 and 74, 174 n.78
Henry, the young 71–2
Henry of Huntingdon 67, 86–8, 91, 94–5, 153
  Historia Anglorum 87
Herbert of Bosham 72–3
Herman of Tournai 29, 31, 32, 34, 37, 39
  De miraculis S. Mariae Laudunensis 26–7, 29–30, 32, 37–8
Hiatt, Alfred 4 n.11, 107 n.62, 174 n.83
Higden, Ranulph 69, 100, 113, 115, 119, 133
  Polychronicon 93–5, 98, 102, 118, 121, 129 n.82
Higham, Nicholas 3, 7, 22 n.4, 25 n.65, 37
Historia Brittonum 3, 7, 9–18, 20–1, 61 n.21, 86–7, 153, 169 n.31
  Arthur in 11–18, 28
  Authorship 22 n.2
  Emrys in 11
  Mirabilia 3, 9, 17
Historia ecclesiastica gentis anglorum see Bede
Historia Meriadoci 3, 132–3, 136–8, 140–1
  Authorship 136
  Sources and analogues 137
Historia regum Britannie see Geoffrey of Monmouth
History (genre) 1–3, 4 n.11, 46–7, 83–4, 102, 150–1
Hoak, Dale 168 n.14
Hoel 161
Holdenried, Anke 78 n.21, 82 n.78
Holinshed, Raphael 123
  Chronicles 123–4, 160
Hopkins, Amanda 142, 145 nn.40 and 42
Horn 137
Horsa 51
Horte, Roger 76
Howard, Thomas, duke of Norfolk 151–2, 155, 168 nn.17 and 19, 168 n.21, 169 n.23, 170 n.35, 171 n.50, 174 n.83
Hugh of Ireland 176 n.98
Hughes, Kathleen 18, 30
Humphrey, duke of Gloucester 121
Huws, Daniel 169 n.31
Hywel Dda 18

Iago, king of Gwynedd and Powys 18
Ida, king 12, 13, 20
Igerne *see* Ygerna
Illtud, saint 26–7, 32–4, 36–7, 39
India 115
Ingham, Patricia 62 n.30
Ingledew, Francis 60
Innocent III, pope 90
Inuentio fortunatae 164
Ireland 35, 36, 54, 70, 98, 104 n.20, 107 n.60, 125 n.7, 166
Irish chronicles 18–21
Irish hagiography 14, 34
Irish narrative 9, 17, 33
Irish people 10, 11, 88, 98
Isidore of Seville 74
Isle of Man 10
Italy 70, 77 n.15, 155

Jackson, Kenneth Hurlstone 17, 24 n.50, 25 n.72, 29, 31
Jaeger, C. Stephen 65 n.61
James I, king of Scotland 119, 121, 130 n.92, 160, 174 n.78
James IV, king of Scotland 172 n.60
James V, king of Scotland 172 n.60
James VI, king of Scotland 165–6, 173 n.66
Jarman, A. O. H. 64 n.40
Jeremiah, prophet 99
Jerome, saint 74
Jerusalem 99, 135
Jervaulx Abbey 153
Jkas, W.-V. 105 n.38
Joachim of Fiore
Vita sancti Benedicti 70
Joannes Historici 115
Johannes de Hauvilla
  Architrenius 2
Johansson, Karl G. 79 n.41
John de Bruges 75
John, king 80 n.47, 104 n.20
John of Cornwall 69, 70
John of Fordun
  Chronica gentis Scotorum 98
John of Glastonbury 118, 120, 124
  Cronica sive antiquitates Glastoniensis ecclesie 109, 117–18
John of Salisbury 47, 72, 73, 75
  Policraticus 46
Johnson, Lesley 114, 126 n.29
Jones, Thomas 24 n.53, 31, 32
Joseph of Arimathea 101, 109, 116–24
  see also Glastonbury; Grail
Joseph of Arimathie see Robert de Boron
Julius Caesar 50
Justice, Steven 82 n.81
Justinian, pope 94
Justus, emperor 94

Kalendre of the New Legende of Englande 123
Kampers, Franz 78 n.28

Karnein, Alfred 145 n.35
Kaup, Matthias 70
Kay *see* Cai
Kellar, Clare 172 n.62
Keeler, Laura 85, 119
Kelley, Edward 165
Kelly, Susan 107 n.60
Kelton, Arthur 171 n.44
Kendrick, Thomas D. 125 n.18, 126 n.28, 172 n.52
Kenilworth 177 n.110
Kennedy, Edward Donald 3, 108 n.84, 114, 126 nn.27 and 29, 127 n.42, 129 n.82, 130 n.87, 131 nn.103 and 107, 174 n.83
Kenney, James 28
Ker, Neil 175 n.93
Kingsford, Charles Lethbridge 120, 121, 130 nn.86 and 89
King's Oven, Dartmoor 29, 37
Kirby, David P. 22 n.11
Kittredge, G. L. 145 n.40
Koble, Nathalie 81 n.70
Koch, John 35
Koebner, Richard 150, 154, 168 n.20
Kynoc 99

La Belle Hélène de Constantinople 137
Lagorio, Valerie 116–18, 120, 122
Lai le Freine 137
Lambard, William 173 n.65
  Archaionomia 176 n.103
Lampeter 26
Lancelot 109, 117, 139
Lancelot (*Chevalier de la Charette*) *see* Chrétien de Troyes
Lancelot en prose 117
Lancelot Compilation (Dutch) 142
Langtoft, Peter (Pierre) 71, 79 n.41, 114, 115
Langland, William
  Piers Plowman 145 n.48
Lanval see Marie de France
Lapidge, Michael 34, 106 n.55, 107 n.57
Latin *Brut* 109, 119–22, 124, 130 nn.86, 88 and 90
Latin language, status of 1, 2, 4 n.2, 132, 136
Laurent de Premierfait 101
La Vengeance Raguidel 142
La3amon (Lawman) 37, 113–14, 127 n.33
  Brut 113–14
Lawton, David A. 116
Leges Edwardi boni Regis 173 n.65
Leges Edwardi Confessoris 173 n.65
Leicester 50
Leifsson, Gunnkaugr 79 n.41
Leir, king 50, 55
Leland, John 111, 152–3, 156–63, 165, 169 n.31, 170 n.43, 173 nn.74 and 77, 174 nn.78 and 79, 175 n.93, 177 n.124
  Antiphilarchia 158
  Assertio inclytissimi Arturii regis Britanniae 157–8, 161, 166, 169 n.27, 170 n.43, 172 nn.52 and 59, 175 n.93
  Codrus, Siue Laus & Defensio Gallofridi Arturii Monumetensis contra Polydorum Vergilium 157–8
  Cygnea cantio 167
  De uiris illustribus 152–3, 157, 158, 170 n.43
Leo, emperor 92–3, 166
Leo, pope 94
Le Saux, Françoise 127 n.30
Les enfances Gauvain 134
Levine, Joseph 150
Lewis, C. S. 32, 87, 102, 138
Lewis, Lionel Smithett 125 nn.3 and 4
Life of Joseph of Arimathy 123
Lifris 30–5, 37–9
Llanbardarn Fawr 34, 39
Llancarfan 33, 35, 39
Llandaff 65 n.59, 89, 90, 97, 100
Llangrannog 34
Llantwit Major 34
Llewellyn, David 100
Lloyd, Sir John 30
Lloyd-Morgan, Ceridwen 36, 170 n.43
Llwyd, Humphrey 171 n.49, 175 n.93, 177 n.115
Loathly lady motif 3
Logres 47
London 97, 152, 166
  Named for Lud in *HRB* 50
Loomis, Grant 29
Loomis, R. S. 29–30, 33, 37–8
Loth, king 98, 101, 134, 176 n.103
Lothian 98
Lovelich, Harry 116
Luard, H. R. 127 n.38
Lucan
  De bello civili 96
Lucius, emperor 57, 99, 155, 169 n.28
Lucius, king 90, 117, 120, 173 n.65
Lud, king 50
Lupack, Alan 37–8
Luscombe, David 80 n.58
Luxford, Julian M. 121–2
Lydgate, John 99
  Fall of Princes 101, 116
Lyfe of Joseph of Arimathia 123
Lynn, Nicholas 176 n.98

Mabinogion see Four Branches of the Mabinogi
Mac Cana, Proinsias 30

MacColl, Alan 62 n.30, 172 n.63
Macsen 31
Maelgwn, king of Gwynedd 19, 21, 27, 31–2, 34, 37
Magna Carta 82 n.79
Mair, John 176 n.96
Major, John 115, 116
Malmesbury abbey 119
Malone, K. 24 n.61
Malory, Thomas 118, 127 n.34, 128 n.52, 149, 150
  Morte Darthur 116, 123, 128 n.52
Manchester 165
Mandeville, John 101
Mann, Jill 145 n.48
Mannyng, Robert 114, 126 n.29
Map, Walter 143
  De nugis curialium 133
Marie de Champagne 138, 139
Marie de France 126 n.25
  Bisclavret 142
  Lanval 135
Martin of Troppau 105 n.38
  Chronicle of the Popes 94
Marvin, Julia 76 n.2, 77 n.6, 78 n.21
Marx, William 120, 130 n.88
Mason, R. A. 165, 172 n.60, 173 n.63, 174 n.88, 177 n.112
Matheson, Lister 118, 127 n.42, 130 nn.87 and 88
Matilda, empress 46
Matthew of Westminster 93, 94, 127 n.38
Maximilian I, emperor 165
McCauley, Barbara Lynn 103 n.16
McKisack, May 62 n.30
Mead, William Edward 169 n.27
Medraut (Mordred) 88, 96, 98–9, 102, 114, 130 n.92, 155
  In *AC* 20
  In *HRB* 45, 58, 87
Meecham-Jones, Simon 143
Meleagant 30
Meleager 134
Melion 142
Melkin the Bard 152
Melwas 30, 36, 38
Mempric 100
Merfyn, king of Gwynedd 9, 10, 20, 22 n.11
Mercator, Gerard 163
Mercia 10, 18, 21
Merlin 3, 43, 45, 67–82, 101, 110, 125 n.7, 132, 145 n.44
  Confusion of Merlinus Ambrosius and Merlinus Celidonius/Silvestris 69, 89
  In *HRB* 50, 51, 53–4, 59, 67, 69, 74, 87
  see also Geoffrey of Monmouth: *Prophetia Merlini*
Merlin (Vulgate) 118
Miller, Molly 24 n.51, 25 n.67
Millican, Charles Bowie 150, 177 nn.119 and 123
Moll, Richard 108 n.76
Mommsen, Theodor 22 nn.5, 6
Monmouth 26, 30, 37, 46
Mont de Chat, Savoy 115
Mont Saint Michel, abbey 23 n.42, 133
Mont Saint Michel, giant of 48, 56–7
Moranski, Karen R. 63 n.38
Mordred *see* Medraut
Morey, Adrian 80 nn.49 and 56
Morgan, king of Morgannwg 18
Morgan le Fay 111, 115, 125 n.9
Morison, Richard 157–8
  An Invective agenste the Great and Detestable Vice, Treason 158
  Exhortation to Styrre up All Englishment to the Defence of their Country 158
  Lamentation in whiche is Shewed what Ruyne and Destruction Cometh of Seditious Rebellyon 157
  Remedy for Sedition 157
Morland, Stephen 112, 126 n.23
Morris, John 22 n.5, 33, 38
Morris, Rosemary 63 n.36, 106 n.50
Morse, Ruth 60 n.12
Mort Artu 102, 126 nn.27 and 29, 128 n.52, 130 n.92
Mottram, Stewart 154–5, 157–8, 168 n.19, 170 n.35, 171 n.50
Mount Etna 115
Mulcaster, Richard 167

Narratio de Arthuro rege Britanniae et rege Gorlagon lycanthropo see Arthur and Gorlagon
'Nennius' *see Historia Brittonum*
New Croniclys compendyusly idrawn of the Gestys of the Kynges of England 120, 122
Nicholson, Graham 168 n.17
North America 164
Northampton 98
Northumbrians 10
Norway 56, 164, 175 n.94, 176 n.103
Norwich 164

Octa 12
Octavian 137
Oeric 12
Offa, king of Merica 16
Oswald, saint 80 n.47
Otter, Monika 60 n.12
Orderic Vitalis 68, 77 n.9
Orme, Nicholas 107 n.67

Ourcamp interpolator 92, 93, 105 n.36
Outigern 11
Ovid
 Metamorphoses 134
Owain, king of Dyfed 18, 20, 25 n.73
Oxford 46, 99, 100

Padarn, saint 26–8, 31–5, 37, 38–9
Padel, Oliver J. 24 n.61, 35–7, 38, 64 n.40, 77 n.16, 144 n.13
Padua 157
Paris 154
Paris, Matthew 71, 79 n.45, 94, 114, 118, 127 n.38
 Chronica maiora 79 n.43, 93
 Historia anglicana 71
Parker, Matthew, archbishop 166, 174 n.88
Parry, Glyn 165, 175 n.91, 176 n.101, 177 nn.104, 107 and 110
Parsons, John Carmi 173 n.65
Partholaym 98–9
Parkes, Malcolm B. 78 n.35
Partner, Nancy 4 n.11, 60 n.13
Patrick, saint 16, 18
 In *AC* 20
 In *HB* 11, 13, 14–18, 20
Peden, Alison M. 81 n.65
Penda, king of Mercia 12
Perceval (Percival) 128 n.54, 145 n.44; *see also* Grail
Perlesvaus 109, 134
Perseus 134
Peter of Blois 73
Philip, saint 117, 120
Phillips, Gervase 172 nn.60 and 62
Picts 98
Pighius, Albertus
 Hierarchiae ecclesiasticae assertio 158
Pilgrimage of Grace 157, 158, 171 n.53
Plummer, Charles 131 n.96
Pollard, A. F. 172 n.62
Powell, David
 The Historie of Cambria, now called Wales 177 n.115
 Pontici Virunii viri doctissimi Britannicae historiae 177 n.115
Powys 18
Pratt, Karen 144 n.13
Priam, king of Troy 100
Priscian 35
Prise, Sir John 163, 169 n.31
 Historiae Brytannicae defensio 175 n.93
prophecy *see* Geoffrey of Monmouth, Sibyl
Prophetia Merlini see Geoffrey of Monmouth
Prose *Bruts* 92, 115, 121, 130 n.91
 Anglo-Norman 114, 120
 Middle English 118–20, 122, 124, 127 n.42, 130 n.92
 see also Latin *Brut*
Purdie, Rhiannon 107 n.59
Putter, Ad 3, 104 n.21, 107 n.62, 114, 126 n.29
Pynson, Richard 123

Queste del saint graal 101, 109, 117, 118, 126 n.29

Radford, C. A. Ralegh 112, 124 n.1
Raedwald, king of East Anglia 12
Rahtz, Philip 126 nn.21 and 22
Ralph of Coggeshall 115
Ralph of Diceto 72, 115
Ramsey 82 n.79
Rank, Otto 144 n.12
Rastell, John 155, 170 n.43
 The Pastime of People 155
Red Sea 115
Rees, Rice 26
Rees, William Jenkin 26
Reeve, Michael D. 4 n.15, 62 n.31, 143 n.3
Reeves, Marjorie 63 n.38
Renaut de Beaujeu
 Bel Inconnu 135
Rhodes, Dennis E. 169 n.25
Rhodri Mawr, king of Gwynedd 18
Rhun 11
Rhygyfarch 33
Richard II, king 130 n.92
Richard III, king 159
Richard, duke of York 122
Richard of Cirencester 115
Richard the Lionheart (Richard I, Richard count of Poitou) 85, 104 n.20, 111, 114, 125 n.15, 175 n.94
Richmond 72
Riddy, Felicity 114, 126 n.29
Rider, Jeff 34
Ridpath, George
 Scotland's soveraignty asserted 173 n.66, 176 n.103, 177 n.112
 see also Craig, Sir Thomas
Rigg, A. G. 3
Robert de Boron 79 n.41, 116
 Joseph of Arimathie 128 n.54
Robert de Chesney, bishop 69
Robert of Avesbury 101, 109, 176 n.97
 Historia de mirabilibus gestis Edwardi III 101, 109
Robert of Exeter 69
Robert of Gloucester 46, 114, 115, 118, 122
Robert of Torigni 86, 133, 134
Roberts, Brynley F. 34, 61 n.16

Robinson, Benedict Scott 174 n.88
Robinson, J. Armitage 125 n.3
Robinson, Richard 166, 174 n.82, 177 nn.114 and 116
A learned and true assertion of the original, life, actes, and death of the most noble, valiant, and renoumed Prince Arthure 169 n.27
The aucient order, societie, and unitie laudable, of Prince Arthure 166–7
Rodarch, king 43, 52
Roger of Howden 71, 175 n.94
Roger of Wendover 127 n.38
roi fainéant 135
romance (genre) 3, 83–4, 101, 113–14, 117, 118, 122–3, 126 n.29, 128 nn.52 and 54, 132–45
Rome 45, 49, 67, 90, 134, 151, 153, 162, 163
Roper, William
Life of Thomas More 130 n.86
Rous, John 98–101
Historia regum Angliae 99–101
Royan, Nicola 107 n.59
Ruthin 27, 31
Sackur, Ernst 76 n.3
St Alban's 76, 78 n.35, 93, 127 n.38
St Asaph 46, 89
St David's 18, 20, 65 n.59, 89–91, 97, 105 n.30
St Peter's Abbey, Gloucester 33
St Werburgh's Abbey 94
Samson, saint 91
Sargent-Baur, Barbara 60 n.12
Saxons 7, 10, 11, 17, 21, 35, 37, 94, 94, 99, 111, 153–5, 162, 172 n.63
As God's punishment 7, 9
In *HB* 12–16, 21, 23 n.32
In *HRB* 45, 50–1, 54–5, 58, 65 n.53, 67, 89, 94, 95
In *VM* 52–3
Scarisbrick, J. J. 152
Schlauch, Margaret 29
Schulz, A. 76 n.3
Schwyzer, Philip 175 n.93
Scotland 31, 35, 47, 72, 77 n.13, 98, 107 n.60, 112, 115, 122, 159, 160–5, 172 n.63, 174 nn.81, 83, 84 and 89
see also Arthur: Conquests: Scotland
Scota 98
Scotus, John 99
Scott, John 125 n.10
Selden, John
Mare clausum 176 n.103
Sergius, pope 99
Servius 74
Seven liberal arts 35
Severn, river 28
Seymour, Edward, duke of Somerset 161, 172 n.63, 174 n.82
Sharpe, Richard 34, 176 n.98
Sherborne abbey 121–2
Sherman, William H. 174 n.78, 176 n.101
Shichtman, Martin B. 60 n.13
Short Metrical Chronicle 114
Sibyl 76 n.3, 78 n.21
Sidney, Sir Henry 166, 177 n.115
Sigebert of Gembloux 92, 105 n.34
Chronographia 92–3
Sims-Williams, Patrick 23 n.28
Sir Isumbras 137
Skeat, W. W. 131 n.105
Smythe, Sir Thomas 166
Somerset 26, 28, 33, 38
Southern, R. W. 60 n.13, 63 n.38, 69, 75, 81 n.71
Spain 77 n.15, 98, 99
Spanish Netherlands 164, 177 n.110
Spenser, Edmund 149, 166–7, 177 n.124
Faerie Queene 149, 166
Prothalamion 167
Spiegel, Gabrielle M. 4 n.1, 60 n.12, 76 n.3
Sprott, Thomas 114
Stamford 101
Stanzaic *Morte Arthur* 128 n.52
Starkey, David 150
Statius
Thebaid 96
Stein, Robert M. 61 n.13, 65 n.53
Stephen of Blois (Stephen, king) 46, 70–1
Stephen of Rouen *see* Étienne de Rouen
Stonehenge (Giant's Ring) 54, 125 n.7
Stow, John 166
Strathclyde 9, 29
Strong, Sir Roy 177 n.108
Stuart, John, duke of Albany 159
Suger, abbot 69
Sulpicius, pope 94
Summit, Jennifer 60 n.5, 177 n.124
Swansea 31

Tadecho 31
Talgarth 27
Taliesin 52
Tancred, king of Sicily 125 n.15, 175 n.94
Tatlock, J. S. P. 29, 30, 32, 48, 61 n.16, 61 n.18, 65 n.59
Taylor, E. G. R. 176 n.98
Taylor, John 106 n.44, 129 n.82
Thomas of Britain 126 n.25
Thompson, Aaron 60 n.5, 147
Thompson, Raymond 144 n.12
Thorpe, Lewis 89

Tintagel 29
Tirechan
  Memorandum 14
Titchfield, abbey 82 n.79
Tolstoy, Nikolai 64 n.40, 77 n.16, 78 n.23
Totnes 48
Tours 47
Trachsler, Richard 63 n.38, 77 n.15, 105 n.38, 108 n.77
Treaty of Greenwich 161
Tredunnock 27, 35
Treharne, R. F. 125 n.3
Trevisa, John 94, 95, 129 n.82
Tristan 135
Tristram (Tristan) 118, 126 n.25
Tritheim, Johann (Johannes Trithemius) 152, 165
  De septem secundeis 165
Tudor, Margaret, queen of Scotland 172 n.60
Tudor-Craig, Pamela 172 n.59
Tuke, Sir Brian 175 n.93
Tunstall, Cuthbert 153, 168 n.19
Turner, Sharon 111
Twyne, John 156–7
Twyne, Thomas 171 n.49

Ullmann, Walter 168 nn.14 and 20
Urien 10, 11, 23 n.40
Uther Pendragon 103 n.6, 127 n.34, 136
  In *HRB* 51, 54, 58, 125 n.7
Usk 27

Valentine and Orson 137
van den Brincken, Anna-Dorothee 105 n.36
van der Lugt, Maaike 81 n.65
van Hamel, A. G. 35
van Maerlant, Jacob 105 n.38
Vera historia de morte Arthuri 3, 49, 58, 83, 95, 97
Vergil, Polydore 2, 153, 155–8, 162–3, 170 nn.33 and 35, 171 n.44, 174 n.84, 175 n.96
  Anglica historia 153–7, 170 n.35
Veysseyre, Géraldine 78 n.32, 79 n.42
Victory, Siân 33
Vigilius, pope 94
Vincent of Beauvais 105 n.38
  Speculum historiale 92–3
Virgil 86
  Aeneid 48, 51, 96
  Georgics 86
Vita Henrici Quinti 121
Vita Merlini see Geoffrey of Monmouth
Vogt, George McGill 177 n.116
Vortigern 23 n.42, 100
  In *HB* 11, 13, 14
  In *HRB* 50, 51, 53–4, 58, 87, 89–90
  In *Life* of Goeznovius 37
  In *VM* 53
Vortimer 10, 13, 17, 18, 23 n.39
Vortiper 11
Vulgate cycle 101, 116
  see also Estoire del saint graal, Lancelot, Merlin, Mort Artu, Queste del saint graal

Wace 68, 73, 92, 100, 101, 114, 115, 139
  Roman de Brut 100, 113, 126 n.25, 138
Wade-Evans, A. W. 29, 34
Wales 9, 39, 47, 71, 89–91, 97, 159, 160
Walsh, P. G. 139
Walsingham, Thomas 163
Walter, archdeacon of Oxford 1, 58
Walter of Châtillon
  Alexandreid 96
Walter of Guisborough 159
Walter, Philippe 143, 145 nn.44 and 47
Warbstow 37
Ward, H. D. L. 76 n.3
Warin (Waurin) 68, 86–8
  Chronicle 79 n.43
Warner, Lawrence 65 n.53
Warwick 99, 100
Watkin, Aelred 112
Watts, Lorna 126 nn.21 and 22
Wedding of Sir Gawain and Dame Ragnell 142
Weiss, Judith 138
Wells Cathedral 111
Welsh literature 2, 7, 16–17, 46, 141
  see also Culhwch and Olwen; *Four Branches of the Mabinogi*; Welsh triads
Welsh nationalist prophecy 46, 52, 69
Welsh people 31, 85–6, 112, 114, 127 n.33
  see also Britons
Welsh saints' lives 24 n.51, 26–41, 135
Welsh triads 29, 33
werewolf stories 141–2
  see also Arthur and Gorlagon; *Bisclarel*; *Bisclavret*
Wessex 95
Westminster 155, 168 n.17, 170 n.43
Whitland 81 n.66
Whitman, Jon 60 n.12
Wickham-Crowley, Kelley M. 37
Widow, Robert 174 n.82
Wille, Claire 79 n.37, 79 n.38, 81 n.73
William IV, king of Scotland 72
William of Malmesbury 94, 110, 112, 113, 119, 132, 152, 156, 162, 170 nn.33 and 41, 174 n.84, 177 n.117
  De antiquitate Glastoniensis ecclesiae 117–18
  Gesta regum Anglorum 110, 170 n.33

William of Newburgh 2, 3, 47, 48, 74, 85–6, 113, 132, 158
  Historia rerum Anglicarum 85
William of Rennes 3, 51, 97
  Gesta regum Britannie 95–7
Williams, Hugh 26, 27
Williams, Janem Mary 40 n.26
Williams, J. E. Caerwyn 61 n.16
Wilson, R. M. 32
Winchester 101, 150
Windsor 160, 174 n.78
Winterbotton, Michael 22 n.6
Wiseman, H. 25 n.75
Withrington, John 128 n.51
Wolfe, John 166
Wolsey, Thomas 151, 159
Wood, Charles T. 117, 123
Wood, Juliette 107 n.59
Worcester Cathedral 175 n.90
Worcestre, William 121
Wright, Neil 77 n.10, 77 n.12, 81 n.66, 87, 96, 103 n.15, 106 n.50, 143 n.3
Wulfstan, bishop 80 n.47
Wynkyn de Worde 123, 129 n.82

Ygerna (Igerne) 54, 103 n.6, 109, 125 n.7
York 89, 91, 161, 172 n.60

Ziolkowski, Jan 53
Zumthor, Paul 69, 76 n.4, 77 n.11, 77 n.15